IPv6:
Theory,
Protocol,
and
Practice

SECOND EDITION

IPv6:
Theory,
Protocol,
and
Practice

SECOND EDITION

Pete Loshin
Internet-Standard.com

ELSEVIER

AMSTERDAM • BOSTON • HEIDELBERG • LONDON
NEW YORK • OXFORD • PARIS • SAN DIEGO
SAN FRANCISCO • SINGAPORE • SYDNEY • TOKYO

Morgan Kaufmann Publishers is an imprint of Elsevier

MORGAN KAUFMANN PUBLISHERS

Senior Editor	*Rick Adams*
Publishing Services Manager	*Simon Crump*
Production Editor	*Troy Lilly*
Associate Editor	*Karyn Johnson*
Cover Design	*Cate Rickard Barr*
Cover Illustrator	*Yvo Riezebos Design*
Cover Image	*Cydney Conger*
Composition	*Cepha Imaging Pvt. Ltd.*
Copyeditor	*Deborah Prato*
Proofreader	*Phyllis Coyne et al. Proofreading Service*
Indexer	*Northwind Editorial Services*
Interior printer	*The Maple-Vail Book Manufacturing Group*
Cover printer	*Phoenix Color Corp.*

Morgan Kaufmann Publishers is an imprint of Elsevier
500 Sansome Street, Suite 400, San Francisco, CA 94111

This book is printed on acid-free paper.

Library of Congress Cataloging-in-Publication Data

Loshin, Peter.
    IPv6 : theory, protocol, and practice/Pete Loshin.—2nd ed.
    p. cm.
    Rev. ed. of: IPv6 clearly explained. c1999
    Includes bibliographical references and index.
    ISBN-13: 978-1-55860-810-8   ISBN-10: 1-55860-810-9 (pbk. : alk. paper)
    1. TCP/IP (Computer network protocol) I. Loshin, Peter. IPv6 clearly explained. II. Title

    TK5105.585.L66   2003
    004.6'2—dc22

                                                                                        2003058303

ISBN-13: 978-1-55860-810-8
ISBN-10: 1-55860-810-9

For information on all Morgan Kaufmann publications,
visit our website at *www.mkp.com*

Printed in the United States of America
06 07 08   5 4 3 2

Contents

Preface

"To boldly go where no man has gone before."
Mission statement for *Star Trek*, the original television series (TOS).

"To boldly go where no one has gone before."
Mission statement for *Star Trek, the Next Generation* television series (NG).

Early in the history of the development of IPv6, before a version number had even been chosen—about the time the original *Star Trek* television series was being resurrected with a new series, *Star Trek, the Next Generation*—members of the informally constituted Internet standards body, the Internet Engineering Task Force (IETF), dubbed the working group charged with designing a new version of the Internet Protocol *IPng*, with the "ng" standing for "next generation."

Then, as now, most everyone used IP version 4; the first three version numbers had apparently been expended in the research and development process that resulted in IPv4, published as a standard in 1981. Version 5 had been reserved for use with another protocol,[1] so once the broad outlines of IPng were settled, so too was the version number.

---

[1] The Internet Stream Protocol, Version 2 (ST-II), an experimental protocol that is described in RFC 1190, "Experimental Internet Stream Protocol, Version 2 (ST-II)." Because this protocol operated at the Internet layer (layer 3 in the OSI model), it required its own protocol version to interoperate within TCP/IP networks.

IPv6 can be considered an upgrade to IPv4 in the same sense that personal computing was an upgrade to mainframe computing. IPv4 is such an integral part of global networking, so entrenched both in organizational infrastructures and the products they use, that there will be no massive shift from support to IPv6 from IPv4. Nor will there be any thought of tossing out the older protocol entirely and replacing it with the new. Just as large companies continue to rely on their mainframes for mission critical computing facilities, so too will organizations continue to depend on IPv4 for their networks as time goes on.

This book will help anyone involved in the process of evaluating, deploying, implementing, maintaining, or managing IPv6 for their own networks or for network products or services. The book is divided into three parts, the first outlining the insurmountable problems with IPv4 and the solutions that IPv6 provides; the second, outlining the protocols that have been devised to solve those problems; and the third, providing practical information and hands-on instructions for setting up and managing IPv6-capable systems and networks.

About the Reader

This book is written for readers who already know something about IPv4 and TCP/IP networking in general. Although a brief refresher section on IPv4 is included in Chapter 2, if you don't already understand the fundamentals you may want to build an understanding of TCP/IP networking using some other resource.[2] Rather than attempt to recapitulate such a broad topic here, this book focuses on IPv6, how it works, and how to use it.

It is also assumed that the reader knows what a Request for Comments (RFC) document is[3]; if you don't already know how to read RFCs, this may be a good opportunity to learn. Although books and articles provide important tools for understanding Internet protocols, there is no substitute for reading the source documents such as RFCs, Internet-Drafts (works-in-progress that may eventually be published as RFCs), and even working group mailing lists.

---

[2] "TCP/IP Clearly Explained" by Pete Loshin provides a good introduction.

[3] See Appendix for more details about RFCs as well as resources for finding, reading, and understanding them.

About the Book

Rather than concentrating on protocol specifications, this book presents in its first half the argument for IPv6 and shortcomings of IPv4, and only then does it present the new and updated protocols. The second half should prove helpful for those in the process of deploying IPv6, with chapters on planning and using IPv6 on production networks. John Spence and TK contribute their expertise in designing and implementing actual IPv6 networks.

For a complete introduction to the theory and history behind the need for IPv6 networking, read Part I. For a complete introduction to IPv6 protocols, read Part II. For a practical hands-on guide to running IPv6, read Part III.

PART I: THEORY

1: *The Disruptive Protocol.* Disruptive technologies, as described by Christensen in *The Innovator's Dilemma*, are sometimes characterized as brilliant solutions to problems that don't yet exist, but that become enormously successful despite the lack of existing market opportunities. This chapter explores the question of whether and how IPv6 might come to succeed despite years of indifference from existing network markets.

2: *What's Wrong with IPv4.* Over a quarter century, the Internet Protocol as we know it (IPv4) has enabled growth of as much as seven or eight orders of magnitude. Today's global and commercial Internet dwarfs the original U.S. Department of Defense–funded ur-Internet. This chapter highlights the reasons IPv4 is approaching the end of its useful life. The very short answer—lack of address space and explosion of non-default routing table—summarizes a quarter century of unprecedented scalability.

3: *Patching IPv4.* For the IETF, patching IPv4 has been a priority, alongside the priority of developing a successor protocol, since the early 1990s. The efforts to extend IPv4's useful life may have been too successful, having pushed the imminent demise of the IPv4 addressing space from 1994 to as far out as 2011 or even further. A variety of strategies, including conservation, rationing, and replacement, have been used over the

years, and for many network experts these efforts have succeeded far
beyond their goals of stopgap, short-term, solutions.

4:    *The Road to Next Generation.* This chapter highlights the process by which
      IPv6 has taken shape within the Internet community. From the time the
      need for a new version of IP was first recognized to the most recent
      refinement of the current Draft Standard protocols, choices have been
      made in the shaping of that new protocol. This chapter examines those
      options and explains why IPv6 looks the way it does now.

5:    *IPv6 Transition Issues.* The Internet has always been a multiprotocol
      network, being shared by systems transporting packets across a variety
      of networks. This chapter examines migration and transition scenarios
      as proposed in IETF working groups and RFCs.

PART II: IPv6 PROTOCOLS

6:    *The IP Security Protocol (IPsec).* Claims that IPv4 security was neglected
      by the founders are based on the argument that early IPv4 networks
      were insecure things strung together on trust between naive but ulti-
      mately honorable academicians. However, at the very start the Internet
      Protocol was defined as a DoD Standard, and security was certainly
      a consideration. Nevertheless, the IETF has given considerably more
      explicit attention to IPv6 security than was accorded to IPv4 during
      its development. This chapter provides an overview to the security
      issues that are, and can be, addressed within the IP Security Protocol
      framework.

7:    *IPv6 Protocol Basics.* What does IPv6 look like? This chapter introduces
      the new protocol, its features, and its functions.

8:    *IPv6 Addressing.* The most obvious difference between IPv4 and IPv6
      is in their addressing formats. IPv4 uses 32-bit (4-byte) addresses to
      uniquely identify nodes within the global Internet; IPv6 uses 128-bit
      (16-byte) addresses to uniquely identify nodes within the global
      Internet. This chapter examines the IPv6 address space, how it is allo-
      cated, how it is used, different types of addresses, and how to work
      with them.

9:    *IPv6 Options and Extension Headers.* One option open to IPng develop-
      ers was to simply expand the IP address space and leave the rest of

IPv4 alone—but that approach was rejected. As long as such a major change was necessary, it was reasoned, why not fix some of the things that needed fixing in IPv4? This chapter describes how the IPv6 packet headers differ from IPv4's. Inasmuch as the protocols themselves process data in those headers, the behavior of the protocols are defined by the protocol headers, so this chapter also introduces IPv6 protocol changes.

10: *IPv6 Multicast.* Although the fundamentals of multicast are unchanged, IPv6 offers significant improvements in the way multicast is specified and implemented. In this chapter, IPv6 multicast addressing is examined in detail, as are the mechanisms such as Multicast Listener Discovery (MLD) that have been introduced to improve multicast under IPv6.

11: *IPv6 Anycast.* Something new in IPv6 is the inclusion of anycast, a type of address that is like multicast in that more than one node can respond to packets sent to the anycast address. The difference is that packets sent to multicast addresses are delivered to *all* the nodes listening to those addresses; nodes send packets to an anycast address when they only need one of a group of nodes to respond. This chapter introduces the IPv6 anycast address type as well as examines how anycast works and what anycast can be used for.

12: *IPv6 Internet Control Message Protocol (ICMPv6).* Simpler is better, and ICMPv6 represents a significant change in the way network metadata is exchanged among IPv6 nodes. This chapter introduces ICMPv6 and discusses how it differs from the versions of ICMP specified for IPv4. ICMPv6 incorporates functions that were formerly performed by the Internet Group Management Protocol (IGMP), Address Resolution Protocol (ARP), and other protocols or mechanisms, and these new functions are introduced in this chapter.

13: *IPv6 Neighbor Discovery.* One of the most important changes in IPv6 is the inclusion of the Neighbor Discovery (ND) protocol. Using ICMPv6 messages, ND allows nodes to discover not just what nodes are on the same local link network as themselves, but also determine when nodes are unreachable, values for Internet parameters on their link, and much more. This chapter introduces ND and examines how it works and what it does.

14: *IPv6 Routing.* Scalability issues have long driven development of new techniques for Internet routing, and some of those existing solutions have been designed for use with IPv6. This chapter discusses how internal and external routing protocols can be used with IPv6, as well as issues of routing within a multiprotocol Internet.

15: *IPv6 Quality of Service.* One of the more intractable of problems with IPv4 has been the question of how to provide different treatment to different packets as they are forwarded through internetworks. While an egalitarian approach, in which all packets are treated identically, may be philosophically appealing, in practice network service providers need mechanisms that can allow them to assign priority (or at least mandate levels of service) to certain subsets of the packets they handle. Despite many years of working the problem for IPv4, IPv6 is, by design, better adapted to provide Quality of Service differentiation—as is explained in this chapter.

16: *IPv6 Autoconfiguration.* Network scalability requires the use of automatic mechanisms rather than manual procedures for configuring and updating the configuration of IP nodes. Again, the IPv6 specifications provide an inherently easier approach to doing autoconfiguration than IPv4. As will be explained in this chapter, special features of IPv6 make autoconfiguration easier.

17: *Mobile IPv6.* Nodes, whether laptop computers or devices such as PDAs and mobile telephones, often move from network to network. As these devices, and the networks, become more ubiquitous, the ability to transit from network to network without dropping connectivity to a specific IP address becomes more and more useful. Mobility under IPv6 is made simpler than under IPv4 through the use of IPv6 header extensions and Neighbor Discovery.

18: *IPv6 and DNS.* To avoid extensive updates to related protocols, IPv6 relies on DNS to link domain names with IPv6 addresses. Despite two different approaches to adapting DNS to work with IPv6, each of which has a loyal following, the current status of DNS for IPv6 is stable and reliable—and straightforward, as will be seen after reading this chapter.

19: *Next Generation Protocols.* Some Internet protocols will have to be adapted for use with IPv6; others can be used without any modification. This chapter introduces the so-called *next-generation* protocols and discusses how Internet protocols in general will interoperate with IPv6.

PART III: PRACTICE

20: *IPv6 Transition Tactics and Strategies.* The theory behind the knotty problem of IPv4/IPv6 coexistence, migration, and transition was discussed in Chapter 5. This chapter offers real-world blueprints for IPv6 planning. Contributed by IPv6 and IP security expert John Spence, this chapter gives you practical, no-nonsense approaches to supporting IPv6 in the enterprise.

21: *Configuring IPv6 on Server Operating Systems.* This chapter provides hands-on instructions for configuring IPv6 on your organization's or your testing lab's server operating systems, including Windows NT, FreeBSD, and Solaris 8.

22: *Configuring IPv6 Routers.* This chapter provides hands-on instructions for configuring IPv6 on your organization's or your testing lab's routers, including Cisco 2611, Cisco 7200, Hitachi GR2000 series, and NEC IX5010 series routers.

23: *Practical IPv6 Security Solutions.* This chapter provides hands-on instructions for setting up working IPv6 security solutions, from IPv4/IPv6 packet-filtering firewalls on Solaris and FreeBSD to configuring IPsec support and TCP wrappers on Solaris.

24: *Email and DNS Under IPv6 .* This chapter provides hands-on instructions for setting up IPv6 applications, including installing and configuring BIND, configuring a DNS server for an IPv6 networks, and setting up an IPv6-compatible email server.

25: *The Present and the Future of IPv6.* Crystal ball gazing is a risky proposition at best, but it becomes even riskier the nearer you get to the future. In this brief chapter, we'll look at existing IPv6 implementations and applications and at some possible futures for IPv6.

PART IV: APPENDIX

IPv6 RFCs and other Resources

Acknowledgments

This book would literally not have been possible without John Spence, CISSP and Senior IPv6 Engineer at Native6 Inc. (www.native6.com). Not only did he actually write important chapters, but he also helped by making accessible work done by former Zama Networks employees Robert C. Zilbauer, Jr., Grant Furness, Gerald R Crow, IV, Megan Ewers Roede, Jim Van Gemert, Brian Skeen, and Steve Smith.

Thanks go also to Morgan Kaufmann staff including Karyn Johnson, Rick Adams, Troy Lilly, and all the others who helped put this book together. Likewise, thanks go to manuscript reviewers Adrian Farrel, Dale Finkelson, Richard Nieporent and Peter Samuelson for their pungent and timely comments.

I

Theory

Part I introduces the challenges facing IPv4 and the forces at work in the development of a successor protocol. The reader should understand the following topics after reading Chapters 1 through 5.

- How new technologies can overshadow strongly entrenched existing technologies without ever seeming to present any direct competition.
- The problems inherent in IPv4 and why they herald an end to Internet growth.
- The mechanisms already designed and deployed to extend IPv4's useful life, and the problems those mechanisms have introduced.
- The steps taken in the development of IPv6.

1

The Disruptive Protocol

This chapter discusses one of the greatest challenges facing IPv6: market acceptance. That this problem is economic rather than technical may be surprising, but as technologies and the markets for them mature, those markets start to behave just like any other commodity market. As founders of so many Internet companies discovered in the first year or so of this decade, it is just not possible to build a sustainable business unless the business generates more in revenue than it costs to run.

At the same time, every once in a while the big companies manage to miss out on a key new technology because it doesn't fit into any existing market. IPv6 may be an example of just such a *disruptive technology* in large part because it meets a need that consumers are not demanding. A discussion of disruptive technologies and IPv6 is, therefore, appropriate before delving into the technical details of IPv6. Understanding first what IPv6 will eventually make possible helps focus on the relevant parts of the technology.

1.1   Disruptive Technologies

The term *disruptive technology* comes from Clayton Christensen's book *The Innovator's Dilemma*.[1] It seems as if every high-tech industry marketeer immediately latched onto the new phrase, hoping to link their products with the excitement that Christensen's ideas generated. Unfortunately for most, disruptiveness is rarely recognizable except in hindsight: Disruptive technologies are not always recognizable until after the fact, and for the very good reason that disruptive technologies are most often adopted for applications different from those originally intended.

Anyone working with technology can benefit from a quick read of Christensen's book if only to better understand how technical developments can have economic impact. In large part based on studies of the hard disk drive industry over several years and several generations of drive technologies, the book presents a compelling argument that when engineers develop a new technology they cannot always anticipate how that technology will be used. Over and over, Christensen found, serious disruptions in the disk drive markets occurred when products were improved in ways that previously would not have been viewed as key to increasing sales.

For example, a hard drive manufacturer with a new, smaller disk drive with lower power requirements would have a hard time selling it to a workstation manufacturer—especially if the price per megabyte was higher. But that same drive might be just the thing for someone who is thinking about designing a powerful laptop computer. And, in fact, the development of small, sturdy, low-power-consumption hard drives made explosive growth in the previously nonexistent laptop market possible.

That particular train has already left the station, but as barriers of performance and price are broken, technologies developed for one market often find their greatest success in some entirely different market. And many disruptive technologies were not even developed for any existing market, which means many will at first look just like conventional flops. These technologies cause market disruption because they essentially create vast new markets out of what were previously insignificant niche markets, and disrupt the business of most of the leading firms in the industry. If your

---

[1] Harvard Business School Press, 1997.

business plan depends on building and selling millions of 8-inch floppy diskette drives just as 5.25-inch drives become popular, your business will be in serious trouble.

However, most technologies can be considered *sustaining* rather than disruptive. A sustaining technology is one that, instead of disrupting things, helps sustain the status quo. Established firms spend millions on research and development in order to generate incremental improvements in their products that will make them more profitable in several ways.

- *By reducing cost of production.* The same products become available at a lower cost to the manufacturer, who can either gain market share by lowering prices or increase profit by keeping prices steady and pocketing the savings. Sustaining technologies don't generally introduce trade-offs, such as very low price in exchange for reduced performance, although disruptive technologies may do so. Automobile manufacturers have increasingly incorporated plastics and recycled materials in new vehicles, thereby incrementally reducing their own costs of production. These technologies are sustaining. A new process for building cars for one-tenth the current cost, using inexpensive plastic injection mold technologies, would be considered disruptive.
- *By improving performance.* If 50 Mhz is good, then 100 Mhz is twice as good and worth three times the price. Hardware, software, and network vendors are constantly seeking ways to improve performance that matter to customers; performance improvements don't always matter. For example, vendors of military GNC (guidance, navigation, and control) systems discovered that there was little enthusiasm for enhancing the accuracy with which nuclear missiles could be targeted. A big one dead center on the Kremlin, they reasoned, will be only marginally more effective than a big one that misses by 50 yards. Yet, improved guidance systems have found applications both in the military, which uses them for precision targeting of conventional weapons, and in the civilian world, where GPS systems are used for driver assistance systems, navigation aids for back-country hikers and skiers, and dozens of other applications.
- *By adding features.* The better a software company is at adding features or locking in users for successive upgrades, the more likely they are to be successful; Microsoft is superb. The more

features, the more likely the product will meet your needs. And if you bought the first version because it met 80% of your needs and the closest competitor met only 75% of those needs, then when the upgrade comes around you'll be likely to go for it as long as the feature list continues to expand. At the same time, feature-rich software that uses proprietary standards is vulnerable to software that is disruptive in supporting open standards and allowing users to choose their own features. By gaining early control of the operating system for computers based on the Intel 8086/08x86 processor family, Microsoft's Disk Operating System (MS-DOS) disrupted the way Apple Computer did business. Apple has always been, fundamentally, a software company that uses its own hardware as its package. It took Microsoft over 10 years to offer the same OS features that Apple did in 1983, but by then Microsoft dominated the industry.

Thus, disruptiveness does not always mean a product that is better than what is already offered by the leading firms in the industry. IPv6 may very well be a far better protocol for the Internet as we know it now and as we hope it continues to grow over the coming years. But barring some compelling new application that requires IPv6 rather than IPv4 for use on conventional routers, workstations, or servers, we will likely not see IPv6 used in any significant way on the Internet or out of North America for at least a few years.

And that is the best news possible, because that's the way a truly disruptive technology behaves. And disruptive technologies don't just change the dynamics of a market, making and breaking individual companies, but they often create great big new markets that can dwarf the original market.

1.2   IPv6: Disruptive or Sustaining?

Sustaining technologies advance the state of the art without radically changing the way the state of the art is implemented. For example, Intel and AMD keep enhancing the design of CPUs to make them faster and faster—but the basic way computers are made and sold doesn't change. Improving CPU performance is a sustaining technology for computers.

On the other hand, some new technology—let's say biological computing—that offers no significant economic or performance advantage over microprocessor would likely be a disruptive technology. After all, why would anyone go to the trouble of creating a computer based on this new technology when doing so would only invite trouble? You don't have any existing infrastructure to support such computers (and you do have a massive infrastructure for the mainstream microprocessor-based computers). And there's no real benefit from building that infrastructure.

But let's say this biological computing technology can be used elsewhere—not for computers but maybe some small niche. Let's say it works great for controlling in-ground sprinkler systems because it interfaces directly to the grass and can tell when it needs water.

Now, Intel, Microsoft, AMD, Apple, Compaq, and Gateway (among many others) will get very interested and sponsor research into how to incorporate it into their product lines. But while the big guys are studying and developing, the sprinkler guys are going to be actually selling it and maybe even expanding into houseplant watering systems and from there into household environmental control systems.

And while the big guys are still trying to figure out how to make these things work in desktop computers or servers, the sprinkler guys will have already created an entirely new market. And they'll have squeezed out the big guys in the process.

At the same time, the upstart sprinkler guys may have turned these household controllers into devices that don't just keep the temperature just right but also manage complex communications networks within and outside the household. This is pretty much what most computing technology is all about these days, and that means that by then the sprinkler company will be bigger than Intel, Microsoft, et al. combined.

That's a disruptive technology.

How does IPv6 fit in? It's kind of like that brand new technology that doesn't really provide any significant advantage over the existing state of the art IPv4 but that can probably do lots of things you can't do with IPv4. We don't know exactly what they are, but the one thing we do know is that IPv6 networks can be immensely huge—so big as to almost be beyond the imagination. This is not the same thing as the IPv4 Internet, which is quite big, but at least we can still get our arms around the concept.

Even if everyone on earth owned a home and work PC, personal laptop, and a dozen or so other high-tech gadgets with connectivity, there
is no intrinsic reason we couldn't use various workarounds (such as
Network Address Translation and Realm-Specific IP, to be discussed in
Chapter 3) to keep IPv4 going. It might be messy, but it's pretty safe to
suggest that the majority of the world's population is too poor for that
scenario.

But as the cost of building a networkable device continues to drop, the
potential for really big networks becomes more interesting. Computers
and other devices for which IPv6 is most often suggested (the most ridicu-
lous being, perhaps, the Internet Refrigerator) are expensive. There is
probably a practical ceiling on the number of networked "things"[2] the
world's economies can produce and maintain, based on the added cost of
network-enabling those things.

If the cost to network-enable a thing falls to the $100 level, $600 billion
would be sufficient to network-enable every individual in the world—
quite a lot, but not an unprecedented sum to spend on such a huge project.
Drop the price to $1 per thing and you can network-enable everyone in
the world for the quite reasonable sum of $6 billion. A single organization
could conceivably underwrite such a venture on its own, or at least form
a consortium to do so.

But things get really interesting the more the price drops. At the $0.01
level, all of a sudden you can start network-enabling some very interesting
things, depending on form factors and processing capabilities. Wiring the
world's population now costs only $60 million, well within the reach of
hundreds and perhaps even thousands of individuals.

At that price, though, there is almost no manufactured product that can
afford to *not* be wired, from produce to pencils.

The implications are staggering: Antitheft applications would not only
eliminate traditional shoplifting but would also eliminate employee

---

[2] A networked "thing" being anything to which a working network interface can be
grafted. Mostly, we think of networked things as computers cabled to a LAN or a telephone
line; increasingly, networked things can be wireless devices such as pagers, PDAs, and cell
phones. For now, though, the cost of adding connectivity hardware, software, and services
is still prohibitively expensive to consider for most of the things we use daily.

"borrowing" of corporate-owned pencils. Inventory and package tracking systems could enable frighteningly accurate global just-in-time manufacturing applications. You don't need very much CPU to tell whether an orange is ripe or rotten, to activate a radio beacon printed on the back of a postage stamp to locate lost mail, or to arm (or disarm) a piece of military ordnance.

Researchers continue to progress in developing devices that are cheap (printed on paper instead of printed circuit boards), powerful enough to do simple processing and store data statically, and small enough to be incorporated into almost any product or device. That's what I call a disruptive technology.

1.3   The Value of the Network

As of early 2003, the first IPv6 production deployments have been in the 3G or third generation wireless mobile phone system. Early estimates of the size of that network predicted hundreds of millions to a billion or more nodes, or roughly an order of magnitude larger than the IPv4 Internet, although so far those predictions are proving too optimistic. However, IPv4 cannot support such large networks, and indications are that wireless communications will only get bigger with time.

But after all, how many wireless devices can one person use? And where else could we see IPv6 deployed any time soon? IPv6-capable toothbrushes are still in the science fiction phase, after all. And how can we evaluate the opportunity that IPv6 represents? Ethernet inventor and former 3Com chief Robert Metcalfe has written, "The value of a network grows by the square of the size of the network." Like Moore's Law, this is more of a rule of thumb, but it can still be quite useful in determining the relative worth of two networks. Here's this conjecture expressed as an equation.

$$Network\ value\ of\ X - node\ network = X^2$$

Let's say the Internet has 100,000,000 nodes and is worth X, which according to Metcalfe's Conjecture is actually a value that equals

$$X = Y * 100,000,000^2$$

Let's assign Y the arbitrary value of 1 IVU (Internet Value Unit), and we've got a value to place on the IPv4 Internet.

$$10,000,000,000,000,000$$

or, to make it easier, 10 million billion IVU.

Let's also posit 100,000 nodes on IPv6 networks around the world today, which, using the same formula, yields a total value for the IPv6 Internet of 10 billion (10,000,000,000) IVU, or one millionth the value of the existing IPv4 Internet.

What happens when the 3G networks come up with 100 million users? The value of the two networks, according to Metcalfe, would be more or less equivalent. Although one could argue that unless IPv6 enables more valuable communication among those nodes than is already being transacted pre-IPv6, there has been no real value added at all.

Nevertheless, in 2002 the impact of IPv6 on existing network markets is still negligible. The opportunities become clear only by looking to future growth. IPv4 won't support much more growth, and it certainly won't support scalability beyond the current types of network applications. Apply the network value conjecture to a future IPv6 network to get an idea of the magnitude of the opportunity.

IPv6 enables much larger networks than the Internet—larger on almost unimaginable scales. For example, individuals and small business receiving the smallest IPv6 address allocation could easily manage networks with 100 billion times as many nodes (and much bigger, perhaps) as the Internet does now. And billions upon billions of organizations and individuals could be accommodated with those network allocations.

A 10-billion-node IPv6 network uses only a minuscule fraction of the total available IPv6 address space; its value would be roughly 10,000 times greater than today's IPv4 Internet. Every time the IPv6 Internet grows by a factor of ten, it becomes 100 times as valuable.

What would a 1-trillion-node (the equivalent of 10,000 Internets) network be worth? The answer is 1,000,000,000,000,000,000,000,000 IVU, or 100 million times today's Internet.

At some point it becomes economically feasible to spend the money to network-enable everything, even if the cost is more than $0.01 or even $1.

1.4 Driving IPv6 Growth

Since 1994, IPv6-related hype has been accelerating. It would be hard to imagine anyone in the networking business who has not at least heard something about IPv6 by now. The reports never question why organizations would make the move to support IPv6, but concentrate on how IPv6 will differ from IPv4, how the technology will change, and how to go about installing and configuring the technology.

Far less frequently does anyone talk about why an organization could gain competitive advantage over others by migrating sooner. Not only do network buyers fail to see any pressing need for IPv6, but the vendors have only recently recognized that the time has come to stop stringing along the IPv6 community with beta, evaluation, and research versions of their products.

What will drive IPv6 growth? Organizations that migrate to IPv6 will do so out of either fear or greed—fear of IPv4 address space exhaustion and Internet backbone meltdowns, and greed for the new killer application that makes IPv6 worth all the trouble it will take to deploy.

1.4.1 CRISIS OR BOONDOGGLE?

Migrating to an IPv4/IPv6 world implies that IPv6 offers something special, something unavailable with IPv4. Sometime soon, the Cassandras of IT exclaim, the IPv4 Internet will run out of address space. But even if you have enough IP addresses, you're still facing a future where the ballooning of the nondefault routing tables cause the Internet backbone routers to melt down.

For those who believe in an IPv6 future, that is enough to start work on an IPv6 plan. But anyone bamboozled by the drivers of the Y2K consulting gravy train needs more than doubtful claims about falling skies. With costs of IPv6 migrations expected to dwarf the Y2K expenditures, CIOs are going to demand that IPv6 bring more to the table than the prospect of fending off yet another vague threat.

IPv4 is unlikely to be sufficient to carry the Internet very far into the future. Yet, few IT departments are embracing IPv6 to coexist with IPv4. Choosing IPv6 as an enterprise solution offers organizations all the address space they can handle, but they must still deal with IPv4 somehow. IPv6 then either functions as a network address translator (NAT), isolating an IPv6-only organization network behind a protocol translator, or else requires that all systems support not just IPv6 but also IPv4.

1.4.2   KILLER APPLICATIONS

No sane person buys something he or she doesn't need, at least not usually. Why buy IPv6 if it doesn't do any more than you can do with IPv4? People bought into IPv4 because it allowed them to access the Internet and the Web. Those were killer applications, and it is the applications that drive demand for new technologies. Demand is just a nicer word that economists use instead of greed.

There is no killer app for IPv6 in the enterprise—not yet anyway. Not only isn't there any demand, but there is also the strong desire to keep what you've got by not spending it on foolish things—another manifestation of greed.

What benefits does IPv6 bring? Perhaps, it might possibly just help with performance; maybe, it could conceivably cut down somewhat on administrative costs. Those rather vague and plausibly deniable assertions come from experts within the IPv6 community who would rather not take the heat when a CIO complains that she spent $100 million on IPv6 and all she got was a lousy 4% improvement in throughput.

IPv6 is unlikely to lower costs over any but the longest time frames by migrating, and perhaps costs will rise.

- Implementing IPv6 may require significant changes and upgrades to existing systems and infrastructure.
- Supporting IPv4 and IPv6 during migration (perhaps over the course of decades) is expensive.
- Technical staffs that are already strained must allocate time and resources for training.

What about security? Is that the killer app for IPv6? Hardly: IPv6 is seen as an improvement largely because the use of the IP Security Protocol (IPsec) is mandatory for IPv6 but optional for IPv4. IPv4 can be made just as secure simply by updating all nodes to include IPsec support.

Stateless autoconfiguration (see Chapter 16) has also been proposed as candidate for killer IPv6 application. Although certainly useful and worthwhile, stateless autoconfiguration is hardly sufficient on its own to drive acceptance. Clearly, some other IPv6 application that does something unimaginably great must surface eventually or else IPv6 may be doomed.

1.4.3 PRODUCTS AND TECHNOLOGIES

It's easy for engineers and managers at leading networking vendors to confuse technologies with products, since so many of them have been involved in the business from the early days when the product *was* the technology. As new technologies come to market, they often do start out as explicit products like steam engines, electric motors, and even computers. General-purpose implementations of new technologies are marketed as products, to be bought and adapted for specialized or personal uses.

Until Microsoft bundled IP support into Windows 95, TCP/IP was treated as a product too. There were a dozen or more companies selling their own implementations of the protocol suite to be installed on Windows, DOS, Macintosh, and other platforms. As Microsoft and other network software vendors increasingly built their business on IP, it stopped being a product and became a feature of other products. Although vendors still sell IP stacks as standalone products, most people are happy to use what comes with Windows or Linux or MacOS or Solaris or whatever OS they're using. If you buy a box, it's almost assumed that it will run IP. Eventually, IP support will be an assumed part of networkable devices in the same way that optical media manufacturers don't list "electric motor included" or "with LASER light!" on their features lists.

Distinguishing between product and technology is important because brand new technologies are often packaged as products for early implementers: Electric motors were originally sold by themselves, and you could either build your own application or buy products into which your motor would fit. Over time, the cost of the motors dropped and manufacturers realized that it would be much easier to sell appliances with the motors built in—and invisible.

Early implementers were happy to install TCP/IP stacks on their own up through the mid-1990s because they got a real benefit: IP-enabled platform independent interoperability, and it enabled the Internet.

However, once that killer app—the Internet, and particularly the Web—came on the scene, IPv4 changed. At first a disruptive technology, it morphed into a sustaining technology. While IP was percolating along its little academic research/university niche, IBM, Microsoft, Novell, and many others were moving proprietary network products into the marketplace. Those companies all eventually had to seriously modify their businesses and products in order to catch up with IP. Now, those companies all support IP in their network products; can they be blamed for not wanting to add support for IPv6, a new protocol?

As IPv4 products started entering the marketplace, the network business was in its infancy. Many companies had not yet added Local Area Networks (LANs) to their IT infrastructure, and there was plenty of room for growth. As IPv4 gained penetration, companies could build their first networks with it at a lower cost than converting large networks to it.

Networking vendors, focused on their own existing product lines, are incorporating IPv6 into IPv4 products. IP is a computer networking protocol, so IPv6 should, vendors seem to be reasoning, be a simple upgrade to existing IPv4 products. Vendors *should* focus on their products, but IPv6 is a hard sell. Most network vendors have not yet promoted IPv6 as a realistic tool for production networks. Most customers are not interested in IPv6 either, and they're certainly put off by the thought of having to replace their already extensive infrastructure, or at least build a parallel infrastructure to coexist with IPv4.

1.4.4   IPv6 as a Sustaining Technology

One possibility unmentioned so far is that maybe IPv6 is a sustaining technology, something that will somehow expand and extend the embrace of network industry giants. Some experts prefer to call IPv6 a revision or update or upgrade of IPv4, with the implication being that it is still IP no matter what version, and it still works the same way (more or less). That position is at best disingenuous. Version numbers to the contrary, IPv6 really is a different protocol from IPv4; it's got a different address space, a different header format, a different set of rules on how to handle packets, and much more.

IPv6 could be a sustaining technology only if it met a currently unmet *need* in IPv4. *Need* being the operative word. Customers who do not perceive any need for IPv6 will be unlikely to buy it.

Even so, IPv6 may ultimately be viewed as a sustaining technology—if its use extends the life of the Internet Protocol.

1.5   A Possible IPv6 Future

As a classic disruptive technology, applications for IPv6 should be expected to crop up unexpectedly; that means leading network industry companies can be expected to completely overlook those applications.

One good candidate is everywhere in the world except North America. With more than enough IPv4 address-allocated space for North America, there is little frustration there when it comes to getting IPv4 network addresses. The rest of the world is not so fortunate, with Asia particularly affected by the address shortage. As China continues to computerize, it will be hard-pressed to effectively network with the meager portion of IPv4 address space that it is likely to be granted. IPv6, therefore, could be a crucial enabler to modernizing much of the world.

At the same time, until these often poorer nations can pay for expensive routers and servers or else generate demand for lower-cost alternatives in sufficient volume, the big vendors will continue to concentrate on their high-ticket, high-margin products. Introduction of low-cost network computers could spur demand in the developing areas of the world and create greater need for IP addresses.

The result could be creation of a new, IPv6-based Internet serving the rest of the world, working in parallel with the existing IPv4 Internet serving the developed nations.

Perhaps mobile wireless devices will develop to the point at which they are cheap enough to be everywhere and smart enough to give users reason to interact with them over an IPv6 Internet. Or maybe something else entirely will come along: small and cheap inventory tags that can display prices and interface directly with a store's database system, massively parallel nanocomputers, or smart paper.

Whatever the killer app turns out to be, the end result will be that the niche-based IPv6 application will grow into a mainstream market before the IPv4 network is eventually enfolded by it.

Right now, IPv6's best bet is to be treated as a disruptive, rather than a sustaining, technology. Expecting existing IPv4 users to upgrade their networks to support IPv6 without providing significant benefits is probably unreasonable. And although many organizations may actually reap benefits through lowered costs of support (from continually fixing broken NATs, for example), IPv6 is still more likely to gain ground through the niches than by frontal assault.

One time line for IPv6 allows a transition period of 10 to15 years (from the mid-1990s when the first IPv6 RFCs were first getting published). By that timetable, something should happen between 2004 and 2009.

I plan on being ready.

2

What's Wrong with IPv4?

It almost, but not quite, goes without saying: Within the Internet, every host must have access to at least one interface to the network that can be uniquely identified through a globally unique IP address. Once you run out of IP addresses, you can't add any more nodes to the network. IPv4 has a theoretical upper limit of about 4 billion (4,000,000,000) unique addresses—but in practice IPv4 is unlikely to support a sustainable population of no more than about 250 million uniquely addressed nodes. To many of those who fear the possibility that we will eventually have to do without the Internet, IPv6 represents the last and best hope for continued, unencumbered Internet growth; even those who prefer the status quo will acknowledge that something must be done.

This chapter takes a look at the problems with IPv4 for which IPv6 is considered a solution.

- The imminent exhaustion of the IPv4 addressing space.
- The imminent collapse of the Internet routing structure due to explosive growth of the nondefault routing table.

- The problem of end-to-end interoperability across routing domains in which IP addresses may not be globally unique.

A working understanding of TCP/IP networking fundamentals is a prerequisite for understanding these issues; the Appendix should help whether you need a crash course or a quick refresher.

2.1   Protocol Life Expectancy

Despite an active development community and enthusiastic supporters for over a decade, as of 2002 the vast majority of Internet traffic continues to rely on the version (version 4) of the Internet Protocol (IP) published in 1981 in RFC 791, "Internet Protocol." Despite the rapid product lifecycles we've become accustomed to as a result of Moore's Law and software vendors who rely on it to inflate their products, network administrators would much rather find a good protocol and stick with it. Patching or tweaking a protocol makes far more sense than trying on a new one every few years.

Internet protocols tend to be long-lived, with many of the most important ones still going strong after close to 20 years, including SMTP, TCP, UDP, ICMP, FTP, Telnet, and others. Many implementations of those protocols current in 1984 would likely still work in the Internet of today.

Software and hardware vendors depend on rapid change and Moore's Law to drive a continuous cycle of highly profitable upgrades, but such recklessness is not practical for network protocols. Although networks cannot do without protocols, they can certainly make the ones we've got continue to work. When some part of any Internet protocol doesn't work as it is supposed to, the IETF is far more likely to create a workaround than to replace it. That is why so many of these venerable specifications are updated over the years but not entirely replaced.

For various reasons, IPv4 is approaching the end of useful life. It still works and should continue to work for the foreseeable future—as long as the Internet stops growing. IPv4 is bumping against the upper limits of its capacity. Despite (and in part because of) the best efforts of the IETF to extend IPv4's useful life through various workarounds, patches, and administrative efforts, the only way the Internet can continue to grow is to introduce a new Internet layer protocol that will support growth.

Most of the people who oppose IPv6 believe the status quo, IPv4, is just fine for now and perfectly adequate going forward as long as proper precautions are taken, and there is no good reason to change. As a result, there is no other candidate internetwork protocol capable of supporting the kind of growth the Internet has long experienced. If you don't like IPv6, it's because you don't want to change from IPv4, not because you like some other option.

IPv6 is the *only* practical and sustainable option.

At the same time, IPv6 will likely never replace IPv4. It must somehow coexist with IPv4 as it gains ground. There will be no cutover date, with all IP nodes switching from IPv4 to IPv6; IPv4 and IPv6 will likely always coexist. The question is what share each protocol holds. While the Internet will never cutover from v4 to v6, there will certainly be smaller networks that do change all at once, and others that will make the complete switch more slowly. As that happens, those networks will either maintain a connection to the IPv4 Internet or just go on their own separate way. Should that happen, parallel IPv4 and IPv6 Internets could replace today's single interoperable and universal Internet.

Any organization that relies on the Internet for any reason should be prepared for an IPv6 future. With the Internet, as well as untold numbers of smaller, private networks using IP for its basic network infrastructure, everyone should at least be aware of what IPv6 brings to the table and what steps must be taken to interoperate with, implement, deploy, and support IPv6.

IPv4 has been an incredibly successful protocol, able to scale from connecting hundreds of hosts on handfuls of networks to linking the hundreds of millions of hosts estimated to be part of the global Internet. First designed in the mid-1970s, IP is showing its age in several ways, to be introduced later in this chapter and examined in greater detail throughout this book. Like a heavily used highway or bridge, IPv4 is reaching the end of its useful lifespan and must be upgraded soon.

2.2 What's Wrong with IPv4

Saying that IPv4 has limitations and shortcomings is very much like saying that the internal combustion engine is a flawed power source for cars and trucks. Certainly, there are flaws: expensive, wasteful of nonrenewable resources, dangerous. Yet, there is no denying that internal combustion engines power a significant portion of the developed and undeveloped world.

IP is an incredibly scalable protocol that has proved itself on countless hosts connected to networks ranging in size from two nodes to hundreds of millions in the global Internet. However, consumers are free to choose alternatives to internal combustion-based vehicles without adversely affecting anyone else; a change in IP has the potential to affect everyone connected to the Internet.

The Internet community recognized the imminent need for a revision to IPv4 as early as the late 1980s, when it became apparent that the existing IP address space would support continued Internet growth for only a relatively short time. This section introduces the reasons that IP must be upgraded; the next section addresses the measures that have been taken to fix these problems in the short-term at least. The last section of this chapter examines why some of these measures must be considered stopgaps as opposed to long-term fixes.

Most discussions about IPv6 focus on a laundry list of problems with IPv4 and benefits of IPv6 that should motivate everyone to demand IPv6 support from all their vendors. Yet, if you hold their feet to a fire, IPv6 experts will admit that there are really only three, maybe four, issues that make IPv6 inevitable.

Addresses IPv4 addresses have been in short supply since the early 1990s, when then-current growth curves showed them being depleted before the end of the decade. A variety of short-term, stopgap, and temporary measures have been instituted over the years to successfully (so far) forestall such a depletion, but some experts have suggested that the need to employ these measures itself is an indication that the address space has been exhausted for all practical purposes.

Routing Although IPv4 continues to hold up well under considerable pressures of growth, the routing tables of the Internet's *nondefault routers* have been growing at alarming rates. These are the backbone routers whose routing tables must reflect routing information for every connected network in the world, and some experts have suggested that more than any address shortage, the size of the nondefault routing tables will ultimately drive the acceptance of IPv6.

End-to-Endness One of the most controversial of the patches on IPv4 has been the use of private network address space[1] and network address translators (NATs). The problem is that the *end-to-end* nature of IP computing, under which all interaction between the source and destination nodes is done without any intermediate mediation, is broken when a system starts changing stuff as it passes between the nodes. There are reasonable workarounds for most applications, but security poses a problem because the Internet Security Protocol (IPsec) relies on the global uniqueness of the nodes' IP addresses to ensure that packets are not being spoofed. And not all applications can work around NATs. By providing plentiful new addresses, IPv6 is seen as a way to at least reduce the number of new NATs being deployed and, by extension, guarantee end-to-end interoperability.

IPv6 OFFERS THREE ADVANTAGES OVER IPv4

1. PLENTIFUL ADDRESSES

2. ROUTING SCALABILITY

3. EASIER END-TO-END SUPPORT

Any other reasons for migrating that you may have read elsewhere in books or magazines are pure speculation. Anyone who claims that IPv6 will be more secure, easier to administer, cheaper to manage, more efficient, or better at brightening and whitening is on shaky ground. It is true that the design of an updated version of IPv4 provided some opportunities to improve on the original design.

The possible fourth advantage over IPv4 is better performance as a result of streamlined headers, no fragmentation, and no header checksums. "Possible" because the increases in transmission rates continue to advance in parallel (if not in lockstep) with increases in processing power. If processing IP packets becomes a bottleneck, then it is possible IPv6 will be

---

[1]See RFC 1918, "Address Allocation for Private Internets," and RFC 3022, "Traditional IP Network Address Translator (Traditional NAT)," as well as Chapter 3.

required to speed things up. However, the performance advantage may also be solvable by upgrading system processing power.

Some of the issues that IPv6 promoters point to include the following.

Security The IPv6 specification mandates that IPv6-enabled nodes support the IP Security Protocol (IPsec), thus making IPv6 nodes more secure than IPv4 nodes. Although this appears to be a reasonable argument, IPsec is specified to work with both IPv4 and IPv6 (and, presumably, other versions of IP to come in the future). IPsec is widely implemented under IPv4 and works the same under any version of IP.

Autoconfiguration IPv4 provides two mechanisms for configuring nodes: static configuration under which nodes are assigned IP addresses that they "own" and that don't change over time; and dynamic configuration under which previously recognized and authorized nodes are given IP addresses as they request them and that may vary from session to session. Dynamic autoconfiguration for IPv4 is sometimes referred to as *stateful autoconfiguration* because some status information about configured nodes must be maintained (especially IEEE media access control or MAC addresses). IPv6 includes a feature called *stateless autoconfiguration* that lets users plug-and-play in networks without prior contact with the network administrator. Although this is a powerful tool, the savings possible from stateless autoconfiguration are hardly likely to convince any CIO to underwrite the astronomical expense of adding IPv6 to a large network.

Mobility Another very nice feature of IPv6 is its improved handling of mobile IP nodes, but as with stateless autoconfiguration this may not be enough to convince anyone to migrate to IPv6.

Performance IPv4 header options vary the size of the packet header and have often been avoided or ignored in the past. The conventional wisdom said these oddly sized (at least, odd relative to the standard 20-octet header without options) packets would be shunted to the side by busy routers, only to be ignored until the router is caught up with normal traffic. In practice, however, this has not been the case and it has not deterred anyone from deploying IPsec over IPv4 for virtual private networks (VPNs).

Some supporters point to improved performance in IPv6 routers over IPv4 routers due to differences in the way addresses and routes are handled. In fact, this is probably one area where IPv6 will provide an advantage—but this is still speculative inasmuch as no IPv6 network has as many routes as are found in the Internet's backbone networks.

Cost IPv6 supporters have suggested that IPv6 will reduce costs in various ways, including the reduced costs of administration, improved security, better performance, and lower cost for actual registration of IP addresses. Any savings would have to be balanced against the added costs of hiring and educating staff to support organizations during their addition of IPv6 connectivity, the costs of upgrading and replacing hardware and software, and the unexpected costs that invariably occur during such large projects. Perhaps IPv6 will reduce costs over the very long term, but that is far from clear.

These areas may indeed prove to be strong selling points for IPv6; but there is currently no evidence that IPv6 will offer significant improvements over IPv4 in any of them.

However, IPv6 does provide relief for IPv4 networks groaning under a shortage of addresses, an explosion in routing tables, and concerns about end-to-end interoperability.

2.3   IPv4 Addressing Crisis

It never hurts to understand how things got to be the way they are, and IPv4's address space is no exception. RFC 33, "New HOST-HOST Protocol," published in 1970, described an early precursor to the Internet Protocol that used only 8 bits for the host address but used 24 bits for the "user number," which seems to have been used similarly to today's transport layer ports. Such a small addressing space was just fine for 1970, given the relative handful of large mainframes available to the researchers.

By the time that IP took its modern form, network addresses ranged from fairly short (8 bits) to fairly long (48 bits or longer). Only a year or so before RFC 791 describing this modern IPv4 was published, IPv4 used a 32-bit address that allocated only 8 bits to the network identifier—meaning that no more than 256 networks could be linked in an RFC 760 IP Internet.

But RFC 790, "Assigned Numbers," added the concept of network classes, permitting many little networks and a few very big ones. Quite possibly the change was made to accommodate the potentially large new networks built from the newest technologies: personal computers and Ethernet networks. In any case, the decision to go with a 32-bit address space was discussed in the 1978 document "The Catenet Model for Internetworking," in which Vint Cerf[2] described the immediate predecessor to modern IP, using 32-bit addresses. According to Cerf, the notion of variable-length addresses had been given serious consideration but was rejected.

> At one point, it appeared that addresses might be as long as 120 bits each for source and destination. The overhead in the higher level protocols for maintaining tables capable of dealing with the maximum possible address sizes was considered excessive.[3]

At the same time, the first octet of the 32-bit addresses was used to identify the network on which the source and destination hosts were connected, with the remaining 24 bits used to identify hosts on individual networks. This protocol could link no more than 256 different networks. This addressing scheme was carried forward into the subsequent versions of the U.S. Department of Defense specifications for the Internet Protocol, including RFC 760; only with the publication of the spec for the IPv4 we know and love in RFC 791 was the notion of network classes introduced.

Figure 2–1 shows how the IP network classes were depicted in RFC 791. The objective was to provide some mechanism for aggregation similar to that described in IEN 46, "A PROPOSAL FOR ADDRESSING AND ROUTING IN THE INTERNET," by David Clark and Danny Cohen, published in 1978.

Rather than insist on limiting the number of permitted networks in an Internet to only 256, the proposal suggested a future in which there were many more than 256 networks connected to a single Internet, with some of them very large and others much smaller. The report even pointed to potential routing issues related to larger numbers of interconnected networks: When there are only 256 or fewer networks, all routers can easily manage the nondefault routing tables. But when there are many more networks,

---

[2]Internet Engineering Note (IEN) 48, published July 1978 and available at http://www.isi.edu/in-notes/ien/ien48.txt
[3]IEN 48, p. 7.

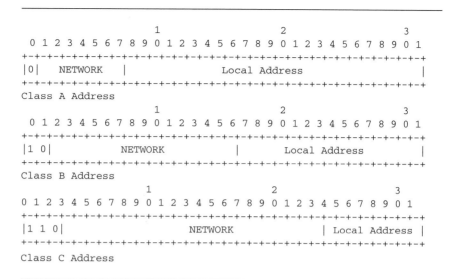

```
                        1                   2                   3
   0 1 2 3 4 5 6 7 8 9 0 1 2 3 4 5 6 7 8 9 0 1 2 3 4 5 6 7 8 9 0 1
  +-+-+-+-+-+-+-+-+-+-+-+-+-+-+-+-+-+-+-+-+-+-+-+-+-+-+-+-+-+-+-+-+
  |0|    NETWORK    |                 Local Address                |
  +-+-+-+-+-+-+-+-+-+-+-+-+-+-+-+-+-+-+-+-+-+-+-+-+-+-+-+-+-+-+-+-+
  Class A Address
                        1                   2                   3
   0 1 2 3 4 5 6 7 8 9 0 1 2 3 4 5 6 7 8 9 0 1 2 3 4 5 6 7 8 9 0 1
  +-+-+-+-+-+-+-+-+-+-+-+-+-+-+-+-+-+-+-+-+-+-+-+-+-+-+-+-+-+-+-+-+
  |1 0|          NETWORK          |          Local Address         |
  +-+-+-+-+-+-+-+-+-+-+-+-+-+-+-+-+-+-+-+-+-+-+-+-+-+-+-+-+-+-+-+-+
  Class B Address
                        1                   2                   3
   0 1 2 3 4 5 6 7 8 9 0 1 2 3 4 5 6 7 8 9 0 1 2 3 4 5 6 7 8 9 0 1
  +-+-+-+-+-+-+-+-+-+-+-+-+-+-+-+-+-+-+-+-+-+-+-+-+-+-+-+-+-+-+-+-+
  |1 1 0|                  NETWORK                 | Local Address |
  +-+-+-+-+-+-+-+-+-+-+-+-+-+-+-+-+-+-+-+-+-+-+-+-+-+-+-+-+-+-+-+-+
  Class C Address
```

Figure 2–1: Internet address classes, from RFC 791.

many of them with internal routers, aggregation provides a mechanism for inferring at least part of an IP destination's route based on its address.

Thirty-two bits can represent over 4 billion unique values, so (in theory, at least) an IPv4 Internet could grow considerably before a lack of available addresses would force any change in the protocol. Yet, in the space of just 25 years, the Internet grew from an experiment with a few dozen networks into a global network upon which hundreds of millions of people rely. The growth has been astronomical, from roughly 10^2 to roughly 10^9—that's seven orders of magnitude. The Internet today is roughly 10 million times the size it was in 1981.

This was a sustained rate of growth that had not been anticipated. Because of the way the IPv4 address space was originally conceived and implemented, the address space could be considered exhausted even though the majority of the address space was not actually being used. Looking at Figure 2–1, one reason for the IPv4 address space squeeze may become apparent. The lower half of the address space is reserved for no more than 126 very large networks. All 32-bit values starting with "0" will be assigned to just 126[4] networks, each with enough local address space to handle

---

[4]Why 126 and not 127? The loopback interface on 127.0.0.0 ties that address up. The all-zeroes address (0.0.0.0) is a reserved value used to indicate "all hosts on this network."

2^{24} nodes—no more than 16,777,216 globally unique addresses within each Class A network.

Assume for the moment that this is the correct size network address allocation for very large organizations (of which, presumably, no more than about 100 or so were expected in the foreseeable future). Once you've handed out half of the Class A networks, you've pulled a full 25% of the entire address space out of circulation. Not only that, but even if these huge organizations each managed to field a million nodes on every one of their Class A nets, they would still be leaving each Class A network 94% vacant.

By 1991, the IETF had already begun actively looking "Towards the Future Internet Architecture" in RFC 1287. In August 1990, during the Vancouver Internet Engineering Task Force (IETF) meeting, attendees projected that the current rate of assignment would exhaust the Class B space by March of 1994.[5] One result of that warning was the creation of the Classless Inter-Domain Routing specification (CIDR) to replace the old Class A/B/C categories[6] with a more flexible system that increased the efficiency with which IP addresses could be allocated as well as reduced some of the burden on routers as the number of Class C networks exploded. However, attendees at the July 1994 Toronto meeting of the IETF predicted that even with CIDR the IPv4 address space would still be exhausted sometime between 2005 and 2011.

Class A recipients include MIT, Apple Computer Inc., General Electric Company, Ford Motor Company, IBM, Xerox, Boeing Computer Services, and even pharmaceutical firms Eli Lilly and Company, and Merck and Company, Inc. By May 1993, 38% of the Class A networks had been allocated, as well as 45% of the Class Bs; Class C was relatively untouched, with only 2% of the total space allocated (over 44,000 networks).[7]

Note: RFC 1715, "The H Ratio for Address Assignment Efficiency," an Informational RFC published in 1994 by Christian Huitema, discussed the creation of a ratio for determining how efficiently an address space is being used; the IPv4 space was even then rapidly approaching saturation. RFC 3194, "The Host-Density Ratio for Address Assignment Efficiency: An update on the H ratio," revises that document with a refinement on

---

[5]RFC 1752, p. 3.

[6]Class D was allocated for IP multicast addresses, and Class E was reserved for future use.

[7]RFC 1466, "Guidelines for Management of IP Address Space," p. 3.

the calculation of address density, reaching the conclusion that the IPv4 address space continues to draw near to practical exhaustion. Both of these documents provide excellent insight into the growth of the Internet and the difficulty of efficiently using the IPv4 address space.

Class A networks accounted for half of the entire IPv4 address space; Class B networks accounted for 25% and Class C networks for 12.5%. A full one-eighth of the address space was reserved for future use (with half of that later allocated for IP multicast addresses), right off the top. Most firms of any size at all wanted Class B networks, and up until the early 1990s they could justify one as long as they had several hundred hosts, more than could fit in a single Class C network.

But Class B networks were almost as underutilized as the Class As, and with only 16,383 available, fully 45% had been allocated. With over two million Class C nets available, 44,000 or so networks barely made a dent in the total. Although the Class C allocation accounted for one-eighth of the total space, it was likely the most densely populated with hosts.

The year 1993 was pivotal: the U.S. government started the process of privatizing the Internet and making possible endless commercial possibilities. The land rush for IP address space (not to mention domain names) was about to begin, and IETF leaders knew that something drastic would have to be done—but the problem was clear well before that.

The strategy for dealing with the address space crisis included two urgent missions: First, design and deploy short-term, stopgap mechanisms that could be used to immediately and easily slow down the rapid rate of IPv4 address consumption; and second, design and deploy a successor protocol that would ultimately replace IPv4.

2.4 The IPv4 Routing Crisis

Although the imminent exhaustion of the IPv4 address space poses a devastating challenge, all the IP addresses in the world will not forestall another potential showstopper: ballooning default routing tables. IPv6 experts suggest that IPv4 routing scalability presents a more disturbing problem than address space issues.

2.4.1 IPv4 Internet Routing

Routers determine the paths by which IPv4 packets arrive at their
destinations. IP routing protocols may use dynamic mechanisms for maintaining information about available routes or may depend on statically
configured tables, but any packets intended for destinations across an
Internet backbone must eventually be routed through a *nondefault router*,[8]
a router that uses a master list of all known Internet routes. These routers
run Border Gateway Protocol version 4 (BGP-4), and the nondefault routing table, referred to as the Routing Information Base (RIB), effectively
describes the topology of the Internet.

Each RIB entry describes a single route, a BGP route being defined as "a
unit of information that pairs a destination with the attributes of a path to
that destination",[9] and as the number of entries in the RIB increases, so too
does the complexity of the router's task.

Most organizations use default routers, routers to which packets are sent
if they are not destined for local delivery; these routers usually have their
own default routers to fall back on when handling nonlocal packets. The
BGP routers have no fall-back position: If a packet's destination network
is not in the RIB, then the packet cannot be routed.

More networks means more routes. Classless Inter-Domain Routing
(CIDR) was instituted in the early 1990s to address the problem of misalign-
ment between the Internet address class structure. As will be discussed in
Chapter 3, CIDR allows more granularity in the assignment of network
address space.

2.4.2 IPv4 Route Aggregation

Instead of being locked into assigning Class A (8-bit network address
with 24-bit host addresses), Class B (16-bit network addresses, 16-bit host
addresses), or Class C (24-bit network, 8-bit host addresses), CIDR allowed
the aggregation of Class C addresses to provide variable network address
allocations. In other words, with CIDR you can make allocations of any
number of bits of network space, from a single Class A on up. A 23-bit

---

[8]Also known as exterior or BGP routers, the Border Gateway Protocol being the protocol
used to route packets outside the local autonomous system.

[9]RFC 1771, "A Border Gateway Protocol 4 (BGP-4)," Yakov Rekhter and Tony Li, 1995.

allocation gives you the equivalent of two Class C networks; a 22-bit allocation gives you four Class C's; and an 18-bit allocation gives you the equivalent of 64 Class C networks (or the equivalent of one quarter of a Class B network). Instead of allocating network address space in only three sizes (Classes A, B, and C), CIDR supports up to 16 different allocation sizes, from a single Class C up to half of a Class A.

The happy result was that now a company with 400 nodes to support could manage without getting two separate Class C networks (adding complexity all around) or trying to get a Class B network address. Less salutary was the resulting complexity added to the routing task: When all network addresses were 8, 16, or 24 bits long, routers could more easily identify the network portion of an address just by looking at the first few bits of each address that indicate the network class. The *network mask* indicates how much of the address is to be considered the network and how much is reserved for local assignment to host addressing.

By the mid-1990s, the convention of expressing network addresses in the form of 192.168.0.0/22, where the first part represents an IP address and the second part indicates how much of that address should be treated as a network address (the rest being reserved for host identification within that network), came about. That network includes the four Class C networks 192.168.0.0, 192.168.1.0, 192.168.2.0, and 192.168.3.0.

This formulation allows routers to more quickly compare the relevant pieces of the address to its routing table.

Aggregation improves matters considerably, but the situation continues to deteriorate as more of the IPv4 address space is assigned and put into service. The more networks there are, the longer the routing list becomes. And the longer the routing list, the longer (on average) it will take the router to figure out where to send the packet. This is not a problem if you have 10, or 100, or 1000 networks to keep track of. But when you get into the higher numbers, as we have now with the Internet, with backbone routers routinely carrying explicit routes for over 110,000 different network addresses,[10] routing can become a nightmare.

---

[10] The Asia Pacific Network Information Centre (APNIC) maintains graphical reports on the state of the BGP routing table at http://www.apnic.net/stats/bgp/; ARIN provides weekly ASCII reports on its mailing list at http://www.arin.net/mailinglists/rtma/.

2.4.3 IPv4 Routing Scalability

RFC 3221, "Commentary on Inter-Domain Routing in the Internet," provides detailed discussion of the problem. As the routing table grew from about 60,000 entries in early 1999 to as many as 110,000 to120,000 entries in 2002, the problem became more than simply handling the number of entries. Geoff Huston, member of the Internet Architecture Board (IAB), cites several disturbing trends in RFC 3221, including the following.

- *Growth in route announcements.* Measured from January 1999 through December 2000, the routing table increased at a rate of 42% per year. Drops in the size of the table during 2001 can be attributed to instances where large numbers of more specific network routes were aggregated into more general routes—for example, when several contiguous Class C (/24) addresses are aggregated into a single /20 route.
- *The 16-bit address space for autonomous system (AS) numbering,* uniquely identifying discrete networks connected to the Internet, supports only 65,535 unique values. Although work is in progress to increase the AS address space to 32-bits, Huston reported over 10,000 autonomous systems across the Internet as of May 2001—then growing at a rate of 51% per year. This rate of growth would exhaust the 16-bit numbering space by August of 2005.
- *IPv4 address consumption,* measured strictly in terms of how much of the address space is being advertised as routable, has been leveling off at a bit more than a quarter of the entire address space. Recent growth reported by Huston showed a 7% annual increase in total address space consumption. Seen in light of the growth in both routes and ASs, this may indicate that most IP host growth is being hidden behind NATs. Alternatively, this data can be explained by organizations applying more specific policies on their exterior routing (i.e., rather than using a single exterior router to mediate all Internet traffic, a multinational might have separate routers serving separate ASs on different continents).
- *Increasing granularity of routing entries.* The amount of IPv4 address space served within the average AS or the average BGP route is dropping. An average route in September 2001 served networks with total capacity of 10,700 IP addresses—a considerable drop from the average 16,000 in November 1999. The average AS in December 1999 had a capacity of 161,900 IP

addresses; by January 2001, the average had dropped to 115,800. Increasingly detailed routing data is being pumped into the global routing domain, in part due to an increase in complexity resulting from decreased reliance on hierarchical routing and increased use of multi-homing (linking to multiple networks).

- *Prefix length distribution is increasing.* The prefix length is a function of the specificity of the network address; a /24 (24-bit) prefix is far more specific than a /8 (8-bit) prefix. Huston reports significant increases in the number of routes with a prefix length of /24 or more over recent years. This ties in with the increased granularity of routing entries.

- *Exceptions to aggregations,* or holes in an aggregation, occur when all of the networks within a particular prefix are routed in the same way except for one or more subsets of the aggregated network. Huston reports that 55% of the then-current routing table entries were of this type, and over two-thirds of those routes used distinct AS paths.

It is not even clear that IPv6 will solve all these problems: BGP is intended for exterior routing with IPv6 as well as IPv4, and fragmentation of aggregates can occur in the IPv6 address space as easily as in the IPv4 space. However, IPv6 does provide a better framework for aggregation than IPv4, as we'll see later.

2.5 The End-to-End Problem

End-to-endness or *transparency* is what you get when endpoints in a network are able to interoperate without any knowledge of the intervening network and without any intervention or interference from intermediate systems. Transparency makes network application development much simpler, for one thing. The developer need only program an application to interface with the network cloud; when transparency is absent, the developer must deal with intermediate systems such as firewalls, NATs (network address translators, see Chapter 3), and caching proxies. Security, in particular, is sensitive to transparency.

NATs compromise end-to-endness because they modify inbound and outbound packet headers. When packet headers are modified, network layer security protocols become useless. There is no qualitative difference between a NAT modifying packet headers on a secured packet and an attacker modifying packet headers in order to *spoof* (send packets from one host that purport to be from another host) the recipient. Both appear to be attacks. In practice, the growth of the NAT-ed Internet has slowed growth of applications that require transparency.

The reason NATs modify packet headers is that the original headers, from inside the NAT-ed network, use the private (NET-10) addresses that are not unique across the global Internet. Using globally unique addresses means that there is an unambiguous way to address each and every network node, no matter where the node is. Once you start numbering nodes ambiguously, NATs and other intermediary systems must be used to prevent confusion and allow nodes with the same addresses to communicate.

Transparency guarantees that communicating nodes communicate directly, no matter what happens within the network cloud. When a NAT or other intermediate system fails, the sessions it mediates also fail. There is no easy way for hosts communicating through that NAT to route around the failure, as there would be in the event that some intermediate router failed.

End-to-end interoperability was a key design feature of the original Internet. As the IPv4 address pool dries up and more networks rely on NAT, proxies, and other gateway devices, the nature of the Internet is changing. Rather than being a robust network, able to route around failures, today's Internet is becoming less reliable while performance degrades. Rather than being a scalable network, capable of supporting new applications without requiring network infrastructure upgrades, today's Internet tends to limit applications to piggybacking on Web services—and at the same time, changes in the network infrastructure sometimes necessitate changes in node software and configuration.

RFC 3424, "IAB Considerations for UNilateral Self-Address Fixing (UNSAF) Across Network Address Translation," discusses the issues raised when network traffic must traverse multiple NAT domains, particularly as they relate to network transparency.

As we'll see later on, IPv6 eliminates NAT and replaces it with a concept of *link-local* and *site-local* network addresses. These local addresses can be thought of (for now) in the same way as telephone extensions might be: Callers from outside may have to dial a country code, area code, exchange, and extension, while callers from inside a single office (link-local) or organization (site-local) can reach the same destination by dialing an extension.

It should be noted that the loss of transparency is only a symptom of the disease—if the Internet had not grown so fast and so large, it would still be a transparent network with end-to-end interoperability the norm. The threat to transparency is due to the same growth that has caused the shortage in IPv4 addresses and the increasing reliance on NAT as a conservation tool.

2.6 Summary

There are many reasons cited by IPv6 supporters for migrating from IPv4 to IPv6, from general ones—such as reduced costs of operation, improved performance, and increased security—to specific ones—such as support for some "killer app" like mobile IP or plug-and-play interoperability. However, all of them can be directly linked either to the huge demand for and dwindling supply of IPv4 network addresses or to the problems associated with creating a scalable routing infrastructure. The next chapter illustrates the approaches over the past decades as short-term fixes for the IPv4 address shortage; Part II will show how IPv6 resolves these problems more permanently.

3

Patching IPv4

Large networks with many endpoints, such as the Internet, are economically viable only if the cost of maintaining those endpoints is manageable. Network upgrades that require modification of the endpoints are to be avoided at all costs, if only because of the difficulty of tracking down every node. Backward compatibility in the Internet is mandatory to avoid the cost of maintaining IP implementations on obsolete or custom-built computers. Even if all nodes ran the same operating system, attempting to upgrade all of them at once with network stack updates is a daunting task.

Protocol designers, whether they've designed protocols for transmission of electricity, telecommunications, or the Internet, must live with the shape of their networks. That means a minimal number of options for the designers of electrical appliance plugs, telephone cabling, or Internet applications. If the basic interface is not suitable, the application must be adapted to the interface rather than vice versa. To the extent that changes have been made to IPv4 over the years, most of the changes have been in the network routing infrastructure rather than in the way IPv4 has been implemented on network endpoints.

In this chapter, we examine four basic strategies that have been used to allow IPv4 to cope with its unprecedented growth and then look at how those strategies have been implemented.

Many of the key features of today's Internet landscape owe their origins to initiatives intended to extend the usable lifetime of IPv4. These measures fall into one or another of these four categories of responses to shortages of limited resources.

Rationing   When a shortage in a particular resource becomes apparent, rationing is often the first response. Survivors on a lifeboat are well advised to identify all their food and water resources and impose a reasonable rationing regime on all. Once it became clear that IPv4 addresses would soon be in short supply, the IETF recommended that regional Internet registries (RIRs) imposed more stringent controls over assignment of large blocks of IP addresses. Until 1992, organizations could relatively easily justify a Class B network allocation as long as they had (or expected to have) more than a few hundred hosts. Since then the IETF and RIRs have repeatedly raised the bar for justification of IPv4 assignments.

Rethinking   Conservation efforts are the result of rethinking the way resources are used. Carpools are one response to gasoline shortages; people must rethink the way they solve the problem of getting to and from their workplaces. The IETF, network managers, and vendors have all applied their creative powers to rethinking their use of IP addresses and coming up with ways to conserve the resource. These efforts yielded the use of subnets,[1] Classless Inter-Domain Routing (CIDR), the Dynamic Host Configuration Protocol (DHCP), and several versions of network address translation (NAT).

Recycling   The allocation of IPv4 network addresses by class left a legacy of vastly underutilized Class A networks. The IETF put out a call to organizations with unused or underused network addresses to return them for reuse in 1996,[2] many cable broadband providers use such space for their home-based customers. Recycling addresses

---

[1] Arguably, the use of subnetting was instituted more as a way to improve routing efficiency, but routing and address space exhaustion are two faces of the same coin.

[2] In RFC 1917 (BCP 4), "An Appeal to the Internet Community to Return Unused IP Networks (Prefixes) to the IANA."

in this way can never offer more than a marginal improvement in the address shortage situation. One potential problem with recycling addresses derives from the practice of hard-coding IP addresses into applications, rather than relying on DNS. If clients always use DNS to reach host *hostname.example.com*, they'll always reach that host; if they use an IP address that someday is recycled, the application will fail. This problem should be insignificant unless developers try to bypass DNS to improve performance at the cost of standards compliance.

Replacement Usually, a piece of infrastructure is replaced entirely only after all other remedies are exhausted. It is just too expensive and cumbersome to pull out the old and put in the new and make sure it all works. However, IPv6 is, ultimately, a replacement for IPv4. We'll touch on options, other than IPv6, that have been proposed to replace IPv4.

The rest of this chapter introduces the most important responses to the IPv4 address space shortage made by the Internet community. It is tempting to put these efforts in chronological order, but doing so can be difficult. For example, not only was Classless Inter-Domain Routing (CIDR) developed roughly in parallel with new rationing policies, but CIDR made such rationing more feasible.

3.1 Network Address Rationing

When demand for a necessity increases suddenly but supply stays inflexibly the same with no change in sight, rationing kicks in. This was one of the first steps taken to address address space shortage, and it resulted in the creation of the three regional Internet registries (RIRs), which were advised to clamp down on who gets IP address space and who doesn't. Published in 1990, RFC 1174, "IAB Recommended Policy on Distributing Internet Identifier Assignment and IAB Recommended Policy Change to Internet 'Connected' Status," called for the Internet registry (IR) function to be delegated by the IANA, so as to better manage distribution of Internet addresses.

Further modifications—in particular the call for creation of Regional Internet Registries (RIRs)—followed in 1992, when RFC 1366, "Guidelines for Management of IP Address Space," was published. RFC 1367, "Schedule for IP Address Space Management Guidelines," was published at the same time and defined a schedule as well as a set of guidelines for address allocation.

RFC 1366 recommended that the remaining Class A network addresses (77) be assigned only by the IANA and that all Class A network addresses over 64/8 be frozen. At the time, it was expected that no Class A addresses would be granted to anyone, but if an organization wanted one, they would have to provide technical details of their proposed network in their petition. As for Class B addresses, the recommendation was to grant them only to organizations that required at least 32 subnets and over 4096 nodes.

Prior to the early 1990s, network address assignment was done on a less formal basis; subsequent to the implementation of the RIRs and the address space management guidelines, address space allocation followed a more formal process under which requesting organizations were required to justify their requests. RIRs also currently assess fees for the use of network address space, adding a market-driven form of rationing. Unlike the early days, holders of large portions of the network address space are now under increasing financial pressure to either use their addresses or trade them in.

3.2   IP Subnetting

The original standard for IPv4 as defined in RFC 791, "Internet Protocol: DARPA Internet Program Protocol Specification," doesn't mention the term *subnet*. As originally defined, the Internet was to be a two-level hierarchy, in which individual nodes (the bottom level) were connected to various networks (the upper level). The Internet was a *classful* network, with smallish networks to be assigned Class C network addresses, large networks assigned Class B network addresses, and the very largest networks assigned Class A network addresses.

It wasn't long after RFC 791 was implemented that the flaws in this addressing approach became evident. Networks that used different media needed to be treated differently; not all nodes within a network would fit on a single cable; organizations spread across large physical plants often required more than one physical LAN; and popular networking technologies such as Ethernet placed limits on the number of nodes on the same network. It was all very well to allow Class B networks 16 bits of address space and over 65,000 uniquely addressable nodes, but the LAN technologies most often used (Ethernet and Token Ring) limited the practical number of nodes on a network to well under 1000.

The solution was to provide a way to subdivide Internet addresses in such a way that a large network could be made to appear to consist of several smaller *subnetworks* or *subnets*. As originally defined in RFC 791, IP nodes interpreted IP addresses by comparing the higher-order bits to determine what address class the address belonged to. Class A addresses have their highest-order bit set to 0 (first octet is in the range of 0 to 127), Class B addresses have their two highest-order bits set to 10 (first octet is in the range of 128 to 191), and Class C addresses have their three highest order bits set to 110 (first octet is in the range of 192 to 223).

Early IP routing depended on nodes interpreting IP addresses classfully so that routers would consider only the first octet of an address as the network and treat the rest of the address as a unique identifier for nodes on that network. Clearly this approach could complicate matters for Class A networks with many thousands of nodes, because routers within the organization would be required to keep track of the locations of all of them.

By 1984, when RFC 917, "Internet Subnets," was published, the two-level approach to internetworking was proving insufficient. RFC 917 documented an approach that was being taken within larger networks, where Class A and Class B networks were using artificial subdivisions to improve internal routing. Published a year later, RFC 950, "Internet Standard Subnetting Procedure," codified an approach to subnetting based on RFC 917.

Although Internet addresses are not, strictly speaking, hierarchical, they are interpreted as if they are. In other words, addresses sharing some number of higher-order bits can be considered to be on the same network. Thus, as just noted, classful network addresses sharing the first three octets, with the first octet in the range of 192 to 223, are treated as being on the same Class C network; network addresses sharing a first octet in the range of 0 to 127 are treated as being on the same Class A network. Figure 3–1 shows how routing occurs to a typical Class B address: 172.16.0.0. The external router accepts all packets destined for any node with an address starting with 172.16.x.x.

The practice of subnetting allows the owner of a Class A address to partition that address space and create logical subnets. A typical use of subnetting,

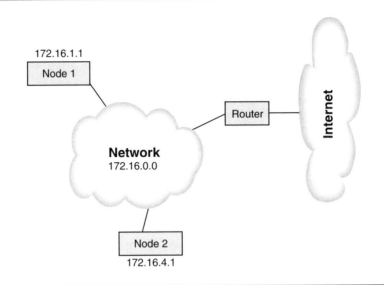

Figure 3–1: External routing of classful Internet addresses.

circa 1988, would see a Class B address with 8 bits of subnet. In all cases, the first 16 bits of the Class B address would be shared by all nodes on the network, but the third octet (bits 17–24) would be used to specify a unique subnet within the Class B network. External routing decisions of packets sent to any node within that Class B address would be identical, but once the packets entered the subnetted network, routers would examine the subnetted portion of the addresses to determine how to route them internally.

As Figure 3–2 shows, subnets allow for more structured internal routing in a Class B network. The internal router is configured to examine the third octet of the network address (the 8 high-order bits of the local part of addresses in the 172.16.x.x network) as a subnet. The external router passes traffic to the appropriate internal router, based on the subnet. For clarity, only one internal router is shown in Figure 3–2, but there could be many others in a large network.

Further subnetting within each subnet is also possible, so complex routing architectures can be created within large organizations. At the same time, it is not necessary for the outer layers of routers to be aware of the

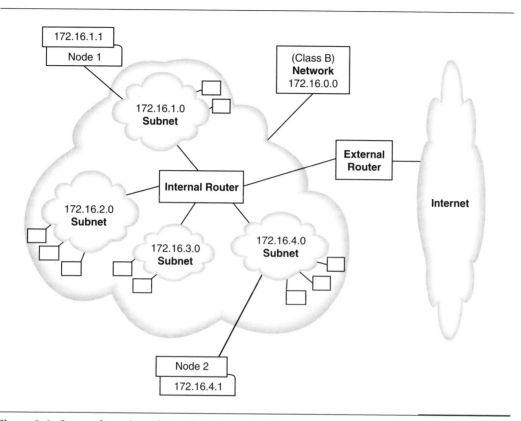

Figure 3–2: Internal routing of classful Internet addresses.

existence of nested sub-subnets. In the example shown here, the external router does need to be configured to route to 8 bits of internal subnet—but any of those subnets could further partition their address space, interpreting 9 or more bits as the subnet address within their network clouds.

Subnetting doesn't increase the number of IP addresses available for use, but it does make it possible to use the address space within any network more efficiently.[3] The idea of using parts of the local address space to form logical subnets also led to the use of parts of the network address

---

[3]Networks of any class may be subnetted, although Class C network subnetting requires a more delicate touch to avoid wasting space or running out of subnets.

space to combine Class C networks to simplify networking in organizations too large for a single Class C but not large enough for a Class B network.

3.3   Classless Inter-Domain Routing (CIDR)

When most computers in use were mainframes costing at least tens or hundreds of thousands of dollars, Class C networks capable of supporting up to 254 uniquely addressed nodes were originally viewed as sufficient for all but the largest corporations. But starting in the early 1980s the growth in popularity of networked PCs within even moderate-sized organizations meant that the concept of "large-" and "moderate-sized" networks changed radically. A Class C network could easily accommodate most smaller businesses, but demand for Class B addresses skyrocketed through the 1980s, and the small supply (just over 16,000) meant that rationing of Class B addresses started very early.

During the early 1990s, experts were concerned about rapid growth in nondefault routing tables, and RFC 1519 includes a discussion of the impact CIDR could have on nondefault routing tables. For example, the authors cite a backbone router (on NSFNET) with approximately 4700 routing table entries as of January 1992—a number that grew to roughly 8500 routes by December 1992.

Subnetting was one way to increase efficiency in the allocation of network addresses within large networks by partitioning large chunks of network address space. By the time the Class B network supply was clearly being rapidly depleted, Class C networks were (and still are, for the most part) plentiful. What would happen if small chunks of network address space—for example, contiguous Class C networks—were aggregated together and treated as if they were a single network?

The result is called *Classless Inter-Domain Routing* (CIDR), sometimes called *supernetting* (in contrast to subnetting). CIDR has become a key mechanism for moderating the effects of Internet growth, and it is defined in RFC 1519, "Class Inter-Domain Routing (CIDR): an Address Assignment and Aggregation Strategy." Rather than specifying some number of bits of subnet to be considered as the network part of an address in addition to the official, classful, network address, CIDR masks specify how many bits of a Class C address to consider too. The allocation size is specified using the form

```
192.168.128.0/17
```

to specify that the high-order 17 bits of the address identify the network, and the rest of the address is used to identify internal nodes. Thus, classful network addresses can be specified as follows.

```
Network Class   Network Address   Mask
-------------   ---------------   ----
Class A         10.0.0.0          /8
Class B         172.16.0.0        /16
Class C         192.168.1.0       /24
```

Classful addressing has long been obsolete, and this form has been used to allow a higher degree of aggregation of routes as well as for indicating subnets. When a number of Class C networks, for example, are aggregated by supernetting with CIDR, routers need only examine the number of high-order bits specified in the mask before looking for a network route to match the address. As Table 3–1 shows, you can supernet 16 Class C networks into a single /20 network capable of supporting no more than 4096 unique node addresses;[4] a /16 allocation gives you the equivalent of a Class B network.

The advantage of the CIDR approach is that it delegates not just the task of routing many smaller networks but also the task of allocating address space to large ISPs. The large ISPs are allocated chunks of the former Class C network address space, and they assign chunks to their customers as needed. An organization that needs the equivalent of four Class C networks can get that many, while organizations that only need a dozen addresses can also be accommodated.

The ISP providing Internet backbone access can advertise itself as being a single supernetted network instead of advertising a separate network route for each customer. Doing this collapses the size of the nondefault routing table, often dramatically.

---

[4]Actually, no more than 4094 addresses; all-ones and all-zeros addresses are reserved addresses.

Mask	# of Class C Networks	# of Host Addresses
/20	16	4094
/19	32	8190
/18	64	16,382
/17	128	32,766
/16	256	65,534
/15	512	131,070
/14	1024	262,142

Table 3–1: As a CIDR allocation mask decreases in size, the number of /24 networks (equivalent to a Class C network) and number of host addresses available increase.

Another result of the deprecation of network classes is that Class A network space (such as 24.0.0.0, as noted earlier) can be allocated in much smaller chunks. For example, the network address 10.4.37.0 /24 may appear to be a subnet of a Class A network, but it actually refers to the equivalent of a Class C network using the newer orthography.

Despite the best efforts of the IETF, nondefault routing tables have grown up to 30-fold since 1992. Although the situation would be much worse without supernetting, CIDR can no longer be considered a long-term solution.

3.4   Dynamic Host Configuration Protocol (DHCP)

One of the early obstacles to IP network scalability was the need to manually configure network nodes with their IP addresses. Based on the Bootstrap Protocol (BOOTP; see RFC 951), the Dynamic Host Configuration Protocol (DHCP; see RFC 2131) provides an automated mechanism for assigning and managing IP address assignment. DHCP has become vital to the operation of large networks, particularly because it allows nodes to "lease" IP addresses: When the lease period is up, the node "returns" the address so it can be reused by some other node.

DHCP is mandatory for networks that may consist of more nodes than allocated IP addresses, such as those offering dial-up access where users log on and off the network regularly. For example, if an ISP offers dial-up access to its Class C network with DHCP, and the average user connects for only two hours a day (distributed evenly, an admittedly unreasonable expectation in real life), the ISP could support roughly 3000 users with only 254 IP addresses.

Although DHCP is also an important tool for providers of "always-on" services such as broadband Internet connectivity, it does not do anything to improve address utilization efficiency in those networks. Every user whose computer is always connected to the network ties up a single IP address; there can be no sharing of addresses as with the more fleeting connections common to dial-up users.

3.5   Recycling Unused IP Networks

RFC 1917 (BCP 4) "An Appeal to the Internet Community to Return Unused IP Networks (Prefixes) to the IANA," demonstrates a slightly different approach to shortage: recycling. Many large chunks of the IPv4 address space have been allocated to organizations that no longer exist or that could never use all of their allocations. Several of these pieces have been recovered, since their previous owners have done the right thing and allowed some or all of their allocation to revert to the registries.

Over the years, Class A networks have been returned to IANA, some of which have simply changed hands (in the 1980s), but mostly as they come in, they are reserved. Some networks of note include the following.

> **10/8:** originally assigned to DARPANET
> **31/8:** originally assigned to University of California
> **36/8:** originally assigned to Stanford University
> **49/8:** Joint Technical Command
> **50/8:** Joint Technical Command

The 024/8 network, at one time administered by Bolt, Beranek, and Newman (the firm responsible for much of the original work on the Internet), was reregistered to the IANA in 1995 and has been recovered for use as the "ARIN Cable Block." North American cable network ISPs are now able to assign numbers out of the subnetted 024/8 block, demonstrating both the use of subnetted Class A network addresses and successful recycling of underused addresses.

3.6   Subnetting Class A Networks

With the deprecation of classful internetworking and the gradual return of sizable chunks of network address space in the form of recycled Class A networks, CIDR, and subnetting provide an excellent and efficient approach to reusing this formerly wasted resource.

In April 1995, experimental RFC 1797, "Class A Subnet Experiment," documented the experimental use of network 39/8 for subnetting. As reported in RFC 1879, "Class A Subnet Experiment: Results and Recommendations," during trials the approach proved successful, and in 1996, the IANA recommended that Class A addresses be used in this way as soon as possible.

The experiment was designed to determine whether the then-current routing software would correctly interpret subnetted Class A addresses. The Class A network 39/8 was chosen for the experiment and divided into two parts designated by the value of the high-order bit of the local part of the address (see Figure 3–3). If that bit is 0, the next 15 bits of the address are to correspond to the low-order 15 bits of the autonomous system[5] (AS) number assigned to an existing network. By using existing ASs, the experimenters were able to populate the network quickly and without any explicit action on the part of the owners of the ASs.

```
+--------+-+-------+--------+--------+
|   39   |0| low 15 bits AS | local  |
+--------+-+-------+--------+--------+
         ^
         |
          \
           high order bit of the
           local part of the address
```

Figure 3–3: "Case 1" from RFC 1797.

---

[5]An AS on the Internet is a backbone-routed network. In other words, there is a single, well-defined routing policy applied when routing external traffic to and from any nodes or networks within the AS. For example, an ISP may provide connectivity for dozens of different customer networks, but all those networks will fall within the ISP's AS for the purpose of routing. Packets moving from one customer network to another are routed internally, and external packets bound for any of the customer networks are routed in the same way.

```
+--------+-+-------+--------+--------+
|   39   |1| variable prefix + local |
+--------+-+-------+--------+--------+
         ^
         |
         \
           high order bit of the
           local part of the address
```

Figure 3–4: "Case 2" from RFC 1797.

Setting the high-order bit of the local part of the address to 1 for the purposes of this experiment would have signified that the address space would be allocated explicitly by the IANA (see Figure 3–4). This option was not used during the experiment.

As reported in RFC 1879, existing router software was capable of handling subnetted Class A networks and even includes examples to be used to configure typical routers.

3.7   Network Address Translation (NAT)

By the late 1980s, a significant segment of the IPv4 market deployed their internetworks with minimal or even no connectivity to the global Internet. Managers of these private networks might isolate them with firewalls or even keep them completely separate, forbidding all external contact other than email exchanged through an application gateway with an air-gap (when the gateway connects with the outside, the internal connection is broken and restored only when the external link is completed).

By the early 1990s, the process of applying for an official and globally unique IPv4 address had become sufficiently arduous, particularly for larger networks, that an alternative came into general use. A set of *private network addresses* was set aside officially in RFC 1597, "Address Allocation for Private Internets," and RFC 1631, "The IP Network Address Translator (NAT)," elaborated on the idea of reusing IP addresses originally suggested by Van Jacobson.

NATs have been hailed by some as the remedy for some if not all of what ails the Internet and IPv4, whereas others consider them the network equivalent of kudzu: a hardy and fast-growing plant that was imported to parts of the southeast United States to alleviate soil erosion earlier in the 20th century. Despite the lofty goals, kudzu turned out to be a superweed, and with no natural checks on its growth, kudzu has displaced almost everything in its path. It grows so quickly that visitors may be cautioned not to nap on the porch unless they want to wake up tangled in the vines that are known to grow as much as a foot or more in a day.

3.7.1 Reasons for NAT

There are times when it is preferable for packets not to be forwarded directly from inside an internetwork. Network address translation (NAT) is an approach used for those instances. The two most commonly cited reasons for using NAT are for security and to map a large network onto a small IP address space.

Perhaps more common is the use of NATs to preserve IP address space. As the IP address space is depleted, more and more organizations have been denied Class B or even Class C networks. One solution is to use the private network space allocation to set up a private network with a Class A, B, or C network address. Routers within the private network can route packets within the network, and packets destined for the global Internet are passed through a network address translator that acts on behalf of the internal systems when interacting with Internet hosts.

NATs were originally introduced to help alleviate network address allocation shortages so organizations could build their intranets as large as they wanted without going through a lengthy and largely pointless process of trying to get an appropriate allocation from a service provider or regional registry. In the meantime, they have propagated across the Internet and have been incorporated into networks as simple and small as single-system home networks and as complicated as any that requires a full Class A–equivalent network address.

Much of the controversy over the need for IPv6 revolves around the question of whether NATs make things better or worse. In the meantime, people continue to deploy private networks and NAT boxes of various types, while the IETF continues to publish RFCs that attempt to clarify matters or even to solve the entire problem with ever more end-to-end friendly versions of NAT.

3.7.2   NAT BASICS

Whether you call it a network address translator or NAT box, a NAT acts as an old-fashioned telephone operator, mediating all inbound and outbound traffic through a switchboard. Inside the NAT, private IP addresses are used for all internal communications; outside the NAT, standard global Internet addresses are used. The NAT box has one interface on the internal network with a private IP address and another interface on the global Internet with a globally unique IP address.

When a node in the private network wants to send a packet to a node on the outside, it creates a packet with its own private IP address as the source and the remote node's IP address as the destination. Following the rules of IP routing, the privately addressed node will determine that the destination is on a different network and therefore the packet must be sent to a router.

NAT boxes often double as routers, to both reduce costs and simplify their function. When the NAT box/router receives the outbound packet, it takes that packet and rewrites it so that the original source address (which will not be usable outside the private network) is replaced with the NAT box's own global Internet IP address. The packet is then sent along to its destination. The destination node perceives the packet as originating with the NAT box.

Any response to the packet is addressed to the NAT box, which keeps track of the internal hosts for which it is serving as go-between. When a packet comes in, the NAT box accepts it, repackages the packet for delivery on the private network, and sends it along to the original source node.

Basic NAT poses difficulties when it is necessary to host Internet servers within the private network: There is only one well-known port for each service available on the NAT box, which makes it difficult when more than one Web server is inside the network. All NAT boxes map the ports as well as IP addresses from the external session onto appropriate ports and addresses for the internal network.

There is another problem: dealing with a network in which more than one server responding to requests on the same well-known port. When there is a single NAT box in front of those servers, the Network Address Translation/Port Translation (NAT/PT) adds a port translator module onto the NAT box so it can differentiate requests to the different servers.

Various other developments and proposals to make NAT friendlier have been considered and implemented over the years, more or less successfully. Some indication of these developments can be inferred from the quantity and titles of the NAT-related RFCs listed later in this section.

3.7.3 NAT ISSUES AND MISCONCEPTIONS

Rather than attempting to cover NATs exhaustively here, we list relevant and current RFCs after a short list of NAT-related problems and concerns.

NATs break IPsec   IPsec (see Chapter 6) is not made any easier by NATs, but it is still often usable. When packets from inside the private network are tunneled securely with IPsec (that is, IPsec secures packets, which are then encapsulated in unsecured IP packets), NATs do not modify the tunneled packets and thus do not harm them. However, end-to-end, untunneled authenticated packets cannot be carried intact across a NAT. Another area where NATs affect IPsec is in the reuse of the private IP addresses. Nonunique addresses can result in confusion, at the least, especially when security information is linked with IP addresses.

NATs complicate organization change   NATs provide a limited number of options for network addressing to the network designer. The odds of having address space collisions are great. Most people naturally assign the network address 192.168.0.0 to their small private network and assign hosts to IP addresses starting at 192.168.0.1 and increasing by one. When two such networks are merged, pandemonium ensues as networked systems stop working and network engineers rush madly to renumber at least one of the original networks.

NATs break applications   Most NAT-related problems with Internet applications are manageable and have been or will be imminently resolved through one fix or another. One notorious application broken by NAT so far has been the multiplayer game, Quake. More relevant to corporate network administrators, FTP was originally specified to allow inbound connections from servers to clients, and in so doing, has broken in that type of implementation used across a NAT.

NATs improve security   IP routers are not supposed to forward datagrams addressed in the private address ranges. If a backbone router receives a datagram bound for one of these addresses, it is supposed to drop it. However, these addresses can be used within an organizational internetwork. Allowing outsiders access to information about a network's host names and IP addresses can expose that network to security risks. Some network administrators prefer to put their entire network behind a network address translator, which accepts datagrams from outside the internetwork and translates them to the NAT addresses used by the hosts inside the private network. However, NATs can often open more holes than they close, especially when routers are not properly configured to drop packets addressed from or to private networks—or when routers can be reconfigured by an attacker. Likewise, network administrators typically use a fairly predictable set of addresses for NAT-ed networks, so attackers may have an easier time locating sensitive systems.

NATs are easy   Solid-state NAT/router/hub/firewall/Internet appliances capable of linking small numbers of systems in home office/small office environments are widely available at reasonable prices. These devices often include a Dynamic Host Configuration Protocol (DHCP) server, making the NAT a plug-and-play as well as an install-and-forget proposition.

NATs are complicated   Deploying NATs in complex Internet environments, can generate network administration nightmares, particularly if there are other NATs already in the network (such as in branch offices). Some engineers have reported that the actual cost of maintaining such a network far exceeds the cost of paying for enough globally unique Internet address space to serve the organization's needs—if that address space were available.

All NATs are pretty much the same   As already noted, there are basic network address-only translators as well as network and port translators; a NAT box may be an inexpensive solid-state appliance, a piece of software running on a PC, or a dedicated router. There are many different types of NATs, and there are many of each type already in use throughout the world.

3.7.4   NAT AND RELATED RFCs

As of 2002, these RFCs had been published about NAT and the issues related to its use. A good place to start is RFC 3022, "Traditional IP Network Address Translator (Traditional NAT)," defining traditional NAT functions. RFC 2663, "IP Network Address Translator (NAT)

Terminology and Considerations," is another good basis for discussion of NAT issues, as are RFC 3027, "Protocol Complications with the IP Network Address Translator," and RFC 2993 "Architectural Implications of NAT."

RFC 1631 *The IP Network Address Translator (NAT)* INFORMATIONAL (obsoleted by RFC 3022)

RFC 2391 *Load Sharing Using IP Network Address Translation (LSNAT)* INFORMATIONAL

RFC 2663 *IP Network Address Translator (NAT) Terminology and Considerations* INFORMATIONAL

RFC 2709 *Security Model with Tunnel-Mode IPsec for NAT Domains* INFORMATIONAL

RFC 2766 *Network Address Translation—Protocol Translation (NAT-PT)* PROPOSED STANDARD

RFC 2962 *An SNMP Application Level Gateway for Payload Address Translation* INFORMATIONAL

RFC 2993 *Architectural Implications of NAT* INFORMATIONAL

RFC 3022 *Traditional IP Network Address Translator (Traditional NAT)* INFORMATIONAL

RFC 3027 *Protocol Complications with the IP Network Address Translator* INFORMATIONAL

RFC 3102 *Realm Specific IP: Framework* EXPERIMENTAL

RFC 3103 *Realm Specific IP: Protocol Specification* EXPERIMENTAL

RFC 3104 *RSIP Support for End-to-End IPsec* EXPERIMENTAL

RFC 3105 *Finding an RSIP Server with SLP* EXPERIMENTAL

RFC 3235 *Network Address Translator (NAT)—Friendly Application Design Guidelines* INFORMATIONAL

RFC 3257 *Stream Control Transmission Protocol Applicability Statement* INFORMATIONAL

This list does not necessarily include every RFC that mentions NAT, only those that are particularly relevant. Only one of these, RFC 2766, is published as a proposed standard; that the rest are all either experimental or informational RFCs shows the degree to which NAT is still very much a topic of research and discussion.

3.8 Realm-Specific IP (RSIP)

The greatest problem with NAT is that lacking a globally unique address to link to a privately addressed node, "end-to-endness"—the quality of having data transmitted directly, without modification, and with assurance of data integrity from source node to destination node—becomes difficult to impossible.

Having been proposed as a method to avoid depleting the IPv4 address space, NAT has been an easy and safe answer for some years now. The only alternatives for much of the late 1990s seemed to be either further rationing of IPv4 addresses or a rapid migration to IPv6 support. Neither of those options is particularly appealing, but there was no other mechanism by which the existing IPv4 Internet infrastructure could be preserved while at the same time relieving the address squeeze by adding new globally unique addresses.

That is, until the Realm-Specific IP (RSIP) protocol arrived, published in late 2001 in a series of four experimental RFCs (see the RFC list for the titles of RFCs 3102 through 3105). As explained in RFC 3102, "Realm Specific IP: Framework," NAT "has become a popular mechanism of enabling the separation of addressing spaces. A NAT router must examine and change the network layer, (and possibly the transport layer) header of each packet crossing the addressing domains that the NAT router is connecting. This causes the mechanism of NAT to violate the end-to-end nature of the Internet connectivity and disrupts protocols requiring or enforcing end-to-end integrity of packets."

Rather than depending on an artificial pool of nonunique IP addresses and the NAT to interoperate with the global Internet from inside a private network, RSIP defines a mechanism by which a host in one addressing realm (that is, a private network) can be allowed to use network resources from a second addressing realm (that is, the global Internet).

RSIP gateways, which replace the NAT boxes, must have the ability to permit the use of those resources—"addresses and other routing parameters," according to RFC 3102—and the (private) RSIP node can interoperate directly with an Internet node without any lower-layer protocol tinkering, as is done by a NAT. An added benefit is that using RSIP depends on the network edges (the RSIP gateways) rather than the interior of the network. Nodes need not be updated to support RSIP as long as RSIP is added to the internetworking infrastructures.

In other words, there is no longer any single, global, IPv4 network but rather a set of networks using IPv4 addresses. Each network uses the standard IPv4 address space, so there may be as many nodes assigned to a single IPv4 address as there are realms (separate IPv4 networks).

On the global IPv4 Internet, any given network interface can be accessed with the 32-bit IPv4 address assigned to that interface. On an RSIP-enabled IPv4 Internet, two or more routing realms can be defined. In any given realm, the 32-bit IPv4 address will be sufficient to uniquely identify any given interface. For the interface to be globally targeted, however, requires the use of the address of the node plus the RSIP realm identifier.

This turns out to be a possible solution to some of the problems that NATs pose in terms of end-to-end interoperability. However, as the authors of the specification make quite clear, RSIP is not intended to replace NAT or to solve the IPv4 address shortage. At best, they write, RSIP is a stopgap measure (as NAT was when it was first proposed).

However, RSIP does offer an interesting solution to the problem of interoperating between networks using different Internet layer protocols, such as IPv4 and IPv6, or even IPv4 and some other as yet undetermined protocol.

When petroleum-based fuel runs out, we'll have to find a replacement. When IPv4 stops working, we'll have to replace it too. Right now, the only two viable options are IPv6 and, maybe, Realm-Specific IP (RSIP).

3.9   Summary

The true cost of IPv6-enabling any particular server, host, router, or network is difficult if not impossible to calculate. However, experts have predicted that enterprises can anticipate price tags for the task to be as much as 10 times greater than the cost of their Y2K preparations. As time goes on, the costs will only increase, yet few if any organizations have committed themselves to migrating to IPv6 support—at least not publicly. And IPv6 is not the only possible response to the problems posed by continued use of IPv4, just the most widely known.

Organizations have limited options as they plan for the future.

- Do nothing. Continue to use IPv4, along with all its fixes and patches, and any additional ones that come out in the future.

NATs will help enable continued growth, and work on maintaining end-to-end networking through NATs should yield solutions to that problem soon enough.

- Plan to deploy RSIP as a replacement for IPv4 NATs, and continue to rely on IPv4 within internal networks.
- Develop a plan for migrating to IPv6 support in a multiprotocol environment, with the goal being to bring new networks online that support IPv6.
- Do nothing and plan on using some other protocol that will come along to replace IPv4 (this is not recommended, considering that there aren't really any alternatives to IPv6 at this point).

Quite a few short-term approaches to the continuing shortage of IPv4 network addresses have been taken since the problem was first recognized in the late 1980s. In this chapter, we've examined the most important of them, including the following.

- Tightening of requirements for network address allocation, effectively imposing rationing on consumers of those addresses.
- IP subnetting
- CIDR
- NAT
- Subnetting of Class A networks
- Recycling of underused/returned allocations

The degree to which each of those strategies has been successful is a testament to the ingenuity of the implementers and deployers of the technologies as well as an indication of how well IPv4 has scaled beyond the wildest imaginings of the early Internet engineers. At this point, however, the only long-term solutions to Internet growth are to replace IPv4 with IPv6 or to devise mechanisms such as RSIP to avoid wholesale system upgrades.

At the same time Internet engineers were grappling with technologies intended to extend the lifetime of IPv4, others were working on the next generation of the Internet Protocol: IPv6. IPv6 is the next step for growing IP networks, and the next chapter highlights the process by which IPv6 was created.

4

The Road to Next Generation

No matter how successful IPv4 has been, in hindsight there's no denying that it could have been a better protocol. As its popularity increased, replacing or updating it has become increasingly more problematic. Lack of network address space is very likely the engine driving adoption of IPv6, but there are other reasons being proposed for moving to support IPv6. This chapter opens with a discussion of some of the improvements that have been proposed for the next generation of IP, followed by a brief history of the development effort for IP Next Generation (IPng).

4.1   Early Assumptions About the Internet Environment

Once it became clear that the Internet would soon grow beyond the capacity of IPv4, RFC 1287, "Towards the Future Internet Architecture," was published (December 1991). This document outlined the results of

a January 1991 meeting of the Internet Activities Board (IAB)[1] and the
Internet Engineering Steering Group (IESG), including the basic assumptions that could (it was thought) be made about the future of the Internet
and what were the most important areas for development of the Internet
protocols.

The group's four broad assumptions were meant to characterize the best
guess about what networking would be like during the next 5 to 10 years.
Agreement on what the networking environment would be like led to
appropriate planning for the future. The assumptions (and the eventual
realities) were as follows.

- The TCP/IP protocol suite would coexist with its main
  rival, OSI, for some time. The International Organization for
  Standardization (ISO) developed the Open Systems Inter-
  connection (OSI) architecture (source of the famous seven-
  layer OSI network protocol model). In fact, TCP/IP quickly
  gained the lion's share of the internetworking market. OSI continued to have influence only insofar as it had been chosen for
  use by government organizations.
- The Internet itself would become more complex, incorporating
  more diverse and a greater number of different types of networking technologies. In other words, instead of settling on
  one or a handful of network connectivity media, an increasing
  population of network connectivity media would become
  available and used over time. In fact, this is the case—
  sort of. Ethernet has come to dominate the LAN market, while
  a handful of other networking technologies (*ATM, Frame
  Relay, wireless Ethernet) have become dominant in other
  segments of the market.
- Access to the Internet would be provided by a variety of
  different carriers, including both public and private providers,
  for a wide variety of different networks. In other words, networks for many different types of organizations, including
  corporations, government agencies, educational institutions,
  and public services, will be connected through common carrier
  service providers as well as by privately maintained network connections. In fact, this assumption has also proven

---

[1]The IAB was later renamed the Internet Architecture Board, allowing the acronym to
remain unchanged.

itself with some qualification. What might be called *ad hoc internetworking*—where one organization provided connectivity to one or more other organizations or individuals by routing those others' packets—was common in the early days of the Internet. However, by the mid-1990s backbone-oriented routing—where global Internet connectivity is offered to consumers, whether individuals, organizations, or government agencies—became the dominant model.

- The Internet must be able to interconnect as many as one billion (10^9) networks, although the consensus seemed to encompass a relatively broad range of anywhere from ten million to ten billion networks.

Even before NATs began masking untold numbers of hosts from any automated surveys, estimates of the global number of TCP/IP nodes were best-guesses. Organizations rarely advertise host IP numbers anymore, and with most new computers shipping with TCP/IP installed (whether Microsoft Windows, Apple, or *nix operating systems), the number of TCP/IP nodes can be assumed to approach the number of computers currently in use. By 2004, I doubt anyone would argue that there are fewer than 100 million or more than 1 billion IP nodes currently in operation. Thus, this assumption (the need to support as many as 1 billion networks or more) is clearly still within range.

The number of networks to be interconnected is still not entirely clear, although it has become clear that the IPv4 address space is insufficient. On the one hand, we could allot one network address to every computer in the world and still be well under the high-end estimate of networks needed. On the other hand, further rapid decreases in cost and size coupled with increases in the distribution of personal computers could create demand as high as (or higher than) one network for every human in the world, thus requiring on the order of at least 10 billion networks just to be assigned to individual people. Factoring in unforeseeable circumstances such as these led some to call for an address space that can handle at least a trillion globally unique networks.

4.2 Designated Areas for Internet Evolution

The January 1991 IAB/IESG meeting generated another list, this one of the areas that were deemed most important to further architectural growth.

The intention was to identify the areas on which development efforts should be focused. These included the following.

- Routing and addressing concerns
- Multiprotocol architecture
- Security architecture
- Traffic control and state
- Advanced applications

These areas, approaches to development, and other issues are discussed next.

4.2.1 ADDRESSING AND ROUTING

The address space was already clearly a problem, but the issue of ballooning routing tables was also of great concern. Another RFC published at about the same time cited routing tables with 5000 and 7000 entries as a looming impediment to performance on networks that were still growing rapidly. The authors of RFC 1287 suggest not only that the IPv4 address space will be depleted but also that at some point before then IPv4 routing algorithms will fail due to the large number of networks. They also suggest that multiple routes between sources and destinations will make possible type of service (ToS) variations and therefore require some mechanisms to control route selection.

Aggregation of network routes, through some mechanism to be determined, is suggested as one possible solution to the explosion of routes. Using some method of defining boundaries between large routing domains would help improve routing efficiency. Another suggestion solicits some efficient mechanism for the computation of network routes, as well as some mechanism for routers to maintain state associated with specific streams that are routed in some special way.

Potential addressing fixes include the use of the existing 32-bit address space as a nonglobally unique identifier. In other words, addresses might be reused in different parts of the network that don't interoperate directly. For example, dividing the world into different routing domains would allow a host address to be used once in each domain, with interoperation between the domains mediated by protocol gateways that rewrite the addresses as they pass over domain boundaries.

Another suggestion for addressing simply increased the size of the host address. A third suggestion expands the host address field and uses the entire field as a nonhierarchical address space, with a connection setup that gives routers the opportunity to map a host address to an administrative domain.

4.2.2 MULTIPROTOCOL ARCHITECTURE

Support for interoperable transmission of OSI as well as TCP/IP traffic was thought to be an important criterion for further development. The perception at the time (up to 1991) was that Internet connectivity meant a host had an Internet address. If you didn't have an IP address and weren't running IP, you weren't connected. This viewpoint was already eroding by 1991, with the authors of RFC 1287 suggesting that connectivity could be based on access to the Internet through email gateways or, more simply, through some application. For example, users on NetWare networks at the time could run Internet applications like web browsers and email clients on their systems but use the Internetwork Packet eXchange (IPX) protocol to transport the data on their local Novell NetWare networks.

In practice, acceptance of TCP/IP as an internetworking protocol suite by most software and hardware vendors during the 1990s has largely driven out competing internetworking protocol suites. Even Novell finally deployed its NetWare network operating system as a native TCP/IP product by 1998.

More important, at least in hindsight, was the comment that TCP/IP could integrate or cross-pollinate with other application protocols. Inter-operability, particularly between applications rather than at the lower layers of the protocol stack, was deemed to be a good thing.

4.2.3 SECURITY ARCHITECTURE

Department of Defense funding of significant research and development work that produced IP meant that the protocols were (at least according to the authors of RFC 1287) built with military security in mind. Although a set of vaguely military priority levels were defined for a first pass at quality of service at the IP layer (in RFC 791), there are no mechanisms for strong cryptographic authentication, access control, authorization, or confidentiality evident at the IP layer until the early 1990s, when work on the IP Security Architecture (IPsec, see Chapter 6) began.

One specific suggestion for a desired security service is the use of *distinguished names* (an OSI construct used in X.500 directory specifications) that can be authenticated in order to implement access controls. Integrity enforcement was also suggested, with mechanisms to prevent modification of transmissions, spoofing of transmission origins, and defense against *replay attacks* (attacks in which an interceptor replays data stolen from an authorized stream). Other services include confidentiality (encrypted transmission), nonrepudiation (use of digital signature algorithms to prevent a sender from denying having sent a message), and protection from denial of service (DoS) attacks.

Other security issues raised in RFC 1287 include router/gateway protocol filtering (in other words, packet filtering firewalls) and encryption key management/storage.

4.2.4 TRAFFIC CONTROL AND STATE

IPv4 is a connectionless protocol, but some applications—audio and video, for example—depend on some degree of traffic control to work properly. A video stream must arrive at its destination at a relatively dependable and predictable rate, not too fast (which might overwhelm the recipient node's buffers) and not too slow (which would degrade the quality of the transmission).

The authors of RFC 1287 suggest the need for some sort of packet queuing mechanims to provide traffic control; they also state that there should be some mechanism by which nodes can maintain status information for different *streams* of packets to more readily enable real-time applications to be carried over IP packets.

Noting that IPv4 implements a Type of Service (ToS) field, the authors also note that not only is ToS not generally implemented, it is not even clear how it could be implemented.

4.2.5 ADVANCED APPLICATIONS

Rather than suggesting new applications, the authors of RFC 1287 suggest that improving and simplifying the processes involved in developing new and advanced applications would be a more productive path. As a starting point, they suggest that the creation of common data formats for different types of data, particularly text, images and graphics, audio and video, workstation displays, and data objects. Also important to developing advanced applications are mechanisms for the exchange of these different types of data.

Suggested mechanisms include *store and forward* services, global file systems, interprocess communications, data broadcast, and a standardized method for accessing databases.

4.3   Room for Improvement

Other areas in which IPv4 could stand some improvement have been cited over the years as providing good reasons to upgrade the protocol. As it became more apparent that IPv4 could use some additional, or at least different, functionality, upgraders were faced with the opportunity to enhance IP in ways that go beyond adding network addressing capacity. This section highlights some of the areas where there is room for improvement, from network administration and automatic node configuration to rethinking ToS and IP options.

4.3.1   Network Administration and Configuration

IPv4 and most of the rest of the TCP/IP application protocol suite were never designed, by themselves, to be easy to use. For example, raw FTP (File Transfer Protocol) depends on what appear to be very arcane request and reply codes and uses a set of cryptic-seeming commands. Why do I mention this? Simply because these apparently complicated command and control mechanisms are actually designed to be standard across all platforms and to simplify access to software that understands the protocols. A system running IPv4 must be configured, correctly, with an apparently complicated set of parameters. These usually include a host name, IP address, subnet mask, default router, and some others (depending on the implementation). This is complicated—it means that the person who does the configuration must understand all these parameters or at least be given them by someone who does understand. What it means is that getting a system connected to an IPv4 network can be very complicated, time-consuming, and costly.

The Boot Protocol (BOOTP) took a first step toward simplifying the process of connecting a host to a network. This relatively simply protocol provided a mechanism for a host with minimal preconfiguration (often simply a terminal) to query a BOOTP server to get its IP configuration parameters. This approach failed to solve the entire problem because it only provided a mechanism for the BOOTP server to map IP address and other configuration information to a link layer address (for example, an Ethernet card interface address). To manage 100 hosts with BOOTP, you must assign each host its own IP address.

Address management and host configuration pose at least two big problems. First, if it is difficult to configure hosts, it costs money; second, if each host must tie up an IP address, whether or not it is connected, it costs address space. It would be nice if we could make host configuration a plug-and-play operation—in other words, so simple that you simply plug the system into the network and it is automatically configured. It would also be nice if we could figure out a way to share IP addresses among many hosts, so that if no more than half of our 100 hosts were connected at any given time, we could get away with sharing 50 IP addresses among them.

As it turns out, another protocol, called the Dynamic Host Configuration Protocol (DHCP), was built on top of the BOOTP framework in an attempt to address these issues. Still using a client/server model, clients can use DHCP to query a server for configuration information, just as with BOOTP. However, DHCP adds more flexibility in terms of what kind of configuration information can be provided as well as how IP addresses are allocated. There are three mechanisms for allocating addresses.

- Using *automatic allocation*, hosts request an IP address and are given a permanent one that they use each time they connect to the network.
- Using *manual allocation*, the server assigns specific IP addresses to individual hosts based on a list provided by a network administrator. These IP addresses are reserved, whether or not the hosts request them.
- Using *dynamic allocation*, the server doles out IP addresses on a first-come, first-served basis; hosts are allowed to use the addresses for a specific time period after which the address "lease" expires.

Both automatic and manual allocation will tend to inefficiently distribute IP addresses; using automatic allocation may tend to tie up IP addresses.

If an organization has more hosts than users, it could burn up as many IP addresses as it has hosts with this scheme. Manual allocation means network administrators must configure an IP address for each host, whether it connects once an hour or once a year to the network. Dynamic allocation, however, enables a relatively large population to share a relatively small number of IP addresses.

Unfortunately, DHCP falls short of enabling true plug-and-play configuration because it is stateful. That is, DHCP maintains the status of different IP addresses and the hosts using them. You have to explicitly set up a DHCP server that knows about your hosts, and the host to be configured with DHCP must know about the nearest DHCP server. True plug-and-play, which is a big part of the portability issue, doesn't happen with IPv4. As we'll see following, the inability of IPv4 to adequately support portability and network administration issues helps prompt the calls for upgrade to IPv6.

4.3.2 Type of Service (ToS)

IP uses a packet-switched network architecture. This means that a packet might take any of a number of different routes to reach its destination. Those routes differ: Some might cost more, some might allow greater throughput, some might have lower latency, and some might be more reliable than others. IPv4 provides a mechanism, the Type of Service field (ToS) that allows applications to tell IP how to handle their data streams. An application that needs lots of throughput—for example, FTP—might force the ToS to favor routes that have lots of bandwidth; an application that needs fast responses—for example, Telnet—might force the ToS to favor routes that have low delays.

This was a good idea that never really caught on that well with implementers. For one thing, it requires routing protocols to incorporate notions of preferential routes based on costs as well as the need to track values for latency, throughput, and reliability for available routes. For another thing, it requires that developers implement a function in their application that might request service that, ultimately, could affect performance. ToS is a choice of one, so if you decide that low latency is most important to your application, it might affect your ability to get higher bandwidth or more reliable routes for your application's packets.

4.3.3 IP Options

The IPv4 header includes a variable-length options field. IP options were meant to be the way to handle certain special functions. The original specifications left these options undefined, but eventually options for things like security as well as certain routing functions were added. Routing options include one (record route) to have each router handling the packet to record its address and another (timestamp) to have each router record its own address as well as the time it handles the packet. Source routing options are also available: Loose source routing specifies a list of routers that the packet must pass through on its way to the packet's destination, whereas strict source routing requires that the packet be routed only by the routers listed.

Options are an important part of IP, but the IPv4 implementation is not ideal. Although they are not often used, it is not because they are not useful so much as that the specification is suboptimal. Rather than throw options out, IPv6 improves the way they are used.

The problem with options is that they are special cases. IP datagrams without options are the vast majority and are the type of datagrams vendors optimize their routers to handle. The IP header without options is always five bytes long and is easy to process—especially when the router design optimizes for the processing of such headers. Performance is key to router sales, and because most traffic does not use IP options, the routers tend to handle those packets as exceptions, shunting them off to the side to be handled when it is convenient—and when it won't affect the router's overall performance.

Despite the benefits of using IPv4 options, the cost in terms of performance has been enough to keep them from being used very often.

4.4 IPng Candidates

Up to 1994, quite a few different proposals were made for the successor to IPv4. By 1992, the three dominant proposal families that would eventually be considered by the IETF in 1994 had already taken shape. RFC 1347, "TCP and UDP with Bigger Addresses (TUBA), A Simple Proposal for Internet Addressing and Routing," outlines one. *TUBA* can be characterized as simply replacing IP with the OSI internetwork protocol, *Connection-Less Network Protocol* (*CLNP*). CLNP uses *Network Service Access* (*NSAP*) addresses that can be any length but that are often implemented in 20 bytes, providing more than enough address space. Furthermore, using CLNP would help IP and OSI to converge, while at the same time eliminating the need to build an entirely new protocol.

Another proposed IPng candidate was first known as IPv7 in 1992, and in 1993 was described in detail in RFC 1475 under the title "TP/IXTP/IX: The Next Internet." It is not clear what TP/IX stands for; according to Christian Huitema in *IPv6: The New Internet Protocol* (Prentice Hall PTR, 1998), the name expresses the desire of its proposer, Robert Ullman, to change not only IP but also TCP with the upgrade. TP/IX uses 64-bit addresses and adds an addressing layer to the hierarchy, above organizations, for administrations.

Under IPv7, eight-byte addresses are used to allocate three bytes to administrative domain, three to the organization's network, and two bytes for the host identifier. The IPv7 datagram header simplifies the IPv4 header, while adding a forward route identifier to be used by intermediate routers to determine how to handle datagrams. For example, the forward route identifier may be associated with a particular route based on certain values relating to the route itself (throughput or value) or to be associated with a particular datagram stream or even to be associated with data from a mobile host—that is, a host that moves from one network to another while maintaining open TCP connections. TP/IX not only modified TCP and UDP, but it also included a new routing protocol called *RAP*.

TP/IX later evolved into another proposal, described in RFC 1707, "CATNIP: Common Architecture for the Internet." CATNIP seems to have little in common with TP/IX, however, except that it retains the IPv7 designation. In its goal of providing a common architecture, the CATNIP specification makes allowances for the three most commonly used internetwork architectures: TCP/IP, OSI, and IPX, as well as discussion of how to integrate a competing proposed standard for the next generation of IP. The stated objective is to make it possible for all existing systems to continue to interoperate with **/no/** modifications, no changes in address, and no software upgrades for individual hosts. By making allowance for different network architectures, the CATNIP proposal meant to minimize impact on the actual infrastructure; however, it meant adding a layer of complexity in order to implement true interoperable internetworking.

The third proposal stream started out as something called *IP in IP*, or *IP Encaps* (for IP encapsulation). Under this proposal, there would be two layers of IP: One would be used for a global backbone, while the other would be used in more limited areas. The IP to be used in limited areas could continue to be IPv4, while the backbone would use a new layer with different addressing. Ultimately, this evolved and merged with other proposals to become the *Simple Internet Protocol Plus* (*SIPP*) proposal.

As explained in RFC 1710, "Simple Internet Protocol Plus White Paper," the SIPP working group grew from three different IETF working groups focused on developing an IPng. The first group was working on a version called *IP Address Encapsulation* (*IPAE*); the working group, chaired by Dave Crocker and Robert Hinden, proposed extensions to IPv4 that would carry larger addresses, and the group focused on developing transition mechanisms.

Somewhat later, Steve Deering proposed a new protocol evolved from IPv4 called the *Simple Internet Protocol* (*SIP*). A working group was formed to work on this proposal, which was chaired by Steve Deering and Christian Huitema. SIP used 64-bit addresses, a simplified header, and options in separate extension headers. After lengthy interaction between the two working groups and the realization that IPAE and SIP had a number of common elements and the transition mechanisms developed for IPAE would apply to SIP, the groups decided to merge and concentrate their efforts. The chairs of the new SIP working group were Steve Deering and Robert Hinden.

In parallel to SIP, Paul Francis (formerly Paul Tsuchiya) had founded a working group to develop the "P" Internet Protocol (Pip). Pip was a new Internet protocol based on a new architecture. The motivation behind Pip was that the opportunity for introducing a new Internet protocol does not come very often and given that opportunity important new features should be introduced. Pip supported variable-length addressing in 16-bit units, separation of addresses from identifiers, support for provider selection, mobility, and efficient forwarding. It included a transition scheme similar to IPAE.

After considerable discussion among the leaders of the Pip and SIP working groups, they came to realize that the advanced features in Pip could be accomplished in SIP without changing the base SIP protocol as well as keeping the IPAE transition mechanisms. In essence, it was possible to keep the best features of each protocol. Based on this, the groups decided to merge their efforts. The new protocol was called Simple Internet Protocol Plus (SIPP). The chairs of the merged working group are Steve Deering, Paul Francis, and Robert Hinden.

Briefly, SIPP offers several changes from IPv4, including the following.

Routing and addressing expansion SIPP specifies 64-bit addresses, double the size of IPv4. The intention is to provide greater degrees of hierarchy within which routing can be accomplished. Another feature is the addition of *cluster addresses*, which identify regions of the network topology. SIPP address extensions, available in units of 64 bits, work with the cluster addresses to create the possibility of a much larger address space.

IP header simplification SIPP does away with some IPv4 header fields, while streamlining the structure to help improve routing efficiency.

Improvement in option implementation SIPP uses a more flexible approach to encoding and implementing IP options.

Quality of service SIPP makes it possible to label datagrams as belonging to specific data flows. Hosts can request special handling for the routing of these flows, especially useful for applications that depend on real-time delivery like that required by video or audio transmission.

Authentication and privacy SIPP adds extensions for authentication, data integrity, and confidentiality.

SIPP was the result of many people from several different groups working together. The finished specification includes many interesting new mechanisms, while still not straying too far from the goal of being an upgrade to IPv4 rather than an entirely new protocol built from the ground up. Notable is the use of routing similar to that in IPv4, still using CIDR to add flexibility and improve routing performance. Also important are new routing extensions that allow choice of routes from different providers based on various criteria (including performance, cost, provider policies for traffic, and so on). Other routing extensions include support for mobile hosts as well as automatic readdressing and extended addressing.

One other notable mechanism is the SIPP approach to IP options: Rather than including them as part of the basic IP header, SIPP segregates any

IP options from the main header. The options headers, if any, are simply inserted into the datagram after the header and before the transport layer protocol header. This way, routers can process datagrams without having to process the options headers unless it is necessary—thus improving performance overall for all datagrams.

RFC 1710 provides both a technical overview to the SIPP specification and a readable justification and narrative of the protocol. It is worth a look, if only to see how IPv6 as we know it came to be—because SIPP, with some modifications, was the specification recommended to and accepted by the IESG as the basis for IPng.

4.5 IPv6, The Next Generation

RFC 1752, "The Recommendation for the IP Next Generation Protocol," published in January 1995, is a fascinating document that outlines clearly what was needed and what was available, in terms of the candidate proposals for successors to IPv4. In its summary, the authors of RFC 1752 describe what IPng would look like.

This protocol recommendation includes a simplified header with a hierarchical address structure that permits rigorous route aggregation and is also large enough to meet the needs of the Internet for the foreseeable future. The protocol also includes packet-level authentication and encryption along with plug-and-play autoconfiguration. The design changes the way IP header options are encoded to increase the flexibility of introducing new options in the future while improving performance. It also includes the ability to label traffic flows.

The fifth item in a long list of specific recommendations is that IPng be based on SIPP with 128-bit addresses. The rest of the RFC provides an excellent resource for further historical background on how the Internet research community identified and approached the problems associated with IPv4, as well as detailed analysis of the three contenders, TUBA, CATNIP, and SIPP. The RFC examines each proposal and discusses how it meets (or fails to meet) the requirements and also presents the results of the proposal review process.

All three proposals are praised in some way, and all ultimately contributed something to the final recommendation. For example, SIPP did not include a strong transition plan or a totally acceptable mechanism for autoconfiguration, so the recommendation draws on the TUBA proposal for those areas. And SIPP was not accepted in all its glory: The concept of address extensions was ultimately considered too experimental and potentially risky to incorporate into the IPng work, while the 64-bit address space was replaced with a 128-bit address space to cope with any future uncertainties.

The recommendations described in RFC 1752 include a variety of further tasks related to the actual design of the IPng and related protocols. SIPP and the others could be considered only as starting points, particularly if IPng were to be sufficiently robust to serve the Internet for years to come.

The first proposed standard RFCs (RFCs 1883 through 1887) to describe IPv6 and supporting protocols were published by early 1996, but they were not entirely complete and were soon followed by various additions and some slight modifications. By the end of the summer of 1998, new IPv6 RFCs were being approved for publication. In particular, RFC 2373, "IP Version 6 Addressing Architecture," replaced RFC 1883 and RFC 2374, "An IPv6 Aggregatable Global Unicast Address Format," replaced RFC 2073. Other newer RFCs approved for publication describe ICMPv6, neighbor discovery, and stateless autoconfiguration for IPv6.

Even as this book is going to press, the second round of IPv6 RFCs are being updated and in some cases replaced by a third wave of specifications. For example, RFC 2373 has been replaced with RFC 3513; other updates are still works-in-progress but can be expected to further hone IPv6 and related specifications over the coming years.

4.6   Summary

Few, if any, efforts in Internet engineering history have taken so long and involved so many different ideas, people, and groups as the project to upgrade the Internet Protocol. The process is instructive for students of networking history, network protocols, and the network protocol specification process. The result, IPv6, may ultimately be considered an improvement over IPv4—but as the product of many committees, there will invariably be those who feel that IPv6 could have been better than it is.

However, before IPv6 can be fully judged, it must be implemented. IPv6-related working groups have come up with a variety of approaches to the process of migrating from IPv4-only environments to networks capable of supporting IPv6. The next chapter discusses how IPv6 support may be deployed in existing networks.

5

IPv6 Transition Issues

The Internet has always been a multiprotocol network, shared by systems transporting packets across a variety of networks. This chapter examines migration and transition scenarios as proposed in IETF working groups and RFCs. These transition scenarios are largely theoretical in nature and reflect proposed solutions more than reality. We will discuss the practical aspects of rolling out support for IPv6 later in Part III.

5.1   Upgrading IP

One might imagine that moving to support IPv6 would require that all hosts on a network be upgraded—a daunting challenge to network managers responsible for global corporate internetworks with tens of thousands of hosts in hundreds of networks. However, this is not the case. Migration to IPv6 support is anticipated to be a gradual process, and mechanisms to gracefully support IPv6 in IPv4 networks have been an important part of the IPv6 development project from the start.

RFC #	Title
2071	Network Renumbering Overview: Why would I want it and what is it anyway?
2072	Router Renumbering Guide
2185	Routing Aspects of IPv6 Transition
2529	Transmission of IPv6 over IPv4 Domains without Explicit Tunnels
2767	Dual Stack Hosts Using the Bump-in-the-Stack Technique (BIS)
2893	Transition Mechanisms for IPv6 Hosts and Routers
3056	Connection of IPv6 Domains via IPv4 Clouds
3142	An IPv6-to-IPv4 Transport Relay Translator

Table 5–1: RFCs Addressing the IPv6 transition process.

Table 5–1 lists some of the key source documents for transition and migration to IPv6 support.

The IPv6 transition will by necessity be gradual and not just because there are many who believe it will be unnecessary. A massive, cutover-style upgrade would not only be unacceptable, considering the huge numbers of networks and nodes already connected to the Internet—it would be impossible. It would require network administrators to find and install new versions of networking software for every host and router on the Internet. Considering the number of different platforms running IPv4, plus the number of nodes connecting using IP and the lack of any central authority to mandate and oversee such a transition, IPv6 is by necessity a protocol that can be implemented only in stages and only in tandem with existing IPv4 implementations.

The transition to IPv6 is taking place slowly, as vendors and developers gradually introduce versions of IPv6 for different platforms and as network managers determine that they need the functions IPv6 provides. IPv4 and IPv6 will have to coexist for a long time, perhaps forever. Most strategies for the transition rely on the two-pronged approach of protocol tunneling, where IPv6 packets are encapsulated within IPv4 packets for transmission from IPv6 islands through IPv4 oceans. At least at first—after the early stages of the transition period—more and more of the IP population will be IPv6-capable. Even in the later stages of the transition, IPv6 encapsulation will continue to be useful for connectivity across IPv4-only backbones and other holdout networks.

The other prong of the strategy is the dual-stack approach, in which hosts and routers run IPv4 and IPv6 stacks on the same network interfaces. This way, a dual-stack node can accept and transmit both IPv4 and IPv6 packets, so the two protocols can coexist on the same networks.

5.2   The IPv6 Protocol Tunneling Approach

Tunneling requires that an IPv6 node at one end of the tunnel be capable of transmitting IPv4 packets (dual-stack node, see next section) and that there be another dual-stack node at the other end of the tunnel. Encapsulating IPv6 within IPv4 is a similar process to any other protocol encapsulation: A node at one end of the tunnel takes the IPv6 datagrams and treats them as payload data intended to be sent to the node at the other end of the tunnel. The result is a stream of IPv4 datagrams that contain IPv6 datagrams. As shown in Figure 5–1, node A and node B are both IPv6-only nodes. To get an IPv6 packet from A to B, node A simply addresses the packet to node B's IPv6 address and passes it to router X. This router encapsulates the IPv6 packet intended for node B and sends it to the IPv4 address of router Y. Router Y receives the IPv4 packet or packets and unwraps them. On finding the encapsulated IPv6 packet intended for node B, router Y forwards the packet appropriately.

There is a set of IPv6 addresses that contain IPv4 addresses (see Chapter 8 for details). One is the *IPv4-compatible address* and the other is the *IPv4-mapped address*.

IPv4-compatible addresses are 128-bit addresses, of which the highest-order 96 bits are set to zero and the last 32 bits contain an IPv4 address. These addresses are intended to be used by dual-stack IPv4/IPv6 nodes capable of automatically tunneling IPv6 packets through IPv4 networks.

The dual-stack node thus is able to use the "same" address for both IPv4 and IPv6 packets. IPv4-only nodes can send packets to the dual-stack node using its IPv4 address, whereas IPv6-only nodes can send packets to the IPv6 address (the IPv4 address padded out with zeros to make it 128 bits long).

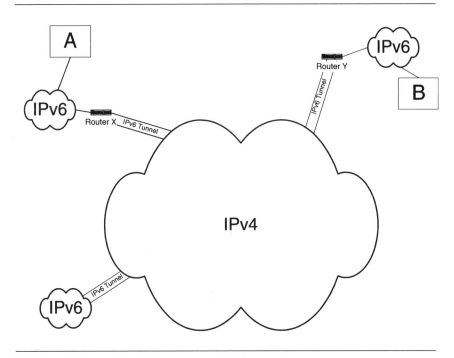

Figure 5–1: Tunneling IPv6 across an IPv4 Internet.

The IPv4-mapped address is similar to the IPv4-compatible address, except that only the highest-order 80 bits are set to zero, with the next 16 bits set to 1. The low-order 32 bits are the IPv4 address of an IPv4 node; that node does not have to support IPv6. The IPv4-mapped address is used to represent an IPv4 node address in a format that an IPv6 node can understand.

In general, the kind of node using these IPv4-compatible addresses would be routers linking IPv6 networks using automatic tunnels through IPv4 networks. The router would accept IPv6 packets from its local IPv6 networks and encapsulate them in IPv4 packets intended for another dual-stack router also using an IPv4-compatible address on the other side of the IPv4 network. The encapsulated packets are then forwarded through the IPv4 network cloud until they arrive at the dual-stack router at the other end of the tunnel, where the IPv4 packets are unwrapped to reveal IPv6 packets that the router then forwards on its local IPv6 networks.

5.2.1   IPv6 Tunnel Types

The following are the different types of tunnels using the internetwork pictured in Figure 5–2. However to differentiate the different types of tunneling, the entities in the figure may be IPv4-only, IPv6-only, or IPv4/IPv6 dual-stacks, depending on the type of tunneling being demonstrated.

Router-to-router tunneling   In Figure 5–2, router X and router Y tunnel IPv6 packets through network O, which is an IPv4-only network. Host A can send IPv6 packets to host B transparently; neither host

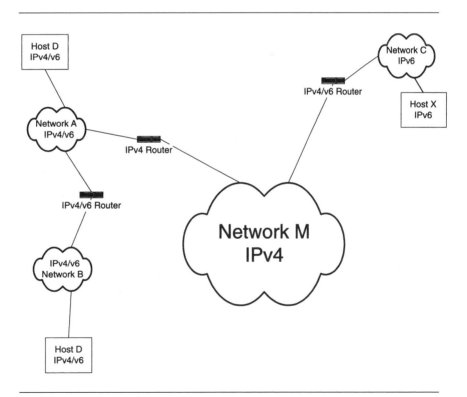

Figure 5–2: Generic network devices illustrating different types of networks.

needs to be concerned with the existence of an intervening IPv4 network (network O). In this case, both host A and host B are IPv6-only nodes.

Router-to-host tunneling In this case, network N in Figure 5–2 is an IPv4-only network, but host B runs IPv4 and IPv6; the rest of the network is IPv6-only. In this case, the tunneling takes place between router Y and host B. IPv6 packets flow freely along the rest of the network, but router Y must encapsulate them in IPv4 in order to deliver them across network N, which is IPv4-only.

Host-to-host tunneling In this case, only host A and host B support IPv6 (they are dual-stack IPv4/IPv6 nodes). The rest of the entities in Figure 5–2 for this illustration are IPv4-only. The tunneling occurs between host A and host B, the two hosts encapsulating their IPv6 packets in IPv4 so as to pass through the IPv4-only routers and networks.

Host-to-router tunneling Finally, consider what happens when host A and router X are dual-stack IPv4/IPv6 nodes, network M is an IPv4-only network, and the rest of the networks support IPv6 only. In this case, host A must tunnel its packets only to router X; once past the IPv4-only network M, router X can unwrap the tunneled packets and forward them normally across the IPv6 networks.

5.2.2 EXPLICIT TUNNELING

Explicit tunneling of IPv6 through IPv4 occurs when the IPv6 packets are encapsulated in IPv4 packets that are addressed using either IPv4-compatible addresses or by configuring a set of IPv4 addresses (indicating the two IPv4 endpoints of the tunnel). The first approach is called *automatic tunneling* because there is no need to configure anything—IPv6-capable nodes will automatically encapsulate IPv6 packets with IPv4-compatible addresses.

When IPv4-compatible addresses are not being used, IPv6 nodes can communicate using a *configured tunnel*. The endpoints of the tunnel must be configured so that the nodes doing the IPv6 encapsulation will be able to properly address the resulting IPv4 packets. Configured tunneling requires that the tunnel endpoint nodes acquire their IPv4 address through some other mechanism (for example, through DHCP, manual configuration, or any other IPv4 configuration mechanism).

5.2.3   IPv6 over IPv4 Without Explicit Tunnels

The problem with tunneling is that in either case (configured or automatic) some special case support must be built into the nodes linking the IPv6 domains across the IPv4 domain. Configured tunnels require a mechanism to configure the tunnel, whereas automatic tunnels require IPv4-compatible IPv6 addresses. A different way to tunnel IPv6 over, described in RFC 2529, "Transmission of IPv6 over IPv4 Domains without Explicit Tunnels," requires only that IPv4 multicast be supported in the infrastructure.

Known as *6over4*, this approach allows IPv6 nodes to treat IPv4 as a link layer protocol for the purpose of locating other IPv6 nodes. In the same way that nodes on an Ethernet network emit broadcast or multicast packets to identify themselves or locate other nodes, an IPv6 node using 6over4 transmits IPv6 packets encapsulated in IPv4 to a multicast group whose members are IPv6 nodes. The encapsulated packets are treated much the same way as an IPv4 node's packets that have been encapsulated in an Ethernet frame. Members of the IPv6 multicast group would be the only ones accepting those packets, and they would respond (or ignore) the encapsulated data, as appropriate.

5.2.4   The Trouble with Tunnels

None of the approaches to tunneling described so far is perfect.

Automatic tunnels   require IPv4-compatible addresses, requiring IPv6 network administrators to acquire at least one such address for each tunnel.

Configured tunnels   require some mechanism to keep tunnel endpoints' configurations up to date and working. They also require humans to configure them at some level and thus are not expected to scale well.

6over4 tunnels   require that the IPv4 infrastructure through which they operate support IPv4 multicast, a specification that is often not implemented in the public Internet. Another problem is scalability, inasmuch as these tunnels treat the global IPv4 Internet as a broadcast medium. Any significant deployment is likely to affect performance on the IPv4 Internet.

In addition to tunnels, IPv6/IPv4 interoperability requires the use of nodes that can handle both protocols at the same time, as discussed next.

5.3   IPv4/IPv6 Dual-Stack

The tenacity of legacy systems, as demonstrated by the years of preparation required to allay Year 2000 fears, should be underestimated at our peril. IPv4 will be with us for a long time, even as some or all of the rest of the networked world upgrades to IPv6. During that time, the upgraded systems will need to maintain interoperability with IPv4 systems; as time goes on, the burden of interoperability will be shifted from the early implementers to the maintainers of legacy systems. In any case, systems capable of supporting both IPv4 and IPv6 will be necessary.

The concept of dual-stack nodes is not new. Many, if not most, corporate hosts that support connectivity to the Internet as well as connectivity to corporate LANs using older versions of Novell's NetWare (in NetWare 5, IP replaces IPX as the native network layer protocol), for example, already support two disparate network stacks. Internet connectivity is provided through the TCP/IP stack, whereas the NetWare connectivity is provided by an IPX stack. As segments are received at the link layer and unwrapped, the headers indicate whether the datagram is intended for the TCP/IP stack or the IPX stack—and the packet is then passed to the appropriate stack for processing.

IPv4/IPv6 dual-stack nodes can work much the same as other types of multiple-stack nodes. The data link layer header contains a field in which an *ethertype* (a value specifying network protocol) indicates the type of protocol being carried in the link layer protocol data unit's payload. Just as Novell IPX/IPv4 dual-stacks differentiated between the two protocols by ethertype (the IPX ethertype value is 0x8137; IPv4 ethertype is 0x0800; and IPv6 ethertype is 0x86DD).

Figure 5–3 shows an example in which dual-stack node D can interoperate with IPv4 or IPv6 nodes on networks A and B and all IPv4 nodes on network M, but not with any nodes on network C, which is strictly IPv6. There is

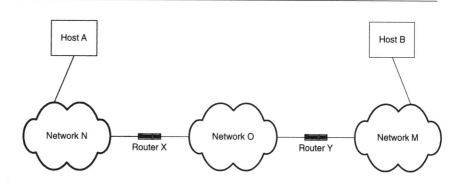

Figure 5–3: Dual-stack systems can interoperate with IPv4 and IPv6 nodes.

no IPv6 routing path from network A to network C. The router linking networks A and M supports only IPv4 and thus cannot forward any IPv6 packets to network C (via network M).

Dual-stack nodes that can perform tunneling add the ability to interoperate over IPv4 networks without any additional IPv6 routers. Tunneling IPv6 over IPv4 can change the connectivity picture in Figure 5–3. For example, if node D is able to tunnel IPv6 over IPv4, then it can use its local IPv4 router to forward packets to network C. If the nodes both support automatic tunneling, the interoperability is seamless; otherwise, some configuration of the link may be necessary.

5.4   Connecting IPv6 Domains via IPv4 Clouds

Another short-term approach to the transition from IPv4-only to IPv6 is known as *6to4* and is described in RFC 3056, "Connection of IPv6 Domains via IPv4 Clouds," a standards track RFC published in 2001. Rather than require previously configured tunnels, 6to4 treats the IPv4 network as a "unicast point-to-point link layer," through which IPv6 networks and nodes can communicate by relay routers.

6to4 requires at least one globally unique IPv4 network address and allocates interim IPv6 network addresses to sites using that method. The globally unique IPv4 network address becomes a part of the network address prefix assigned to the 6to4-based IPv6 network, and edge routers

```
+---+------+-----------+--------+-------------------------------+
| 3 |  13  |    32     |   16   |            64 bits            |
+---+------+-----------+--------+-------------------------------+
|FP | TLA  |  V4ADDR   | SLA ID |          Interface ID         |
|001|0x0002|           |        |                               |
+---+------+-----------+--------+-------------------------------+
```

Figure 5–4: 6to4 transitional addresses take this form (from RFC 3056).

can be configured to encapsulate IPv6 packets using those addresses into IPv4 packets.

Figure 5–4 shows how those IPv4 addresses (signified by V4ADDR) are made a part of the interim 6to4 IPv6 addresses. Those encapsulating IPv4 packets use the protocol type 41 to indicate they are carrying IPv6 trafffic (this is the same protocol type used to indicate the presence of tunneled IPv6 packets).

5.5   Summary

Although there are many nontechnical issues involved in the transition from an IPv4-only world to one in which IPv6 is an important (if not dominant) protocol, the technical issues must be resolved before taking up the task of implementing and deploying IPv6. In this chapter, we have looked briefly at some of the technical approaches to supporting IPv6 in IPv4-only networks.

Although it is necessary to have at least some nodes that can support both IPv4 and IPv6, as well as mechanisms by which IPv6 packets can be carried through, over, or across IPv6 networks, these are not sufficient to enable an organization or individual to migrate to an IPv6 environment. The chapters in Part III offer more specific and more practical advice about this transition.

One issue often cited (generally incorrectly) as a primary reason for migrating to IPv6 support is security. The next chapter introduces the IP Security Protocol (IPsec), an optional part of IPv4 but a mandatory protocol for all IPv6 implementations.

IPv6 Protocols

IPv6, like IPv4, is a protocol defined by a set of addressing protocols, a set of protocol headers, and a set of protocol behaviors. Part II begins with a chapter on the Internet Protocol Security Architecture (IPsec), a protocol that is defined for use with both IPv4 and IPv6. The rest of this section of the book details IPv6 by first defining the rules for IPv6 addressing in Chapter 7; defining the protocol headers in Chapter 8; and discussing additional protocol behaviors as represented by routing protocols in Chapter 9. Chapter 10 discusses the changes and additions necessary for making existing upper- and lower-layer protocols work well with IPv6.

After reading Part II, you will be able to do the following.

- Understand IP security issues and explain how IPsec works
- Discuss and differentiate IPv6 address types
- Refer to IPv6 nodes and networks by their addresses
- Identify IPv6 packets and use packet header information for troubleshooting purposes
- Understand how the new features of IPv6 work, from Neighbor Discovery to IPv6 autoconfiguration
- Understand IPv6 routing behavior
- Identify modifications and additions to existing protocols necessary for IPv6 support

If you don't have the time (or need) to understand the precise differences between IPv6 and IPv4, it is possible to summarize IPv6 as being an update of IPv4 with 128-bit addresses, streamlined headers, and a few changes in the information contained in the headers and the functions possible with the protocol. However, some of the changes noted in the next chapter have significant implications, as the remainder of Part II will demonstrate.

6

The IP Security Protocol (IPsec)*

Claims that IPv4 security was neglected by the founders are based on the argument that early IPv4 networks were insecure things strung together on trust between naive but ultimately honorable academicians. However, at the very start the Internet Protocol was defined as a U.S. Department of Defense (DoD) standard, and security was certainly a consideration. Nevertheless, the IETF has given considerably more explicit attention to IPv6 security than was accorded to IPv4 during its early development.

The desirability and utility of authentication and security features at the IP layer have been debated for years. This chapter discusses how authentication and security, including secure password transmission, encryption, and digital signatures on datagrams, are implemented under IP through the *Authentication Header* (*AH*) and *Encapsulating Security Payload* (*ESP*) options. Before examining the *IP Security Protocol* (*IPsec*), however, we will take a look at the IP security architecture described in RFC 2401,

---

*This chapter is adapted from Chapter 26 of *TCP/IP Clearly Explained* (4th edition).

"Security Architecture for the Internet Protocol," and the different pieces of that architecture.

IPv4 as originally designed offered no real security features; it was intended simply as an internetworking protocol. While not necessarily a problem for a networking protocol used largely in research and academic settings, the increase in importance of IP networking to the general business and consumer networking environments makes the potential harm resulting from attacks more devastating than ever. This section examines the following.

- Issues of security for IP
- Security goals defined for IP
- Cryptographic elements of IPsec
- Protocol elements of IPsec
- Implementing IPsec

The next section takes a look at the specifics of IPsec, as well as some of the tools being assembled to achieve these goals.

6.1   IP Security Issues

IPsec as defined in RFC 2401 provides a security architecture for the Internet Protocol—*not* a security architecture for the Internet. The distinction is important: IPsec defines security services to be used at the IP layer, both for IPv4 and IPv6. It is often said that IPv6 is "more secure" than IPv4, but the difference is that IPsec is required for all IPv6, whereas it is optional for IPv4 nodes.

The IP Security Protocol (IPsec) provides an interoperable and open standard for building security into the network layer rather than at the application or transport layer. Although applications can benefit from network layer security, the most important application IPsec enables is the creation of virtual private networks (VPNs) capable of securely carrying enterprise data across the open Internet.

IPsec is often used in conjunction with tunnel management protocols, including the Layer 2 Tunneling Protocol (L2TP), the Layer 2 Forwarding (L2F) protocol designed by Cisco Systems, and Microsoft's Point to Point

Tunneling Protocol (PPTP). RFC 2661, "Layer Two Tunneling Protocol 'L2TP,'" defines L2TP as a standards track specification for tunneling packets sent over a PPP link.

While the tunnel management protocols offer access security services, they don't provide authentication or privacy services, so they are often used in conjunction with IPsec—which does provide those services. However, saying that IPsec specifies protocols for encrypting and authenticating data sent within IP packets is an oversimplification and even obscures IPsec's full potential. IPsec enables the following.

Encryption of data passing between two nodes, using strong public and private key cryptographic algorithms

Authentication of data and its source, using strong authentication mechanisms

Control over access to sensitive data and private networks

Integrity verification of data carried by a connectionless protocol (IP)

Protection against *replay* **attacks,** in which an intruder intercepts packets sent between two IP nodes and resends them after decrypting or modifying them

Limitation of *traffic analysis* **attacks,** in which an intruder intercepts protected data and analyzes source and destination information, size and type of packets, and other aspects of the data, including header contents that might not otherwise be protected by encryption

End-to-end security for IP packets, providing assurance to users of end-point nodes of the privacy and integrity of their transmissions.

Secure tunneling through insecure networks such as the global Internet and other public networks

Integration of algorithms, protocols, and security infrastructures into an overarching security architecture

As defined in RFC 2401, "Security Architecture for the Internet Protocol," the goal of the IP security architecture is "to provide various security services for traffic at the IP layer, in both the IPv4 and IPv6 environments." This means security services that have the following features.

Interoperable   As with all Internet protocols, interoperability is a fundamental goal. This means that any IP node supporting IPsec can communicate with any other node supporting IPsec. There is a basic

set of cryptographic algorithms for encryption and integrity checking, which all IPsec nodes must support, although individual nodes
and implementations may support many more, optional, algorithms.
Although some nodes are configured to prefer newer or less open
algorithms, all nodes are required to support the basic ones.

High quality The baseline for security through IPsec must be set
high enough to guarantee a reasonable degree of actual security.
Algorithms and key lengths that are to be vulnerable to attack are not
acceptable. For example, data encrypted with 40-bit encryption keys
can be *brute-forced* or successfully and quickly decrypted by trying
every combination. The number of possible keys is $2^{40} - 1$, or roughly
1000 billion; on average, the correct key will be discovered after trying
half (about 500 billion) of those combinations. Such attacks are almost
trivially easy with commercial off-the-shelf hardware, and thus 40-bit
keys are not considered to provide "high-quality" security.

Cryptographically based Cryptographers work with algorithms for
encryption, secure hashing, and authentication. Encryption algorithms allow regular data to be transformed into *cyphertext*, data
scrambled so that only the entity holding an appropriate *key* can
decrypt it. Secure hash algorithms operate on any size chunk of data
to generate a fixed-length sequence of bits (the hash). An entity can
confirm the integrity of the data by running the hashing algorithm on
received data; if the transmitted hash and the calculated hash agree,
the data is verified as having been sent without change. Authentication of entities through the use of digital signatures depends on public
key algorithms. Data encrypted with the public key of a public/
private key pair can be decrypted only by an entity with access to
the private key; likewise, if an entity encrypts something (such as the
text of a message) with their *private* key, then anyone with access to
the public key can decrypt the message and confirm that the sender
has access to that key.

By basing IPsec on cryptography rather than on any other mechanisms for security, the protocol designers place limits on the security
goals possible to attain through its use while at the same time ensuring that those security goals will be achieved through the use of
verifiable and reliable mechanisms.

The IP security architecture allows systems to choose the required security protocols, identify the cryptographic algorithms to use with those

protocols, and exchange any keys or other material or information necessary to provide security services.

As may be evident from its highly qualified description, public key cryptography-based mechanisms require that all participants can be confident that public keys are issued only to the entities identified with those keys. When a public key is published purporting to represent Microsoft Corporation, the possibility that the key has been properly issued to Microsoft and not to a computer criminal should approach 100% certainty. Unfortunately, as was demonstrated in early 2001 when it was reported that leading public key infrastructure vendor Verisign, Inc., issued two public key certificates to an impostor claiming to represent Microsoft, this is not always possible.

As a network layer protocol, IPsec provides security only at the network layer. This means that packets can be protected from the point at which they enter the IP network (the source node's IP interface) to the point at which they leave the IP network (the destination node's IP interface). IPsec cannot substitute for proper application or transport layer security mechanisms, and IPsec cannot protect against attackers taking control of the source or destination nodes or processes.

6.2   Security Goals

Computer security can be said to embody three general goals.

Authentication   The ability to reliably determine that data has been received as it was sent and to verify that the entity that sent the data is what it claims to be. Successful authentication means preventing attackers from impersonating an authorized entity.

Integrity   The ability to reliably determine that the data has not been modified during transit from its source to its destination. Successfully maintaining data integrity means preventing an attacker from modifying authentic data without detection as well as preventing the acceptance of data that has been corrupted somewhere in the network clouds (as happens occasionally).

Confidentiality   The ability to transmit data that can be used or read only by its intended recipient and not by any other entity.

Successfully maintaining data confidentiality means preventing anyone other than the intended recipient(s) from being able to access
private data.

Developments in modern cryptography, specifically in the use of *public
key cryptography* (discussed in the next section), make possible the combination of these three goals in one set of functions. These goals—authentication, integrity, and confidentiality—are achieved through three related
functions.

Digital signatures   unequivocably link the holder of a particular secret
with data represented as having been *signed* by that entity.

Secure hashes   digitally "summarize" a sequence of data using a repeat-
able process that will produce identical results only if the data
sequence being verified matches the data sequence produced by the
sender.

Encryption   is the process of performing a reversible transformation on
readable data so as to render it unreadable by anyone other than the
holder of the appropriate decryption key.

Some or all of these functions are possible in combination or individually
in protocols at every layer of the TCP/IP stack, from IP (through IPsec) to
the transport layer (through TLS, the Transport Layer Security protocol)
to security functions provided through applications.

The goal of IPsec is to provide security mechanisms for all versions of IP.[1]
IPsec provides security services at the IP layer, and systems may require
other systems to interact with it securely with IPsec and a particular set
of security algorithms and protocols. While IPsec mandates support for
a basic set of algorithms, it also allows nodes to negotiate acceptably secure
interaction with other systems with optional algorithms. IPsec provides
the framework within which nodes can negotiate appropriate algorithms,
protocols, key lengths, and other aspects of secure communication.

IPsec allows maintenance of the following.

Access control   IPsec allows security protocols to be invoked governing
the secure exchange of keys, allowing authentication of users for
access control purposes.

---

[1]IPsec support is mandatory for IPv6 nodes, but optional for IPv4 nodes.

Connectionless integrity   IPsec allows nodes to validate each IP packet independent of any other packet. There is no need to verify sequences of packets or even to have access to other packets exchanged by the same nodes. Connectionless integrity is enabled through use of secure hashing techniques, similar to the use of check digits but with greater reliability and less likelihood of tampering from unauthorized entities.

Data origin authentication   Identifying the source of the data contained in an IP packet is another security service provided by IPsec. This function is accomplished through the use of digital signatures.

Defense against packet replay attacks   As a connectionless protocol, IP is subject to the threat of replay attacks, where an attacker sends a packet that has already been received by the destination host. Replay attacks can harm system availability by tying up receiving system resources. IPsec provides a packet countermechanism that protects against this ploy.

Encryption   Data confidentiality—keeping access to data from anyone but those with proper authorization—is provided through the use of encryption.

Limited traffic flow confidentiality   Encrypting data is not always sufficient to protect systems; merely knowing the endpoints of an encrypted exchange, the frequency of such interaction, or other information about the transmissions can provide a determined attacker with enough information to disrupt or subvert systems. IPsec provides some limited traffic flow confidentiality through the use of IP tunneling, especially when coupled with security gateways.

All of these functions are possible through proper use of the Encapsulating Security Payload (ESP) Header and the Authentication Header (AH). A handful of cryptographic functions is specified for IPsec and is described briefly in the next section.

Public key encryption provides a mechanism for performing almost all of these functions with a single set of processes. AH provides mechanisms for applying authentication algorithms to an IP packet, whereas ESP provides mechanisms for applying any kind of cryptographic algorithm to an IP packet including encryption, digital signature, and/or secure hashes.

IPsec is aimed at eliminating certain types of attacks, including the following.

Denial of service (DoS) attacks   These occur when an entity uses network transmissions to prevent legitimate users from using network resources. For example, an attacker may flood a host with TCP SYN requests and thereby crash a system, or the attack may consist of repeated transmission of long mail messages with the intention of filling up a user's or site's bandwidth with nuisance traffic.

Spoofing attacks   These occur when an entity transmits packets that misrepresent the packets' origins. For example, one type of spoofing attack occurs when the attacker sends a mail message with the From: header indicating the source of the message as, say, the president of the United States. More insidious and almost as easy to engineer are those attacks that occur when packets are sent out with an incorrect source address in the headers.

Man-in-the-middle attacks (MITMs)   These occur when an attacker (Alice) positions herself between two communicating entities (call them Bob and Carol) and intercepts all their transmissions. Alice poses as Bob when communicating with Carol, and as Carol when communicating with Bob. Alice, as a result, is able to send whatever data she wants to Bob instead of what Carol wants to send to Bob. MITM attacks are relatively easy when transmissions are not encrypted or authenticated. However, Alice can successfully attack even a protected data stream if she is able to either gain access to Carol's secret keys (or be issued a set of her own public/secret key pairs that is sufficiently similar to Carol's that Bob will be fooled).

This last attack is important because it raises the issue of handling keys. As just noted, encryption and digital signature functions require the use of *keys* to decrypt and/or verify data, and *digital certificates* are one mechanism by which public keys can be distributed. Although all *public key infrastructure* (*PKI*) providers, including Verisign, make their own efforts to validate all applications, the problem is not a matter of technology. As noted earlier, Verisign issued two digital certificates to someone who improperly posed as a representative of Microsoft; a sufficiently motivated attacker will presumably use every possible tactic to get a desired certification. An attacker's ability to forge credentials (from letterhead on which to type a request for a corporate digital certificate to passport, birth certificate, or other documents submitted to support a fraudulent application) may exceed the ability of the PKI provider to detect them.

As a result of this potential vulnerability, IPsec requires a mechanism by which keys can be securely administered and distributed in a way that associates public keys with the entities that are supposed to own them.

As just noted, IPsec secures IP—*not* the Internet and certainly not the systems connected to the Internet or the processes running on those systems. IPsec must be considered only one part of the organizational security strategy. While IPsec-protected traffic may pass unscathed across the global Internet, before it leaves its source and after it arrives at its destination, that traffic will be vulnerable to attacks on local links, local systems, processes, and the protocols used there.

6.3   Encryption and Authentication Algorithms

Rather than relying on secrecy to protect an encryption or authentication scheme (an approach known as "security through obscurity"), TCP/IP security protocols always specify that cryptographic algorithms be well known and accessible. This is done for several reasons, not the least of which is that as an open protocol suite, TCP/IP protocol specifications must be published freely. The most important reason, however, is that secrecy is a poor safeguard over security.

Attempting to keep an encryption algorithm secret is almost impossible, particularly if it is being used by anyone other than the person who knows the secret. Attackers have many cryptanalysis tools at their disposal for breaking codes, and they need only have access to ciphertexts to break them. Having access to the software used to encrypt and/or decrypt data with the secret algorithm makes the task much easier: the attacker must only determine what the software does to the data to figure out how to reverse the operation.

The greatest advantage that published algorithms provide is the benefit of scrutiny by researchers and others seeking to find ways to further improve or break the algorithms. The more trained experts examine an algorithm, the less likely they are to overlook an "obvious" attack.

Security algorithms and protocols are hard to design because there are so many different ways to attack them—and designers can't always imagine them all. Although national security organizations as well as corporations may have their own top-secret codes, secrets are hard to keep. Spies and other criminals are well known for their skill at motivating (through bribery, extortion, or other means) people who know secrets to share them.

The prevailing wisdom in security holds that a good encryption or authentication algorithm should be secure even if an attacker knows what algorithm is being used. This is particularly important for Internet security, since an attacker with a sniffer will often be able to determine exactly what kind of algorithm is being used by listening as systems negotiate their connections.

In this section we'll cover five types of important cryptographic functions.

- Symmetric encryption
- Public key encryption
- Key exchange
- Secure hashes (message digests)
- Digital signature

6.3.1   SYMMETRIC ENCRYPTION

Most people are familiar with *symmetric encryption*, if only at a visceral, intuitive level: Plaintexts are encrypted with a secret key and some set of procedures, and they are decrypted with the same key and the same set of procedures. If you have the key, you can decrypt all data that has been encrypted with that key. Sometimes known as *secret key encryption*, symmetric encryption is computationally efficient and it is the most frequent type of encryption for network transmission of volumes of data.

In October 2000, the National Institute of Standards and Technology (NIST) announced that the *Rijndael*[2] data encryption algorithm had been selected for the *Advanced Encryption Standard* (*AES*), replacing the outdated *Data Encryption Standard* (*DES*) algorithm originally developed during the 1970s by IBM. DES uses 56-bit keys, although a variation called *triple DES*

---

[2] According to an FAQ at the NIST Web site, "The algorithm's developers have suggested the following pronunciation alternatives: 'Reign Dahl,' 'Rain Doll,' and 'Rhine Dahl.'" The AES home page is http://csrc.nist.gov/encryption/aes/.

encrypts data three times with the DES algorithm, providing improved security.

Using a secure encryption requires using sufficiently long keys. Shorter keys are vulnerable to brute-force attacks, in which an attacker uses a computer to try all the different possible keys. Key lengths on the order of 40 bits, for example, are considered insecure because they can be broken by brute-force attacks in very short order by relatively inexpensive computers. Single-DES has been brute-forced as well; in general, 128-bit and longer keys are likely to be secure against such attacks for the immediate future.

Symmetric encryption algorithms can be vulnerable to other types of attacks. Most applications that use symmetric encryption for Internet communications use session keys, meaning that the key is used for only a single-session data transmission (sometimes several keys are used in one session). Loss of a session key thus compromises only the data that was sent during that session or portion of a session.

These are some of the other symmetric encryption algorithms that have been or are currently being used for Internet applications.

RC2/RC4   These commercial symmetric encryption algorithms were developed and marketed by cryptography firm RSA.

CAST   Developed in Canada and used by Nortel's Entrust products, CAST supports up to 128-bit keys.

IDEA   The International Data Encryption Algorithm supports 128-bit keys. It was patented by Swiss firm Ascom, which granted permission for IDEA to be used for free noncommercial use in the seminal and open source encryption program Pretty Good Privacy (PGP), written by Philip Zimmermann and published for a time by Network Associates, Inc.

GOST   This algorithm was reportedly developed by a Soviet security agency.

Blowfish   This algorithm was developed by Bruce Schneier and released to the public domain.

Twofish   This was Bruce Schneier's submission to the AES competition.

Skipjack   This algorithm was developed by the National Security Agency for use with the Clipper chip's escrowed key system.

6.3.2   PUBLIC KEY ENCRYPTION

Public key encryption, also called *asymmetric encryption*, uses pairs of keys: One, the *public key*, is associated with the other, the *secret key*. The public key is intended to be made public. Any data encrypted with the public key can only be decrypted with the secret key and any data encrypted with the secret key can be decrypted with the public key.

Anyone can get a public key and encrypt some data with it. That data can be decrypted only by the holder of the secret key. As long as an entity can keep its secret key a secret, other entities can be sure that any data encrypted with the public key will be accessible only to the holder of the associated secret key. The holder of the secret key can encrypt something using that secret key and make it available to another entity. That entity can verify the first entity as holding the secret key of a particular public key pair by decrypting the data with the public key.

Public key encryption tends to be computationally intensive and is most often used to encrypt session keys for network transmissions as well as for digital signatures.

The most commonly used type of public key encryption is the *RSA* algorithm developed by Ron Rivest, Adi Shamir, and Len Adleman. RSA defines a mechanism for choosing and generating the secret/public key pairs, as well as for the actual mathematical function to be used for encryption.

6.3.3   KEY MANAGEMENT

One of the most complex issues facing Internet security professionals is how to manage keys. This includes not only the actual distribution of keys through a key exchange protocol but also the negotiation of key length, lifetime, and cryptographic algorithms between communicating systems.

An open channel (an open communication medium over which transmissions can be overheard) like the global Internet complicates the process of sharing a secret. This process is necessary when two entities need to share a key to be used for encryption. Some of the most important cryptographic algorithms relate to the process of sharing a key over an open channel securely, in a way that keeps the secret from anyone but the intended recipients.

Diffie-Hellman key exchange is an algorithm that allows entities to exchange enough information to derive a session encryption key. Alice (the customary entity name for the first participant in a cryptographic protocol) calculates a value using Bob's public value and her own secret value (Bob is the second participant in cryptographic protocols). Bob calculates his own value and sends it to Alice; they each then use their secret values to calculate their shared key. The mathematics are relatively simple (but outside the scope of this book); the bottom line is that Bob and Alice can send each other enough information to calculate their shared key but not enough for an attacker to be able to figure it out.

Diffie-Hellman is often called a public key algorithm, but it is not a public key *encryption* algorithm. Diffie-Hellman is used to calculate a key, but that key must be used with some other encryption algorithm. Diffie-Hellman can be used for authentication, though, and is also used by PGP.

Key exchange is integral to any Internet security architecture, and candidates for the IPsec security architecture include the *Internet Key Exchange* (*IKE*) protocol and the *Internet Security Association and Key Management Protocol* (*ISAKMP*).

ISAKMP is an application protocol, using UDP as its transport, which defines different types of messages that systems send to each other to negotiate the exchange of keys. The mechanisms and algorithms for doing the actual exchanges, however, are not defined in ISAKMP—it is a framework to be used by the specific mechanisms. The mechanisms, often based on Diffie-Hellman key exchange, have been defined in a number of different proposals over the years. These are some of them.

Photuris Based on Diffie-Hellman, *Photuris* adds the requirement that the requesting node send a *cookie*, a random number that is used as a sort of session identifier. The cookie is sent first, and the server acknowledges the request by returning the cookie. This reduces the risk from denial-of-service attacks made by attackers forging their source addresses. Photuris also requires all parties to sign their negotiated key to reduce the risk of a man-in-the-middle attack (in which an attacker pretends to be Bob to one system's Alice, while pretending to be Alice to the other system's Bob).

SKIP Sun Microsystems' *Simple Key-management for Internet Protocols* (*SKIP*) is also based on Diffie-Hellman key exchange, but rather than requiring parties to use random values to calculate their keys, SKIP calls for the use of a secret table that remains static. The parties look up secret values in this table and then transmit calculated values based on some secret value from the table.

OAKLEY Although this mechanism shares some features with Photuris, it provides different modes of key exchange for situations where denial-of-service attacks are not a concern.

By defining a separate protocol, ISAKMP, for the generalized formats required to do key and Security Association exchanges, it can be used as a base to build specific key exchange protocols. The foundation protocol can be used for any security protocol, and it does not have to be replaced if an existing key exchange protocol is replaced.

It should be noted that manual key management is an important option and in many cases is the *only* option. This approach requires individuals to personally deliver keys and configure network devices to use them. Even after open standards have been firmly determined and implemented, particularly as commercial products, manual key management will continue to be an important choice.

As more research is done with IPsec, work on an IKE successor protocol (sometimes called *Son-of-IKE*) is ongoing, with IKEv2 one candidate protocol that (as of 2002) is a work-in-progress.

6.3.4 SECURE HASHES

A hash is a digital summary of a chunk of data of any size. Simple types of hashes include check digits; secure hashes produce longer results (often 128 bits or longer). Good secure hashes are extremely difficult for attackers to reverse-engineer or subvert in other ways. Secure hashes can be used with keys or without, but their purpose is to provide a digital summary of a message that can be used to verify whether some data that has been received is the same as the data sent. The sender calculates the hash and includes that value with the data; the recipient calculates the hash on the data received. If the results match the attached hash value, the recipient can be confident in the data's integrity.

Commonly used hashes include the MD2, MD4, and MD5 message digest functions published by Network Associates. The *Secure Hash Algorithm* (*SHA*) is a digest function developed as a standard by NIST. Hashes may be used on their own or as part of digital signatures.

6.3.5   DIGITAL SIGNATURE

Public key encryption, as noted previously, relies on key pairs. Digital signatures rely on the property of public key encryption that allows data encrypted with an entity's secret key to be decrypted with the public key of the pair. The sender calculates a secure hash on the data to be signed and then encrypts the result using a secret key. The recipient calculates the same hash and then decrypts the encrypted value attached by the sender. If the two values match, the recipient knows that the owner of the public key was the entity that signed the message and that the message was not modified during transmission.

The RSA public key encryption algorithm can be used for digital signatures: The signing entity creates a hash of the data to be signed and then encrypts that hash with its own secret key. The certifying entity then calculates the same hash on the data being received, decrypts the signature using the signing entity's public key, and compares the two values. If the hash is the same as the decrypted signature, then the data is certified.

Digital signatures carry with them several implications.

- A signature that can be certified indicates that the message was received without any alteration from the time it was signed to the time it was received.
- If a signature cannot be certified, then the message was corrupted or tampered with in transit, the signature was calculated incorrectly, or the signature was corrupted or tampered with in transit. In any case, an uncertifiable signature does not necessarily imply any wrongdoing but does require that the message be resigned and resent in order to be accepted.
- If a signature is certified, it means that the entity associated with the public key was the *only* entity that could have signed it.

In other words, the entity associated with the public key cannot deny having signed the message. This is called *nonrepudiation* and is an important feature of digital signatures.

There are other mechanisms for doing digital signatures, but RSA is probably the most widely used one and is implemented in the most popular Internet products.

6.4   IPsec: The Protocols

IPsec is a security tunneling protocol, defining a mechanism that allows a node to encrypt and/or authenticate packets and encapsulate the secured packets (which may now be literally indecipherable, having been encrypted) into new packets. Figure 6–1 illustrates the basic idea behind IPsec and other security tunneling protocols.

IPsec depends on the use of *security gateways*, which encapsulate IP packets on behalf of their clients. In Figure 6–1, the security gateway labeled "X" serves, among others, hosts A′, B′, and C′; "Y" serves hosts A, B, and C. The PC off on the side has its own, software, security gateway. In this example, the tunnel from X to Y carries all secured traffic between the two pictured Internets. In this case, each security gateway integrates all traffic for its local network and encrypts and/or authenticates all of it between itself and the security gateway at the other end. If all traffic is being encrypted (a good bet), then any attacker sitting inside the public Internet could intercept these packets but would get relatively little information from them. At best, the attacker would discover that there is a secure tunnel between X and Y, but she would likely learn only how much traffic was being sent between the two security gateways.

The security gateways create secure tunnels, as shown in Figure 6–2, by accepting IP packets sent from one node (A) to another (B). A sends off the packets as if they were going to be delivered directly to B; the security gateway X then takes those packets (along with any others from the same network) and treats them as raw data to be sent to security gateway Y. The packets sent by A are shown as open envelopes to signify that they have not been encrypted, while the packets sent from X are shown as

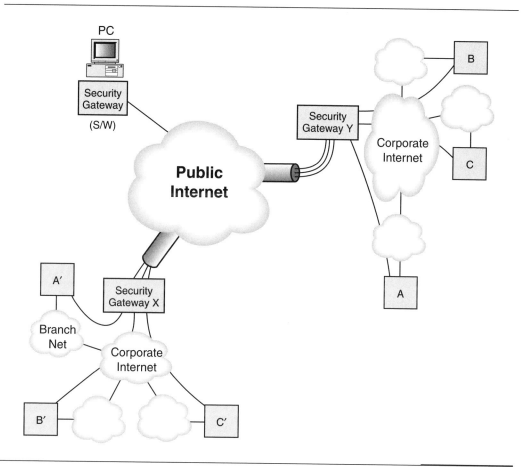

Figure 6–1: Security tunneling across a hostile network.

sealed envelopes to indicate that they contain the encrypted packets sent from A.

The original IPsec specifications define security protocols for the Authentication Header (AH) and the Encapsulating Security Payload (ESP) IP options, as header options (for IPv4) or header extensions (for IPv6). As their names imply, AH provides an authentication mechanism, whereas ESP provides an encryption ("encapsulated security") mechanism for privacy.

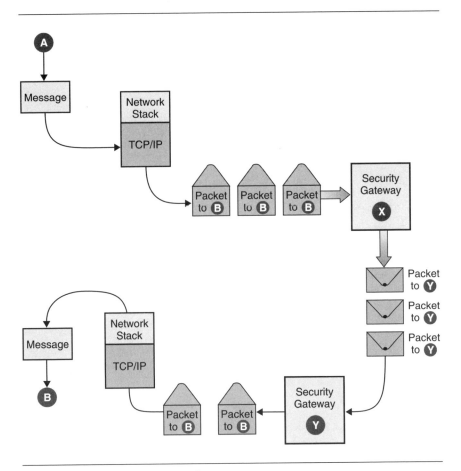

Figure 6–2: Using a secure tunnel.

6.5   IP and IPsec

IPsec provides security services for either IPv4 or IPv6, but the way it provides those services is slightly different in each. When used with IPv4, IPsec headers are inserted after the IPv4 header and before the next-layer protocol header.

IPv6 simplifies header processing: Every IPv6 packet header is the same length, 40 octets, but any options can be accommodated in extension headers that follow the IPv6 header. IPsec services are provided through these extensions.

The ordering of IPsec headers, whether within IPv4 or IPv6, has significance. For example, it makes sense to encrypt a payload with the ESP Header and then use the Authentication Header to provide data integrity on the encrypted payload. In this case, the AH Header appears first, followed by the ESP Header and encrypted payload. Reversing the order, by doing data integrity first and then encrypting the whole lot, means that you can be sure of who originated the data but not necessarily certain of who did the encryption.

6.5.1   SECURITY ASSOCIATIONS

The *Security Association (SA)* is a fundamental element of IPsec. RFC 2401 defines the SA as "a simplex 'connection' that affords security services to the traffic carried by it." This rather murky definition is clarified by a description; an SA consists of three things.

- A Security Parameter Index (SPI)
- An IP destination address
- A security protocol (AH or ESP) identifier

As a simplex connection, the SA associates a single destination with the SPI; thus, for typical IP traffic there will be two SAs: one in each direction that secure traffic flows (one each for source and destination host). SAs provide security services by using either AH or ESP but not both (if a traffic stream uses both AH and ESP, it has two—or more—SAs).

The *Security Parameter Index (SPI)* is an identifier indicating the type of IP header the security association is being used for (AH or ESP). The SPI is a 32-bit value identifying the SA and differentiating it from other SAs linked to the same destination address. For secure communication between two systems, there would be two different security associations, one for each destination address.

Each security association includes more information related to the type of security negotiated for that connection, so systems must keep track of their SAs and what type of encryption or authentication algorithms, key lengths, and key lifetimes have been negotiated with the SA destination hosts.

6.5.2   USING SECURITY ASSOCIATIONS

As mentioned earlier, ISAKMP provides a generalized protocol for establishing SAs and managing cryptographic keys within an Internet environment. The procedures and packet formats needed to establish, negotiate, modify, and delete SAs are defined within ISAKMP, which also defines payloads for exchanging key generation and authentication data. These formats provide a consistent framework for transferring this data, independent of how the key is generated or what type of encryption or authentication algorithms are being used.

ISAKMP was designed to provide a framework that can be used by any security protocols that use SAs, not just IPsec. To be useful for a particular security protocol, a *Domain of Interpretation*, or *DOI*, must be defined. The DOI groups related protocols for the purpose of negotiating security associations—security protocols that share a DOI all choose protocol and cryptographic transforms from a common namespace. They also share key exchange protocol identifiers, as well as a common interpretation of payload data content.

While ISAKMP and the IPsec DOI provide a framework for authentication and key exchange, ISAKMP does not actually define how those functions are to be carried out. The IKE protocol, working within the framework defined by ISAKMP, does define a mechanism for hosts to perform these exchanges.

The sending host knows what kind of security to apply to the packet by looking in a *Security Policy Database* (*SPD*). The sending host determines what policy is appropriate for the packet, depending on various selectors (for example, destination IP address and/or transport layer ports), by looking in the SPD. The SPD indicates what the policy is for a particular packet: Either the packet requires IPsec processing of some sort—in which case it is passed to the IPsec module for processing—or it does not—in which case it is simply passed along for normal IP processing.

Outbound packets must be checked against the SPD to see what kind (if any) of IPsec processing to apply. Inbound packets are checked against the SPD to see what kind of IPsec service should be present in those packets.

Another database, called the *Security Association Database* (*SAD*), includes all security parameters associated with all active SAs. When an IPsec host wants to send a packet, it checks the appropriate selectors to see what the SAD says is the security policy for that destination/port/application. The SPD may reference a particular SA, so the host can look up the SA in the SAD to identify appropriate security parameters for that packet.

6.5.3 TUNNEL AND TRANSPORT MODE

IPsec defines two modes for exchanging secured data: *tunnel mode* and *transport mode*. IPsec transport mode protects upper-layer protocols and is used between end-nodes. This approach allows end-to-end security because the host originating the packet is also securing it, and the destination host is able to verify the security, either by decrypting the packet or certifying the authentication.

Tunnel mode IPsec protects the entire contents of the tunneled packets. The tunneled packets are accepted by a system acting as a security gateway, encapsulated inside a set of IPsec/IP headers, and forwarded to the other end of the tunnel, where the original packets are extracted (after being certified or decrypted) and then passed along to their ultimate destination.

The packets are only secured as long as they are "inside" the tunnel, although the originating and destination hosts could be sending secured packets themselves, so that the tunnel systems are encapsulating packets that have already been secured.

Transport mode is good for any two individual hosts that want to communicate securely; tunnel mode is the foundation of the *Virtual Private Network* or *VPN*. Tunnel mode is also required anytime a *security gateway* (a device offering IPsec services to other systems) is involved at either end of an IPsec transmission. Two security gateways must always communicate by tunneling IP packets inside IPsec packets; the same goes for an individual host communicating with a security gateway. This occurs anytime a mobile laptop user logs into a corporate VPN from the road, for example.

Tunneling, shown in Figure 6–3, allows two systems to set up SAs to enable secure communications over the Internet. Network traffic originates on one system, is encrypted and/or signed, and is then sent to the destination system. On receipt, the datagram is decrypted or authenticated, and the payload is passed along up the receiving system's network stack where it

Figure 6–3: A pair of hosts using IPsec to communicate transparently across the Internet.

is finally processed by the application using the data. This is a *transparent mode* use of security associations, because the two hosts could be communicating just as easily without security headers—and because the actual IP headers of the datagrams must be exposed to allow them to be routed across the Internet.

An SA can also be used to tunnel secure IP through an internetwork. Figure 6–4 shows how this works. All IP packets from system A are forwarded to the security gateway X, which creates an IP tunnel through the Internet to security gateway Y, which unwraps the tunneled packets and forwards them. Security gateway Y might forward those packets to any of the hosts (B, C, or D) within its own local intranet, or it could forward them to an external host, like M. It all depends on where the originating host directs those packets. Whenever an SA destination node is a security gateway, it is by definition a tunneled association. In other words, tunneling can be done between two security gateways (as shown in Figure 6–4), or it can be done between a regular node and a security gateway. Thus, host M could create a tunneled connection with either security gateway, X or Y. It is tunneled by virtue of the fact that datagrams sent from M are passed first to the security gateway, which then forwards them appropriately after decrypting or authenticating.

6.5.4 Encapsulating Security Payload (ESP)

Specified in RFC 2406, "IP Encapsulating Security Payload (ESP)," the ESP Header allows IP nodes to exchange datagrams whose payloads

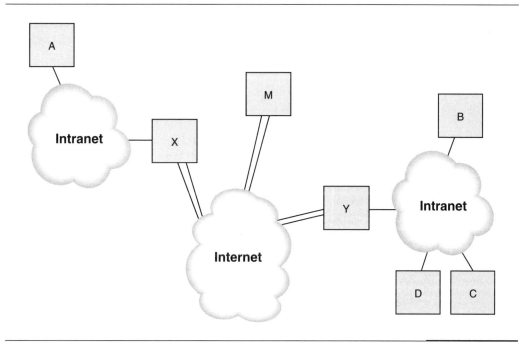

Figure 6–4: IP security tunneling.

are encrypted. The ESP Header is designed to provide several different services (some overlapping with the Authentication Header), including the following.

- Confidentiality of datagrams through encryption.
- Authentication of data origin through the use of public key encryption
- *Antireplay services* through the same sequence number mechanism as provided by the Authentication Header
- Limited traffic flow confidentiality through the use of security gateways

The ESP Header can be used in conjunction with an Authentication Header. In fact, unless the ESP Header uses some mechanism for authentication, it is recommended that the Authentication Header be used with the ESP Header.

The ESP Header must follow any headers that need to be processed by nodes intermediate to the destination node—all data that follows the ESP Header will be encrypted, with the encrypted payload beginning directly after the last ESP Header field (see following).

ESP can be used in tunnel or transport mode, similar to the Authentication Header. In transport mode, the IP Header and any Hop-by-Hop, Routing, or Fragmentation Extension Headers precede the Authentication Header (if present), followed by the ESP Header. Any Destination Options Headers can either precede or follow the ESP Header, or even both; any Headers that follow the ESP Header are encrypted.

The result appears, in many respects, to simply be a regular IP datagram transmitted from source to destination, with an encrypted payload. This use of ESP in transport mode is appropriate in some cases, but it allows attackers to study traffic between the two nodes, noting which nodes are communicating, how much data they exchange, when they exchange it, and so forth. All this information may potentially provide the attacker with some information that helps defeat the communicating parties.

An alternative is to use a security gateway, much as just described for the Authentication Header. A security gateway can operate directly with a node or can link to another security gateway. A single node can use ESP in tunnel mode by encrypting all outbound packets and encapsulating them in a separate stream of IP datagrams that are sent to the security gateway. That gateway then can decrypt the traffic and resend the original datagrams to their destinations.

When tunneling, the ESP Header encapsulates the entire tunneled IP datagram and is an extension to the IP Header directing that datagram to a security gateway. It is also possible to combine ESP Headers with Authentication Headers in several different ways; for example, the tunneled datagram may have a Transport-Mode Authentication Header.

The following ESP Header format (taken from RFC 2406) includes the Next Header field, which appears near the end of the ESP Header and indicates the presence (and identity) of any other headers (such as AH) that may follow. The rest of the ESP Header consists of the following.

Security Parameter Index (SPI)   This is the same 32-bit value referred to in the section on the Authentication Header. This value is used

```
 0                   1                   2                   3
 0 1 2 3 4 5 6 7 8 9 0 1 2 3 4 5 6 7 8 9 0 1 2 3 4 5 6 7 8 9 0 1
+-+-+-+-+-+-+-+-+-+-+-+-+-+-+-+-+-+-+-+-+-+-+-+-+-+-+-+-+-+-+-+-+ ----
|               Security Parameters Index (SPI)                 | ^Auth.
+-+-+-+-+-+-+-+-+-+-+-+-+-+-+-+-+-+-+-+-+-+-+-+-+-+-+-+-+-+-+-+-+ |Cov-
|                    Sequence Number                            | |erage
+-+-+-+-+-+-+-+-+-+-+-+-+-+-+-+-+-+-+-+-+-+-+-+-+-+-+-+-+-+-+-+-+ | ----
|                  Payload Data (variable)                      | |  ^
~                                                               ~ |  |
|                                                               | |Conf.
+                   +-+-+-+-+-+-+-+-+-+-+-+-+-+-+-+-+-+-+-+-+-+-+ |Cov-
|                   |          Padding (0-255 bytes)            | |erage
+-+-+-+-+-+-+-+-+-+-+               +-+-+-+-+-+-+-+-+-+-+-+-+-+-+ |  |
|                                  | Pad Length | Next Header   | v  v
+-+-+-+-+-+-+-+-+-+-+-+-+-+-+-+-+-+-+-+-+-+-+-+-+-+-+-+-+-+-+-+-+ ------
|                Authentication Data (variable)                 |
~                                                               ~
|                                                               |
+-+-+-+-+-+-+-+-+-+-+-+-+-+-+-+-+-+-+-+-+-+-+-+-+-+-+-+-+-+-+-+-+
```

by the communicating nodes to refer to a security association, which can be used to determine how the data should be encrypted.

Sequence Number   This 32-bit value is set to zero to start and is incremented by one with each datagram sent. As just described for the Authentication Header, the sequence number can be used to protect against replay attacks, and a new security association must be set up before this value cycles through all 2^{32} values.

Payload Data   This is a variable-length field and actually contains the encrypted portion of the datagram, along with any supplementary data necessary for the encryption algorithm (e.g., initialization data). The payload begins with an *initialization vector*, a value that must be sent in plaintext; encryption algorithms need this value to decrypt the protected data.

Padding   The encrypted portion of the header (the payload) must end on the appropriate boundary, so padding may be necessary.

Padding Length   This field indicates how much padding has been added to the payload data.

Next Header This field operates as it normally does with other IPv6 extension headers; it just appears near the end of the header (where it can be given confidentiality protection) rather than at the beginning so that the next layer protocol can be hidden from any unauthorized third parties.

Authentication Data This is an *Integrity Check Value* (ICV) calculated on the entire ESP Header (except for the authentication data). This authentication calculation is optional. The ICV is discussed at greater length following.

6.5.5 AUTHENTICATION HEADER

The Authentication Header can be used to do the following.

- Provide strong integrity services for IP datagrams, which means the AH can be used to carry content verification data for the IP datagram.
- Provide strong authentication for IP datagrams, which means that the AH can be used to link an entity with the contents of the datagram.
- Provide nonrepudiation for IP datagrams, assuming that a public key digital signature algorithm is used for integrity services.
- Protect against replay attacks through the use of the sequence number field.

The Authentication Header can be used in tunnel mode or in transport mode, which means that it can be used to authenticate and protect simple, direct datagram transfers between two nodes, or it can be used to encapsulate an entire stream of datagrams that is sent to or from a security gateway.

AH is specified in RFC 2402, "IP Authentication Header," and the header is shown on page 115 (taken from RFC 2402).

In transport mode, the Authentication Header protects the payload of the original IP datagram as well as the parts of the IP Header that do not change from hop to hop (e.g., the Hop Limit field or Routing Headers). Figure 6–5 shows what happens to a transport-mode IP datagram as the Authentication Header is calculated and added to it (the Destination Options Header may also appear before the Authentication Header).

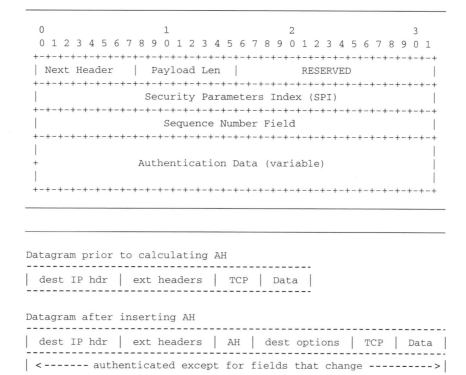

Figure 6–5: Adding an Authentication Header to an IP datagram in transport mode.

The destination IP address and extension headers are protected only insofar as they do not change from hop to hop.

When the Authentication Header is used in tunnel mode, however, it is used differently. Figure 6–6 shows the difference. The original destination IP address, along with the entire original IP datagram, is encapsulated into an entirely new IP datagram that is sent to the security gateway. Thus, the entire original IP datagram is fully protected, as are the portions of the encapsulating IP Headers that don't change.

AH header fields include the following.

Payload length   This 8-bit field indicates the entire length of the Authentication Header in units of 32-bit words, minus 2.

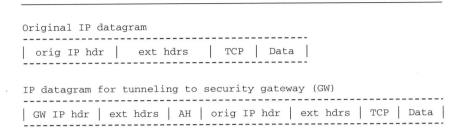

```
Original IP datagram
---------------------------------------------
| orig IP hdr |    ext hdrs    |  TCP |  Data |
---------------------------------------------

IP datagram for tunneling to security gateway (GW)
-------------------------------------------------------------------------
| GW IP hdr | ext hdrs | AH | orig IP hdr | ext hdrs | TCP |  Data |
-------------------------------------------------------------------------
```

Figure 6–6: Adding an Authentication Header to an IP datagram in tunnel mode.

As originally defined, the Authentication Header consisted of 64 bits of header, with the rest devoted to authentication data (see the following). Thus, the payload length field merely indicated the length (in 32-bit words) of the authentication data. With the addition of the Sequence Number field (see the following), this value now equals the length of the authentication data plus the length of the Sequence Number field.

Reserved   The next 16 bits are reserved for future use; at present, they must be set to all zeros.

Security Parameter Index (SPI)   This 32-bit value is an arbitrary number. Together with the destination IP address and security protocol (in this case, AH to indicate the Authentication Header), the SPI uniquely identifies the security association to be used for the Authentication Header. An SPI value of zero is for local use only and should never be transmitted; values from 1 through 255 are reserved by the Internet Assigned Numbers Authority (IANA) for future use.

Sequence Number   This 32-bit value is a mandatory counter; it is also included by the sender, although it may not always be used by the recipient. Starting from zero, this counter is incremented with every datagram sent and is used to prevent replay attacks. When the recipient is using it for antireplay purposes, it will discard any datagrams that duplicate a sequence number that has already been received. This means that when the counter is ready to cycle through (when 2^{32} datagrams have been received), a new security association must be negotiated—otherwise, the receiving system will discard all datagrams once the counter is reset.

Authentication Data   This field contains the Integrity Check Value (ICV), which is the heart of the Authentication Header. The contents must be a multiple of 32 bits in length and may contain padding to attain that length. Calculation of this value is discussed in the next section.

6.5.6   CALCULATING THE INTEGRITY CHECK VALUE (ICV)

The Authentication Data fields in the AH and ESP Headers are variable-length fields, each of which contains an Integrity Check Value (ICV). The field is variable length to accommodate variations from ICV algorithms, and the length is specified by the selected function. This is an optional field: It is included only when an authentication service is in use for the SA that corresponds to the header, and information about the ICV function in use is maintained along with the rest of the SA data.

The ICV calculation is a bit tricky in that some of the data being authenticated may be modified en route, such as IP header hop counts. According to RFC 2402 the AH ICV is computed on the IP header fields that either don't change in transit or whose values on arrival can be predicted, the AH header itself (though the Authentication Data field is set to zero for the calculation), and the upper-level protocol data that is being authenticated (this is assumed to be unchanged in transit).

The ESP ICV, according to RFC 2406, is computed on the entire ESP packet, excluding the Authentication Data field. This includes the SPI, Sequence Number, Payload Data, Padding (if present), Pad Length, and Next Header; the last four fields will be in ciphertext form, since encryption is performed prior to authentication.

These are the suggested algorithms for ICV.

Message Authentication Codes (MACs),   the results of which are then encrypted with an appropriate symmetric encryption algorithm (for example, AES)

Secure hash functions,   such as MD5 or SHA-1 (an updated version of SHA)

To comply with the standard, implementations must support MD5 and SHA-1 keyed hashing, at least.

6.5.7 IPSEC HEADERS IN ACTION

IPsec security services are provided through the AH and ESP Headers in conjunction, of course, with appropriate and relevant key management protocols. The AH protocol is specified in RFC 2402, "IP Authentication Header"; ESP is specified in RFC 2406, "IP Encapsulating Security Payload (ESP)."

Either security header may be used by itself, or both may be used together in various combinations of transport or tunnel modes. When used together with AH encapsulating ESP, packet authentication can be checked prior to decrypting the ESP Header payload. These headers can also be nested when using IPsec tunneling: An originating node can encrypt and digitally sign a packet, and then send it to the local security gateway. That gateway may then reencrypt and resign the packet as it sends it off to another security gateway.

The ESP and AH authentication services are slightly different: ESP authentication services are ordinarily provided only on the packet payload, whereas AH authenticates almost the entire packet including headers.

The Sequence Number field is mandatory for all AH and ESP Headers and is used to provide antireplay services. Every time a new packet is sent, the Sequence Number is increased by one (the first packet sent with a given SA will have a Sequence Number of 1).

When the receiving host elects to use the antireplay service for a particular SA, the host checks the Sequence Number: if it receives a packet with a Sequence Number value that it has already received, that packet is discarded.

The Authentication Data field contains whatever data is required by the authentication mechanisms specified for that particular SA to authenticate the packet. The ICV may contain a keyed Message Authentication Code (MAC) based on a symmetric encryption algorithm (such as AES or Triple-DES) or a one-way hash function such as MD5 or SHA-1.

The most obvious difference between ESP and AH is that the ESP Header's Next Header field appears at the end of the security payload. Of course, since the header may be encapsulating an encrypted payload, you don't need to know what next header to expect until after you've decrypted the payload—thus, the ESP Next Header field is placed after rather than before the payload.

ESP's authentication service covers only the payload itself, not the IP headers of its own packet as with the Authentication Header. And the confidentiality service covers only the payload itself; obviously, you can't encrypt the IP headers of the packet intended to deliver the payload and still expect any intermediate routers to be able to process the packet. Of course, if you're using tunneling, you can encrypt everything, but only everything in the tunneled packet itself.

6.6   Implementing and Deploying IPsec

IP layer security protects IP datagrams. It does not necessarily have to involve the user or any applications. This means users may be merrily using all of their applications without ever being aware that all their datagrams are being encrypted or authenticated before being sent out to the Internet (of course, that situation will only occur as long as all the encrypted datagrams are properly decrypted by hosts at the other end).

As a result, one question that comes up is how to implement IPsec. RFC 2401 suggests several strategies for implementing IPsec in a host or in conjunction with a router or firewall.

Integrated implementation   Integrate IPsec into the native IP implementation. This approach is probably the best, but also the most difficult, as it requires rewriting the native IP implementation to include support for IPsec. Integrating IPsec into the IP stack adds security natively and makes it an integral part of any IP implementation. However, it also requires that the entire stack be updated to reflect the changes.

"Bump-in-the-stack" (BITS)   Implement IPsec "beneath" the IP stack and above the local network drivers. The IPsec implementation monitors IP traffic as it is sent or received over the local link, and IPsec functions are performed on the packets before passing them up or down the stack. This works reasonably well for individual hosts doing IPsec.

This approach inserts special IPsec code into the network stack just below the existing IP network software and just above the local link software. In other words, this approach implements security through a piece of software that intercepts datagrams being passed from the existing IP stack to the local link layer interface. This software then does the necessary security processing for those datagrams and hands them off to the link layer. This approach can be used to upgrade systems to IPsec support without requiring that their IP stack software be rewritten.

"Bump-in-the-wire" (BITW)   Implement IPsec in a hardware cryptographic processor. The crypto processor gets its own IP address; when used for individual hosts, the bump-in-the-wire acts much like a BITS implementation, but when the same processor provides IPsec services to a router or firewall, it must behave as a security gateway—meaning that it must do IPsec security protocols in tunnel mode.

This approach uses external cryptographic hardware to perform the security processing. The device is usually an IP device that acts as a sort of a router or, more accurately, security gateway for all IP datagrams from any system that sits behind it. When such a device is used for a single host, it works very much like the BITS approach, but implementation can be more complex when a single BITW device is used to screen more than one system.

These options differ more in terms of where they are appropriate than in subjective terms. Applications that require high levels of security may be better served with a hardware implementation. Applications that run on systems for which new IPsec-compliant network stacks are not available may be better served by the BITS approach.

6.7   Summary

Network security is probably the subject of as many books and chapters within technical books as IP. This chapter provides a concise introduction to IP security issues and security goals, starting with the definition of the challenges facing security managers and the tools at their disposal. IPsec provides authentication services through the use of public key encryption, digital signature, and secure hashing tools; it provides privacy services through the use of public and secret key encryption as well.

On top of these cryptographic tools, however, IPsec requires additional protocols to handle the secure and verifiable distribution and management of encryption keys. IPsec combines these cryptographic and security protocols with IP, using security associations to link packets with hosts and a pair of optional IP security headers (ESP and AH) to transmit IP packets securely.

IPsec is often linked to IPv6 because while IPsec support in IPv4 is optional, it is mandatory for all IPv6-capable hosts. Although some cite "security" as a reason to prefer IPv6 over IPv4, to a great degree the same level of security is possible if IPsec were mandatory for all IPv4 nodes.

IPv6 protocols are introduced in the next chapter.

7

IPv6 Protocol Basics

IPv6 embodies change in several important areas.

- Expanded addressing
- Simplified header format
- Improved extension and option support

These changes to IP succeed at achieving most of the goals originally charted by the IAB back in 1991 (see RFC 1287, "Toward the Future Internet Architecture"). The expanded IPv6 address space means IP can continue to grow without concern about depletion of resources; the addressing architecture helps improve the situation for routing efficiency.

The simplified header format improves routing efficiency by requiring less processing of packets, whereas the improvements in extension and option support mean that special needs can be accommodated without significantly affecting performance either of routing of normal packets or of the special-needs packets. Flow labeling provides another mechanism for treating streams of packets efficiently, particularly useful for real-time applications. Required support of IPsec, providing authentication and privacy, also makes IPv6 a more desirable protocol for commercial uses that require special treatment of sensitive information or resources.

7.1   The IPv6 Address Space

The designers of IPv6 could have simply grafted a larger address space onto the existing IPv4 addressing architecture—but doing so would cause us to miss out on a huge opportunity for improving IP. Changing the entire addressing architecture provides an incredible opportunity not only for improving efficiency of address allocation but also for improving IP routing performance.

The IPv4 address space was divided into several different classes based on the values of their high-order bits. The IPv6 address space is also divided into different categories based on high-order bits, as shown in Table 7–1, although most of the address space is unassigned as of yet. The global unicast address space takes up fully one-eighth of the entire address space, with all global unicast addresses sharing the three high-order bits 001. Other allocations are discussed later. All these allocations still leave roughly 85% of the IPv6 address space unassigned, with no current plans to assign them for now. At the same time, the allocations that have been made should be more than ample for the foreseeable future.

As of 2003, the Regional Internet Registries (RIRs) are allocating /32 network prefixes to organizations requesting them, and those allocations may be expanded in the future if necessary. So far, there is no provision for suballocations of network blocks smaller than /48, although there are proposals on the table that would permit such "micro-allocations."

7.1.1   PROVIDER-BASED AGGREGATION

In 1995, RFC 1884, "IP Version 6 Addressing Architecture," allocated a full quarter of the address space for two different types of unicast addresses: one-eighth for provider-based unicast addresses and one-eighth for geographic-based unicast addresses. The intent was to offer addresses that could be assigned based either on who provided network service to the address holder or where the subscribing network was located. *Provider-based aggregation* would have required networks to take on aggregatable IP addresses based on the source of their Internet access. However, this

Allocation	Prefix (binary)	Fraction of address space
Unassigned	0000 0000	1/256
Unassigned	0000 0001	1/256
Reserved for NSAP Allocation	0000 001	1/128
Unassigned	0000 01	1/64
Unassigned	0000 1	1/32
Unassigned	0001	1/16
Global Unicast	001	1/8
Unassigned	010	1/8
Unassigned	011	1/8
Unassigned	100	1/8
Unassigned	101	1/8
Unassigned	110	1/8
Unassigned	1110	1/16
Unassigned	1111 0	1/32
Unassigned	1111 10	1/64
Unassigned	1111 110	1/128
Unassigned	1111 1110 0	1/512
Link-Local Unicast Addresses	1111 1110 10	1/1024
Site-Local Unicast Addresses	1111 1110 11	1/1024
Multicast Addresses	1111 1111	1/256

Table 7–1: Initial IPv6 address space allocation map, from RFC 3513.

approach was seen to be less than a perfect solution for very large organizations with far-flung branches, some of which would require service from different providers. Provider-based aggregation would add even more IP address management headaches for these large organizations.

7.1.2   GEOGRAPHIC-BASED AGGREGATION

Steve Deering proposed *geographic-based allocation* as an alternative in the Simple Internet Protocol (SIP, a precursor to SIPP, see Chapter 4). These addresses, unlike provider-based addresses, would be allocated on a permanent basis much as IPv4 addresses have been allocated. These addresses would be based on geographic location, and providers would have to maintain additional routes to support these networks outside the aggregatable portion of the IPv6 address space.

The ISP community dislikes geographic-based allocations because it means significantly more complexity (and cost) to manage geographic address allocation. Since most objections to provider-based allocation grew out of difficulties of configuring and reconfiguring nodes with provider-based addresses, geographic address allocation has been dropped in favor of developing improved automatic and dynamic host configuration under IPv6—including the ability to automatically renumber entire networks when providers are changed.

7.1.3   IPv6 AGGREGATION

With the goal of avoiding complicating the IPv6 routing tables, the current approach to aggregation is based on having routes aggregated by the service providers. The addition of stateless autoconfiguration and renumbering protocols to IPv6 will serve to make some types of aggregation unnecessary.

7.2   IPv6 Header Format

Network protocols can be said to consist of the set of rules that govern exchanges of information between nodes and the information itself. IP packet headers contain the information and constrain that information in most cases to valid values. Once it is clear what information is contained in the headers and what values are valid, the rules of the exchanges become self-evident.

Figure 7–1 shows the IPv4 packet header structure, and Figure 7–2 shows the IPv6 packet header structure. Compare the two, and it becomes clear that IPv6 should be a simpler protocol if only because they carry less information. However, the fields that have been dispensed with are either no longer needed or wanted, and IPv6 provides at least as much functionality to network nodes as IPv4.

IPv6 headers consist of 8 fields (2 of which are source and destination addresses) spread over 40 bytes. Contrast this with IPv4 headers, which contain at least 12 different fields and may be as short as 20 bytes if no options are in use or as long as 60 bytes if options are being used. Routing is thought to be more efficient with a uniformly sized header and with fewer fields to examine and process.

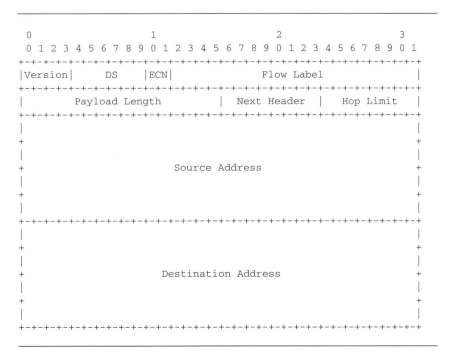

```
 0                   1                   2                   3
 0 1 2 3 4 5 6 7 8 9 0 1 2 3 4 5 6 7 8 9 0 1 2 3 4 5 6 7 8 9 0 1
+-+-+-+-+-+-+-+-+-+-+-+-+-+-+-+-+-+-+-+-+-+-+-+-+-+-+-+-+-+-+-+-+
|Version|  IHL  |Type of Service|          Total Length         |
+-+-+-+-+-+-+-+-+-+-+-+-+-+-+-+-+-+-+-+-+-+-+-+-+-+-+-+-+-+-+-+-+
|         Identification        |Flags|     Fragment Offset     |
+-+-+-+-+-+-+-+-+-+-+-+-+-+-+-+-+-+-+-+-+-+-+-+-+-+-+-+-+-+-+-+-+
|  Time to Live |    Protocol   |        Header Checksum         |
+-+-+-+-+-+-+-+-+-+-+-+-+-+-+-+-+-+-+-+-+-+-+-+-+-+-+-+-+-+-+-+-+
|                        Source Address                         |
+-+-+-+-+-+-+-+-+-+-+-+-+-+-+-+-+-+-+-+-+-+-+-+-+-+-+-+-+-+-+-+-+
|                      Destination Address                      |
+-+-+-+-+-+-+-+-+-+-+-+-+-+-+-+-+-+-+-+-+-+-+-+-+-+-+-+-+-+-+-+-+
|                    Options                     |    Padding    |
+-+-+-+-+-+-+-+-+-+-+-+-+-+-+-+-+-+-+-+-+-+-+-+-+-+-+-+-+-+-+-+-+
```

Figure 7–1: IPv4 packet headers (from RFC 791).

```
 0                   1                   2                   3
 0 1 2 3 4 5 6 7 8 9 0 1 2 3 4 5 6 7 8 9 0 1 2 3 4 5 6 7 8 9 0 1
+-+-+-+-+-+-+-+-+-+-+-+-+-+-+-+-+-+-+-+-+-+-+-+-+-+-+-+-+-+-+-+-+
|Version|    DS   |ECN|                Flow Label                |
+-+-+-+-+-+-+-+-+-+-+-+-+-+-+-+-+-+-+-+-+-+-+-+-+-+-+-+-+-+-+-+-+
|        Payload Length         |   Next Header |   Hop Limit   |
+-+-+-+-+-+-+-+-+-+-+-+-+-+-+-+-+-+-+-+-+-+-+-+-+-+-+-+-+-+-+-+-+
|                                                               |
+                                                               +
|                                                               |
+                        Source Address                         +
|                                                               |
+                                                               +
|                                                               |
+-+-+-+-+-+-+-+-+-+-+-+-+-+-+-+-+-+-+-+-+-+-+-+-+-+-+-+-+-+-+-+-+
|                                                               |
+                                                               +
|                                                               |
+                     Destination Address                       +
|                                                               |
+                                                               +
|                                                               |
+-+-+-+-+-+-+-+-+-+-+-+-+-+-+-+-+-+-+-+-+-+-+-+-+-+-+-+-+-+-+-+-+
```

Figure 7–2: IPv6 packet headers (from RFCs 2460 and 2474).

The header could be simplified as a result of some changes in the way IP works. For one thing, making all headers the same length eliminates the need for the header length field. For another, by changing the rules about packet fragmentation, several fields can be removed from the header. Fragmentation in IPv6 may only be done by source nodes: Intermediate routers along the packet's path can no longer fragment them. Finally, while eliminating the IP header checksum will definitely improve performance, it shouldn't affect reliability in any way, particularly because header checksums are performed by higher-level protocols (UDP and TCP).

7.3   IPv4 Versus IPv6

The IPv4 header shown in Figure 7–1 is superficially similar but only the version field is completely unchanged in IPv6. The version field must remain unchanged to allow IPv4 and IPv6 to coexist in the same local link. The rest of the header fields have been changed or modified in IPv6 as follows.

Version   is a four-bit value, and for IPv4 must be equal to four.

Header length   is irrelevant to IPv6 because all IPv6 headers are the same length. IPv4 requires this field because its headers can be as short as 20 bytes and as long as 60 bytes to accommodate IP options.

Type of Service (ToS)/Differentiated Services   Unlike most other IPv4 header fields, the IPv4 ToS field has changed significantly since it was originally specified in 1982 to be used to tag packets for different kinds of handling by routers (see RFC 791). As of 1989, when RFC 1122, "Requirements for Internet Hosts—Communications Layers," specified host requirements, the ToS field had yet to be used to any significant degree. Further modification came when an additional flag bit was assigned in 1992 in RFC 1349, "Type of Service in the Internet Protocol Suite."

However, in 1998 the ToS field became the *Differentiated Services* field, to be used in both the IPv4 and IPv6 headers. The DS field consists of 6 bits that are used to specify, broadly, how a packet should be treated by routers to provide it an appropriate Quality of Service (QoS). RFC 2474, "Definition of the Differentiated Services Field (DS Field) in the IPv4 and IPv6 Headers," defines how the field works for both

IPv4 and IPv6. This specification calls for replacing both the IPv4 ToS and the IPv6 *Traffic Class* fields with the DS field.[1]

Datagram length   becomes the *payload length* field in IPv6. IPv4's datagram length field specifies the length of the entire datagram, including the IP headers. Thus, routers can calculate the length of the IPv4 datagram payload by subtracting the header length from the datagram length; this calculation is unnecessary in IPv6 because the IPv6 payload length includes extension headers.

Datagram identification   is used to identify a datagram as being part of a fragmented source packet. This is useful only in instances where packet fragmentation is permitted, as in IPv4; because IPv6 does not permit intermediate node fragmentation this field is unnecessary.

Flags   are also used to enable fragmentation.

Fragment offset   is also used to enable fragmentation.

Time-to-live (TTL)   has morphed slightly into the IPv6 *hop limit* field. TTL was originally meant to be an upper bound, in seconds, of the lifetime of a packet in the Internet cloud. IP packets must be assigned a finite lifetime in order to avoid undeliverable packets clogging networks as they shuttle back and forth among routers. If the IPv4 time-to-live counter reaches zero, the packet is discarded. The rationale was that packets might be caught in circular routes, and if they did not expire in some way, they would continue to be routed forever (or until the network crashed). The original specification called for routers to decrement this value by the number of seconds it took from receipt of a packet until the packet was forwarded. In practice, most routers have been implemented to simply decrement this value by 1 rather than attempting to measure the actual time spent in the router.

Protocol field   refers to the next-higher-layer protocol encapsulated within the IPv4 packet. The values for different protocols are available through IANA. This field evolved into the *next header* field in IPv6, where it specifies the next header, whether an IPv6 extension header or another layer's protocol header.

---

[1]RFC 3168, "The Addition of Explicit Congestion Notification (ECN) to IP," traces the development of the ToS field.

Header checksum is a reasonably robust approach to avoiding the processing of packets that have had their headers mangled en route
to their destination. However, with upper-layer protocols like TCP
and UDP calculating their own checksums on headers, the IPv4
header checksum was deemed superfluous. The cost of checking
the checksum en route is outweighed by the ease with which the
destination node can quickly determine that a packet has been
damaged by using transport or application layer checks. For those
applications that do actually require content authentication at the network layer, the much more robust authentication header is available
in IPv6.

Source/destination addresses go from 32 bits for IPv4 packets to 128 bits
each for IPv6 packets.

IP options in IPv4 are replaced in IPv6. IPv6 options exist as separate
headers after the main IPv6 header but before the packet payload.

Although all the IPv4 header fields were thought to be useful as defined
originally (and as tested in early experiments with IP networking), almost
all of them have undergone changes of one kind or another in IPv6. The
fragmentation-related fields are out, as are the header checksum and
IP options. Likewise, the TTL, protocol, and header length fields have
mutated to a greater or lesser degree. And the rest have been modified to
support IPv6 addresses and functions.

7.4 IPv6 Header Fields

The IPv6 header is clearly new and improved, if only because it has fewer
fields. As just noted, the version field is unchanged from IPv4, and the
Differentiated Services field (which replaces the original IPv6 Traffic Class
field) is defined identically for IPv4 and IPv6.

IPv6 header fields include the following.

Version is a 4-bit value, and for IPv6 it must be equal to 6.

Differentiated Services (DS) contains a 6-bit value (2 bits are reserved
for future use). Since 1994, this field has evolved from the 4-bit

Priority field; later, the name was changed to Traffic Class. See Chapter 15 for more about differentiated services and IPv6.

ECN These 2 bits are used as Explicit Congestion Notification (ECN) flags (see Chapter 15 for more about ECN and IPv6).

Flow label is a 20-bit value used to identify packets that belong to the same *flow* (see the next section for more about flows). A node can be the source for more than one simultaneous flow. The flow label and the address of the source node uniquely identify flows. This field was originally (in RFC 1883) set to 24 bits, but when the DS field was increased in size to 8 bits, the flow label field was decreased to compensate (see Chapter 15 for more about IPv6 flows).

Payload length is a 16-bit field containing an integer value equal to the length of the packet payload in bytes—in other words, the number of bytes contained in the packet after the end of the main IPv6 header, including any IPv6 extension headers. This means that IPv6 extensions are included as part of the payload for the purposes of calculating this field.

Next Header indicates what protocol is in use in the header immediately following the IPv6 packet. Protocols are identified with standard 8-bit values defined and managed by the IANA. The value of this field may refer to a higher-layer protocol like TCP or UDP, or indicate the existence of an IPv6 extension header.

The value 59 in the Next Header field of an IPv6 header or any extension header indicates that there is nothing following that header. This field will otherwise contain ethertype values (see Chapter 5) specifying the next header's protocol.

Hop limit Every time a node forwards a packet, it decrements this 8-bit field by 1. If the hop limit reaches zero, the packet is discarded. Unlike in IPv4, where the time-to-live field fulfills a similar purpose, sentiment is currently against putting a protocol-defined upper limit on packet lifetime for IPv6. That is not to say that packets with infinite lifetimes will be permitted, but rather that the maximum hop limit can vary from network to network.

Source address is the 128-bit address of the node originating the IPv6 packet.

Destination address   is the 128-bit address of the intended recipient of the IPv6 packet. This address may be a unicast, multicast, or anycast address. If a routing extension is being used (which specifies a particular route that the packet must traverse), the destination address may be one of those intermediate nodes instead of the ultimate destination node.

The Differentiated Services field and the concept of IPv6 flows are discussed in greater depth in Chapter 15. In the absence of support for intermediate IP fragmentation, determining the Path MTU becomes more important than ever to ensuring that IPv6 packets are no bigger—and no smaller—than necessary. Path MTU discovery is discussed at greater length later in this chapter.

7.5   Option Headers

IPv4 options change the shape of the IP headers: A packet with an IPv4 option has as much as 40 octets more data in its header than an unoptioned header. This physical difference between regular packets and packets using options means the optioned packets must be treated as special cases by routers, which are usually optimized to handle standard packets. As a result, datagrams with options tend to be delivered more slowly, not so much because they require special processing as because they tend to be shunted off to the side to be handled when the router is not busy forwarding normal packets.

IPv6 *extension* or *option* headers can drastically reduce the performance hit on packets that use options. Except for Hop-by-Hop Options, which by definition must be processed by each forwarding router, options on IPv6 packets are hidden from intermediate routers and thus can have no effect on how the packets are forwarded.

Another of the benefits of IPv6 is that it simplifies the process of defining new options. As of 2003, a number of options have been defined.

Hop-by-Hop Options Header   This header always appears immediately after the main IPv6 header and contains optional data that every node on the packets path must examine. So far, two Hop-by-Hop Options have been specified: the Jumbo Payload Option and the Router Alert Option.

The Jumbo Payload Option identifies the payload of the packet as being longer than 65,535 octets (including the Hop-by-Hop Option Header). If a router is unable to handle a jumbogram, it returns an ICMPv6 error message.

The other Hop-by-Hop Option is the Router Alert Option. This is used to notify routers that information inside the IPv6 datagram is intended to be viewed and processed by an intermediate router even though the datagram is addressed to some other node (for example, control datagrams that contain information pertaining to bandwidth reservation protocols).

Routing Header   This header causes the packet to visit specific nodes, specified in the header, on its route to its destination. The initial destination address of the IPv6 header is not the same as the ultimate destination of the packet, but rather the first address in the list contained in the Routing Header. When that node receives the packet, it processes the IPv6 header and the Routing Header and resends the packet to the second address listed in the Routing Header. This process continues until the packet reaches its ultimate destination.

Fragment Header   The Fragment Header contains all the information about IP fragments that formerly would be stored in the main IPv4 header fields. This extension includes fields for a fragment offset, a More Fragments flag, and an identification field; it is used to allow a source node to fragment a packet too large for the path MTU between the source and the destination.

Destination Options Header   This header stands in for the IPv4 options field. At present, the only destination options specified are padding options to fill out the header on a 64-bit boundary if the (future) options require it. The Destination Options Header is meant to carry information intended to be examined by the destination node.

Authentication Header (AH)   This header provides a mechanism for calculating a cryptographic checksum on some parts of the IPv6 header, extension headers, and payload.

Encapsulating Security Payload Header (ESP)   This header will always be the last, unencrypted header of any packet. It indicates the rest of the payload is encrypted, and provides enough information for the authorized destination node to decrypt it.

Chapter 9 provides more complete details about what IPv6 options are and how they are used.

7.6   IPv4 Packet Size Limits

IPv4 packet size is restricted by a number of factors, including the following.

Total length field   This IPv4 header field is 16 bits, restricting the total size of any IPv4 packet to 65,575 octets or fewer.

Up to 576 octets   The IPv4 specification in RFC 791 requires that all nodes be capable of accepting packets of any size up to 576 octets. Thus, although there is an upper bound on packet size, very small packets (even packets with no payloads) are permitted. Packets with a maximum-sized IPv4 header (60 octets) are thus able to carry a 512 octet payload, that number of octets representing a manageable block of data ($512 = 2^9$ octets).

Over 576 octets   RFC 791 recommends that datagrams larger than 576 octets only be sent if the source is assured that the destination will accept larger datagrams.

While IPv4 packets are limited based on the length of the entire packet, IPv6 packets are limited on the payload length. When IPv6 extension headers are present, the packet header can be considerably longer than the standard IPv6 header length (40 octets)—but the header extensions are considered to be part of the payload when calculating payload length. A new set of factors govern the length of IPv6 payloads, as described next.

7.6.1   IPv6 MTU Requirements

Requiring nodes to assume that the maximum transmission unit (MTU) of the Internet is 576 octets affects performance to the extent that systems capable of handling more are forced to accept less. IPv6 changes that by requiring every link in the Internet to have an MTU of 1280 octets or more. Where the MTU on a local link is less than 1280 octets, there must be some link-specific fragmentation and reassembly mechanism incorporated into a link layer protocol.

While 1280 octets is the required minimum MTU for links carrying IPv6 traffic, RFC 2460 recommends that wherever possible the MTU should be set to 1500 octets or more. The higher the MTU, the less likely the need for fragmentation will arise when IPv4 (or other protocols) are encapsulated within IPv6 packets.

7.6.2 FRAGMENTATION

Although IPv6 forbids intermediate nodes from fragmenting packets that are too large for the local link, end-to-end fragmentation is permitted. Source nodes may fragment packets that are reassembled only by the recipient when using the Fragment Header (see Chapter 9).

However, implementors are urged to use Path MTU discovery (PMTUD; see Chapter 12) to determine an appropriate MTU rather than fall back on fragmentation. Where minimal implementations are desired, such as for booting a node from the network, RFC 2460 suggests using the minimum MTU of 1280 octets rather than attempt to implement either PMTUD or fragmentation support.

7.6.3 JUMBOGRAMS

IPv6 adds support for extra-large packets called *jumbograms*, having a payload larger than 65,575 octets. Documented in RFC 2675, "IPv6 Jumbograms," jumbograms are considered useful and relevant only for nodes connected to local links whose MTU is 64K octets or larger. Jumbograms are implemented in an IPv6 extension header (see Chapter 9).

7.7   Other IPv6 Features

The changes in IPv6 go beyond the larger address space and streamlined packet headers. As private IPv4 Internets as well as the global Internet have grown, shortcomings in the ability of IPv4 to scale have arisen. The lack of automatic tools for configuring and maintaining IP nodes and networks has held back IP deployment and required untold expenditures of network support time and effort.

Although some of the updates to IPv6 have been tried in IPv4, the improvements in the base protocol mean that the new functions work better. This
section introduces these functions, all of which will be discussed at greater
length later on.

7.7.1 AUTOCONFIGURATION

The original automatic IP configuration protocol was the Boot Protocol
(BOOTP), specified in RFC 951, "Bootstrap Protocol (BOOTP)," back in
1985. This protocol defines a mechanism for nodes to query their local
link with broadcasts requesting an address from which they can load
boot images over from BOOTP servers. The Dynamic Host Configuration
Protocol (DHCP), specified in RFC 2131, "Dynamic Host Configuration
Protocol," is based on BOOTP but provides a mechanism by which nodes
can load their configurations from DHCP servers.

Both BOOTP and DHCP are considered *stateful autoconfiguration* protocols
because they require that nodes on a network be configured by a
BOOTP/DHCP server that maintains state about the address allocations
it makes. In other words, the configuration server is allocated a block of
addresses from which to assign addresses to nodes requesting them. If the
configuration server offering IP addresses on a network is unavailable,
hosts are not able to connect at all. As networks grow larger, redundant
configuration servers must each be allocated its own block of addresses
to assign, creating new problems of balancing demand across those
servers.

A *stateless autoconfiguration* protocol, in which nodes can connect to a network without depending on any server, can permit much greater flexibility
and scalability as networks grow in size or as network nodes move around
more frequently.

As will be made clear in the next chapter and in Chapter 13, IPv6 addresses
make stateless autoconfiguration easier because node interface identifiers
are unique on each link (as well as, usually, globally unique).

IPv6 features a Stateless Autoconfiguration Protocol, specified in RFC 2462,
"IPv6 Stateless Address Autoconfiguration," as well as an updated version
of DHCP, called DHCPv6, that is still (officially, at least) a work-in-
progress.

7.7.2   NETWORK RENUMBERING

One of the ongoing problems with IPv4 results from the way network addresses are allocated to networks: Most organizations are assigned their network addresses by their network service providers. If the organization wishes to change providers, they must either transfer their network with addresses intact from one provider to another. In that case, aggregated routing is defeated. While the original provider could aggregate routes to that network with all its other customers' networks, the new provider cannot—a new route must be added for that single network. Figure 7–3 shows what happens using IPv4 addresses in this way.

As already noted, automatic network renumbering as well as autoconfiguration allows IPv6 to use a single type of route aggregation. In Figure 7–3, before the customer switches ISPs, the nondefault router table includes two routes for ISP A and ISP B: All packets addressed to 10.X.X.X go to ISP A, and all packets addressed to 192.168.X.X go to ISP B. But when the customer switches ISPs while retaining its original network address, non-default Internet backbone routers must add an extra route to indicate that

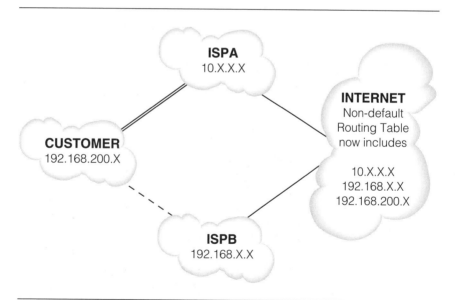

Figure 7–3: Changing network providers means either adding complications to the default routing table or renumbering the customer's network.

packets going to network 192.168.X.X are routed through ISP B *except* for packets addressed to 192.168.200.X.

7.7.3 NEIGHBOR DISCOVERY

RFC 2461, "Neighbor Discovery for IP Version 6 (IPv6)," is a draft standard that specifies, according to the abstract, a mechanism for IPv6 nodes on the same link to "use Neighbor Discovery to discover each other's presence, to determine each other's link-layer addresses, to find routers and to maintain reachability information about the paths to active neighbors."

The Neighbor Discovery for IPv6 protocol, by adding new messages for ICMPv6, effectively replaces the Address Resolution Protocol (ARP) for associating link layer network addresses with IPv6 addresses, as well as some router-related ICMP messages used with IPv4. At the same time, it adds new features such as neighbor unreachability. Neighbor Discovery is discussed in greater detail in Chapter 13.

7.7.4 ANYCAST

Although specified in RFC 2373, "IP Version 6 Addressing Architecture," in 1998, the anycast address is still a relatively murky concept. A unicast address points to a single network interface; a multicast address points to a group of network interfaces, with packets addressed to that address delivered to all group members. In contrast, an anycast address is indistinguishable from a unicast address except that a group of two or more interfaces can be configured to respond to packets sent to the anycast address—with only one of the group members responding to any particular anycast packet.

Packets sent to a multicast address are delivered to multiple nodes (all members of the multicast group identified with the address). Packets sent to an anycast address are sent to any one (but only one) of the group of nodes that are members of the anycast group.

The "closest" anycast member node responds to anycast packets, with closeness determined by the shortest route between the requesting and responding nodes. Figure 7–4 shows how anycast might work in an IPv6 internet. When Node X sends out a packet to an anycast address, any of the anycast nodes could respond—but if all the anycast nodes are available,

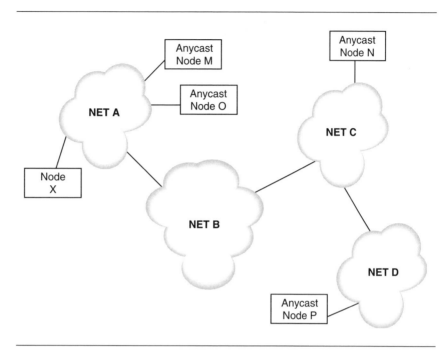

Figure 7–4: Anycast function in an IPv6 internet.

Nodes M and O would normally be the only ones to respond to Node X (because they are "closest," being on the same link). If those nodes are unavailable, Node N would probably respond to an anycast from X; if N is unavailable as well, then Node P becomes the closest anycast responder.

A more detailed discussion of IPv6 anycast (and IPv4 precursors) is provided in Chapter 11, including the fundamentals of anycast, limitations placed on anycast in its original specification, perceived problems with implementing anycast in usable applications, and possible future directions for IPv6 anycast.

7.7.5   MOBILE IPV6

The desktop computer is, in many instances, giving way to laptops, notebooks, and palmtops. Given the degree to which these end-user computers are mobile, how can they be connected to an IP network and responsive to a single IP address even as they are moved from one subnet to another? This problem is distinguishable from that of cellular mobile nodes, which must be capable of maintaining a virtual circuit as the nodes move from one cell to another, in several important ways. First, the mobile IP node must be able to support a more formal definition of a virtual circuit, capable of transmitting data with error detection. Also, the mobile IP node is not expected to be quite as continuously or rapidly mobile as a mobile telephone, for example.

The problem of mobility for IPv4 was first addressed in a standards track specification, RFC 2002, "IP Mobility Support," in 1996. Not long after, work on extending IP mobility to IPv6 was begun—but as of early 2003, the IPv6 mobility specification, while considerably more mature, is still a work-in-progress.

In simple terms, the mobile IP node receives packets sent to its home address from anywhere. When the mobile node is on its home network, it behaves like any other IP node. When the mobile node is "away," the mobile node stays in touch with its *mobility agent*, letting it know where it is (a *care-of address*) when it is not attached to the home network. The mobility agent sits on the mobile node's home network and resends packets sent to the mobile node's home address to the mobile node out on the road.

Unfortunately, IP mobility turns out to be somewhat more complicated, especially as requirements for performance, robustness, and security increase. IPv6 mobility is defined in a separate protocol, using IPv6 option headers, and will be discussed in greater detail in Chapter 17.

7.8   Summary

After reading this chapter, you should have a good overall picture of how IPv6 works, from its address space and architecture to special features and functions that have been added or updated in IPv6. Keeping in mind this overview of the IPv6 header, option headers, and the differences between IPv4 and IPv6, the next chapter probes more deeply into IPv6 addressing, from address representation to address types to the addresses each IPv6 node must recognize.

8

IPv6 Addressing

One might suppose that the most obvious difference between IPv4 and IPv6 is the address space: IPv4 addresses are only 32 bits long, and IPv6 addresses are 128 bits long. And there are more differences in the way IPv6 uses those addresses. However, in another sense, address length will be the least obvious change because it will be invisible to most users. Applications carried over IPv6 networks must rely completely on the Domain Name System (DNS) to correctly link IP host names to IPv6 addresses and networks. DNS and IPv6 will be discussed in detail in Chapter 18.

In this chapter, we begin with a discussion of the IPv6 addressing architecture, as designed by the original IPng working groups. Next, we look at the IPv6 address space, address formats, and the way in which addresses are intended to be allocated. IPv6 does away with broadcasts and relies instead on unicast and multicast, and adds a new category: anycast addresses.

The IPv6 addressing architecture was first published as a proposed standard in 1995, in RFC 1884, "IP Version 6 Addressing Architecture." As originally formulated, IPv6 addresses were defined to be "128-bit

identifiers for interfaces and sets of interfaces." Three types of addresses—
unicast, *multicast*, and *anycast*—were defined, with unicast defined as "an
identifier for a single interface. A packet sent to a unicast address is delivered to the interface identified by that address." Multicast and anycast
addressing will be discussed later in this chapter and in more detail in
later chapters.

Since 1995, the IPv6 addressing architecture specification has been updated
twice, first in 1998, with the publication of RFC 2373, "IP Version 6 Addressing Architecture," and later with RFC 3513 in mid-2003. This section begins
with the basics as first defined in RFC 2373, followed by a discussion of
the current standard as defined in RFC 3513.

8.1   IPv6 Address Types

There are three types of IPv6 address.

Unicast   An identifier for a single interface. A packet sent to a unicast
address is delivered to the interface identified by that address.

Multicast   An identifier for a set of interfaces (typically belonging to different nodes). A packet sent to a multicast address is delivered to all
interfaces identified by that address.

Anycast   An identifier for a set of interfaces (typically belonging to different nodes). A packet sent to an anycast address is delivered to one of
the interfaces identified by that address (the "nearest" one, according
to the routing protocols' measure of distance). Any unicast address
could be specified as an anycast address, as long as all nodes configured to respond on that address are aware of its status as anycast
rather than unicast.

Broadcast addresses have been deprecated, their functions having been
replaced by multicast and anycast.

Broadcast created problems for IPv4 networks almost from the start.
Intended to carry information destined for more than one node,[1] broadcast

---

[1]As when a node attempts to request network booting information and has not been
configured for the local link.

can place a drag on network performance. As the number of broadcasts on a local link increases, the burden on every node on the link to process all broadcasts also increases. And as networks become larger, the number of such burdened nodes not only increases but so too does the likelihood that any individual node will ever have to actually process any particular broadcast packet. Finally, the practice of improperly forwarding broadcasts across subnets can overwhelm routers.

With IPv6, the broadcast function is accomplished by sending packets to the *all nodes* multicast address. More limited sets of multicast groups, such as "all routers on the local link," provide broadcast functionality much more efficiently. Nodes interested in the traffic formerly carried in broadcasts can subscribe to a multicast address; all other uninterested nodes can ignore packets sent to that address. Broadcasts never adequately solved the problem of propagating information across the Internet—for example, routing information—but multicast permits a more scalable, and acceptable, solution.

8.1.1 NETWORK AND NODE ADDRESSING

IPv6 addresses are usually divided into two equal parts with the high-order 64 bits usually identifying a network address and the low-order 64 bits usually identifying the node with a *modified EUI-64* address. This *extended unique identifier* is defined by (and is a trademark of) the IEEE and is based on the IEEE Registration Authority's 24-bit *Organizationally Unique Identifier (OUI)*, plus a 40-bit extension identifier assigned by the organization assigned the OUI. These values are based on the same data used to generate 48-bit *Media Access Control (MAC)* addresses associated with Ethernet and other LAN interface cards.

Interface addressing and the EUI-64 address are discussed in greater detail later on in this chapter, as are IPv6 address types that don't conform to the typical 64/64 address division.

8.1.2 AGGREGATABLE ADDRESSING

IPv6 addresses are *aggregatable* in the same sense that Classless InterDomain Routing (CIDR) addresses are aggregatable: addresses sharing the same prefixes can be forwarded over the same routes. RFC 2374 defines a fairly strict regime for this aggregation, setting up three levels at which aggregation can be accomplished (aggregation and aggregation entities will be discussed later in this chapter). However, these predefined aggregation levels were made obsolete with publication of a revision to RFC 2374, RFC 3587, "IPv6 Global Unicast Address Format," published as this book went to press.

RFC 2374 also defines two types of aggregatable addresses. *Provider-based aggregatable addresses* have to be changed when the provider is changed, but *exchange-based addresses* are allocated directly by an IPv6 exchange entity that is independent of the network provider. The exchange entity provides an address block, while the subscriber contracts with a separate provider for actual network access. The network access is provided either directly, through the provider, or indirectly, through the exchange, but routing is done through the exchange. This makes possible arrangements by which the subscriber can change providers without address renumbering. It also allows the subscriber to use more than one Internet service provider to handle a single block of network addresses.

As with the detailed aggregation entity layers, exchange-based addresses are likely to disappear in IPv6 standards after 2003.

8.1.3 IPv6 Address Representation

IPv4 addresses are typically represented in *dotted quad* format, four decimal values (0 through 255) separated by periods, as in the following.

```
10.0.0.1
192.168.1.50
```

IPv6 addresses, four times as long as IPv4 addresses, are four times as cumbersome and potentially confusing. In RFC 3513, three approaches to representing IPv6 addresses are suggested. The preferred method is to represent them as a sequence of eight 16-bit values, separated by colons.

```
XXXX:XXXX:XXXX:XXXX:XXXX:XXXX:XXXX:XXXX
```

Here is an example.

```
FEDC:BA98:7654:3210:FEDC:BA98:7654:3210
1080:0:0:0:8:800:200C:417
```

Address type	Standard representation	Compressed
Unicast address	1080:0:0:0:8:800:200C:417A	1080::8:800:200C:417A
Multicast address	FF01:0:0:0:0:0:0:101	FF01::101
Loopback address	0:0:0:0:0:0:0:1	::1
Unspecified addresses	0:0:0:0:0:0:0:0	::

Table 8–1: Standard and compressed IPv6 address representations (from RFC 3513).

Due to some methods of allocating certain styles of IPv6 addresses, it will be common for addresses to contain long strings of zero bits. In order to make writing addresses containing zero bits easier, a special syntax is available to compress the zeros. The use of "::" indicates multiple groups of 16-bits of zeros. The "::" can only appear once in an address; the number of bits being compressed can be easily inferred if it is used once, but if it is used more than once, there is no way to tell how many bits are compressed in each use. The "::" can also be used to compress the leading and/or trailing zeros in an address. Table 8–1 lists the addresses provided in RFC 3513 as examples of the compressed representation.

Further confusing matters, although offering some amusement, is RFC 1924, "A Compact Representation of IPv6 Addresses," which defines a set of rules for writing out IPv6 addresses using base85 encoding. Published on April 1, 1996, the joke was that base85 allowed all IPv6 addresses to be fully expressed in precisely 20 characters, considerably fewer than most other representations.

An IPv6 unicast address identifies a single IPv6 interface. As with IPv4, any given IPv6 node may have more than one network interface, but each interface must have its own unicast address associated with it. Unicast addresses can be viewed as containing a single piece of information, contained in a 128-bit field: an address that completely identifies one particular interface.

An anycast address, as already noted, is a unicast address to which two or more interfaces are configured to respond. In this chapter, we look at unicast addresses in greater detail, followed by an introduction to the concept of IPv6 anycast, including a discussion of anycast address allocations and reservations, anycast routing, and analysis of the anycast function.

8.2   Unicast Address Types

Several types of unicast addresses have been defined for use with IPv6.

Global unicast   Formerly known as aggregatable global unicast, these addresses can be routed across the global IPv6 Internet and are globally unique.

Link local unicast   These addresses are for addressing on a single link for purposes such as auto-address configuration, neighbor discovery, or when no routers are present. Packets sent to this address are never supposed to be forwarded across local links.

Site local unicast   These addresses are for addressing packets within an entire site (or network or organization). Packets addressed to site-local addresses must never be forwarded outside the site. Although internal network traffic routing can be done on complete IPv6 addresses, allowing site-local unicast may allow greater routing efficiency. Site-local addresses may include up to 54 bits in the network half of the address to indicate a subnet address.

Unicast addresses with embedded IPv4 addresses or encoded NSAP addresses   IPv6 supports interoperability with other network layer protocols, not just IPv4. For example, a range of addresses was set aside for Novell's NetWare/IPX addresses in RFC 2373. Although the IPX allocation has been dropped in RFC 3513, support for embedding both IPv4 and *Network Service Access Point* (*NSAP*) addresses used with the OSI *Connectionless Network Protocol* (*CLNP*) is provided in RFC 3513.

Table 8–2 shows how to identify different types of IPv6 addresses, including multicast and the unspecified and loopback address. The type of an IPv6 address is identified by the high-order bits of the address, as shown.

Unlike in IPv4, which usually works on one or two interface identifiers for each network connection, in IPv6 a single interface may be required to have several (sometimes many) interface identifiers to which it must respond. All interfaces must respond to a link local address as well as to a globally unique address, and many will have to respond to a third, site-local, address. For systems that are subscribed to multicast or anycast groups, the number of identifiers can be significantly higher (see Chapter 10).

Address type	Binary prefix	IPv6 notation
Unspecified	00...0 (128 bits)	::/128
Loopback	00...1 (128 bits)	::1/128
Multicast	11111111	FF00::/8
Link-local unicast	1111111010	FE80::/10
Site-local unicast	1111111011	FEC0::/10
Global unicast	(everything else)	

Table 8–2: Identifying IPv6 address types (from RFC 3513).

8.3 Special Unicast Address Types

Several different types of special unicast addresses are defined in RFC 3513. They are briefly discussed in this section.

8.3.1 UNSPECIFIED ADDRESS

The address 0:0:0:0:0:0:0:0 is called the unspecified address. It must never be assigned to any node because it indicates the absence of an address. One example of its use is in the Source Address field of any IPv6 packets sent by an initializing host before it has learned its own address.

The unspecified address must not be used as the destination address of IPv6 packets or in IPv6 Routing Headers. An IPv6 packet with a source address of unspecified must never be forwarded by an IPv6 router.

8.3.2 LOOPBACK

The unicast address 0:0:0:0:0:0:0:1 is called the loopback address. It may be used by a node to send an IPv6 packet to itself. It may never be assigned to any physical interface. It is treated as having link-local scope and may be thought of as the link-local unicast address of a virtual interface (typically called "the loopback interface") to an imaginary link that goes nowhere.

The loopback address must not be used as the source address in IPv6 packets that are sent outside of a single node. An IPv6 packet with a destination address of loopback must never be sent outside of a single node and must never be forwarded by an IPv6 router. A packet received on an interface with destination address of loopback must be dropped.

8.3.3 ENCODED NSAP ADDRESSES

NSAP addressing is used for OSI CLNP networks, and a mechanism for encoding NSAP addresses into IPv6 addresses (as well as for encoding IPv6 addresses within NSAP addresses) is defined in the experimental RFC 1888, "OSI NSAPs and IPv6." However, due to the relative scarcity of CLNP networks and the recommendation that existing CLNP networks should reimplement their addressing to support IPv6 directly, the NSAP-encoded IPv6 allocation may suffer the same fate as the IPX allocation.

8.4 IPv6 Address Format

At 128 bits, IPv6 addresses can carry much more information than 32-bit IPv4 addresses. An IPv4 address signifies little more than a unique network layer interface; other than a unique local identifier coupled with a unique network identifier, there is no information implicit in the address. IPv6 addresses, on the other hand, are capable of carrying more data.

The most basic representation of an IPv6 unicast address looks like this.

```
|                             128 bits                             |
+------------------------------------------------------------------+
|                          node address                            |
+------------------------------------------------------------------+
```

Any IPv6 node must be able to interpret an IPv6 address as a series of 128 bits and determine whether the address refers to itself or not. Every IPv6 unicast address is 128 bits long and represents a unique node network interface.

A slightly more sophisticated IPv6 implementation would be able to identify IPv6 addresses as divisible into at least two separate parts.

```
|                     n bits                  |    128-n bits    |
+---------------------------------------------+------------------+
|                  subnet prefix              |   interface ID   |
+---------------------------------------------+------------------+
```

In this case, the subnet prefix, defined by some number ("n") of bits, is identifiable as the local link to which the node is attached. A node capable of making this distinction could perform a very simple routing function, transmitting packets destined for the local subnet locally and forwarding nonlocal packets to some default router.

A more detailed general representation of the IPv6 address provides three parts: a global routing prefix (identifying a nondefault route for the address), a subnet ID, and an interface ID.

```
|          n bits         |  m bits  |      128-n-m bits       |
+-------------------------+----------+-------------------------+
| global routing prefix   | subnet ID|      interface ID       |
+-------------------------+----------+-------------------------+
```

This structure bears a superficial resemblance to the use of subnets in IPv4 addresses, in which a single IPv4 network is subdivided into subnets. However, the IPv6 unicast addressing architecture was intended to be an aggregatable architecture. IPv6 network service providers maintain nondefault routers for their customers to handle external routing, accepting all packets whose addresses' first n bits match the provider's global routing prefix, the same prefix being incorporated into all their customers' IPv6 addresses. Within the service provider's network, internal routers distribute packets based on their destination address subnet ID.

8.4.1   IPv6 Address Aggregation Fields

In RFC 2374, the aggregatable unicast IPv6 address format is defined with a great deal of precision, splitting the 128-bit addresses in half, with the low-order 64 bits representing the interface ID and the high-order 64 bits divided into several fields, in which routing structure information can be recorded.

```
| 3|  13 | 8 |   24   |   16   |              64 bits            |
+--+-----+---+--------+--------+---------------------------------+
|FP| TLA |RES|  NLA   |  SLA   |           Interface ID          |
|  | ID  |   |  ID    |  ID    |                                 |
+--+-----+---+--------+--------+---------------------------------+
```

In this definition, taken from RFC 2374, the *Format Prefix* (*FP*) refers to the three high-order bits of the address; when these bits are 001, the address is considered an aggregatable global unicast address. The other fields refer to routing aggregation: Top Level, Next Level, and Site Level Aggregation identifiers, with an octet reserved for future use.

As defined in RFC 2374, these fields were to be used as follows.

FP   The *format prefix* is the 3-bit prefix to the IPv6 address that identifies where it belongs in the IPv6 address space. The value 001 in this field identifies it as a global unicast address.

TLA ID   The *top-level aggregation identifier* contains the highest-level routing information of the address. This refers to the grossest level of routing information in the internetwork, and as currently defined (at 13 bits), there can be no more than 8192 different top-level routes.

RES   The next 8 bits are reserved for future use, perhaps to expand the top-level or next-level aggregation ID fields.

NLA ID   The *next-level aggregation identifier* is 24 bits long, and it is meant to be used by organizations that control top-level aggregation IDs to organize that address space. In other words, those organizations (probably to include large Internet service providers and others providing public network access) can carve that 24-bit field into their own addressing hierarchy. Such an entity might break itself down into four top-level routes (internal to the entity) by taking 2 bits for those routes and leave itself 22 bits of address space to allocate to other entities (likely to be smaller-scale, more local, service providers). Those entities, in their turn, could also subdivide the space they are allocated in the same way—if there is enough room.

SLA ID   The *site-level aggregation identifier* is the address space given to organizations for their internal network structure. With 16 bits available, each organization can create its own internal hierarchical network structure using subnets in the same way they are used in IPv4. As many as 65,535 different subnets are available using all 16 bits as a flat address space. Using the first 8 bits for higher-level routing within the organization would allow 255 high-level subnets, each of which has as many as 255 sub-subnets.

Interface ID   This 64-bit field uniquely identifies the node.

Although as of 2003 this is the proposed standard documented in RFC 2374, this entire structure of aggregation identifiers is unlikely to be carried forward. The replacement drafts for RFC 2374 dispense entirely with this structure, mostly because its approach to aggregation is similar to the use of network classes in IPv4. By restricting how IPv6 addresses should be used well in advance of any significant deployment, such a structured approach puts IPv6 at risk for restricting the way it can be used. Rather than attempting to impose some "likely" framework for IPv6 aggregation, the update to RFC 2374 will dispense with these layers and define IPv6 unicast more generally, like this.

```
|          n bits        |  m bits  |       128-n-m bits        |
+------------------------+----------+---------------------------+
| global routing prefix  | subnet ID|        interface ID       |
+------------------------+----------+---------------------------+
```

Except for special situations (see following), all IPv6 unicast addresses will be considered aggregatable addresses where the value of n + m always equals 64. (Unless the 3 high-order bits of the address are 000, the interface ID part of the address is required, by RFC 3513, to be 64 bits long and in the modified EUI-64 format.)

8.4.2 GLOBAL ROUTING PREFIX AND SUBNET ID

IPv6 addresses are half interface ID, with the other half identifying routing information. For standard global unicast addresses, the two parts are equal in length: 64 bits. The network part of the address consists of two parts.

Global routing prefix   The highest-order bits of the network part of the address function as an external routing prefix for the global IPv6 Internet. These prefixes can be allocated to individuals, companies, service providers, and any other entity requesting an IPv6 network address space. The global routing prefix carries enough information to allow packets to be routed to the site using the address.

Subnet ID   The remaining, lower-order bits of the network part of the IPv6 address are used to identify subnets within an IPv6 network. With the smallest current assignment of a 48-bit IPv6 global routing prefix, the assignee can allocate up to 16 bits of internal subnets (as many as 2^{16} or 65,536 separate subnets). However, when a packet is being routed across the global IPv6 Internet, the subnet ID can be safely ignored. It is used only for internal routing purposes. Entities requesting IPv6 address blocks directly from RIRs are being given /32 blocks, with the smallest suballocation currently limited to /48 prefixes.

IPv6 address prefixes are represented in a manner similar to that used for IPv4 addresses, in CIDR notation, like this.

```
ipv6-address/prefix-length
```

The IPv6 address can be in any of the defined formats, and the prefix-length is the number of bits used in the address as the global routing prefix, in decimal. The following examples are taken from RFC 3513. First, some valid representations of an IPv6 address using a 60-bit prefix (the hexadecimal value 12AB00000000CD3) include this.

```
12AB:0000:0000:CD30:0000:0000:0000:0000/60
12AB::CD30:0:0:0:0/60
12AB:0:0:CD30::/60
```

Using the same prefix, the following are not permitted representations, along with the reasons for their invalidity.

```
12AB:0:0:CD3/60     may drop leading zeros, but not
                    trailing zeros, within any 16-bit
                    chunk of the address
12AB::CD30/60       address to left of "/" expands to
                    12AB:0000:0000:0000:0000:000:0000:CD30
12AB::CD3/60        address to left of "/" expands to
                    12AB:0000:0000:0000:0000:000:0000:0CD3
```

RFC 3513 also notes that a node's full IPv6 address and its prefix (the subnet prefix) can be combined in this way.

```
node address:    12AB:0:0:CD30:123:4567:89AB:CDEF
subnet number:   12AB:0:0:CD30::/60
abbreviated as:  12AB:0:0:CD30:123:4567:89AB:CDEF/60
```

8.4.3 MODIFIED EUI-64 INTERFACE ADDRESSING

All IPv6 unicast addresses, other than those starting with the 3 high-order bits of 000, are required (by RFC 3153) to use the *Modified EUI-64* format for the lower 64 bits of interface address.[2] The exceptions are discussed in the next section.

---

[2]RFC 2374, page 7: "Interface IDs used in the aggregatable global unicast address format are required to be 64 bits long and to be constructed in IEEE EUI-64 format."

As just noted, EUI-64 interface identifiers are assigned to link layer network interfaces, usually by manufacturers who are assigned OUIs by the IEEE. Each OUI is a 24-bit value that is linked to one and only one entity (usually a manufacturer of networking equipment). Manufacturers of Ethernet (and other network link layer) interfaces burn into each interface a globally unique identifier usually known as a Media Access Control (MAC) address. The high-order 24 bits is the OUI, and the rest of the address (another 24 bits for Ethernet) is assigned by the OUI entity. The result is that all Ethernet cards have a globally unique MAC address[3] that is 48 bits long (MAC-48).

The IEEE defines the EUI-64 interface identifier as consisting of the 24-bit OUI value in the high-order bits followed by 40 low-order bits such that the entire sequence identifies an instance of the implementation (e.g., a network interface card) globally uniquely. However, there are millions of Ethernet cards in use that have only MAC-48 addresses. RFC 3513 specifies methods for supporting IPv6 interface addresses with modified EUI-64 interface identifiers for interfaces with the following types of interface identifiers.

EUI-64 interface identifier If an EUI-64 identifier exists, it can be used as an IPv6 interface identifier simply by inverting the "u" (universal/local) bit of the OUI value (the bit identified as "X" here). The "c" bits represent the OUI, and the "m" bits represent the vendor-supplied (unique) part of the interface ID.

```
|0                 1|1               3|3               4|4               6|
|0                 5|6               1|2               7|8               3|
+-----------------+-----------------+-----------------+-----------------+
|cccccccXgccccccccc|cccccccccmmmmmmmm|mmmmmmmmmmmmmmmmm|mmmmmmmmmmmmmmmm|
+-----------------+-----------------+-----------------+-----------------+
```

MAC-48 interface identifier MAC-48 identifiers can be transformed from their standard format

```
|0                 1|1               3|3               4|
|0                 5|6               1|2               7|
+-----------------+-----------------+-----------------+
|cccccc0gccccccccc|cccccccccmmmmmmmm|mmmmmmmmmmmmmmmmm|
+-----------------+-----------------+-----------------+
```

---

[3]There are reports that some unscrupulous vendors have sold Ethernet cards manufactured with nonunique MAC addresses.

to this format

```
|0                1|1              3|3              4|4              6|
|0                5|6              1|2              7|8              3|
+----------------+----------------+----------------+----------------+
|cccccc1gccccccccc|ccccccccc11111111|11111110mmmmmmmmm|mmmmmmmmmmmmmmmmmmmmm|
+----------------+----------------+----------------+----------------+
```

where the value 0xFF FE is inserted between the OUI and the vendor-supplied part of the interface identifier; the u bit is also inverted (from 0 to 1 in this case).

Nonglobal interface identifier   Some link layer protocols, such as ARCnet and Apple's LocalTalk, don't use globally unique addresses but rather allow each link to assign whatever addresses it wants. An EUI-64 formatted identifier can be generated by taking the link address (unique only on that link) and prefix it with zero so that it is 64 bits long. For example, an 8-bit node identifier whose hexadecimal value is 0x4F becomes the following.

```
|0                1|1              3|3              4|4              6|
|0                5|6              1|2              7|8              3|
+----------------+----------------+----------------+----------------+
|0000000000000000|0000000000000000|0000000000000000|0000000001001111|
+----------------+----------------+----------------+----------------+
```

Note that the universal/local bit (the seventh bit) will always be set to 0 in this type of identifier, resulting in clarification to other IPv6 nodes that this node's interface address is unique only on its own link.

Security identifier   RFC 3041, "Privacy Extensions for Stateless Address Autoconfiguration in IPv6," addresses the concerns of security and privacy experts who point out that the permanent use of the same interface identifier, such as is done with IPv6 addresses based on IEEE MAC 48 addresses, can result in detailed mapping of a user's Internet activities. Cross-referencing of Web server logs with existing information-gathering techniques can produce very precise profiles of these users, from their names, addresses, and credit card and other personal information to inferences made about their personal interests based on the Internet resources they use. Corporate users can also be targeted by attackers seeking to track usage or map networks for criminal activity.

In RFC 3041, a mechanism is defined for randomly generating addresses that conform to the modified EUI-64 format. Hosts using this mechanism may change their interface identifier every time they connect to the network or, more frequently, to thwart illicit (as well as licit, but unwanted) information-gathering activities.

No interface identifier   Point-to-point links and any other configured tunnel links do not need interface identifiers (there are only two end-points, so each node can differentiate itself from the other end node based purely on whether data is going in or out). The only requirement for interface identifiers in these cases is that they be unique on the link. RFC 3513 suggests that in these cases the node assign an identifier that is based on (but not the same as) a globally unique identifier associated with the node in some way—either the identifier of another of that node's interfaces or some identifier defined for the node. Such identifiers may be configured manually, created with a random number generator, based on some other system identifier (serial number) or some other method.

The authors of RFC 3513 recommend strongly that to avoid duplication of identifiers on a link, a collision detection algorithm be implemented for links that do not use their own interface identifiers. Collision detection is a function of neighbor discovery, discussed in Chapter 13.

RFCs specifying "IPv6 Over X" should be consulted for more detail about how to generate the IPv6 interface identifier for any particular link layer protocol. Table 8–3 lists the link layer specifications current as of 2003.

RFC #	Title
2590	Transmission of IPv6 Packets over Frame Relay Networks Specification
2497	Transmission of IPv6 Packets over ARCnet Networks
2492	IPv6 over ATM Networks
2491	IPv6 over Non-Broadcast Multiple Access (NBMA) Networks
2472	IP Version 6 over PPP
2470	Transmission of IPv6 Packets over Token Ring Networks
2467	Transmission of IPv6 Packets over FDDI Networks
2464	Transmission of IPv6 Packets over Ethernet Networks

Table 8–3: Specifications for transmitting IPv6 packets over various link layer protocols.

8.4.4   IPv4-COMPATIBLE ADDRESSES

When IPv4 addresses are encapsulated within IPv6 addresses, a "mixed" format is allowed, in which the IPv4 portion of the address can be represented in standard dotted quad form, while the rest of the address is formatted as a standard IPv6 address, resulting in this form.

`XXXX:XXXX:XXXX:XXXX:XXXX:XXXX:ddd.ddd.ddd.ddd`

These addresses were originally defined to fall into two categories.

IPv4-compatible IPv6 address   The IPv6 transition mechanisms (see RFC 2893, "Transition Mechanisms for IPv6 Hosts and Routers") include a technique for hosts and routers to dynamically tunnel IPv6 packets over IPv4 routing infrastructure. IPv6 nodes that use this technique are assigned special IPv6 unicast addresses that carry a global IPv4 address in the low-order 32 bits.

IPv4-mapped IPv6 address   A second type of IPv6 address that holds an embedded IPv4 address is also defined. This address type is used to represent the addresses of IPv4 nodes as IPv6 addresses.

As of 2003, the IPv4-mapped address appears ready to be deprecated in response to work in progress being done by Jun-ichiro itojun Hagino and Craig Metz, both longtime contributors to the IPv6 effort. The two have determined that IPv4-mapped addresses can be subverted by attackers to trick IPv4 nodes into believing that an attacker's packet actually originated locally.

8.5   IPv6 Node Self-Awareness

The IPv6 address architecture specification defines a set of addresses that every node must be able to recognize as referring to itself. The task is somewhat more complicated under IPv6 than IPv4 because IPv6 nodes must be able to recognize every network interface as being a node on a link, a node within a site, and a node on the global IPv6 Internet. Under IPv4, nodes need only be able to recognize themselves by responding to the loopback address and to addresses configured for any IPv4 interface.

As defined in RFC 3513, a host is required to recognize the following addresses as identifying itself.

- A link-local address for each interface
- All assigned unicast addresses
- The loopback address
- All all-nodes multicast addresses
- Solicited-node multicast address for each of its assigned unicast and anycast addresses
- Multicast addresses of all other groups to which the host belongs

A router is required to recognize all addresses that a host is required to recognize, plus the following addresses as identifying itself.

- The subnet-router anycast addresses for the interfaces it is configured to act as a router on
- All other anycast addresses with which the router has been configured
- All-routers multicast addresses
- Multicast addresses of all other groups to which the router belongs

NOTE: Addressing and routing of multicast packets, including definitions of the multicast-related addresses cited here, will be discussed at greater length in Chapter 10.

Another related issue is which addresses an IPv6 implementation should predefine for all nodes. The specification makes clear that only the following address prefixes should be predefined in an implementation.

- Unspecified address
- Loopback address
- Multicast prefix (FF)
- Local-use prefixes (link-local and site-local)
- Predefined multicast addresses
- IPv4-compatible prefixes

All implementations should assume all other addresses are unicast unless specifically configured as anycast addresses.

8.6   Summary

Although this chapter includes considerable detail about how to differentiate different types of special IPv6 addresses, as well as how to represent them in written documents, the most important facts relate to the way that IPv6 addresses can be aggregated for routing purposes (see Chapter 14 for more on routing) and the general IPv6 unicast address format using the IEEE EUI-64 interface identifier.

The next chapter returns to the IPv6 header, specifically detailing the use of IPv6 header extensions to enable IP options. Unlike IPv4 options, which are limited to no more than 40 octets of data in a special-case header field, IPv6 options work more efficiently and provide greater function than their predecessors.

9

IPv6 Options and Extension Headers

This chapter discusses the implications of the IPv6 extension headers, how they work, and how they differ from the IP option headers used with IPv4. Particular attention will be paid to the proper order and use of header extensions, as well as discussion of the use of jumbograms, hop-by-hop options, destination options, routing, and fragmentation headers.

The most important IPv6 options, the IP Security Protocol (IPsec) headers, have already been introduced in Chapter 6. The ESP and AH headers look the same, whether used in IPv4 or IPv6, but the way those headers are attached to the IP header differs significantly. This chapter introduces the concept of using *extension headers* to carry *optional Internet-layer data*—information about handling packets at the Internet layer that is not always needed but often required for particular applications. Security headers provide one set of examples. Not all packets need to be authenticated or encrypted, but when nonrepudiation or privacy is required, packets must carry additional security information.

Rather than making the length of the IPv6 headers variable, depending on whether optional Internet-layer data must be carried along with the packet (as in IPv4), IPv6 optional data is carried in these supplementary extension headers that are inserted in the packet after the main IPv6 headers.

This chapter provides an introduction to the concept of extension headers, along with the following.

- IPv6 extension header placement in the packet
- IPv6 extension header ordering in the packet
- IPv6 extension header format
- IPv6 extension header creation and modification
- Current IPv6 extension headers

Because the IPv6 specification allows creation of new extension headers as the need arises, the list of current extension headers may be incomplete. The interested reader should check the IANA Web site (www.iana.org) for current values of available IPv6 options.

9.1 IPv6 Options and Extension Headers

RFC 2460 specifies IPv6 extension headers as the mechanism by which "optional Internet-layer information is encoded in separate headers that may be placed between the IPv6 header and the upper-layer header in a packet." Each different type of extension header (the RFC defines five of them, and two others are defined for IPsec) is identified with an 8-bit protocol identifier in the Next Header field of the previous header.[1]

As of early 2003, seven IPv6 extension headers have been defined. Table 9–1 lists all of the valid values for IPv6 Next Header fields. Extension header identifiers are listed in the table along with other valid values.

9.1.1 ADDING EXTENSIONS TO IPv6 HEADERS

Figure 9–1 (from RFC 2460) shows how IPv6 extension headers are incorporated into the packet. The first example shows a TCP/IPv6 packet with

---

[1]If there is only one extension header, the type of header is identified in the Next Header field of the IPv6 packet; if there are two or more extension headers, the second extension header is identified in the Next Header field of the first extension header.

Next Header type	Value	Notes
Hop-by-Hop Options	00	
IPv6	41	For tunneling IPv6 in IPv6
Routing	43	
Fragment	44	
Authentication	51	
Destination Options	60	
Encapsulating Security Payload	50	
No Next Header	59	No header follows this header

Table 9–1: Valid values for IPv6 Next Header fields.

```
+---------------+-----------------------
|  IPv6 header  | TCP header + data
|               |
| Next Header = |
|     TCP       |
+---------------+-----------------------
+---------------+---------------+-----------------------
|  IPv6 header  | Routing Header | TCP header + data
|               |                |
| Next Header = | Next Header =  |
|   Routing     |     TCP        |
+---------------+---------------+-----------------------
+---------------+---------------+-----------------+-----------------
|  IPv6 header  | Routing Header | Fragment Header | Fragment of TCP
|               |                |                 | header + data
| Next Header = | Next Header =  | Next Header =   |
|   Routing     |   Fragment     |     TCP         |
+---------------+---------------+-----------------+-----------------
```

Figure 9–1: Inserting IPv6 extension headers into IPv6 packets (from RFC 2460).

no extension headers. The next example also shows a TCP/IPv6 packet with an added extension header (the Routing Header). Finally, the third example shows a TCP/IPv6 packet with two extension headers, the first a Routing Header and the second a Fragment Header.

The Next Header field is present in all IPv6 headers; the value for this field will indicate "TCP" for all TCP/IPv6 packets that do not use any extension headers. When extension headers are being used, the Next Header field of the last header will always indicate "TCP" for TCP/IPv6 packets.

These are some current (mid-2003) IPv6 extensions.

Routing   Similar in purpose to the *Loose Source and Record Route Option*
defined for IPv4, the Routing Option allows the node sending a packet
to specify one or more routers that must process the packet en route
to its destination.

Hop-by-Hop   Some IPv6 options are logically constrained to being used
only by the source and destination nodes. For example, the ESP
header, which indicates that the rest of the packet is encrypted, can be
safely ignored by intermediate routers. Likewise, other IPv6 options
are logically required to be processed by intermediate nodes. For
example, the Routing Header requires that at least some intermediate routers examine it. The Hop-by-Hop Header is used when one or
more options are present that must be examined by *every* node in the
delivery path from source to destination.

Fragment   Although IPv6 prohibits intermediate nodes from fragmenting packets, end-to-end fragmentation is permitted when the source
node determines it needs to send packets that are larger than the
path MTU (see Chapter 12). The Fragment Header contains information regarding packet fragmentation, intended only for the packet's
destination node.

Destination   Just as the Hop-by-Hop Header is defined to specifically
require all intermediate nodes to process the header, the Destination Header is defined to limit the use of the enclosed options to the
destination node only.

Authentication   When strong (cryptographic quality) authentication is
required, the Authentication Header is used (see Chapter 6).

Encapsulating Security Protocol   When strong encryption is required,
the ESP Header is used (see Chapter 6).

Clearly, there are issues related to the order in which extension headers
are added to a packet header, to be discussed next.

9.1.2   EXTENSION HEADER ORDERING

When an IPv6 packet is transmitted with two or more extension headers,
a choice must be made about the order in which the headers are placed

after the main IPv6 header. The goal of this order is to make sure that all optional data that must be processed by the destination node, as well as by any intermediate nodes, is available, while at the same time allowing those nodes to efficiently process packets with options.

For example, the Hop-by-Hop Header should be placed directly after the main IPv6 header because it must be processed by all intermediate nodes (routers) that process the packet. On the other hand, the Destination Options Header should be placed last, after all other extension headers and just before the upper-layer protocol header. Intermediate nodes do not need to process these options, and other end-to-end options such as fragmentation or security must be processed before the packet's payload can even be interpreted correctly. Taken from RFC 2460, Table 9–2 shows the recommended extension header ordering.

The only header extension that should appear more than once in any given IPv6 packet is the Destination Options Header, and that is permitted only when the extension headers are processed by intermediate nodes. In those

---

Recommended extension header order

IPv6 header
Hop-by-Hop Options Header
Destination Options Header (note 1)
Routing Header
Fragment Header
Authentication Header (note 2)
Encapsulating Security Payload Header (note 2)
Destination Options Header (note 3)
Upper-layer header

Note 1: For options to be processed by the first
        destination that appears in the IPv6
        Destination Address field plus subsequent
        destinations listed in the Routing Header.

Note 2: Additional recommendations regarding the
        relative order of the Authentication and
        Encapsulating Security Payload Headers are
        given in [RFC-2406].

Note 3: For options to be processed only by the
        final destination of the packet.

Table 9–2: Recommended extension header order (from RFC 2460).

cases, a set of options can be attached for the intermediate "destinations" that the packet visits en route to its final destination—where a second Destination Options Header can be processed only by the end-node.

Again, the recommended restriction on having only one of each extension header is based on logic. For example, all Hop-by-Hop Options should be incorporated into a single extension header for efficiency. Likewise, only one each of a Routing, Fragment, or Security Header makes sense for each packet.

It should be noted that the order specified in Table 9–2 is a recommendation and not a requirement.[2] Although IPv6 implementations *should*[3] conform to these recommendations, they are not required to do so. And in keeping with the fundamental Internet liberal/conservative principle ("Be liberal in what you accept, and conservative in what you send"; see RFC 791), IPv6 nodes are required to accept and attempt to process whatever extension headers occur in a packet, whether in the recommended order or not and whether there is only one of each type or more.

9.1.3 IPv6-in-IPv6 Tunneling

The *IPv6* Next Header type is included in Table 9–1, and when it appears, it indicates that IPv6 packets are being tunneled within another stream of IPv6 packets. *Protocol tunneling* happens when datagrams from one protocol are encapsulated within datagrams of another protocol. A concrete example of protocol tunneling might occur when a person has postal mail forwarded from her home office to her branch office by having each piece of mail placed in a new envelope with the branch office address as the new destination. The original piece of mail is unchanged, and it will eventually be delivered to the appropriate person, but it was wrapped (encapsulated) in a different packet before it arrived at its intended destination.

Conceptually, IP-in-IP tunneling is quite similar, and it is often linked with the similar function of mobile IP delivery when a mobile node notifies its home network of a forward-to address. Then, any packets sent to the

---

[2]The exception is the Hop-by-Hop Header, which must appear only immediately after the main IPv6 header. See section 9.4 for more about this type of header.

[3]The term *should* is defined for use in an RFC (see RFC 2119, "Key Words for Use in RFCs to Indicate Requirement Levels") to indicate "that there may exist valid reasons in particular circumstances to ignore a particular item, but the full implications must be understood and carefully weighed before choosing a different course."

mobile node's home address can be encapsulated in a new IP packet for redelivery to the mobile node's current location (see Chapter 17 for more about Mobile IPv6).

When an IPv6 packet is encapsulated within another IPv6 packet, the encapsulated packet may have one set of extension headers that are processed only after the packet arrives at the other end of the tunnel. At the same time, the encapsulating packet can have its own set of extension headers that are added by the node at the transmitting end of the tunnel and processed only by intermediate nodes within the tunnel and/or by the node at the receiving end of the tunnel.

9.1.4 IPv6 Extension Headers and Options

The IPv6 extension headers are intended to carry optional Internet-layer data, so all extension headers are considered to be optional. Two of the originally defined extension headers—the Hop-by-Hop Options and Destination Options Headers—can carry one or more options to be interpreted by the appropriate recipient(s). Unlike the other IPv6 extension headers, which enable specific functions (fragmentation, encryption, etc.) while at the same time being optional (there is no requirement to encrypt packets, for example), the Hop-by-Hop and Destination Option extensions are generalized headers that are distinguished only by the way they are processed.

In other words, Hop-by-Hop Option Headers carry options that are processed at every hop; Destination Option Headers carry options that are processed only at the destination.

In some cases, there is confusion about the nomenclature of IPv6 extension headers. It should be noted here that extension headers contain optional data but are not necessarily options headers. Only the Hop-by-Hop Options and Destination Options Headers are actually "options headers" because they carry unspecified options to be processed by, respectively, nodes at each hop or the destination node(s).

9.2 Routing Header

The IP routing architecture is designed to allow interoperation among nodes without having to program internetwork structure into those nodes.

Once a packet is transmitted by a node into a network cloud, the intermediate nodes doing routing within the cloud make simple decisions about how to forward the packet. Sometimes it is possible that those decisions can produce an unwanted result, in which case it is possible for the sending node to make a better decision about how its packets should be routed.

Source Routing Options allow nodes to specify one or more routers through which the packet must pass on its way to its destination. IPv4 defines a *Loose Source* Routing Option, in which all listed routers must handle the packet, but the packet may pass through other routers as well. This is opposed to *Strict Source* Routing, in which the packet must pass through all the routers listed in the option and *only* those routers. Strict Source Routing is rarely used, and Loose Source Routing is controversial because it can be used to avoid passing through security gateways. However, Source Routing is still useful for routing around network faults, forcing packets through preferred routers, and for trouble-shooting specific routers.

The IPv6 Routing Header is defined in RFC 2460; the value 43 in the Next Header field specifies that a Routing Header follows.

9.2.1 IPv6 Routing Header Format

The IPv6 Routing Header is similar to the IPv4 Loose Source/Record Route Option, in which the routers on the list decrement a field in the header extension to record that they processed the packet. Figure 9–2 shows the general format for this header extension.

After the Next Header[4] and header extension length[5] fields of the Routing Header are the *routing type* and *segments left* fields. Although different types of Routing Headers are possible, as of 2003 only two have been recognized by the IANA: the Source Route type defined in RFC 2460 (Type 0) and another type that was defined in the mid-90s to support the Nimrod network architecture (Type 1).

The *Segments Left* field holds an 8-bit value from 0 to 255 that indicates how many of the nodes listed in the header remain to be visited before the packet arrives at its final destination. For example, if three routers are listed in the header when the packet is sent, the value of the segment's left field will be set to 3.

---

[4]Indicates protocol contents of the header following this one.
[5]Indicates number of 8-octet words in the header, not including the first 8 octets.

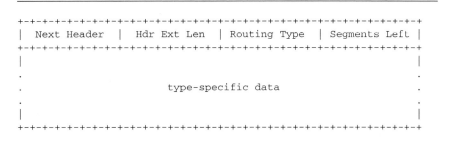

Figure 9–2: Routing Header extension format (from RFC 2460).

9.2.2 SOURCE ROUTE (TYPE 0)

The *Source Route* Routing Header is indicated by the value 0 in the routing type field. Specified in RFC 2460, the format for this header is shown in Figure 9–3 and is similar to the format used by the IPv4 source route option (see RFC 791), consisting of the standard IPv6 Routing Header fields, a 32-bit reserved field (filled with 0 and ignored; these bits pad out the initial 8-octet word of the header extension), and the IP addresses of the nodes through which the packet must be routed.

The destination address of a packet sent with a Source Route Routing Header is initially set to the first node the sender wants the packet to traverse, and the Segments Left field is set to equal the number of addresses in the Routing Header extension. The IPv6 address of the packet's final destination is the last address in the list. The values of the address list items change as the packet passes through the listed nodes; the way they change is discussed later (see Figure 9–4).

The Routing Header is processed only when the packet arrives at the first address in the list; all nodes between the source and that first destination node ignore the Routing Header. When the packet does arrive at the first destination, that node processes the Routing Header by following these steps:

Check value in the Segments Left field

- If Segments Left = 0, meaning the packet has arrived at its final destination, the node can skip the Routing Header and go on to the next header.
- Otherwise, go on to the next step.

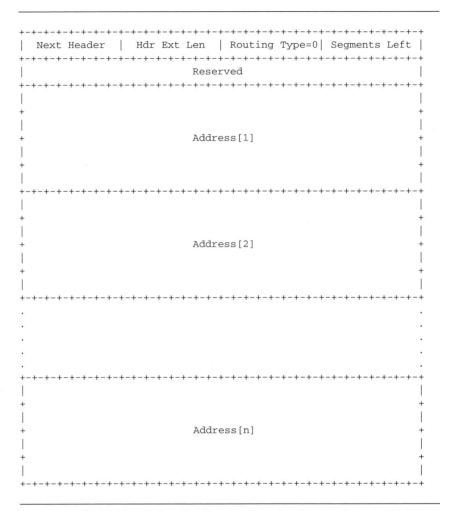

Figure 9–3: Source Route Routing Header extension format (from RFC 2460).

Check the parity of the Header Extension Length field

- If the header length is an odd number (there should be an even number of 8-octet words in the header because all IPv6 addresses are 128 bits, or 16 octets long), send an ICMP error message to the source address, and discard the packet.
- If the header length is an even number, determine how many addresses are in the field by dividing the header length value

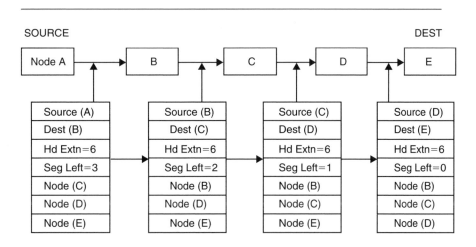

Figure 9–4: Source routing in action, as a packet is moved from Node A to Node E.

by 2 to determine how many IPv6 addresses are carried in the header extension. If the Segments Left field is greater than this computed number of IPv6 addresses, it means the packet headers are not properly formed; an ICMP message must be sent back to the source and the packet discarded. Otherwise, do the following.

• Decrement the Segments Left value by 1, figure out which of the destinations in the list should be the packet's next stop, check to make sure that address is not a multicast address (forbidden in the Routing Header), and then switch the main header destination address with the address of the packet's next stop. Then check the Hop Limit of the main header, if it has been exceeded, send an ICMP error back to the source, and drop the packet.

This algorithm allows intermediate nodes on the list to indicate which nodes have already been traversed and which remain to be traversed. Node A (in Figure 9–4) has a list of nodes for a packet to be routed through on its way to Node E, starting with Node B and going through Nodes C and D. The initial packet is sent to the first node in the list, Node B. Note that Node A does not have to include Node B's address in the Routing Header list of nodes.

When the packet arrives at Node B, it is processed: the Segments Left field is decremented from 3 to 2, and the original destination address (Node B) trades places with the first node on the Routing Header list (Node C). Once this packet is received at Node C, the Segments Left field goes from 2 to 1, and Node C's address goes back to the Routing Header to be replaced by Node D's address. The process repeats for Node E, the final destination, where the Routing Header list contains just the nodes that were originally specified to be stops en route from Node A to Node E.

Routers may be required to modify Routing Headers of the packets they process, but some header extensions may not be modified at all, like the Fragment Header.

9.3   Fragment Header

To send a payload that is too large to be accommodated in a single packet (because the resulting packet would be larger than the path MTU from source to destination), IPv6 permits nodes to break up the packet into two or more pieces and then send each piece (*fragment*) as a separate packet.

The Fragment Header in IPv6 allows only source nodes to fragment packets for reassembly only by the destination node—end-to-end fragmentation. It is useful to understand how IPv4 fragmentation works before looking at IPv6 fragmentation.

9.3.1   IPv4 FRAGMENTATION

IPv4's datagram Fragmentation Option has long caused controversy: It squanders IPv4 header real estate, accounting for 20% of the basic IP header (the datagram ID, fragmentation flags, and fragment offset field). Fragmentation adds a computational burden on routers and destination nodes. Fragmentation makes IPv4 more complicated to implement, as well. IPv6 permits only end-to-end fragmentation—in other words, the source and destination nodes that are communicating are permitted to negotiate the use of fragmentation by the source only. In IPv4, packets could be fragmented by intermediate routers to allow packets larger than the *maximum transmission unit* or *MTU* for some link.

Ultimately, this kind of fragmentation in IPv4 was permitted because the alternatives seemed even less appealing. Placing an upper limit on IP datagram size lower than the smallest allowed PDU on any network medium using IP would unreasonably limit the PDU size for media that can handle very large chunks of data efficiently. Limiting the IP datagram length to under 1500 octets (the maximum allowed size for Ethernet frames) or to 576 octets (MTU for the X.25 wide area network protocol) would likewise limit more efficient network media.

Alternatively, placing a lower limit on the size of PDU of any network medium using IP and thus requiring all network media to support some minimum PDU size determined by the IETF would unnecessarily restrict the types of media capable of carrying IP. Since one of the most basic tenets of IP networking is that it is a universally interoperable protocol, this option is also unacceptable.

IPv4 packets can potentially be fragmented any time they cross different types of network media. For example, a 1492-octet-long IP datagram is just long enough to fit inside an Ethernet frame, but it would have to be fragmented in order to cross an X.25 network, which can handle only datagrams as large as 576 octets.

A node sets the length of its datagrams based on its local MTU. IPv4 has an upper limit on datagram size of 65,535 octets, since the IP header field for datagram length is 16 bits long. However, most common network media have much smaller maximum network frame sizes, as discussed in the previous chapter. When there are several different networks across which network traffic passes, there will be a path MTU. This is the largest unit that can pass unfragmented across all the intervening networks in a datagrams route—in other words, the smallest MTU of any of those networks.

9.3.2 IPv6 Fragmentation Header Fields

The IPv6 header is considerably simplified by the absence of fragmentation-related headers, thus simplifying the task of processing the standard IPv6 header. When fragmentation occurs, the source node inserts a Fragmentation Header (signified by a value of 44 in the preceding header's Next Header field). Figure 9–5 shows the format for this header extension.

The header extension carries the appropriate data for fragmentation but only when it is needed. The fields in this header extension include the following.

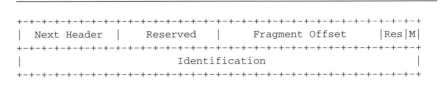

Figure 9–5: IPv6 Fragmentation Header (from RFC 2460).

Next Header   The standard next header field, an 8-bit value identifying
   the protocol contained in the headers following this one.

Reserved   Initialized to zero for transmission; ignored on reception.

Fragment Offset   A 13-bit integer that indicates, in units of 8 octets, the
   relative position in the unfragmented packet of the data that follows
   the header. A Fragment Offset value of 0 means the first fragment of
   a packet; a value of 100 means that the following fragment follows
   800 octets of data carried in some other fragment(s).

Res   A 2-bit reserved field that is initialized to zero for transmission and
   ignored on reception.

M flag   When set to 1, this flag indicates that there are more fragments
   on their way; when set to 0, it indicates that this fragment is the last
   fragment.

Identification   This 32-bit field identifies every fragmented packet
   uniquely—during the lifetime of the packet. All fragments from
   the same packet share the same value in this field, allowing the
   destination node to identify different pieces of the same packet for
   reassembly, as well as to quickly discard fragments that have already
   been received.

   The lifetime of the packet is considered to include the time it takes to
   transmit the network from source to destination as well as whatever
   time is required to wait for the rest of the original packet fragments.
   Since this field is limited to more than 4 billion unique values, it
   should be capable of supporting even high-performance network
   links for any reasonable packet lifetime.

By shifting the Fragment Offset field to the left (and the More flag to the right), the header becomes easier to process. The Fragment Offset is a value specifying the number of 8-octet words to be offset; that value is stored in a 13-bit field. Ignoring the low-order 3 bits of that part of the header (that is, the 2 reserved bits and the More flag) allows the 13-bit Fragment Offset field to be expressed as a 16-bit value and interpreted as the number of octets specified by the offset.

9.3.3 PACKET FRAGMENTATION

The original packet (before fragmentation) contains two parts.

Unfragmentable Part   The IPv6 header, plus any extension headers that must be processed by nodes other than the final destination node. For example, the unfragmentable part of a packet with Routing and/or Hop-by-Hop Headers would include the IPv6 header plus the Routing and/or Hop-by-Hop Headers.

Fragmentable Part   Everything else. This means any extension headers to be processed by the destination node and the upper-layer headers and data.

The packet can be thought of as looking like this.

```
+------------------+-----------------------//------------------------+
|  Unfragmentable  |                  Fragmentable                   |
|      Part        |                      Part                       |
+------------------+-----------------------//------------------------+
```

Fragments are created by dividing the unfragmentable part up, like this.

```
+------------------+-------------+--------------+--//--+----------+
|  Unfragmentable  |    first    |    second    |      |   last   |
|      Part        |   fragment  |   fragment   | .... | fragment |
+------------------+-------------+--------------+--//--+----------+
```

With each fragment incorporated into its own packet, the resulting packets duplicate the unfragmentable part of the original packet and add a Fragment Header, resulting in a sequence of packets that look like this.

```
+------------------+--------+--------------+
|  Unfragmentable  |Fragment|    first     |
|      Part        | Header |   fragment   |
+------------------+--------+--------------+
```

```
+------------------+--------+-------------+
| Unfragmentable   |Fragment|   second    |
|      Part        | Header |  fragment   |
+------------------+--------+-------------+
                        o
                        o
                        o
+------------------+--------+----------+
| Unfragmentable   |Fragment|   last   |
|      Part        | Header | fragment |
+------------------+--------+----------+
```

Each of the fragment-carrying packets has the same unfragmentable part, with the Next Header field of the last header of that part set to 44, indicating that the next header is a Fragment Header.

At the destination node, the process is reversed as fragment packets begin arriving; if all the fragments have not been received within 60 seconds, the packets that have been received are discarded, and if the first (offset = 0) fragment was received, the receiving node sends an ICMP error message.

9.4   Hop-by-Hop and Destination Options Headers

Unlike the other header extensions discussed so far, the Hop-by-Hop and Destination Options Headers are generalized extensions that carry options intended to be processed either at every stop that the packet makes en route to its destination (Hop-by-Hop) or only on receipt at the packet's destination. The various different options that have so far been defined are discussed in the next section; other options will invariably be defined in the future.

9.4.1   OPTIONS HEADERS FORMAT

Both options headers share the same general format, as shown in Figure 9–6. The only fields required for all options headers are the Next Header (8 bits indicating the protocol of the header that follows) and the Hdr Ext Len (8 bits indicating the length of the header in 8-octet words, excluding the first 64 bits). The Options field is left wide open and can be filled with up to 2040 octets of option data (the Hdr Ext Len maximum value 255 eight-octet units).

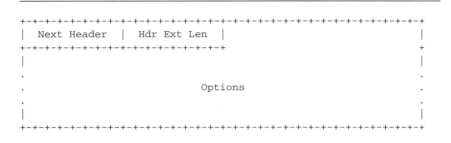

Figure 9–6: General Options headers format (from RFC 2460).

The Next Header field value of 0 indicates that a Hop-by-Hop Options Header follows; a value of 60 indicates that a Destination Options Header follows.

9.4.2 DESTINATION OPTIONS FUNCTIONS

If a Destination Options Header option type is not recognized by the destination node, the default behavior is to discard the packet and send an ICMP message to the sender. If the destination address is a multicast, the packet is discarded silently.

Optional data carried in a Destination Options Header may sometimes be just as easily carried in some other type of header extension. For example, it is possible to define a Fragmentation Option for the Destination Option Header that accomplishes the same function as the Fragmentation Header. The authors of RFC 2460 note that the choice may depend on which approach uses fewer octets or is easier to process. However, when the implementation requires that nodes not recognizing the option do something other than the default (discard and then send an ICMP message[6] if possible), the Destination Options Header extension must be used. As will be explained in the next section, Destination Options may be encoded with three alternative responses to unrecognized options.

9.4.3 OPTIONS SPECIFICATION AND ENCODING

The options in the options extension headers are encoded in a standard format, where the *type*, *length*, and *value* are defined for each option.

---

[6]Unrecognized Type message, see Chapter 12.

```
   0              7 8              15 16
+-+-+-+-+-+-+-+-+-+-+-+-+-+-+-+-+- - - - - - - - -
|  Option Type  |  Opt Data Len |  Option Data
+-+-+-+-+-+-+-+-+-+-+-+-+-+-+-+-+- - - - - - - - -
```

Figure 9–7: Format for options carried in IPv6 options extension headers (from RFC 2460).

Figure 9–7 shows how these values are formatted, as specified in RFC 2460.

The first octet identifies the option using an 8-bit *option type* value. These values are maintained by the IANA, and values identified by the IANA as valid as of early 2003 are shown in Table 9–3.

The second octet, *opt data len*, is an 8-bit unsigned integer that defines the length of the *option data field* in octets. The option data field is a variable-length field in which optional data for that option type is carried.

The option type octet is further subdivided to allow the use of the three high-order bits to specify how nodes should handle the attached packet in certain circumstances. The two highest-order bits indicate what a node should do with the packet if the node doesn't recognize the option type.

00 skip the option, but continue processing the rest of the header normally

01 discard the packet

10 discard the packet entirely and, for multicast and nonmulticast packets, send an ICMP message[7] to indicate that the option type is unrecognized

11 discard the packet and, for only nonmulticast packets, send an ICMP message[8] to indicate that the option type is unrecognized

For some options, the option data may be modified en route. The third-highest-order bit is used to specify whether an intermediate node can modify this data: 0 in this position indicates that option data does not change, whereas 1 in this position indicates that option data may be changed. When an Authentication Header is present in the packet, for

---

[7]ICMP Parameter Problem, Code 2
[8]ICMP Parameter Problem, Code 2

any option whose data may change en route, its entire Option Data field must be treated as zero-valued octets when computing or verifying the packet's authenticating value.

9.4.4 OPTION PADDING

Protocol headers and options often must be aligned precisely (for example, IP headers typically align on a 32-bit boundary). IPv6 header extensions are typically *padded*—extra space is inserted between parts of the headers, usually set to 0—to be aligned on 8-octet multiples. The very first options defined for IPv6 extension headers solve this problem.

The *Pad1* option is the simplest: The value of 0x00 (binary: 0000 0000) is inserted into the option after the main option body to take up a single octet. This option is recommended for use only when a single octet must be padded.

The *PadN* option is two or more octets long, depending on the amount of padding required. This option is identified by the value 0x01 followed by the option data length and the appropriate padding option data (some number of octets that should be set to 0, but that should be ignored in any case), like this.

```
+-+-+-+-+-+-+-+-+-+-+-+-+-+-+-+-+- - - - - - - -
|       1        |  Opt Data Len | Option Data
+-+-+-+-+-+-+-+-+-+-+-+-+-+-+-+-+- - - - - - - -
```

The first 8 bits of this option are set to 0x01 (binary: 0000 0001), with the next octet used to specify how many octets of data follow. When only two octets of padding are needed, this option would have the value 0x01 00 to indicate the option type (PadN), where required the option fields (option id and option data length) are sufficient to pad out the option.

When more than two octets of padding are required, the option data length field contains an integer with a value from 1 to 5, indicating how many octets are needed to make the entire option contain some multiple of eight octets.[9]

---

[9]Adding six octets of padding would make the entire option eight octets long, indicating that padding was not needed in the first place; seven octets of padding would be equivalent to a single octet of padding.

9.4.5 Current Valid Options

Only a few options have been defined for use in IPv6 extension headers that can carry options. Table 9–3 lists those valid as of 2003.

In addition to the padding options, valid IPv6 extension header options include the following.

Jumbo Payload   (RFC 2675) "IPv6 Jumbograms."

> A "jumbogram" is an IPv6 packet containing a payload longer than 65,535 octets. This document describes the IPv6 Jumbo Payload option, which provides the means of specifying such large payload lengths. It also describes the changes needed to TCP and UDP to make use of jumbograms. Jumbograms are relevant only to IPv6 nodes that may be attached to links with a link MTU greater than 65,575 octets, and need not be implemented or understood by IPv6 nodes that do not support attachment to links with such large MTUs.

NSAP Address   RFC 1888: "OSI NSAPs and IPv6" (experimental) for carrying encapsulating a complete NSAP (Network Service Access Point, see Chapter 8) address in the IPv6 header.

HEX	BINARY			
	act	chg	rest	
0	00	0	00000	Pad1
1	00	0	00001	PadN
C2	11	0	00010	Jumbo Payload
C3	11	0	00011	NSAP Address
4	00	0	00100	Tunnel Encapsulation Limit
5	00	0	00101	Router Alert
C6	11	0	00110	Binding Update
7	00	0	00111	Binding Acknowledgment
8	00	0	01000	Binding Request
C9	11	0	01001	Home Address
8A	10	0	01010	Endpoint Identification

Table 9–3: IPv6 Option Types (from IANA).

Tunnel Encapsulation Limit   RFC 2473, Generic Packet Tunneling in IPv6 Specification.

A tunnel entry-point node may be configured to include a Tunnel Encapsulation Limit option as part of the information prepended to all packets entering a tunnel at that node. The Tunnel Encapsulaton Limit option is carried in a Destination Options extension header [IPv6-Spec] placed between the encapsulating IPv6 header and the IPv6 header of the original packet. (Other IPv6 extension headers may also be present preceding or following the Destination Options extension header, depending on configuration information at the tunnel entry-point node.)

The Tunnel Encapsulation Limit option specifies how many additional levels of encapsulation are permitted to be prepended to the packet—or, in other words, how many further levels of nesting the packet is permitted to undergo—not counting the encapsulation in which the option itself is contained. For example, a Tunnel Encapsulation Limit option containing a limit value of zero means that a packet carrying that option may not enter another tunnel before exiting the current tunnel.

Router Alert   RFC 2711 published in 1999.

New protocols, such as RSVP, use control datagrams which, while addressed to a particular destination, contain information that needs to be examined, and in some case updated, by routers along the path between the source and destination. It is desirable to forward regular datagrams as rapidly as possible, while ensuring that the router processes these special control datagrams appropriately. Currently, however, the only way for a router to determine if it needs to examine a datagram is to at least partially parse upper-layer data in all datagrams. This parsing is expensive and slow. This situation is undesirable.

This document defines a new option within the IPv6 Hop-by-Hop Header. The presence of this option in an IPv6 datagram informs the router that the contents of this datagram are of interest to the router and to handle any control data accordingly. The absence of this option in an IPv6 datagram informs the router that the datagram does not contain information needed by the router and hence can be safely routed without further data-gram parsing. Hosts originating IPv6 datagrams are required to include this option in certain circumstances.

Binding Update/Acknowledgment/Request   Originally identified with IPv6 mobility support; see Chapter 17.

Home Address   Mobile IPv6 defines a Home Address destination option in a work-in-progress on IPv6 mobility.

The Home Address option is carried by the Destination Option extension header (Next Header value = 60). It is used in a packet sent by a mobile node while away from home, to inform the recipient of the mobile node's home address.

Endpoint Identification   Based on a feature used with Nimrod ("a scal-able internetwork routing architecture" from the mid-1990s) to determine endpoints in IPv4/v6 networks.

Others can be expected. One work-in-progress defines a new approach to path MTU discovery (see Chapter 12 for more on PMTU):

IPv6/PMTU Option Header Draft

This document presents a new method for the PMTU discovery for IPv6. To discover the PMTU of a path, a source node mea-sures its actual PMTU using the newly defined Hop-by-Hop Option Header, whereas a source node initially assumes that the PMTU of a path is the known MTU of the first hop in the path in the previous one [1981]. In order to measure the actual PMTU, the source node sends the IP packet with the newly defined Hop-by-Hop Option Header to the destination node with the first data packet when the node is beginning. This can eliminate the chance of occurrence of several iterations of the somewhat complex discovery cycle (sending a packet, receiving a Packet Too Big message, reducing a packet size). Most of all, since existing PMTU has a weak point for security and denial-of-service attacks, this document suggests a security function when PMTU is going on.

9.5   Summary

Although IPv4 options have been defined from the very beginning, their use has never been widespread. IPv6 option header extensions have been designed to remedy the flaws in IPv4 options, and, as demonstrated in this chapter, should gain wider acceptance. Although so far only a few options have been defined, they may be applied in a number of different ways to enable protocol tunneling, routing options, security options, fragmentation, and more.

As we'll see in Chapter 17, the IPv6 mobility protocol uses an extension header, but in the next chapter we examine another function—multicast—that, while present in IPv4, is designed for greater effectiveness and ease of use under IPv6.

10

IPv6 Multicast

Multicast for IPv6 is based on the same principles as multicast in IPv4 or, for that matter, multicast in link layer protocols like Ethernet.

- Nodes that are members of a multicast group receive packets transmitted to the multicast group address.
- The original sender of a multicast packet sends it only once, but the packet will be repeated so as to be delivered to all group members.
- When a multicast packet is transmitted on a multiaccess network, in which all nodes can detect all transmissions but ignore those addressed to nodes other than themselves, group members all process the same packet transmitted by the original sender.
- When a multicast packet is transmitted on a nonbroadcast, multiaccess (NBMA) network like ATM or Frame Relay, an intermediary node accepts the multicast and then repeats it to all nodes subscribed on the network.

Although the fundamentals are quite similar to multicast in IPv4, IPv6 protocols depend to a great degree on the use of multicast for functions such as neighbor discovery (see Chapter 13), node autoconfiguration (see Chapter 16), mobile IPv6 (see Chapter 17), and more.

As part of the renovation and simplification of IPv4-generation protocols, and to improve the efficiency with which the functions just cited are performed, IPv6 multicast has also been streamlined. The Internet Group Management Protocol (IGMP) used in parallel with ICMP in IPv4 has been dropped for IPv6. Instead, IPv6 multicast recipients are detected with the Multicast Listener Discovery (MLD) protocol, which is actually a set of ICMPv6 messages.

This chapter provides a brief look at the IPv6 specifications for multicast, including the multicast address format, multicast scopes, transient/permanent multicast groups, and multicast address allocation. Also covered here are the Multicast Listener Discovery (MLD) protocol and multicast routing under IPv6.

10.1   IPv6 Multicast Address Format

Like all IPv6 addresses, IPv6 multicast group addresses are 128 bits long, but multicast addresses are identifiable because the high-order 8 bits of the address are all 1s. The IPv6 multicast address format, shown in Figure 10–1, consists of four "fields."

High-order octet   This will always be 11111111 for multicast addresses.

Flags   The first three of these four single-bit flags are reserved; the fourth bit specifies whether the multicast group is a *well-known* address (permanently assigned to a defined group of nodes) or *transient* (an address used temporarily with no permanently defined set of members).

Scope   This field contains a value from 0 through 0xF. The multicast address scope indicates the relative size of the domain over which the multicast packet should be propagated (see Table 10–1).

Group ID   The remainder of the multicast address is given over to the *group ID*.

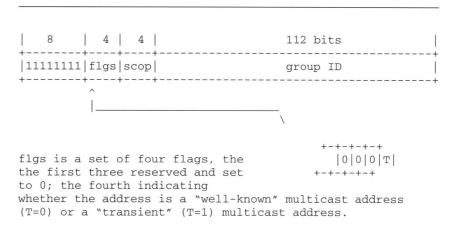

```
|   8    |  4  |  4 |                   112 bits                    |
+--------+-----+----+-----------------------------------------------+
|11111111|flgs|scop|                   group ID                    |
+--------+-----+----+-----------------------------------------------+
           ^
           |_____
                                                \
                                    +-+-+-+-+
flgs is a set of four flags, the    |0|0|0|T|
the first three reserved and set    +-+-+-+-+
to 0; the fourth indicating
whether the address is a "well-known" multicast address
(T=0) or a "transient" (T=1) multicast address.
```

Figure 10–1: IPv6 multicast address format (from RFC 3513).

Value	Scope
0	reserved
1	interface-local scope
2	link-local scope
3	reserved
4	admin-local scope
5	site-local scope
6	(unassigned)
7	(unassigned)
8	organization-local scope
9	(unassigned)
A	(unassigned)
B	(unassigned)
C	(unassigned)
D	(unassigned)
E	global scope
F	reserved

Table 10–1: IPv6 multicast address scope values.

10.2   Multicast Scope Definitions

The *scop* field of the multicast address is used to limit the multicast group scope. Table 10–1 lists the values defined for multicast group scope.

The most local scope, interface-local, specifies a single network interface to be used to transmit multicast packets over the loopback address. The scope can expand to the local link, site, organization, or global IPv6 Internet. As shown in Table 10–1, the all-zeros (0) and all-ones (0xF) values are reserved, with half of the rest of the values unassigned (but available for administrators who want to assign their own regions). Site-local and link-local scopes correspond to the unicast definitions for those scopes (see preceding section).

Beyond the link- and site-local scopes that can be automatically defined by physical connectivity lie the admin-local and organization-local scopes that are administratively configured and can span separate networks. The organization-local scope is meant to be able to cross site boundaries within a single organization.

Most important is the group ID field, which identifies the multicast group within the group's defined scope. As with IPv4 multicast groups, there are permanently assigned IPv6 multicast groups whose IDs have specific meaning. For instance, permanently assigned group IDs of the form ::2 specify "all routers" within the defined scope. So the following addresses specify three different multicast groups that consist of all the IPv6 routers in different scopes.

```
FF01:0:0:0:0:0:0:2
FF02:0:0:0:0:0:0:2
FF05:0:0:0:0:0:0:2
```

The first group includes IPv6 routers within scope 1 (the local interface), the second includes all routers within scope 2 (the local link), and the third includes all routers within scope 5 (site-local). If the high-order octets were FF0E, the group (if it was used) would consist of all IPv6 routers in the global IPv6 Internet. Those packets, however, would not likely be forwarded throughout the IPv6 Internet.

10.3   Reserved and Permanent Multicast Addresses

The group ID has meaning for permanently assigned groups, but transient group IDs have meaning only within their scope. The same transient, site-local, multicast address may be used at any number of separate sites. And FF15::101, a transient site-local address, does not have any relation to the similar permanent site-local scope address FF05::101.

There are other reserved and permanent multicast address allocations. For example, under no circumstances is the "all-zeroes" address a valid one for multicast, no matter what the scope. RFC 3513 explicitly reserves these addresses and states that can never be used.

```
FF00:0:0:0:0:0:0:0
FF01:0:0:0:0:0:0:0
FF02:0:0:0:0:0:0:0
FF03:0:0:0:0:0:0:0
FF04:0:0:0:0:0:0:0
FF05:0:0:0:0:0:0:0
FF06:0:0:0:0:0:0:0
FF07:0:0:0:0:0:0:0
FF08:0:0:0:0:0:0:0
FF09:0:0:0:0:0:0:0
FF0A:0:0:0:0:0:0:0
FF0B:0:0:0:0:0:0:0
FF0C:0:0:0:0:0:0:0
FF0D:0:0:0:0:0:0:0
FF0E:0:0:0:0:0:0:0
FF0F:0:0:0:0:0:0:0
```

This list of reserved addresses should be filtered on all IPv6 routers, just to ensure that packets sent to or from those addresses are not forwarded.

Another set of multicast addresses that have been permanently assigned are the *All Nodes Addresses* for interface-local and link-local scopes.

```
FF01:0:0:0:0:0:0:1  all IPv6 nodes, within scope 1
   (interface-local)
```

```
FF02:0:0:0:0:0:0:1   all IPv6 nodes, within scope 2
   (link-local)
```

These groups are defined as consisting of all IPv6 nodes, within the scope defined.

The *All Routers Addresses* are defined as follows.

```
FF01:0:0:0:0:0:0:2      all IPv6 routers,
   within scope 1 (interface-local)
FF02:0:0:0:0:0:0:2      all IPv6 routers,
   within scope 2 (link-local)
FF05:0:0:0:0:0:0:2      all IPv6 routers,
   within scope 5 (site-local)
```

The *Solicited-Node Address* is used with ICMPv6 to determine whether an IPv6 node is configured with a particular IPv6 address. All nodes are required to subscribe to the solicited-node address for every unicast and anycast address that node responds to. This is the format of this address.

```
FF02:0:0:0:0:1:FFXX:XXXX
```

Solicited-node multicast addresses are computed as a function of the node's unicast and anycast addresses; the address is formed by taking the low-order 24 bits of an address (unicast or anycast) and appending those bits to the prefix FF02:0:0:0:0:1:FF00::/104, resulting in a multicast address in the following range.

```
FF02:0:0:0:0:1:FF00:0000
to
FF02:0:0:0:0:1:FFFF:FFFF
```

Solicited-node addresses and their use are discussed in the next section.

Fixed-scope multicast addresses are permanently assigned over specific scope values. The most current assignments are available through the IANA Web site; those available as of mid-2003 are listed in Table 10–2.

Node-local scope	
FF01:0:0:0:0:0:0:1	All nodes address
FF01:0:0:0:0:0:0:2	All routers address

Link-local scope	
FF02:0:0:0:0:0:0:1	All nodes address
FF02:0:0:0:0:0:0:2	All routers address
FF02:0:0:0:0:0:0:3	Unassigned
FF02:0:0:0:0:0:0:4	DVMRP routers
FF02:0:0:0:0:0:0:5	OSPFIGP
FF02:0:0:0:0:0:0:6	OSPFIGP designated routers
FF02:0:0:0:0:0:0:7	ST routers
FF02:0:0:0:0:0:0:8	ST hosts
FF02:0:0:0:0:0:0:9	RIP routers
FF02:0:0:0:0:0:0:A	EIGRP routers
FF02:0:0:0:0:0:0:B	Mobile-agents
FF02:0:0:0:0:0:0:D	All PIM routers
FF02:0:0:0:0:0:0:E	RSVP-ENCAPSULATION
FF02:0:0:0:0:0:1:1	Link name
FF02:0:0:0:0:0:1:2	All-dhcp-agents
FF02:0:0:0:0:1:FFXX:XXXX	Solicited-node address

Site-local scope	
FF05:0:0:0:0:0:0:2	All routers address
FF05:0:0:0:0:0:1:3	All-dhcp-servers
FF05:0:0:0:0:0:1:4	All-dhcp-relays
FF05:0:0:0:0:0:1:1000	Service location
-FF05:0:0:0:0:0:1:13FF	

Table 10–2: Permanently-assigned fixed-scope multicast addresses.

There are also a number of multicast addresses that are permanently assigned in all scopes; values assigned as of mid-2003 are listed in Table 10–3.

10.4   Solicited-Node Multicast

As part of the neighbor discovery protocol (see Chapter 13), IPv6 nodes are required to join a special multicast group for every IPv6 unicast and anycast to which the nodes have been configured to respond. These addresses

All scope multicast addresses	
FF0X:0:0:0:0:0:0:0	Reserved multicast address
FF0X:0:0:0:0:0:0:100	VMTP managers group
FF0X:0:0:0:0:0:0:101	Network time protocol (NTP)
FF0X:0:0:0:0:0:0:102	SGI-Dogfight
FF0X:0:0:0:0:0:0:103	Rwhod
FF0X:0:0:0:0:0:0:104	VNP
FF0X:0:0:0:0:0:0:105	Artificial Horizons — Aviator
FF0X:0:0:0:0:0:0:106	NSS — name service server
FF0X:0:0:0:0:0:0:107	AUDIONEWS — Audio news multicast
FF0X:0:0:0:0:0:0:108	SUN NIS+ information service
FF0X:0:0:0:0:0:0:109	MTP—Multicast transport protocol
FF0X:0:0:0:0:0:0:10A	IETF-1-LOW-AUDIO
FF0X:0:0:0:0:0:0:10B	IETF-1-AUDIO
FF0X:0:0:0:0:0:0:10C	IETF-1-VIDEO
FF0X:0:0:0:0:0:0:10D	IETF-2-LOW-AUDIO
FF0X:0:0:0:0:0:0:10E	IETF-2-AUDIO
FF0X:0:0:0:0:0:0:10F	IETF-2-VIDEO
FF0X:0:0:0:0:0:0:110	MUSIC-SERVICE
FF0X:0:0:0:0:0:0:111	SEANET-TELEMETRY
FF0X:0:0:0:0:0:0:112	SEANET-IMAGE
FF0X:0:0:0:0:0:0:113	MLOADD
FF0X:0:0:0:0:0:0:114	any private experiment
FF0X:0:0:0:0:0:0:115	DVMRP on MOSPF
FF0X:0:0:0:0:0:0:116	SVRLOC
FF0X:0:0:0:0:0:0:117	XINGTV
FF0X:0:0:0:0:0:0:118	microsoft-ds
FF0X:0:0:0:0:0:0:119	nbc-pro
FF0X:0:0:0:0:0:0:11A	nbc-pfn
FF0X:0:0:0:0:0:0:11B	lmsc-calren-1
FF0X:0:0:0:0:0:0:11C	lmsc-calren-2
FF0X:0:0:0:0:0:0:11D	lmsc-calren-3
FF0X:0:0:0:0:0:0:11E	lmsc-calren-4
FF0X:0:0:0:0:0:0:11F	ampr-info
FF0X:0:0:0:0:0:0:120	mtrace
FF0X:0:0:0:0:0:0:121	RSVP-encap-1
FF0X:0:0:0:0:0:0:122	RSVP-encap-2
FF0X:0:0:0:0:0:0:123	SVRLOC-DA
FF0X:0:0:0:0:0:0:124	rln-server

Table 10–3: Permanently assigned variable-scope multicast addresses.

All scope multicast addresses
FF0X:0:0:0:0:0:0:125 proshare-mc
FF0X:0:0:0:0:0:0:126 dantz
FF0X:0:0:0:0:0:0:127 cisco-rp-announce
FF0X:0:0:0:0:0:0:128 cisco-rp-discovery
FF0X:0:0:0:0:0:0:129 gatekeeper
FF0X:0:0:0:0:0:0:12A iberiagames
FF0X:0:0:0:0:0:0:201 "rwho" Group (BSD) (unofficial)
FF0X:0:0:0:0:0:0:202 SUN RPC PMAPPROC_CALLIT
FF0X:0:0:0:0:0:2:0000-FF0X:0:0:0:0:0:2:7FFD multimedia conference calls
FF0X:0:0:0:0:0:2:7FFE SAPv1 announcements
FF0X:0:0:0:0:0:2:7FFF SAPv0 announcements (deprecated)
FF0X:0:0:0:0:0:2:8000-FF0X:0:0:0:0:0:2:FFFF SAP dynamic assignments

Table 10–3: *Continued*

are based on the low-order 24 bits of each anycast/unicast address, which in most cases will correspond to the unique portion of any interface's MAC address (if present).

Any node attempting to configure itself with an IPv6 address is required to send out a neighbor discovery solicitation on the solicited-node multicast address for that IPv6 address. In that way, if the address is already being used, the node using it will respond to the solicitation, and the requesting node can avoid address collision with the existing node.

The solicited-node multicast address is designed to fulfill this function in the most efficient way possible.

- First, by using the low-order 24 bits of each IPv6 address, each node will likely have to subscribe to only one solicited-node multicast address per IPv6 interface. The same single address can serve for any and all EUI-64-based anycast/unicast addresses, regardless of scope.
- Second, although solicited-node multicast addresses for interfaces owned by two different nodes on the same link are possible, they are minimized by the use of the 24-bit address space. With over 16 million unique addresses, the chance of two IPv6 interfaces on the same link colliding on those bits is low.

The solicited-node multicast address is also used for other neighbor discovery purposes, allowing nodes to more quickly map an IPv6 address to a link layer network address.

10.5 Multicast Listener Discovery (MLD) for IPv6

IPv4 multicast group membership is managed through the use of a separate protocol, the Internet Group Management Protocol (IGMP). Considered part of IPv4, IGMP works much like ICMP in that it permits nodes to exchange network metainformation. IPv4 nodes exchange IGMP messages, usually with routers, to indicate the multicast groups to which they wish to subscribe.

Under IPv6, multicast group management is accomplished with a set of ICMPv6 messages that comprise the Multicast Listener Discovery (MLD) protocol. Like Neighbor Discovery, MLD can be considered a subprotocol of ICMPv6. As stated in the introduction to RFC 2710, "Multicast Listener Discovery (MLD) for IPv6," the purpose of the protocol is to allow a router "to discover the presence of multicast listeners (that is, nodes wishing to receive multicast packets) on its directly attached links, and to discover specifically which multicast addresses are of interest to those neighboring nodes. This information is then provided to whichever multicast routing protocol is being used by the router, in order to ensure that multicast packets are delivered to all links where there are interested receivers."

MLD uses three different types of messages.

Multicast Listener Query The Query message type has two subtypes. The *General Query* is used by routers to discover all the multicast groups that listeners on the link are subscribed to; the *Multicast-Address-Specific Query* is used by routers to discover whether there are any local link subscribers (listeners) to a particular multicast address. Only routers send queries, and usually there is only one router that acts as a querier on each link.

Multicast Listener Report An unsolicited Report message is sent by any node when it begins listening to a multicast address; Report messages are generated in response to a Query message sent by a router (either a query for a specific multicast address or a general query).

Multicast Listener Done The Done message should be sent by a node when it stops listening to a multicast address.

It should be clarified that MLD is not used to identify every node subscribing to every multicast address or to associate link layer addresses with all subscribers, but rather to notify routers of which multicast addresses are of interest to one or more nodes on the local link. In that way, the routers have a simple mechanism for keeping track of multicast addresses *they* must monitor on their other links.

The protocol itself defines a set of behaviors for routers and multicast listeners, with routers periodically sending General Queries to ascertain which multicast addresses they must forward to each of their links, and with multicast listeners sending Reports in response to router queries as well as unsolicited Reports when they begin monitoring a multicast address.

The protocol incorporates a set of timers that multicast listeners use to determine when they must respond to router Queries as well as how frequently a sending router must send General Queries. MLD allows routers to monitor all relevant multicast addresses—but only relevant multicast addresses—so ideally there will be only one node sending one Report for each multicast address.

As described in RFC 2710, MLD messages are sent with a link-local IPv6 Source Address, an IPv6 Hop Limit of 1, and an IPv6 Router Alert option in a Hop-by-Hop Options Header. (The Router Alert Option is necessary to cause routers to examine MLD messages sent to multicast addresses in which the routers themselves have no interest.) The message format is shown in Figure 10–2.

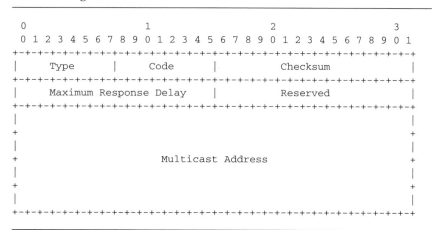

Figure 10–2: Multicast Listener Discovery (MLD) message format (from RFC 2710).

10.6   Summary

The use of scope, especially to differentiate between the local network and the global IPv6 Internet, is an important reason why multicast can be so much more useful in IPv6 networks than it has been in IPv4 networks. An integral part of IPv6 protocols, we will see how multicast performs important functions in ICMPv6 in Chapter 12, as well as related protocols such as Neighbor Discovery (Chapter 13), Mobile IPv6 (Chapter 17), and elsewhere.

Though related to multicast, IPv6 anycast addressing differs in important ways. As will become clear in the next chapter, anycast has the potential to improve IPv6 network efficiency.

11

IPv6 Anycast

One of the more surprising features of IPv6 was the inclusion of an entirely new communication model, anycast, to join the existing unicast and multicast models. Where unicast communication permits the transmission of packets to one specific node, and multicast permits transmission of the same packet to one or more nodes, anycast adds the ability to send a packet to any one—and only one—of a group of one or more destination nodes.

Although first specified in the IPv6 specification in 1995 (RFC 1884, "IP Version 6 Addressing Architecture"), the anycast concept had been around before then. However, despite the longevity of the idea, as of 2003 there has been very little experience with anycast and related applications.

Starting with an overview, including a brief look at the history of anycast, this chapter introduces the current state of the IPv6 anycast specification, followed by summary of some of the work that is currently being undertaken to make anycast work and to exploit anycast for useful applications.

11.1   Anycast Overview

An experimental specification for IPv4 anycasting was defined in RFC 1546, "Host Anycasting Service," in 1993. That document suggested that another address class could be carved out of the IPv4 address space for anycast addresses. In that way, nodes could identify anycast packets simply by looking at their destination addresses and treating them appropriately.

The motivation behind the RFC 1546 anycast experiment was to provide nodes with a simpler way to reach any of a group of interchangeable application servers. For example, rather than requiring a user to choose a particular FTP server from a list, anycast (it was suggested) would allow the user to simply specify the group of FTP servers, any of which would be satisfactory.

Although an interesting idea, RFC 1546 anycast never gained much traction, and it is unlikely that any networks currently support it (if any ever did). However the use of a single unicast address by two or more nodes is considered a type of *pseudo-anycast*, such as when multiple nodes are assigned the same address for the purpose of load balancing or for handling high-demand applications.

Pseudo-anycast can be achieved by distributing servers across the Internet and assigning a provider-independent prefix to the address they all share. Routers local to each of the servers can then advertise different routes to the same prefix, and routers delivering packets to the pseudo-anycast address can then choose the most appropriate route—the "nearest" route, usually.

There are significant differences between IPv6 anycast and pseudo-anycast, including a difference in the problem each tries to solve. Pseudo-anycast was devised as a way to distribute high-demand servers around the global Internet in order to serve DNS data or HTTP content more efficiently using BGP. IPv6 anycast was devised to be a more general solution to reaching any one of a group of servers that exist on the site or even the link, a well as (perhaps) across the global Internet.

11.2   Anycast Motivations

To a certain extent, the problem of choosing the nearest server (described as the motivation for RFC 1546 anycast) has been solved by using pseudo-anycast to distribute servers for load-balancing and responding to high-demand global applications. That did not end the interest in defining an anycast service in IPv6, but it also took away one of the more obvious problems to which anycast offered a potential solution. RFC 2373 states the following.

> One expected use of anycast addresses is to identify the set of routers belonging to an organization providing Internet service. Such addresses could be used as intermediate addresses in an IPv6 Routing Header, to cause a packet to be delivered via a particular service provider or sequence of service providers.
>
> Some other possible uses are to identify the set of routers attached to a particular subnet, or the set of routers providing entry into a particular routing domain.

These functions might be similar to those provided by multicast (see Chapter 10) groups, but there is no reason why anycast could not allow individual nodes to send packets to the nearest gateway or DNS server.

Another suggested use for anycast is cited in RFC 2526, "Reserved IPv6 Subnet Anycast Addresses."

> [A]n anycast address may be used in a source route to force routing through a specific Internet service provider, without limiting routing to a single specific router providing access to that ISP.

Whether or not anycast-based solutions are sufficiently compelling to motivate their deployment for these purposes has yet to be seen.

11.3   Anycast Architectural Issues

IPv6 nodes can differentiate multicast addresses from unicast addresses, and as a result they are able to take certain actions that don't make sense or are not permitted, like not attempting to open a TCP connection with a multicast address. Anycast addresses, when they are indistinguishable from unicast addresses, provide the benefit of transparency to nodes attempting to open communications with anycast nodes—but they also bear the burden of having to deal with the statelessness of the IPv6 (or IPv4) protocol.

When a node sends an IPv6 packet to an anycast address, the packet will be delivered to the nearest node configured to respond to that address. When a node sends 10 or 100 or 1000 packets to an anycast address during an exchange of stateful higher-layer protocols (like TCP), there is always the possibility that more than one node configured to respond to that anycast address will respond. For example, if one anycast node becomes congested, then another anycast node may be temporarily "nearer"; the same goes for congestion over intermediate routes between the requesting node and the anycast nodes.

11.3.1   IPv4 Anycast Issues

The authors of RFC 1546 concluded that raw IPv4 anycasting should be used only by applications that were themselves stateless and sending packets containing UDP messages. In that way, there would be no problem if one anycast node responded to an anycast packet from a client while another anycast node responded to the next request from the same client. For stateful interactions, the authors suggest adding a mechanism that guides all subsequent anycast packets to the first node that responds to a TCP request by allowing only anycast packets carrying a TCP SYN (synchronize) segment requesting that a connection be opened. Once an anycast node responds, it responds using its own unicast address.

The problem with this approach is that it only works when anycast addresses are identifiable as such. The result is that IPv6 anycast faces the same problems (having two different servers/routers responding to two or more sequential packets addressed to a single address) with the added limitation that the node sending those packets is not aware that there is anything special about the address to which it is sending.

11.3.2   IPv6 Anycast Issues

As with IPv4 anycast, IPv6 anycast is also hobbled by the nondeterministic delivery of packets: An anycast packet can be delivered to any of the nodes configured to respond to the anycast address. As a result, all anycast nodes must provide a uniform service, including the same kind of performance as well as the same service. This makes anycast especially suitable for load-balancing and other content delivery functions, but it also complicates matters by requiring that mechanisms be added to allow stateful higher-layer protocols to operate across a group of servers.

Because IPv6 anycast addresses are drawn from the unicast allocation, nodes sending packets to anycast can't tell when they are sending a single packet to a single, unique node (unicast) and when they are sending a single packet to any single node of a group (anycast). As a result, fragment reassembly, as well as any other end-to-end functions like encryption or authentication, becomes all but impossible.

11.3.3   IPSEC AND ANYCAST

As with fragmentation, IPsec requires that the same two nodes be end-points: Security Associations are based on data exchanged by the source and destination nodes, and (by definition) that precludes the ability of two or more anycast nodes to respond on each other's behalf. All the same reasons that make it possible for IPsec to secure packets sent from node to node also make it extremely difficult if not impossible to secure packets sent from one node to any one of a group of nodes.

11.3.4   ANYCAST ADDRESS ASSIGNMENT

As currently specified, only routers should be configured to respond to anycast addresses. Maintaining this restriction simplifies the problem of routing anycast packets, because no additional routing entries are required and there will already be routes existing to the networks served by those routers. When an anycast packet is transmitted, it is simply processed by intermediate routers and forwarded on an appropriate route based on the network prefix. Any router that has been configured to respond to a particular anycast address will do so when it receives a packet sent to that address.

Thus, because global anycast addresses are likely to be restricted, if not forbidden entirely, there is little or no need for exterior routes to be added for anycast, either.

Allowing regular hosts to respond to anycast addresses would complicate matters. Not only would explicit routes to those nodes have to be added to routers, but a new mechanism would have to be added to allow the hosts to advertise their willingness to accept anycast packets, while at the same time prevent them from acting as or being perceived as routers themselves.

Note: The set of nodes that responds to a single anycast address is referred to as an *anycast group*. This term helps emphasize the ways in which anycast and multicast are similar, even though anycast addresses can be indistinguishable from unicast.

11.4   IPv6 Anycast Specification

So far, only a few protocol specifications specifically address IPv6 anycast. Defined as part of the IPv6 addressing architecture in RFC 3513, anycast addresses are taken from the IPv6 unicast address space and are otherwise indistinguishable from IPv6 unicast addresses. These are the primary attributes and rules relating to anycast described in RFC 3513.

Configuration   A unicast address becomes an anycast address whenever it is assigned (on purpose) to more than one network interface. Nodes with such network interfaces must be configured to respond on that interface as an anycast node; the anycast node must be "aware" of its anycast interface.

Scope   All interfaces configured with anycast addresses will share some network prefix in common. For example, consider the case of a group of nodes each configured with the same anycast address within a typical /48 IPv6 network. If those nodes have interfaces configured with the anycast address located on all the network's subnets, the shared prefix will be the network's full /48 network address. That prefix (/48) identifies the network area within which the anycast address routes must be advertised, with a separate route advertised for each network interface across the entire /48 network.

In the event that the shared prefix is null—meaning there is no common identifiable routing prefix in common—the anycast address would be advertised across all routers in the global IPv6 Internet. In general, global anycast addresses would be a severe strain on the routing infrastructure of the Internet and, due to the difficulty of scaling, are expected to be available only on a very restricted basis, if at all.

Restricted use   Until there is more experience using anycast, RFC 3513 restricts the use of anycast addresses in two ways. First, only routers are permitted to have interfaces configured with anycast addresses;

```
|                        n bits                        |   128-n bits   |
+------------------------------------------------------+----------------+
|                    subnet prefix                     | 00000000000000 |
+------------------------------------------------------+----------------+
```

Figure 11–1: Subnet-Router anycast address format (from RFC 3513).

second, anycast addresses may not be used as the source address of a packet.

Required anycast address The Subnet-Router anycast address (see Figure 11–1) is required to allow nodes to send out packets that are to be delivered to one router on the subnet indicated in the destination address prefix. The format is shown in the Figure. Routers are required to be prepared to respond to anycasts sent to the Subnet-Router anycast address for any subnets to which they are linked.

11.5   Reserved IPv6 Anycast Addresses

Although specifications for IPv6 anycast, from the original IPv6 addressing architecture defined in RFC 1884 through to the current version in RFC 3513, define anycast addresses as being structurally identical to IPv6 unicast addresses, several specifications define specific, reserved, anycast addresses that have an explicit meaning and are not to be used for unicast transmission.

The first such address, the Subnet-Router anycast address, is defined in RFC 3513 itself. One potential use for anycast is suggested for the Subnet-Router address, which allows a node to directly interact with one router located on any specified subnet. When mobile nodes that are away from their home networks need to get back in touch with their mobility agent, they can use this anycast address to send packets directly to any router on their home network.

Another anycast address has been reserved for Mobile IPv6 Home-Agents; this address and a group of other addresses that are being reserved for use as anycast addresses are described in RFC 2526. When mobile IPv6 nodes are away from their home network, they may need to discover the addresses of their home network agents (the hosts that coordinate connectivity with the mobile nodes that are away from home). Another anycast address has been reserved for this specific use.

All mobile home agents are required to respond to the anycast address defined for *Mobile IPv6 Home-Agents* when received on any subnet to which they provide mobile services (see Chapter 17 for more about Mobile IP).

The basic format for these reserved anycast addresses when using the basic (EUI-64) IPv6 unicast format is shown in Figure 11–2, along with the more general format for addresses that don't require the EUI-64 format. The 7-bit anycast ID field identifies the type of anycast address in use; there are 128 different values for this field, of which all but the Mobile IPv6 Home-Agents address are reserved for future use (that is, they haven't yet been assigned).

Another reserved anycast prefix is introduced in RFC 3068, "An Anycast Prefix for 6to4 Relay Routers." The *6to4 anycast address* simplifies the configuration and use of 6to4 relay routers and sets aside another reserved prefix to indicate a special anycast address (6to4 routing is discussed in Chapter 20).

```
========================
EUI-64 anycast format:
========================
+------------------------------------+------------------+------------+
|                                    |                  |            |
|              64 bits               |     57 bits      |   7 bits   |
|                                    |                  |            |
+------------------------------------+------------------+------------+
|                                    |                  |            |
|           subnet prefix            | 1111110111...111 | anycast ID |
|                                    |                  |            |
+------------------------------------+------------------+------------+
                                     |                               |
                                     |  interface identifier field   |
                                     +-------------------------------+

========================
General anycast format:
========================
+------------------------------------+------------------+------------+
|                                    |                  |            |
|               n bits               |    121-n bits    |   7 bits   |
|                                    |                  |            |
+------------------------------------+------------------+------------+
|                                    |                  |            |
|           subnet prefix            | 1111111...111111 | anycast ID |
|                                    |                  |            |
+------------------------------------+------------------+------------+
                                     |                               |
                                     |  interface identifier field   |
                                     +-------------------------------+
```

Figure 11–2: Formats for EUI-64 and other reserved IPv6 anycast addresses (from RFC 2526).

11.6   *Making Anycast Work*

Anycast seems to be a fairly straightforward new service, until one recalls that while a node can send a packet to an anycast address, no packets whose source address is an anycast may be sent. Using anycast addresses that cannot be distinguished from unicast further complicates matters.

As with unicast and multicast, anycast addresses must be routed from source to destination; anycast adds these further restrictions.

- Packets must be delivered to one, and only one, of the nodes accepting packets at that anycast address.
- The node to which those packets are delivered must be the "closest" one to the sender.

Using an anycast address as the source of an IPv6 packet poses several difficulties, mostly derived from the need to differentiate "any one node of a group of nodes" from "one and only one specific node." While the destination node may be one of a number of interchangeable nodes, the source (the originator of the packet) can be only the specific node that sent the packet.

This section examines anycast implementation, from routing to determining the appropriate response to anycast packets to using anycast with stateful upper-layer protocols (such as TCP) and stateless upper-layer protocols (such as UDP).

11.6.1   ANYCAST ROUTING

The IPv6 specification suggests (strongly) that only routers be configured to respond to anycast addresses. This restriction simplifies the problem of anycast routing: The packet will be routed as if it is a normal unicast address, and as soon as the packet arrives at a router that is a member of the anycast group (that is, the "nearest" router), it will have been delivered.

No additional routing entries are required—the routers already advertise their willingness to accept packets, including anycast packets, sent to their own network prefix.

In fact, such a mechanism has been proposed. RFC 2710, "Multicast Listener Discovery (MLD) for IPv6," defines a mechanism used by nodes and routers to report their membership in a multicast group.[1] A work-in-progress extends the MLD mechanism to support reporting of anycast group membership. Routers would then be able to act on behalf of anycast nodes in the same way they behave for multicast (see Chapter 10 for more about multicast).

11.6.2   RESPONDING TO ANYCAST PACKETS

Using anycast as a source address results in obviously illogical scenarios such as sending a response or an error message to the wrong node.

More troublesome, perhaps, is that with nodes barred from using anycast addresses as the source of a packet, anycast servers responding to packets from clients must use their own unicast address that is associated with their anycast network interface. Thus, as shown in Figure 11–3, a client sending a packet to "Server X" (acutally one of a number of nodes responding to the anycast address associated with that server) would receive back a packet whose source was Server A. As a result, any upper-layer protocol (such as TCP) that uses source and destination IP addresses would require modification to support anycast.

The problem of how to differentiate anycast from unicast addresses is crucial to implementing anycast because of this problem. Various solutions to the problem of restricting anycast addresses from the IP source header field over the years are discussed in the next section.

In practice, anycast nodes use their unicast addresses when responding to anycast packets. This poses a security risk unless there is some way to authenticate the responding server as being a member of the anycast group.

11.6.3   IDENTIFYING UNICAST ADDRESSES

Although anycast and unicast addresses are by definition structurally indistinguishable, increasingly special anycast addresses are being reserved. In this way, anycast packets can be distinguished from unicast

---

[1]MLD performs the same function that the Internet Group Management Protocol (IGMP) performs for IPv4 and that was previously incorporated into the Internet Control Message Protocol for IPv6 (ICMPv6). MLD is discussed at greater length in Chapter 10, and ICMPv6 is covered in Chapter 12.

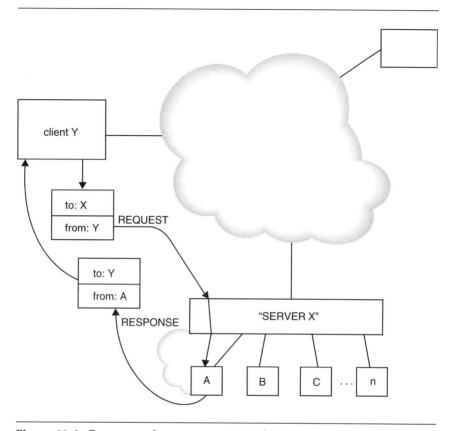

Figure 11–3: Responses from an anycast node arrive with a source address different from what the sender might expect.

and treated appropriately. Already described in this chapter are the anycast prefix for subnet routers, the set of reserved anycast addresses that includes the mobile IPv6 home agent anycast, and the 6to4 relay router anycast.

Other alternatives that have been suggested include the following.

- Modifying the anycast definition so that anycast addresses can be differentiated from unicast addresses. That way, nodes sending to those addresses will expect to receive a packet from an address different from the one they sent to.

- Extend DNS to include resource records that identify anycast addresses.
- Modify upper-layer transport protocols (such as TCP and SCTP) to accommodate unicast source addresses in reply to requests sent to anycast addresses.
- Add a mechanism that allows anycast nodes to respond to anycasts but transfer the session to a unicast interface address.
- Allow the client to continue using the anycast destination address, but use the IPv6 Routing header to specify the address of the server that initially responded.

So far the most manageable solution is to reserve anycast addresses and thereby identify them. It is possible that other protocols such as TCP, SCTP, or DNS will be extended (that is, have new options defined) to enable anycast, but that approach has not yet been specified in any RFC.

11.6.4 THE FUTURE OF ANYCAST

As of 2003, use of IPv6 anycast is limited not just by the difficulty of applying it to stateful upper-layer protocols, but also by a relative lack of infrastructure for deploying anycast applications—and a shortage of applications. A number of proposals have been drafted by individuals as well as IETF working groups to help improve the situation.

Here are some suggestions for improving the way anycast is implemented.

Anycast binding   In their draft "IPv6 Anycast Binding Using Return Routability," Brian Haberman and Eric Nordmark, two long-time contributors to the development of IPv6 and related protocols, proposed using the Mobile IPv6 Return Routability and Binding Update mechanism to allow TCP/SCTP and stateful protocols using UDP to map a unicast address from the anycast address to which a node is sending.

Anycast Address Resolving Protocol   Another approach was outlined in the draft "A Protocol for Anycast Address Resolving," in which an Anycast Address Resolving Protocol (AARP) is defined to permit a unicast address to be mapped to an anycast address prior to beginning the communication. The goal of the protocol—to permit the use of anycast addresses without modifying any existing protocols—is accomplished by having nodes begin all Internet communications with an ICMPv6 probe to the destination address. The sender waits for a response, by which it determines the actual unicast address of the node responding.

Although this would permit nodes to identify themselves as anycast group members, it would likely open up vulnerabilities to denial of service and man-in-the-middle attacks by making it easier for a hostile node to misrepresent itself as a legitimate member of an anycast group.

Furthermore, this approach would also tend to minimize the benefits of using anycast in the first place, since it immediately shifts anycast transmissions to a single unicast address.

Adapting multicast mechanisms to anycast A number of proposals have been made to adapt mechanisms originally designed for multicast for use with anycast. Doing so leverages extensive experience with multicast for use with the less familiar anycast. The difference between multicast and anycast lies mainly in that anycast packets need only be delivered to one node of a group, whereas multicast packets need to be delivered to all members of a group. *Protocol Independent Multicast-Sparse Mode* (*PIM-SM*) mechanisms are readily adapted for use with anycast.

In some ways more important than infrastructure, useful applications help drive demand for support of any new protocol. These are some other works-in-progress that define ways to use anycast.

Anycast and DNS Masataka Ohta, of the Graduate School of Information Science and Engineering of the Tokyo Institute of Technology and working with the IETF working group on DNS operation, proposed using anycast (though not specifically IPv6 anycast) as a solution to reducing the demand on root DNS servers and allowing the closest DNS server to respond on behalf of the root servers for some requests.

Fault tolerance and load balancing Another work-in-progress, "Fault Tolerance and Load Balance Services using IPv6 Anycast," proposes an algorithm by which an anycast client node can maintain communications with an anycast group without interruption by network or system problems. Interestingly, the author, long-time IPv6 contributor and Intel employee Ettikan Kandasamy Karupiah, notes that the application of this algorithm presupposes the existence of some mechanism for managing anycast group membership and that a mechanism is in place for mapping a unicast address to the closest member of the anycast group.

Further work with anycast infrastructure and applications will likely continue to grow, and the interested reader is urged to keep tabs on anycast by reading the latest Internet-Drafts and RFCs as they are published.

11.7   Summary

This chapter provided an overview to the history, use, and problems related to the use of IPv6 anycast. Although widespread use of anycast in the global Internet is unlikely ever to happen, chances are good that anycast will eventually become a useful mechanism within organizations and service providers as support for it grows within IPv6. Fundamental to that kind of support is the need for network control and packet routing mechanisms, such as those used for unicast as well as multicast. The next chapter introduces IPv6 control messages and unicast routing.

12

IPv6 Internet Control Message Protocol (ICMPv6)

Most networking protocols require some channel for the exchange of network meta-data, and IPv6 is no exception. The Internet Control Message Protocol for IPv6 (ICMPv6) is built largely on ICMP as used with IPv4. Unlike ICMP for IPv4, ICMPv6 provides a more complete set of tools for the exchange of meta-information about the Internet layer among nodes. This chapter outlines how ICMPv6 works and how it is used.

12.1 A New Control Message Protocol

IP nodes need a special protocol to exchange messages that pertain to IP-related conditions. The Internet Control Message Protocol (ICMP) defines a set of messages and requests used to report error and informational conditions, as well as for use with diagnostic functions. ICMPv6 is based on ICMP but adds new messages to support IPv6. The specification for ICMPv6 was first published in 1995 in RFC 1885, "Internet Control Message Protocol (ICMPv6) for the Internet Protocol Version 6 (IPv6) Specification," and updated in 1998 with RFC 2463.

Originally, ICMPv6 incorporated IPv6 multicast group management functions provided in IPv4 by the Internet Group Management Protocol (IGMP), but these functions are now performed by the Multicast Listener Discovery (MLD) mechanism discussed in Chapter 10. This chapter focuses on ICMPv6 message definitions, requests and responses, and how ICMPv6 is used.

ICMPv6 represents a fundamentally changed protocol from ICMP. Not only is MLD implemented completely as a subprotocol of ICMPv6, but so is Neighbor Discovery (Chapter 13); many of the other features made possible with IPv6, including stateless IPv6 addressing (Chapter 16) and Mobile IPv6 (Chapter 17), are implemented through the judicious use of ICMPv6.

12.1.1   ICMPv6

IPv6 nodes use ICMPv6 messages to report error conditions encountered when processing IPv6 packets or to solicit a response from a node to gather information. Network diagnostic functions such as ping and traceroute are based on the use of ICMP messages,[1] and other functions such as *Path MTU Discovery* and *Neighbor Discovery* are also based on ICMP. Although not an explicit part of the ICMPv6 specification, these functions can operate only with ICMPv6 and are discussed later.

ICMP is an integral part of IP insofar as it provides a channel for nodes to communicate about problems, but ICMP messages are encapsulated within IP packets, and ICMPv6 messages are identified in the IPv6 Next Header field by the value 58.[2]

The format for ICMPv6 messages is shown in Figure 12–1.

---

[1] Ping uses the ECHO and ECHO REPLY messages to determine whether a node is responding on a particular IP address; traceroute depends on manipulating the Time to Live value of a stream of packets to determine the path taken by those packets from source to destination.

[2] In contrast, ICMP for IPv4 is identified by the value 1.

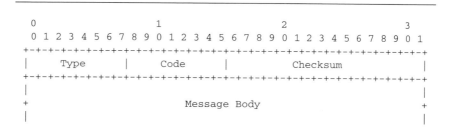

```
0                   1                   2                   3
0 1 2 3 4 5 6 7 8 9 0 1 2 3 4 5 6 7 8 9 0 1 2 3 4 5 6 7 8 9 0 1
+-+-+-+-+-+-+-+-+-+-+-+-+-+-+-+-+-+-+-+-+-+-+-+-+-+-+-+-+-+-+-+-+
|     Type      |     Code      |           Checksum            |
+-+-+-+-+-+-+-+-+-+-+-+-+-+-+-+-+-+-+-+-+-+-+-+-+-+-+-+-+-+-+-+-+
|                                                               |
+                        Message Body                           +
|                                                               |
```

Figure 12–1: ICMPv6 message format (from RFC 2463).

There are only three required ICMPv6 message header fields.

Type   This 8-bit value indicates the specific type of ICMPv6 message being carried. ICMPv6 allows two categories of message type, identified by the value of the high-order bit of the value. A 0 indicates an *error message* (all values from 0 to 127), and a 1 indicates an *informational message* (all values from 128 to 255). Specific message types and their uses are discussed in the next section.

Code   The meaning of this 8-bit value varies depending on the message type and can be used to fine-tune message meanings.

Checksum   This 16-bit field is used to detect corruption of the message. As defined in RFC 2463, "The checksum is the 16-bit one's complement of the one's complement sum of the entire ICMPv6 message starting with the ICMPv6 message type field, prepended with a 'pseudo-header' of IPv6 header fields, as specified in (RFC 2460, section 8.1). The Next Header value used in the pseudo-header is 58." The checksum field itself is set to 0 when calculating the checksum.

The *message body* contains whatever data is appropriate for the message type being used, which may include additional protocol parameters or parts of packets that caused the problem being reported by the message.

12.1.2 INTERNET CONTROL MESSAGES

In general, ICMP messages are generated as a result of some error condition.[3] For example, if a router is unable to process an IP packet, it might

---

[3] They can also be generated to solicit information about a link.

send an ICMP message back to the sender. The sending node could then remedy the error condition being reported. For example, if a router is unable to process an IP packet because it is too large to be sent out on a network link, the router generates an ICMP error message indicating that the packet is too large. The source host, on receiving this message, can use it to determine a more appropriate packet size and resend the data in a series of new IP packets.

The messages defined for ICMPv6 as of 2003 are listed in Table 12–1, with a reference to the document in which each is described. RFC 2463 defines six types of ICMPv6 messages.

Destination Unreachable   A Destination Unreachable message should be generated by a router or by the IPv6 layer in the originating node in response to a packet that cannot be delivered to its destination

Type	Name	Reference
1	Destination Unreachable	[RFC2463]
2	Packet Too Big	[RFC2463]
3	Time Exceeded	[RFC2463]
4	Parameter Problem	[RFC2463]
128	Echo Request	[RFC2463]
129	Echo Reply	[RFC2463]
130	Multicast Listener Query	[RFC2710]
131	Multicast Listener Report	[RFC2710]
132	Multicast Listener Done	[RFC2710]
133	Router Solicitation	[RFC2461]
134	Router Advertisement	[RFC2461]
135	Neighbor Solicitation	[RFC2461]
136	Neighbor Advertisement	[RFC2461]
137	Redirect Message	[RFC2461]
138	Router Renumbering	[RFC2894]
139	ICMP Node Information Query	[RFC2894]
140	ICMP Node Information Response	[RFC2894]
141	Inverse Neighbor Discovery Solicitation Message	[RFC3122]
142	Inverse Neighbor Discovery Advertisement Message	[RFC3122]

Table 12–1: Valid ICMPv6 message types (from IANA).

address for reasons other than congestion. (An ICMPv6 message must not be generated if a packet is dropped due to congestion.)

Packet Too Big A Packet Too Big must be sent by a router in response to a packet that it cannot forward because the packet is larger than the MTU of the outgoing link. The information in this message is used as part of the Path MTU Discovery process.

Time Exceeded If a router receives a packet with a Hop Limit of zero, or a router decrements a packet's Hop Limit to zero, it must discard the packet and send an ICMPv6 Time Exceeded message with Code 0 to the source of the packet. This indicates either a routing loop or too small an initial Hop Limit value.

Parameter Problem If an IPv6 node processing a packet finds a problem with a field in the IPv6 header or extension headers such that it cannot complete processing the packet, it must discard the packet and should send an ICMPv6 Parameter Problem message to the packet's source, indicating the type and location of the problem.

Echo Request Every node must implement an ICMPv6 Echo responder function that receives Echo Requests and sends corresponding Echo Replies. A node should also implement an application-layer interface for sending Echo Requests and receiving Echo Replies, for diagnostic purposes.

Echo Reply Every node must implement an ICMPv6 Echo responder function that receives Echo Requests and sends corresponding Echo Replies. A node should also implement an application-layer interface for sending Echo Requests and receiving Echo Replies, for diagnostic purposes.

12.2 ICMPv6 Messages

All ICMPv6 messages must be processed in much the same way as IPv4-based ICMP messages, and in this section we examine the six basic ICMPv6 messages defined in RFC 2463. It should be noted that ICMPv6 error messages should never be generated when a router or link is congested because doing so could only make things worse (by tying up

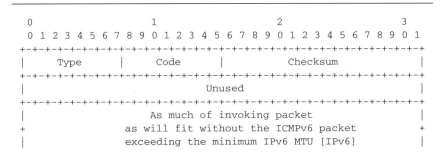

Figure 12–2: ICMPv6 Destination Unreachable Message format (from RFC 2463).

additional router resources). Other mechanisms, typically at the transport or application layers, are available for detecting and remediating network congestion.

Destination Unreachable Message   When a router receives a packet that it cannot deliver, it should generate a Destination Unreachable Message. The format for this message is shown in Figure 12–2 (from RFC 2463). This message is identified by the value 1 in the Type field.

The value in the Code field indicates the reason the destination was unreachable, with five values defined, each of them indicating a different condition.

0   *No route to destination.* This message occurs when a router does not have a route defined for the destination address of the IP packet. This message can only be generated by a router without a default route. The default route is used to route packets being sent to networks that have not been explicitly defined in the router's routing table.

1   *Communication with destination administratively prohibited.* This message may be generated by a packet-filtering firewall when a prohibited type of traffic is sent to a host inside a firewall.

2   *Not currently assigned.*

3   *Address unreachable.* This code signifies that there is some other problem with delivering the packet, perhaps with resolving the destination address into a link layer (network) address or reaching the destination at the link layer on the destination network.

4 *Port unreachable.* This code is generated by the destination node when an upper-layer protocol (e.g., DP) is not listening for traffic on the packet's destination port but only if the transport protocol doesn't have some other mechanism for notifying the source of this problem.

The unused section of the message is padded out with zeros so that the rest of the message begins on an eight-octet boundary.

12.2.1 PACKET TOO BIG

Routers are required to send a Packet Too Big message (identified by type value 2) whenever they receive a packet that cannot be forwarded because it is larger than the MTU of the link onto which it should be forwarded. The message format is similar to that of the Destination Unreachable message, except that the second four octets of the header contain the maximum transmission unit (MTU) of the link for which the packet is too large.

12.2.2 TIME EXCEEDED

Two distinct types of Time Exceeded message (Type value 3) are defined for ICMPv6. The first (defined by Code value 0) is for packets that have been bouncing around the network for too long; the second (defined by Code value 1) is for packets that have exceeded their fragment reassembly time.

Stale packets are purged from the network when their hop limit is exceeded. Routers processing inbound packets whose hop limit field contains a 1 (meaning they've just completed their last permitted hop) or 0 (meaning the packet has been mistakenly forwarded despite having timed out) must drop the packet and generate a Time Exceeded message.

Time Exceeded messages generally indicate either that the default hop limit count is set too low for the network or that there is a routing loop causing the packet to bounce from router to router without arriving at its destination address.

This message is useful for building the *traceroute* function. This function allows a node to identify all routers along the path that a packet takes between the source and the destination. It works like this: First, a packet is sent to the destination with a hop limit of one. The first router it reaches will decrement the hop limit and respond with a Time Exceeded message, and the source node will have identified the first router in the path. The source resends the packet with a hop limit of two, and if the packet must pass through a second router, that router will decrement the hop limit to zero and generate another Time Exceeded message. This continues until the packet eventually reaches its destination; in the meantime, the source node has received a Time Exceeded message from each intermediate router.

12.2.3 PARAMETER PROBLEM

When there is a problem with some part of the IPv6 header or extension headers that keeps a router from completing the processing of the packet, the router must discard the packet. It is recommended that the router implementation should generate an ICMP parameter problem message that indicates the type of problem (bad header field, unrecognized next header type, or unrecognized IPv6 option), with a pointer value that indicates at which byte of the original packet the error condition was encountered.

12.2.4 ICMPV6 ECHO FUNCTION

ICMPv6 includes a function that is not related to error conditions. Two types of messages, the Echo Request and Echo Reply, are required for all IPv6 nodes. The Echo Request message can be sent to any valid IPv6 address and can include an echo request identifier, a sequence number, and some data. The Echo Request identifier and sequence may be used to differentiate replies to different requests, although both are optional. The data is also optional and can be used for diagnostic purposes.

When an IPv6 node receives an Echo Request message, it is required to respond by sending an Echo Reply message. The reply must contain the same request identifier, sequence number, and data as were contained in the original request message.

The ICMP Echo Request/Reply message pair is the basis of the "ping" function. Ping is an important diagnostic function because it provides a method of determining whether a particular host is connected to the same network as some other host.

12.3   Fragmentation and Path MTU

The original IPv4 specification allows nodes to *fragment* packets when a packet arriving on one interface is too large to be transmitted as a single protocol data unit (PDU) on the outgoing interfaces. Figure 12–3 shows an example of where a router accepts packets from a network where the maximum transmission unit (MTU) is 1500 octets but has to forward those packets across a network with an MTU of 576 octets.

The router in this example could notify the sending node that its MTU is too small to handle the large packets, but doing so means the router might have to devote significant resources to notifying nodes all over about the situation; further, the situation might be transient, in which case it would have to notify nodes when the MTU goes back to normal. To avoid sending messages to nodes all over the Internet, it could discard oversized packets quietly (e.g., no messages back to the sender), or it could break the packets up itself to be rebuilt on delivery.

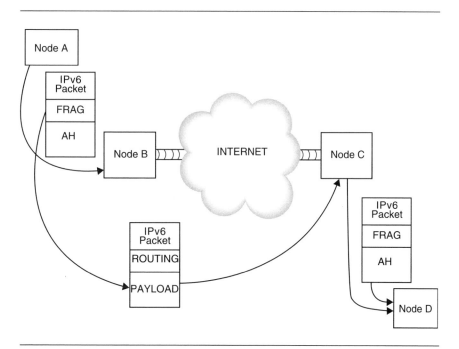

Figure 12–3: IPv4 packet fragmentation.

The process of determining a path MTU—to determine the largest packet that can be carried intact from one node to another—is defined for IPv4 in RFC 1191, "Path MTU Discovery."

12.3.1   FRAGMENTATION AND PATH MTU DISCOVERY

Fragmentation in IPv6 is permitted only between the originating node and the destination; this simplifies the header and reduces overhead for routing. IPv6 nodes may, however, do end-to-end fragmentation if necessary, using the fragmentation option (see Chapter 9), but intermediate routers (or other nodes) are not permitted to break up packets that are too large for their link.

Hop-by-hop fragmentation is considered harmful. For one thing, it can generate more fragments than end-to-end fragmentation. For another, the loss of a single fragment means all the fragments must be retransmitted. IPv6 does support fragmentation through an extension header, though, as described next. Understanding how IPv4 fragmentation works will clarify why it has been changed in IPv6.

IPv4 packet fragmentation happens when the unfragmented packet is too long to traverse a network link along its route from source to destination. To illustrate, a source node may create a packet of 1500 bytes and send it to a remote destination somewhere on the Internet. The packet is transmitted on the source's link layer network to the default router for that node. This router forwards the packet on its link to the Internet, which may be a point-to-point connection with an Internet service provider. Somewhere inside the Internet cloud, or somewhere closer to the destination node, there may be a network link that cannot handle data in chunks that large. In that case, the router using that network link would have to break up the 1500-byte datagram into fragments no larger than the next network's MTU maximum transmission unit (MTU) size. So if the next link could handle packets no larger than, say, 1280 bytes, the router would break up the original packet into two pieces. The first would be 1256 bytes long, leaving 24 bytes for the IPv4 header. The second fragment would be the length of the remainder of the original packet, 244 bytes, plus another 20 bytes for another IPv4 header (plus four octets for padding out the packet to end on an eight-octet word boundary).

Fragmentation in IPv4 is done as needed by intermediate routers along a packet's path. The fragmenting router modifies the packet's header as necessary to include the original packet's datagram identification, as well as setting the fragmentation flags and the fragment offset field appropriately. When the resulting fragmented packets are received by the destination node, that system must reassemble the packets using the fragmentation data in the IPv4 headers of each packet fragment.

Using fragmentation, it is possible to interoperate between nodes that exist on very different types of networks, with any kind of network in between. The source node doesn't need to know anything about the destination node's network, nor does it need to know anything about the networks in between. This has always been considered a relatively good thing, since not requiring nodes or routers to store information or maps of the entire Internet helps make the Internet very scalable. On the other hand, it also poses a performance problem for routers: Fragmenting IP packets costs processing power and time along the route as well as at the destination. There is the overhead of keeping track of IP datagram identifiers, calculating fragment offsets, and actually dividing up a packet into fragments and then reassembling it at its destination.

The problem is, although in any given route the source may know the link MTU, it cannot know ahead of time the *path MTU.* The path MTU, of course, is the size of the largest packet that can be carried over any network along the route between the source and the destination without having to fragment it.

There are, however, two ways to reduce or eliminate the need for fragmentation. The first, which is available in IPv4, is to use a method called *path MTU discovery.* With this approach, a router can send out a packet the size of the link MTU to the destination for the router. If the packet reaches a link at which it must be fragmented, the fragmenting router sends back an ICMP message indicating how much smaller the fragmenting router's link MTU is. This process can be repeated until the router can determine the path MTU.

The other way to cut down on the need for fragmentation is to require that all links supporting IP be able to handle packets of some reasonable minimum size. In other words, if a link MTU could be anything from 20 bytes on up, then all nodes would have to be prepared to do a considerable amount of fragmenting of packets. On the other hand, if you could come up with some reasonable size that all network links could accommodate and set that as the absolute minimum permitted packet size, you could eliminate fragmentation.

12.3.2   IPv6 Path MTU Discovery

IPv6, in fact, uses both these approaches. In the original RFC, the IPv6 specification calls for every link to support an MTU of at least 576 bytes. The resulting payloads for these packets would then be 536 bytes, allowing 40 bytes for the IPv6 headers. Since RFC 1883 was published in 1995, compelling arguments have been made for a larger MTU. Christian Huitema reports (in "IPv6: The New Internet Protocol," 2nd ed., Prentice-Hall) that as of 1997, Steve Deering was campaigning for an MTU of 1500 bytes. By 1998, with publication of RFC 2460, the minimum MTU permitted for IPv6 was set at 1280 bytes.

In part to compensate for what may turn out to be a shorter MTU, the IPv6 specification also strongly recommends that all IPv6 nodes implement *path MTU discovery*. Described first in RFC 1191, "Path MTU Discovery," this mechanism uses the Don't Fragment bit in the fragment flags field to cause intermediate routers to return ICMP error messages indicating that the packet is too large.

The IPv6 version of path MTU discovery is described in RFC 1981, "Path MTU Discovery for IP version 6." This upgrade is largely based on the original RFC 1191 specification, but some changes have been made to make it work with IPv6. Most important, because IPv6 doesn't support fragmentation in its header, there is no Don't Fragment bit to set. The node doing the path MTU discovery simply transmits the largest packet permissible on its own network link to the destination. If an intermediate link cannot handle packets of that size, the router attempting to forward the path MTU discovery packet will return an ICMPv6 error message back to the source node. The source node will then send another, smaller, packet. The process is repeated until no ICMPv6 error messages are received, and the source node then can use the most recent MTU as the path MTU.

12.3.3   PMTU Implementation Issues

The path MTU between any two nodes on a network may vary depending on the routes available and the conditions on those routes at any given time. A path MTU calculated half an hour ago may have been significantly smaller or larger than the value as calculated now. Although the protocol can almost immediately precipitate a recalculation of the path MTU when it becomes smaller (the node sending a packet will receive an ICMPv6 "packet too big" message), there is no obvious way to detect a change that increases the path MTU.

To remedy the situation, RFC 1981 recommends that implementations cache PMTU values and have the values time out after some moderate amount of time (10 minutes is the duration suggested). At that point, the PMTU value can be recalculated.

In this way, packet size efficiency can be maximized. However, there are some situations in which the path MTU value will never change. For example, a node connecting to an FDDI network that is attached to the global Internet through a small MTU fixed serial link will never discover a path MTU greater than the MTU of the serial link. As a result, implementations should incorporate a mechanism for changing the maximum age of cached PMTU values that includes an option for never timing them out.

12.4   Other ICMPv6 Functions

As already noted, ICMPv6 provides a framework for other protocols to operate. The Multicast Listener Discovery (MLD) protocol uses ICMPv6 messages, as discussed in Chapter 10; likewise, ICMPv6 messages are used to perform the functions defined under the Neighbor Discovery (ND) protocol, to be discussed in the next chapter.

12.5   Summary

Although it resembles ICMP in many ways, ICMPv6 has been made more powerful than its predecessor at the same time it has been simplified. The judicious use of multicast, as defined for IPv6, and the elimination of IGMP as a separate protocol make ICMPv6 an even more important part of IPv6. Of particular note is the inclusion of the neighbor discovery protocol as part of ICMPv6.

13

IPv6 Neighbor Discovery

One area in which IPv4 networking is made more complicated is in locating servers, routers, configuration data, and generally in making it possible for nodes to determine what other nodes are nearby (on the same link) and what nodes are remote (off-link). *Neighbor Discovery (ND)* for IPv6 is defined in RFC 2461, "Neighbor Discovery for IPv6," and it provides an important tool that not only simplifies network administration and management but also enables a much greater degree of scaling in IPv6 network size.

This chapter compares how ND is specified and implemented in IPv4 and IPv6, followed by a discussion of some of the roles that ND fulfills for IPv6. The rest of the chapter outlines how ND works, with some example ND messages and protocol interactions.

13.1   The Neighbor Discovery Protocol

As noted in the abstract of RFC 2461, "IPv6 nodes on the same link use Neighbor Discovery to discover each other's presence, to determine each other's link layer addresses, to find routers and to maintain reachability information about the paths to active neighbors." Five types of ICMPv6 messages to be used in neighbor discovery are defined in RFC 2461, including a pair of messages for router solicitation and router advertisement, a pair for neighbor solicitation and advertisement, and a redirect message.

By defining neighbor discovery functions in terms of ICMPv6 messages, additional protocols (such as ARP) are unnecessary—and without a mechanism for doing broadcast (as in IPv4), those protocols would not work anyway. As a mandatory part of any IPv6 implementation, ICMPv6 offers an ideal transport for neighbor discovery messages.

ICMPv6 messages, particularly requests, are usually multicast, whereas responses may be unicast to the requesting node or multicast to the all-nodes multicast address group (equivalent, functionally, to the IPv4 concept of broadcast). Although the neighbor discovery requests may be multicast to the all-nodes group, they can also be restricted to subsets of the all-nodes group such as all-routers on the local link.

The messages defined in RFC 2461 for neighbor discovery are described in that specification as having the following functions.

Router Solicitation   When an interface becomes enabled, hosts may send out Router Solicitations that request routers to generate Router Advertisements immediately rather than at their next scheduled time.

Router Advertisement   Routers advertise their presence together with various link and Internet parameters either periodically or in response to a Router Solicitation message. Router Advertisements contain prefixes that are used for on-link determination and/or address configuration, a suggested hop limit value, and so forth.

Neighbor Solicitation   Sent by a node to determine the link layer address of a neighbor or to verify that a neighbor is still reachable via a cached link layer address. Neighbor Solicitations are also used for Duplicate Address Detection.

Neighbor Advertisement   A response to a Neighbor Solicitation message. A node may also send unsolicited Neighbor Advertisements to announce a link layer address change.

Redirect   Used by routers to inform hosts of a better first hop for a destination.

These five sets of messages solve quite an array of networking problems, as discussed next.

13.2   Solving Networking Problems

IP nodes on the same local link are neighbors on two separate and distinct networks: the local link network, and the Internet on which the nodes are distinguishable through their globally unique IP addresses. Under IPv4, the process of mapping an IP address to a local link layer address was straightforward, with ARP, but limited in scope.

The neighbor discovery protocol in IPv6 allows nodes on the same local links to map their IP addresses to their link layer addresses, but it also allows for the solution of more complicated problems, as described in RFC 2461.

Router Discovery   Hosts need a mechanism for locating a local router.

Prefix Discovery   Hosts need a mechanism for discovering the set of address prefixes that define which destinations are on-link for an attached link. Nodes use prefixes to distinguish destinations that reside on-link from those only reachable through a router.

Parameter Discovery   Hosts need a mechanism for discovering local link network parameters, such as the link MTU, or IP network parameters, such as the hop limit value, to place in outgoing packets.

Address Autoconfiguration   Hosts need a mechanism for configuring an IPv6 network interface address automatically.

Address Resolution   Hosts need a mechanism for determining a link layer address of a neighboring host, given only the destination's IP address. This function is performed by ARP in IPv4.

Next-hop Determination   When sending a packet, a host must determine where to send it. That decision is made based on the destination's IP address; hosts need a way to decide whether the packet should be sent to a router or directly to the destination. The packet is sent to a router if the destination is not local; otherwise, the packet is sent directly to its (local) destination.

Neighbor Unreachability Detection   Hosts need a mechanism by which they can determine that a neighbor is no longer reachable. For neighbors used as routers, alternate default routers can be tried. For both routers and hosts, address resolution can be performed again.

Duplicate Address Detection   Hosts need a mechanism by which they can verify that an address is not already in use by another host.

Redirect   Routers must have a mechanism by which they can notify a host that there is a better-positioned router to be used as the first-hop node to reach some particular destination.

In addition to these basic functions, IPv6 neighbor discovery can solve more complicated problems, as described in RFC 2461.

Link layer address change   A node that knows its link layer address has changed can multicast a few (unsolicited) Neighbor Advertisement packets to all nodes to quickly update cached link layer addresses that have become invalid. Note that the sending of unsolicited advertisements is a performance enhancement only (e.g., unreliable). The Neighbor Unreachability Detection algorithm ensures that all nodes will reliably discover the new address, although the delay may be somewhat longer.

Inbound load balancing   Nodes with replicated interfaces may want to load-balance the reception of incoming packets across multiple network interfaces on the same link. Such nodes have multiple link layer addresses assigned to the same interface. For example, a single network driver could represent multiple network interface cards as a single logical interface having multiple link layer addresses.

Load balancing   Handled by allowing routers to omit the source link layer address from Router Advertisement packets, thereby forcing neighbors to use Neighbor Solicitation messages to learn link layer addresses of routers. Returned Neighbor Advertisement messages can then contain link layer addresses that differ depending on who issued the solicitation.

Anycast addresses Anycast addresses identify one of a set of nodes providing an equivalent service, and multiple nodes on the same link may be configured to recognize the same anycast address. Neighbor Discovery handles anycasts by having nodes expect to receive multiple Neighbor Advertisements for the same target. All advertisements for anycast addresses are tagged as being nonoverride advertisements. This invokes specific rules to determine which of potentially multiple advertisements should be used.

Proxy advertisements A router willing to accept packets on behalf of a target address that is unable to respond to Neighbor Solicitations can issue nonoverride Neighbor Advertisements. There is currently no specified use of proxy, but proxy advertising could potentially be used to handle cases like mobile nodes that have moved off-link. However, it is not intended as a general mechanism to handle nodes that, for example, do not implement this protocol.

13.3   IPv6 Neighbor Discovery Compared with IPv4

Strictly speaking, there is no single, explicit neighbor discovery protocol defined for IPv4. A variety of protocols, including the Address Resolution Protocol (ARP) and parts of the Internet Control Message Protocol (ICMP) for IPv4, serve the function of mapping local link addresses to IP addresses of neighboring nodes.

For example, the ICMP Router Discovery protocol defined in RFC 1256, "ICMP Router Discovery Messages," specifies a mechanism by which IPv4 nodes may multicast (or broadcast) a request on their local link to discover local routers offering forwarding beyond the local link. IPv4 nodes with an IP address known to be local can map a local link network address by querying the local link using an ARP request.

Having supplied such wants with a pastiche of protocols, protocol extensions, and protocol modifications, IPv4 still lacks a standard mechanism for performing many basic functions. For example, no standard mechanism for detecting when a neighbor is *unreachable* has been defined for IPv4. Likewise, some reachability/unreachability functions can be accomplished under IPv4 only by eavesdropping on routing protocol messages exchanged by local routers.

As described in RFC 2461, Neighbor Discovery offers "a multitude of improvements" over the existing solutions in IPv4, including the following.

- Router Discovery is part of the base protocol set; there is no need for hosts to "snoop" the routing protocols.
- Router Advertisements carry link layer addresses; no additional packet exchange is needed to resolve the router's link layer address.
- Router Advertisements carry prefixes for a link; there is no need to have a separate mechanism to configure the "netmask."
- Router Advertisements enable Address Autoconfiguration.
- Routers can advertise an MTU for hosts to use on the link, ensuring that all nodes use the same MTU value on links lacking a well-defined MTU.
- Address Resolution multicasts are "spread" over 4 billion (2^{32}) multicast addresses, greatly reducing address resolution-related interrupts on nodes other than the target. Moreover, non-IPv6 machines should not be interrupted at all.
- Redirects contain the link layer address of the new first hop; separate address resolution is not needed upon receiving a redirect.
- Multiple prefixes can be associated with the same link. By default, hosts learn all on-link prefixes from Router Advertisements. However, routers may be configured to omit some or all prefixes from Router Advertisements. In such cases, hosts assume that destinations are off-link and send traffic to routers. A router can then issue redirects as appropriate.
- Unlike IPv4, the recipient of an IPv6 redirect assumes that the new next-hop is on-link. In IPv4, a host ignores redirects specifying a next-hop that is not on-link according to the link's network mask. The IPv6 redirect mechanism is expected to be useful on nonbroadcast and shared media links in which it is undesirable or not possible for nodes to know all prefixes for on-link destinations.
- Neighbor Unreachability Detection is part of the base significantly improving the robustness of packet delivery in the presence of failing routers, partially failing or partitioned links,

and nodes that change their link layer addresses. For instance, mobile nodes can move off-link without losing any connectivity due to stale ARP caches.

- Unlike ARP, Neighbor Discovery detects half-link failures (using Neighbor Unreachability Detection) and avoids sending traffic to neighbors with which two-way connectivity is absent.
- Unlike in IPv4 Router Discovery the Router Advertisement messages do not contain a preference field. The preference field is not needed to handle routers of different "stability"; the Neighbor Unreachability Detection will detect dead routers and switch to a working one.
- The use of link-local addresses to uniquely identify routers (for Router Advertisement and Redirect messages) makes it possible for hosts to maintain the router associations in the event of the site renumbering to use new global prefixes.
- By setting the Hop Limit equal to 255, Neighbor Discovery can be made immune to off-link senders that accidentally or intentionally send ND messages. In IPv4 off-link senders can send both ICMP Redirects and Router Advertisement messages.
- Placing address resolution at the ICMP layer makes the protocol more media-independent than ARP and makes it possible to use standard IP authentication and security mechanisms as appropriate.

As of mid-2003, the IANA reports 10 different ND option format types, as shown in Table 13–1. The complete specifications for each type of option can be found in the relevant protocol specifications.

- Types 1 through 5 are defined in RFC 2461.
- Type 6, the NBMA Shortcut Limit option, is defined in RFC 2491, "IPv6 over Non-Broadcast Multiple Access (NBMA) networks."
- Types 7 and 8 are defined in "Mobility Support in IPv6," a work-in-progress.
- Types 9 and 10 are defined in RFC 3122, "Extensions to IPv6 Neighbor Discovery for Inverse Discovery Specification."

Rather than reproduce the complete specifications for all these message types, the next section provides an example of a typical and representative ND message exchange: Router Solicitation.

IPv6 Neighbor Discovery Option Formats

The IPv6 Neighbor Discovery has options that are
identified by an option format type field [RFC 2461].

Type	Description
1	Source Link-layer Address
2	Target Link-layer Address
3	Prefix Information
4	Redirected Header
5	MTU
6	NBMA Shortcut Limit Option
7	Advertisement Interval
8	Home Agent Information
9	Source Address List
10	Target Address List

Table 13–1: IPv6 Neighbor Discovery option formats (from www.iana.org).

13.4   Router Solicitation

When a node joins a network, one of the first things it needs to do is discover the address of the nearest router. One way is to wait for the local router to advertise itself on the link, as it must do periodically. However, the Router Solicitation mechanism allows a node to request a router to transmit a Router Advertisement immediately. In this way, the node can record the IPv6 address and, optionally, the link layer address of the router. This transaction illustrates both the Router Solicitation message and the Router Advertisement message.

13.4.1   ROUTER SOLICITATION MESSAGE

The Router Solicitation message format is shown in Figure 13–1. This message is encapsulated in an IPv6 packet that is usually addressed to the all-routers multicast address with the link local or site local scope.

The Message Type field value is set to 133 to indicate the ICMPv6 message is of the Router Solicitation type; the Code value is set to 0 (the only valid value for Router Solicitation messages).

The only valid option defined in RFC 2461 is the *Source Link-layer Address* option; while not mandatory, the node sending the message should include this option with the sender's link layer address. If the sender uses the unspecified address (e.g., no link layer address is available), the sender must not use this option.

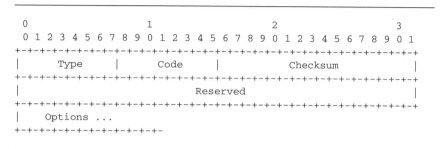

Figure 13–1: Router Solicitation message (from RFC 2461).

13.4.2 ROUTER ADVERTISEMENT MESSAGE

The Router Solicitation is multicast to all the routers in whatever scope was specified in the IPv6 destination address; all the routers in that scope are supposed to respond with their standard Router Advertisement message. Normally, routers transmit advertisements on a regular schedule (according to RFC 2461, the elapsed time between advertisements "MUST be no less than 4 seconds and no greater than 1800 seconds [30 minutes]").

The router will transmit this message once during the prescribed period addressed to the all-nodes multicast address, but if the message is being sent in response to a Router Solicitation message, the packet is addressed to the node making the request. The Router Advertisement message format is shown in Figure 13–2.

The message type is 134 (indicating Router Advertisement), and the only valid Code value is 0. The advertisement includes this other information.

Current Hop Limit   An 8-bit integer indicating the local default value for the Hop Count field in the IPv6 header. The value 0 indicates that the hop limit is unspecified for the router sending the message.

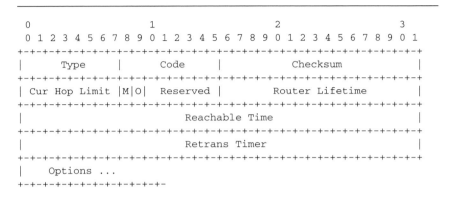

Figure 13–2: Router Advertisement message (from RFC 2461).

Managed Address Configuration Flag (M)   When this flag is set to 1, it indicates that nodes are supposed to use stateful IPv6 autoconfiguration (see Chapter 16) to assign an address to the interface in addition to any statelessly configured IPv6 addresses that have been automatically configured.

Other Stateful Configuration Flag (O)   When this flag is set to 1, it indicates that nodes are supposed to use stateful IPv6 autoconfiguration to configure nonaddress parameters for the interface.

Reserved   These 6 bits are unused and must be set to 0 by the sender and ignored by the recipient.

Router lifetime   This 16-bit integer indicates the number of seconds in the usable lifetime of the advertiser as a default router. The maximum value (2^{16}) is a bit over 18 hours, while a value of 0 indicates that the router is not a default router.

Reachable time   This 32-bit integer indicates the number of milliseconds that a node can assume a neighbor to still be reachable after a *reachability confirmation* has been received. This value must be no greater than 3,600,000 milliseconds (1 hour); it is used for the Neighbor Unreachability Detection algorithm used with Neighbor Discovery.

Retrans Timer   This 32-bit integer indicates the number of milliseconds between retransmitted Neighbor Solicitation messages. This value is used for Neighbor Unreachability Detection as well as for address resolution functions.

Options defined in RFC 2461 for the Router Advertisement message include the source link layer address, the MTU value, and prefix information (indicating which prefixes are local and which are not).

13.5   Summary

An ongoing challenge for IP networking has always been the need to define mechanisms to allow nodes to interoperate across local link networks that are fundamentally different. The use of ARP and its various different flavors on broadcast and nonbroadcast media has required the creation of a whole family of services on nonbroadcast networks.

With the creation of special ICMPv6 messages designed for neighbor discovery functions, IPv6 networking can be accomplished with significantly less interaction between link layer and Internet layer protocols. Not only are there more functions possible using Neighbor Discovery in IPv6, but the ones that have always been necessary for locating routers, neighbors, and configuration parameters are more easily accomplished.

Neighbor Discovery makes it possible for nodes to more easily determine which network prefixes should be considered local and which are not. When nodes send packets to any of the nonlocal prefixes, they must pass them along to a router for routing. As we'll see in the next chapter, IPv6 routing is very much like IPv4 routing—but with some twists.

14

IPv6 Routing

The primary difference between an ordinary host and a router is that the router is configured to accept packets intended for another destination and to forward those packets to what the router determines is the best next hop. The router usually also supports at least one routing protocol through which it can acquire current information about network routes. In this chapter, after an overview of IP routing in general, we'll introduce the changes necessary to support IPv6 routing.

14.1 IP Routing Fundamentals

The simplest of routers are those serving a single network with two interfaces: one for the local network and the other for sending all other traffic. These routers function as *gateways* for the local network. Local hosts recognize two types of destinations: those hosts that are on the local *logical IP subnet* (*LIS*) and that can be reached directly over the local link and those hosts that are not local (everywhere else). Hosts on this network

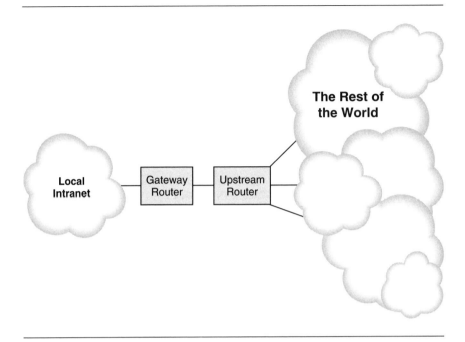

Figure 14–1: Simple local gateway router architecture.

are configured to deliver local packets directly, on their own, over the link layer, and all other packets are sent to the IP gateway system (the local router), which forwards them along its "other" interface.

The typical small office/home office (SOHO) network uses a simple gateway like this, as do almost all networks connected to the Internet via broadband services. The local router (or gateway) will typically be configured to accept inbound packets destined for the local network and to forward any packets it receives from within the network to its own upstream router. If the gateway is on a point-to-point link, as is frequently the case, the gateway does nothing more than pass along packets from the local network to the system on the other end of that link (see Figure 14–1).

14.1.1   ROUTED NETWORKS

As intranets become more complex with more than one internal LIS spanning multiple LANs, MANs, or WANs, internal routers become necessary.

These routers provide connectivity to hosts within the intranet as well as (perhaps) the rest of the global Internet. The number and type of routers, as well as the number of networks each router links, all depend on the intranet's design and organization's goals and requirements for that network. Figure 14–2 shows a simple multirouter intranet, in which internal routers must decide how best to forward packets not intended for the local network.

Using the example in Figure 14–2, it becomes clear that packets sent from a host on network A and destined for a host on network D would have to be sent to Router$_1$, which would then forward it to Router$_5$ on network E; from there the packet is forwarded to Router$_4$ on network D. Router$_4$ then forwards the packet directly to the destination host.

When that same packet is to be delivered but Router$_5$ is unavailable for some reason, Router$_1$ will have to forward the packet to another router that is capable of, ultimately, delivering the packet to network D. The only

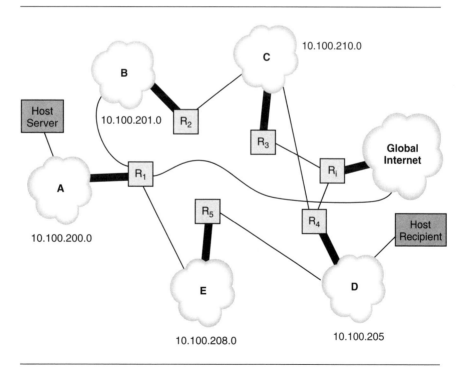

Figure 14–2: Increasingly complicated intranet routing domain.

other options open in that case are to forward the packet to the global Internet (not acceptable) or to Router$_2$ on network B. Router$_2$ forwards the packet to Router$_3$, which forwards the packet to Router$_4$, which delivers the packet to its destination. Router$_i$ is the Internet gateway, forwarding packets to and from the global Internet; Router$_1$ is a backup Internet gateway.

With five internal LISs, plus the global Internet, there are six different LISs to contend with; fully interconnecting them all so that all networks are reachable from each other in one hop requires 15 dedicated links. By permitting more than one hop between local LISs, full interconnectivity can be achieved with fewer links.

However, the routers need information—which of their own links are up and which down, what portions of the network the other routers can reach. The exchange and update of this information are the primary goals of Internet routing protocols; in support of this goal is the corollary need to avoid propagating false information or acting on faulty information, while at the same time optimizing performance (by minimizing the number of hops it takes from source to destination).

The routers in Figure 14–2 are *interior* routers because they route packets inside an AS or other *routing domain*; inside that domain, the LISs are separate *administrative domains* (ADs). An AD is comparable to an AS, except on a smaller scale. As we'll see, *exterior routing*, which occurs between routers linking different ASs through a backbone, requires a different approach to the exchange of information and determination of optimal routes.

14.1.2   INTERIOR AND EXTERIOR ROUTING PROTOCOLS

The two basic routing tasks are, first, making sure that all networks within Internets route traffic appropriately among themselves (interior routing) and second, making sure that all internetworks connected to a large Internet (such as the global Internet) are able to route reliably between each other (exterior routing). Simple routing strategies like default gateways and ICMP route advertising will be sufficient to move network traffic inside most intranets.

However, routing protocols do not define the routing process—they define the process by which routers exchange information about the network.

Routing table information must be kept current, and routers are constantly communicating with each other to announce their own connectivity.

Typically, hosts acquire routing information either as part of their static configuration or through the Dynamic Host Configuration Protocol (DHCP). The host uses ARP to acquire a physical address for all local Internet traffic, and everything else is passed to the default gateway router. In smaller networks, that router connects directly to the ISP's router, connected in turn to an Internet *backbone*, a network linking more than one AS. Routers on backbone networks must maintain far more comprehensive routing tables because they must route between and among all networks. They don't usually have a default gateway specified, and backbone routers are sometimes referred to as *nondefault* routers.

Exterior or backbone routing protocols must allow communicating routers to report frequent changes in conditions and connectivity, quickly and efficiently. An interior routing protocol enables routers within smaller Internets to report their own conditions and connectivity but generally support less complicated routing architectures. The interior routing protocol supported by a router is often referred to as its *Interior Gateway Protocol* (*IGP*), where "gateway" is used as a synonym for router; an exterior routing protocol is likewise called an *Exterior Gateway Protocol* (*EGP*).

14.1.3   ROUTING ALGORITHMS

The simplest formulation of a routing strategy is to opt for the *shortest-path* route whenever there is a choice. How to determine which is the shortest path presents the greater challenge. There are two dominant strategies for determining the shortest path for interior routing, each of which is implemented in its own protocol. The *distance-vector routing* algorithm[1] is described in RFC 1058, "Routing Information Protocol," which also defines the RIP routing protocol for IP networks. Another approach to interior routing is called Dijkstra's Algorithm, and it is also known as the *link state* or *open shortest path first* algorithm. Open Shortest Path First (OSPF) is also the name of the interior routing protocol defined in RFC 2328, "OSPF Version 2," which is also STD 54.

---

[1] This algorithm may also be identified as *Bellman-Ford* or other combinations of the names of the researchers who did the original work on it.

Together, RIP and OSPF represent the IGPs you are most likely to find on an Internet or intranet.

14.1.4 EXTERIOR GATEWAY PROTOCOLS

In today's global Internet, the most important exterior routing protocol is the Border Gateway Protocol (BGP), defined in RFC 1771 "A Border Gateway Protocol 4 (BGP-4)." Unlike interior routing, exterior routing is complicated by the need for backbone routers to connect many different autonomous systems; if those routers were to advertise route availability, packets might be forwarded almost at random to a router connected to almost any AS, whether or not the destination is actually within the AS.

Internet exterior routing protocols have evolved over the years to accommodate increasingly large and complex routing environments. An early such protocol, the Gateway to Gateway Protocol (GGP), was described in RFC 823, "The DARPA Internet Gateway," in 1982. GGP uses a distance-vector routing algorithm similar to that incorporated in RIP: Gateways boot up assuming that all their links are down and no networks are reachable, but as they test out their own links and receive routing updates from other gateways, they are able to build up their routing tables to reflect the current state of the Internet. RFC 823 has been assigned "Historic" status.

Also historic is the Exterior Gateway Protocol (EGP), formally specified in RFC 904, "Exterior Gateway Protocol Formal Specification," in 1984. GGP failed to address the issue of organizational Internets that could not be connected directly to a *core* or backbone router. Extra hops were often added when noncore routers would send traffic to their own local default routers instead of forwarding them to a more appropriate Internet router that might be closer to the destination. Figure 14–3 illustrates the problem.

The figure shows a noncore router that is connected to a backbone on which various core routers are available. All of the core routers are, in theory at least, equally capable of routing any packets from any other routers connected to the backbone. Node X wants to communicate with node Y; ideally, the noncore router sends packets directly to Core Router C, but that can only happen if there is a way for the core routers to advertise their routes directly to noncore routers. EGP provides such a mechanism, by which EGP routers, as they come online, attempt to acquire some other router to act as a *peer*; peers exchange routing information about which

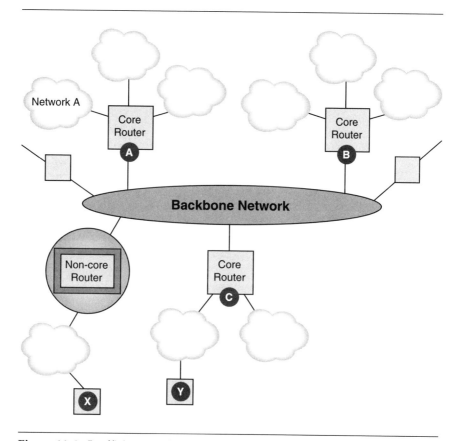

Figure 14–3: Inefficient routing across a backbone.

networks they can reach. One of EGP's flaws was that it provided no way to compare two or more advertised routes to the same destination.

14.1.5 ROUTING IN IPv6

The three most important routing protocols—RIP, OSPF, and BGP—are all used for routing in IPv6 networks with little or no modification, as will become clear by the end of this chapter. Routing in an IP network, whether IPv6 or IPv4, is accomplished using the same mechanisms; the biggest differences are the greater reliance on aggregation and the longer addresses. Once those two factors are accommodated by a routing protocol, IPv6 routing can be accommodated.

14.2   RIP and RIPng

Routing protocols can use two basic methods to measure connectivity across internetworks, as exemplified by the RIP and OSPF protocols. We begin with RIP, which uses the *distance-vector* approach: Routers share their routing tables and make additions and corrections based on reports from other routers.

The distance-vector algorithm takes its name from the way routers share their routing tables. A router expresses each route as a pair of values, the *vector* or destination network, and the *distance* from that router to that network (usually measured in hops, or the number of intermediate routers a packet would have to traverse to arrive at the destination network).

A router sends *advertisements* of its routes, containing all the routes (vectors) and distances to those routes, to neighboring routers. In this way, routes can be propagated across an Internet as can changes in available routes.

14.2.1   THE DISTANCE-VECTOR ALGORITHM

A distance-vector router begins with no knowledge of the Internet other than the networks to which it is directly connected. When it first boots, this router will have a routing table that consists of only as many entries as the router has network interfaces; it might look like this.

```
Destination      Distance      Route
10.0.0.0              0         direct
192.168.100.0         0         direct
```

The router then begins building up its routing table by listening to other router announcements that are broadcast on whatever network interfaces each router is connected to. In other words, routers advertise their routes to any neighboring router, where "neighboring" means connected to the same link.

For example, consider what happens when this router (let's call it router X) receives an announcement from router Y. The announcement lists routes as pairs of destination and distance values, like this.

```
Destination     Distance
192.168.200.0      0
10.5.0.0           0
10.10.0.0          3
10.0.0.0           4
192.168.100.0      4
```

Router X can now update its own routing table by comparing it to the distance-vector data supplied by router Y. The first two distance-vector pairs are not already in router X's routing table, so they can be added; the distance to those networks is 0 hops from router Y, which means they are only one hop from router X (router Y is a neighbor to router X, so it is only one hop away). Router X adds those networks to its routing table, with a distance value of 1.

The third pair is also for a network heretofore unknown to router X, but at a distance of 3 hops from router Y; router X adds this network to its routing table, with a distance value of 4.

The last two routes are the only networks that router X started out with in its routing table; after comparing the distance value, router X ignores those pairs. Router X's routing table now looks like this.

```
Destination      Distance     Route
------------------------------------------
10.0.0.0            0         direct
192.168.100.0       0         direct
192.168.200.0       1         router Y
10.5.0.0            1         router Y
10.10.0.0           4         router Y
```

Distance-vector routers may be thought of as street hawkers who adver-tise their routes by shouting them out to their neighbors; in the preceding example, router Y in effect yelled out, "I can reach 192.168.200.0 in zero hops; I can reach 10.5.0.0 in zero hops; I can reach 10.10.0.0 in three hops; I can reach 10.0.0.0 in four hops; I can reach 192.168.100.0 in four hops!"

Router X, listening to this advertisement, could be anthropomorphized to be thinking, "Y can reach 192.168.200.0 in zero hops, so now I can reach it in one hop; Y can reach 10.5.0.0 in zero hops, so now I can reach it in one hop; Y can reach 10.10.0.0 in three hops, so now I can reach it in four hops; Y can reach 10.0.0.0 in four hops, but I can reach it directly; Y can reach 192.168.100.0 in four hops, but I can reach it directly."

When Router X sends out its route advertisement, router Y will undoubtedly amend its own routes for 10.0.0.0 and 192.168.100.0, changing the distance from those networks from 4 to 1.

14.2.2 BASIC RIP

All systems on an internetwork can use RIP, but hosts generally are passive participants, listening to the routing information and updating their routing tables, whereas routers can both listen to routing broadcasts and transmit routing information. Routes can be propagated on request by a router that has just booted up, although routers typically broadcast their routes every 30 seconds.

Routes are broadcast as distance-vector pairs: a network and a hop count. Other routing protocols use the convention that a hop indicates a transmission to another router, so the hop count from a gateway to a network to which the gateway is connected directly would be 0. RIP counts that as one hop, so the lowest number of hops possible with RIP is one; with other protocols zero hops are possible.

The rules for RIP are fairly simple.

1. Active routers broadcast their routes every 30 seconds by default (although this may vary if the network administrator wishes).
2. All listening systems compare these broadcasts to their own routing tables and update their routing tables IF
   (1) there are routes to new networks previously unlisted,
   (2) there are better (e.g., shorter) routes to existing networks,
   or (3) a route is reported unreachable (it should be removed).
3. A route is kept until a better route is reported.

4. If there are two equivalent routes (same hop count), the first received goes into the routing table.
5. Routes are timed out if they are not updated after three minutes; in other words, a route must be assumed down if it is not being reported.
6. Routers broadcast route changes as they occur, without waiting (triggered updates).
7. A hop count of 16 is considered unreachable (which means RIP is unusable in any intranet wider than 15 hops).

RIP tends not to propagate corrections to routing tables very quickly, although errors are passed along more quickly. RIPs relatively low maximum hop count and the use of triggered updates help minimize some of the inherent problems with the distance-vector method of sharing routing information as described in the next section.

14.2.3 ROUTING WITH RIP

Implemented for IP before any actual standard specifications had been agreed upon, RIP is currently documented in RFC 2453, "RIP Version 2" (also published as STD 56). RIP's success has more to do with the way it was implemented—in the *routed* program that was a part of the original BSD/UNIX distributions—than with its technical merits.

RIP is a protocol implementation of distance-vector routing: RIP messages, encapsulated in UDP datagrams, are sent out with a header and at least one and no more than 25 *RIP entries*. The header has three fields (followed by 1 to 25 RIP entries).

Command   A one-octet field, whose value may currently contain either 1, indicating a request for all or part of a routing table; or 2, indicating a response, containing all or part of a router's routing table. An advertisement is a response, even though it may not have been sent in response to a particular request.

Version   RIP versions 1 and 2 are valid values for this one-octet field.

The RIP entry itself is 20 octets and consists of the *address family identifier*, or *AFI* field, a two-octet value indicating the type of address family (that is, Internet addresses or some other type of address), and a second two-octet field that, for RIPv1, is left set to 0. In RIPv2, this field is the *route tag* field, and it contains a tag that can differentiate internal routes (those pertaining to the local routing domain) from external routes (those imported from adjacent interior or exterior routing domains).

RIPv1 uses the next four octets for network destination IPv4 address, followed by eight octets set to 0, followed by a four-octet *metric* field containing a value from 0 through 15 indicating the "distance" of the route.

This is an important limitation, and it is imposed on RIP rather than imposed by RIP: The field is large enough at 32 bits to accommodate huge distances, but the protocol designers felt that RIP should not be used for networks that have a diameter greater than 15 hops. Routing changes take too long to propagate across a larger RIP network, and the volume of router network traffic also becomes a burden as the Internet grows larger.

The RIP headers are shown in Figure 14–4, from RFC 2453.

As is clear from the differences in the RIP entry formats for RIPv1 and RIPv2, RIPv2 can transmit considerably more information about each route, including a subnet mask value and a next hop value (to be used in concert with the route tag). RIPv2 incorporates an extension facility, and in addition to transmitting more routing information, it uses an algorithm for multicast routing and improved security.

```
RIP headers:

 0                   1                   2                   3
 0 1 2 3 4 5 6 7 8 9 0 1 2 3 4 5 6 7 8 9 0 1 2 3 4 5 6 7 8 9 0 1
+-+-+-+-+-+-+-+-+-+-+-+-+-+-+-+-+-+-+-+-+-+-+-+-+-+-+-+-+-+-+-+-+
|  command (1)  |  version (1)  |         must be zero (2)      |
+---------------+---------------+-------------------------------+
|                                                               |
~                         RIP Entry (20)                        ~
|                                                               |
+---------------+---------------+---------------+---------------+
```

Figure 14–4: RIP headers and RIPv1/v2 message formats.

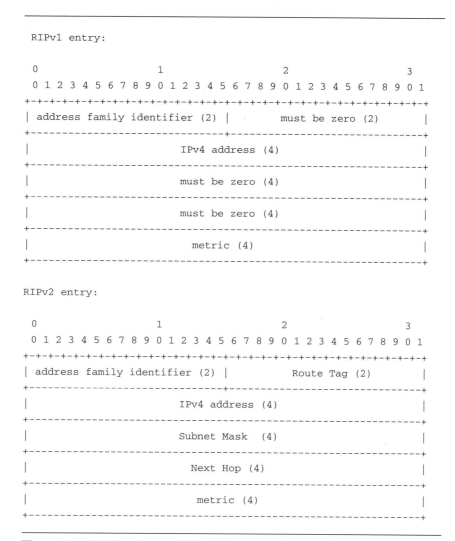

Figure 14–4: RIP headers and RIPv1/v2 message formats. *(Continued)*

RIP does not send subnet mask information in routing updates, so there is the potential for routing problems in internetworks that are highly sub-netted, particularly if more than one subnetworking scheme is being used in the internetwork. RIP-2 addresses many of the shortcomings of RIP and adds support for subnets—something that the original RIP lacks simply because subnets had yet to be accepted as part of the IP networks at the time that RIP was first designed.

Despite RIP's flaws, development of RIP-2 continued for several reasons. RIP is widely implemented on many different platforms, partly because it is an easy protocol to implement. On small intranets, RIP can be a very efficient routing protocol, making few demands on system overhead and bandwidth. Finally, RIP is relatively easy to configure and manage.

14.2.4   RIPng

RFC 2080, "RIPng for IPv6," defines the protocol for use in IPv6 networks. The RIPng routing table contains an entry for each reachable destination; each entry contains at least the following information (as defined in RFC 2080).

- The IPv6 prefix of the destination.
- A metric, which represents the total cost of getting a datagram from the router to that destination. This metric is the sum of the costs associated with the networks that would be traversed to get to the destination.
- The IPv6 address of the next router along the path to the destination (i.e., the next hop). If the destination is on one of the directly connected networks, this item is not needed.
- A flag to indicate that information about the route has changed recently. This will be referred to as the "route change flag."
- Various timers associated with the route, in particular related to when announcements should be sent out and when routes should be timed out.

Routers using RIPng send and receive UDP messages on UDP port 521; the RIPng message is formatted as shown in Figure 14–5.

RIPng Route Table Entries (RTEs) take the format shown in Figure 14–6. These entries carry routing information, specifically the route tag, prefix length, and routing metric for each routed IPv6 prefix. An RIPng message can carry as many RTEs as the local MTU permits. To determine the maximum number of RTEs for a particular MTU, the following steps may be taken.

1. Take the MTU size, in octets.
2. Subtract the IPv6 header size from that value.
3. Subtract the UDP header size from that value.
4. Subtract the RIPng header size from that value.

```
0                   1                   2                   3
0 1 2 3 4 5 6 7 8 9 0 1 2 3 4 5 6 7 8 9 0 1 2 3 4 5 6 7 8 9 0 1
+-+-+-+-+-+-+-+-+-+-+-+-+-+-+-+-+-+-+-+-+-+-+-+-+-+-+-+-+-+-+-+-+
| command (1)   | version (1)   |        must be zero (2)       |
+-+-+-+-+-+-+-+-+-+-+-+-+-+-+-+-+-+-+-+-+-+-+-+-+-+-+-+-+-+-+-+-+
|                                                               |
~                   Route Table Entry 1 (20)                    ~
|                                                               |
+-+-+-+-+-+-+-+-+-+-+-+-+-+-+-+-+-+-+-+-+-+-+-+-+-+-+-+-+-+-+-+-+
|                                                               |
~                            . . .                              ~
|                                                               |
+-+-+-+-+-+-+-+-+-+-+-+-+-+-+-+-+-+-+-+-+-+-+-+-+-+-+-+-+-+-+-+-+
|                                                               |
~                   Route Table Entry N (20)                    ~
|                                                               |
+-+-+-+-+-+-+-+-+-+-+-+-+-+-+-+-+-+-+-+-+-+-+-+-+-+-+-+-+-+-+-+-+
```

Figure 14–5: RIPng message format (from RFC 2080).

```
0                   1                   2                   3
0 1 2 3 4 5 6 7 8 9 0 1 2 3 4 5 6 7 8 9 0 1 2 3 4 5 6 7 8 9 0 1
+-+-+-+-+-+-+-+-+-+-+-+-+-+-+-+-+-+-+-+-+-+-+-+-+-+-+-+-+-+-+-+-+
|                                                               |
~                        IPv6 prefix (16)                       ~
|                                                               |
+---------------------------------------------------------------+
|          route tag (2)        | prefix len (1)|  metric (1)   |
+-+-+-+-+-+-+-+-+-+-+-+-+-+-+-+-+-+-+-+-+-+-+-+-+-+-+-+-+-+-+-+-+
```

Figure 14–6: RIPng Route Table Entry format (from RFC 2080).

5. Divide that result by the size of the RTE, and round down to nearest integer.

Thus, using a standard set of headers for IPv6 (40 octets), UDP (8 octets), and RIPng (4 octets) headers, we must subtract 52 octets from the local MTU. In the event that security headers are also used, the size of those headers would also be subtracted. The RTE length is 20 octets. To illustrate, for a link MTU of 1500 octets the calculation would be as follows.

$$1500 - 40 - 8 - 4 = 1448$$

$$1448/20 = 72.4$$

Thus, as many as 72 RTEs could be transmitted with each RIPng routing message.

The operation of the RIPng protocol is similar to that of RIP; there are two commands defined for the RIPng header.

Request (command type 1)   are used to ask routers to send some or all of their routing tables.

Response (command type 2)   are used to send all or part of a router's routing table. The message may be a response to a particular request, or it may be a regularly scheduled update sent out by the router.

The *route tag field* in the RIPng header is intended to be used to differentiate among routes that are internal to the RIPng routing domain and routes that are imported from other routing domains, including other internal routing domains as well as external routing protocols such as BGP.

Another important feature of RIPng is the ability to specify an IPv6 *next hop* address for any route table entry. This is a feature incorporated into RIP-2 in the form of a next hop field in the RTE, but including a next hop address in RIPng routing table entries would increase the size of the RTE from 20 octets to 36 octets and thus reduce the number of RTEs a router can forward on any given link. The solution is to define a special next hop RTE, shown in Figure 14–7.

The next hop address RTE indicates that all subsequent RTEs until the end of the RIPng message (or until another next hop address RTE is encountered) use the specified next hop address.

```
 0                   1                   2                   3
 0 1 2 3 4 5 6 7 8 9 0 1 2 3 4 5 6 7 8 9 0 1 2 3 4 5 6 7 8 9 0 1
+-+-+-+-+-+-+-+-+-+-+-+-+-+-+-+-+-+-+-+-+-+-+-+-+-+-+-+-+-+-+-+-+
|                                                               |
~                  IPv6 next hop address (16)                   ~
|                                                               |
+---------------------------------------------------------------+
|       must be zero (2)       |must be zero(1)|     0xFF        |
+-+-+-+-+-+-+-+-+-+-+-+-+-+-+-+-+-+-+-+-+-+-+-+-+-+-+-+-+-+-+-+-+
```

Figure 14–7: RIPng Next Hop address RTE format (from RFC 2080).

14.3   OSPF and OSPFng

Defined in RFC 2328 (STD 54) "OSPF Version 2," the current version of the Open Shortest Path First (OSPF) protocol uses the link state method to let routers create their own internetwork maps. Developed partly in response to some of the shortcomings of RIP, OSPF propagates routing information more quickly and stably than RIP, handles subnets appropriately, can balance loads where equivalent routes are available, supports type of service routing, and uses multicasting—all advantages over RIPv1.

Link state routing protocols, of which OSPF is an example, mandate that each router in an AS maintain a *link state database*. This database represents a map of the entire AS's topology, a map that is shared by all routers in the AS. Each router *floods* the AS with its own reachable neighbors and usable network interfaces—known as the router's *local state*. In short order, all routers in the AS can build their own map by aggregating the data in these advertisements and connecting the dots. If router A announces that it is directly connected to routers B, C, and D, on network 10.0.0.0, and router E on network 192.168.100.0, then any router in the AS can start assembling the map. Routers A, B, C, and D all have interfaces on 10.0.0.0; routers A and E have interfaces on 192.168.100.0.

Once the map is assembled, each router calculates the *shortest paths* to any given route by walking the map from its own location in the network. Figure 14–8 shows how a simple network map can be created. The link state approach to routing keeps the volume of information passed along to other routers to a minimum. Each router periodically checks on the status of neighboring routers, reporting which links are alive to all other participating routers. With this information, each router can then create its own map of the internetwork.

Link state routing addresses most of the problems posed by distance-vector protocols like RIP. OSPF adds features not available in RIP, and calculating routes based on the link state database is easier than mapping routes based on periodic RIP advertisements. Link state routing protocols even have less impact on the network because they generate a lower volume of data and because that data is passed to neighboring routers, which pass it on to other routers. By virtue of being a link state protocol, OSPF also makes changes propagate in a more orderly and reliable fashion. Since a link is either up or down, there is no reason for hosts to retain looped routes.

Network A connects to Networks B and C

Network B connects to Networks A and D

Network C connects to Networks A and D

Network D connects to Networks B and C

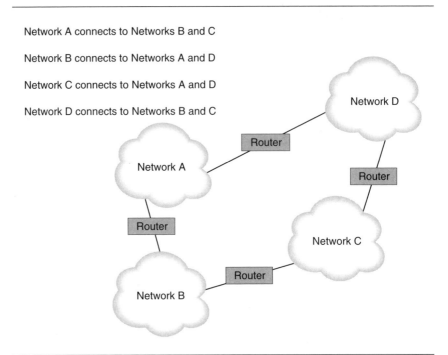

Figure 14–8: Routers using a link state routing protocol can deduce the structure of their AS.

OSPF allows routing decisions to be made explicitly in cases where there are equivalent alternate routes, as is required for applications such as load balancing. Under RIP, the first of any group of equivalent advertised routes is the route that will be recorded; OSPF allows network managers to distribute traffic across these equivalent routes.

Another OSPF feature that offers greater flexibility is the use of separate routes for different types of IP services. For example, it supports routing of FTP traffic over one route (perhaps a faster link, to give better overall file transfer performance) and Telnet over a different route (perhaps a link with lower latency or roundtrip time for better interactive response).

Support of subnet addressing is an important feature, as is the use of multi-casting to routers. OSPF also includes an authentication mechanism that prevents routers from accepting routing information from unauthenticated sources.

14.3.1 Differences from OSPF for IPv4

RFC 2740, "OSPF for IPv6," provides the specification for adapting OSPF to use with IPv6. For the most part, OSPF for IPv6 uses the same mechanisms used in OSPF for IPv4 (defined in RFC 2328, "OSPF Version 2"). As with any IP routing protocol, OSPF was modified for use with IPv6 to accommodate 128-bit (rather than 32-bit) addresses; other changes were required as well. These differences are spelled out in RFC 2740 and include the following.

Link versus subnet processing   Under IPv6, *link* means "a communication facility or medium over which nodes can communicate at the link layer" (RFC 2460). IPv4 routing protocols tend to operate on a per-subnet basis, even though a single link can comprise more than one, unrelated, subnet. OSPF for IPv6 routers connect to the link, not the subnet, so a single interface may suffice for more than one subnet.

Addressing semantics removed   For the most part, IPv6 addresses do not appear in OSPF protocol packets. This allows routers to use OSPF without reference to the network layer protocol (IPv4 or IPv6) in use. Rather than identifying neighboring routers by IP address, they are identified by a Router ID.

Flooding scope   OSPF for IPv6 adds three different scopes for floods, including a link-local scope, an area scope that is valid across links, and an autonomous system (AS) scope, valid across an entire AS.

Several other changes listed in RFC 2740 refer to modification in the way IPv6 works or to the modifications necessary to support IPv6 addresses, but otherwise the protocol works very similarly to OSPF for IPv4.

14.4   IPv6 and BGP

If routing across a single backbone can be complicated, imagine routing over multiple backbones—some of which overlap, and many of which offer routes to the same destination networks. Figure 14–9 illustrates some of the entities involved, as well as the problems.

RFC 2545, "Use of BGP-4 Multiprotocol Extensions for IPv6 Inter-Domain Routing," is a brief document because BGP (and path vector routing protocols in general) is "mostly independent of the particular Address Family for

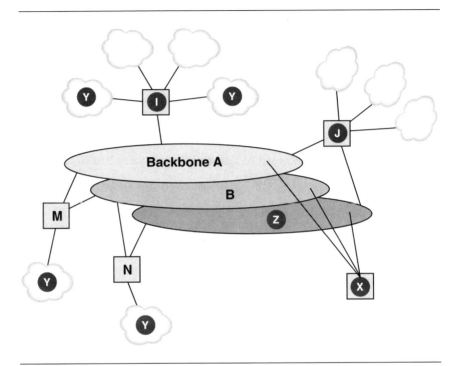

Figure 14–9: Modern Internet topology with multiple backbones.

which the protocol is being used." "Multiprotocol Extensions for BGP-4," RFC 2283, defines a pair of BGP attributes to be used in multiprotocol networks of all kinds; RFC 2545 discusses how IPv6 systems should use those attributes to exchange IPv6 routing information.

In this section we introduce BGP and then take a brief look at how IPv6 interdomain routing is enabled through the use of multiprotocol extensions for BGP.

14.4.1   BGP BASICS

By 1989, a version of today's core Internet routing protocol was published in RFC 1105, "A Border Gateway Protocol (BGP)," as an experimental specification; BGP version 4 is currently an Internet draft standard (one step away from full standard status) and specified in RFC 1771, "A Border

Gateway Protocol 4 (BGP-4)," and RFC 1772, "Application of the Border Gateway Protocol in the Internet."

Backbone Z is operated by a backbone service provider and offers a *transit* service, meaning that they carry packets to and from client networks, such as the Internet service providers I and J. Backbone Z is called a *transit AS*, because it is an autonomous system that moves packets from one AS to another. This implies that it has connections to at least two other ASs. Traffic from one AS to another is called *transit traffic*, to be distinguished from *local traffic*, or traffic that remains within a single AS.

In the modern Internet topology, a routing entity may also be a *multi-homed AS*, which differs from a transit AS because it does *not* carry transit traffic but it does carry local traffic. For example, network X in Figure 14–9 might represent a large organization that maintains connections to several backbone networks but that carries traffic only intended for network X.

Finally, a *stub AS* (like network Y in the figure) is one that can carry only local traffic; a stub router connects a single AS to one other AS.

EGP worked reasonably well, but was unable to differentiate between advertised routes: A router notified other routers only whether or not it could reach an AS. With no basis for comparing directness of routes offered by two or more routers, a border router could only guess at which router was better for a particular packet. Neither the link state nor the distance-vector routing approaches will work well for this kind of network. The complexity is too great for any single router to handle all of the routes between all of the networks.

BGP addresses the problem by extracting the inter-AS routing issues from the intra-AS routing issues. In a BGP-routed network, each AS is connected to the rest of the network by at least one each of two different entities.

BGP speaker Every AS in the network needs at least one BGP representative to exchange reachability information with speakers for the other ASs.

BGP gateway Every AS in the network needs to be connected to the network through at least one BGP gateway.

A gateway and a speaker may be deployed on the same system, but they may be deployed separately. And unlike RIP or OSPF routers, which exchange information about their own connectivity only, BGP routers exchange complete routes. With a RIP-like protocol, a router in network I (Figure 14–9) would have a routing table full of entries from every other router it can reach directly for all the other networks on backbone A. Network X would be reachable in two hops through networks M and J, even though network I can reach X in a single hop on its own.

By including not just the number of hops but also the specific path for each route, BGP routers can eliminate routing loops. Using speakers, separate from routers, to communicate reachability information allows BGP network administrators to implement routing and forwarding policies that affect how packets are routed to and from particular networks that would otherwise be indistinguishable.

The Border Gateway Protocol (BGP) replaced EGP as the current solution to Internet routing. Routers pass along distance-vector reachability information, but instead of just including networks and distances, BGP includes the actual route needed to reach each destination. This allows the router to lay down the distance-vector routes into an actual map of the Internet and eliminate the routing loops to which distance-vector protocols are prone.

14.4.2   BGP Multiprotocol Extensions

Originally, BGP was designed to exchange IPv4 routing information only. RFC 2283, "Multiprotocol Extensions for BGP-4," defined a type of data structure that permitted the use of any network layer protocol, not just IPv4. The key is to define a set of *network layer reachability information* (*NLRI*) that specifies the following.

Address Family Information   Which network layer protocol addresses are being indicated. This could be IPv4, IPv6, IPX, or some other network layer network addressing scheme.

Next Hop Information   The address of the appropriate next hop associated with the BGP route for which the NLRI is being attached.

Network Layer Reachability Information   One   or   more   network addresses associated with the attribute for which the NLRI is being used to advertise.

The *Multiprotocol Reachable NLRI* and *Multiprotocol Unreachable NLRI* attributes contain one or more records that contain these three pieces of information. BGP routers can use the Multiprotocol Reachable NLRI to advertise the availability of a route to a BGP peer, to advertise a network layer address for the router that should be used as the next hop for certain destinations, or to report on Subnetwork Points of Attachment (SNPAs are basically link layer addresses associated with the network layer addresses).

14.4.3 IPv6 Inter-Domain Routing with BGP

BGP routing in IPv6 networks is accomplished, basically, in the same way as in IPv4 (or any other type of) networks. Noting this, RFC 2545 addresses the use of scoped IPv6 addresses—for BGP, the most significant difference between IPv4 and IPv6—with BGP.

Because BGP defines the exchange of routing information across domains, the use of link-local addresses is sometimes necessary but also potentially damagined. As a result, RFC 2545 defines rules to govern the use of link-local addresses when advertising connectivity for IPv6 network addresses.

14.5 IPv6 Routing Issues

Even though interior and exterior routing protocols have been adapted for use in IPv6 networks, and even though there are decades of widespread experience with those protocols in their IPv4 incarnations, it would be presumptuous to suppose that IPv6 routing will hold no surprises. To the contrary, experts anticipate that there will be significant issues to be resolved with IPv6 routing; the unanticipated problems may be even greater.

Subnetting   Network managers must keep in mind that the smallest network allocation currently being made by RIRs is a /48 block. That means IPv6 networks will have 16 bits (or more) of subnet space to play around with. Currently, in IPv4 networks, that much subnet space is available only to networks with the equivalent of a Class A network address block. With the potential for as many as 65,000 or so subnets, network designers must be careful to build their networks and subnetworks in a way that will keep the size of the routing table manageably small. If subnets are assigned haphazardly, they may cause routing structures beyond the capacity of existing interior routing protocols to handle.

Hardware   Many departmental and branch level routers are quite capable of handling typical IPv4 routing needs, but the possibility of having very large routing tables (as just noted) could overwhelm the routers themselves as well as the interior routing protocols.

Multihoming   When an organization receives two or more IPv6 network address allocations from different ISPs, they are said to be multihomed. The goal is to have the network behave as if it is a single system, both when interacting with nodes within the network and when interacting with nodes exterior to the network. A further complication is the desire to minimize the number of routing table entries for each network; solutions proposed so far focus on the use of tunneling between the different allocated networks and incorporating alternate routes within each routing table entry.

As more IPv6 networks are joined together in a global IPv6 Internet, experience with these issues will suggest appropriate solutions.

14.6   Summary

In this chapter, we have introduced the basics of Internet routing, including link state and distance vector routing algorithms, interior and exterior routing, RIP, OSPF, and BGP routing, and how those protocols are adapted for use with IPv6.

In the next chapter we look at how Quality of Service (QoS) is implemented over IPv6 networks.

15

IPv6 Quality of Service (QoS)

Providing Quality of Service (QoS) in IP networks has long been an important but elusive goal for IETF working groups. The original IPv4 header specification included a Type of Service (ToS) field that was rarely if ever implemented: It would have required implementers to make judgments about which of their packets were to be given worse-than-normal treatment. This simplistic approach has been replaced over the years with the Differentiated Services (Diffserv) approach, and the ToS field has been renamed the Differentiated Services (DS) field in RFC 2474, "Definition of the Differentiated Services Field (DS Field) in the IPv4 and IPv6 Headers."

Diffserv allows the use of the DS field for data that indicates how a packet should be treated by routers. Rather than assigning a priority, the DS field is used to assign membership in a group that has a set of policies associated with it. These diffserv *behavior aggregates* (groups of packets that are to be treated in the same way by a router at network boundary) work the same way in both IPv4 and IPv6.

In an effort to remedy the faults of the Type of Service approach used in IPv4, an early goal of the IPv6 effort was to replace ToS with the concept of *flows*, which were to behave somewhat like behavior aggregates. The Flow Label field in the IPv6 header was first discussed in the early 1990s with RFC 1809, "Using the Flow Label Field in IPv6." This specification was published half a year before the original IPv6 specifications in 1995. At that time, the field raised more questions than it answered,[1] including how to determine which packets should be assigned a flow and how routers should handle flows that they didn't have flow routing information for.

By 1998 and the revised IPv6 specification in RFC 2460, the Flow Label field was still considered experimental as the questions regarding its use had yet to be resolved through extensive implementation and experimentation. As of 2003, a new specification that explains appropriate use of the Flow Label in IPv6 is still a work-in-progress but should be published soon as a proposed standard.

Up to the late 1990s, applications that depended on underlying network protocols relied on Transmission Control Protocol (TCP) to respond to network congestion. However, in January 1999, the experimental RFC 2481, "A Proposal to Add Explicit Congestion Notification (ECN) to IP," was published detailing an approach to congestion management that could include the network layer protocol, IP. Updated to proposed standard in September 2001, RFC 3168, "The Addition of Explicit Congestion Notification (ECN) to IP," updates some of the mechanisms discussed in this chapter.

In this chapter we cover the IPv6 approach to QoS, including the use of the diffserv field in IPv6, followed by discussion of IPv6 Flow Labels and the use of Explicit Congestion Notification with IPv6.

15.1   QoS Basics

The IP model is a democratic one: All packets are (in theory) treated equally, getting a "best effort" delivery service from the systems in

---

[1]Including length: Prior to 1995, the Flow Label field was 28 bits long; by 1995 it had shrunk to 24 bits, and in 1998 it reached its current specified size of 20 bits.

the Internet. This has several implications for application performance and in some cases limits applications in a number of ways.

1. Packets may be delivered in order or out of order.
2. Packets may be delivered smoothly or in spurts.
3. Packets may or may not be delivered.

In the case of real-time applications, this can require that receiving hosts buffer data as it comes in, adding delay on top of whatever network delay exists. Instead of passing incoming network data directly to the application, the incoming data is stored temporarily as the host waits for all data, including out of order data and data that may be temporarily delayed, to arrive.

The unpredictability of the IP datagram service is due to the way routers handled traffic: Packets come in from various sources, arriving at the router on different interfaces with different networks, and the router processes those packets in the order they are received.

Despite the first pass at the problem through assignment of Type of Service values, IP as originally defined lacks mechanisms for differentiating between packets that have quality of service requirements and those that don't.

- Transient congestion, such as caused by a surge of packets from one source, can cause unpredictable results. A packet surge may delay other traffic passing through a router. Or it might not.
- All datagrams are created equal, which means that there is no way to give one datagram priority over another.
- Individual routers can be configured to favor packets being sent to or from some particular network interface, but once the packet is routed, it will be treated just like any other packet by other routers. IP lacks a mechanism for flagging packets at their source and indicating that they should be treated differently in some way from source to destination.
- Even if packets can be flagged for special treatment, IP lacks the mechanisms for tracking packets and monitoring performance and resource use.

QoS protocols are intended to differentiate between packets on an end-to-end basis and adding the mechanisms necessary to allocate resources throughout a path for packets that require them.

15.1.1 APPROACHES TO QUALITY

The two basic approaches to adding QoS to the Internet are the Integrated Services (intserv) and Differentiated Services (diffserv) models. Introduced and defined in 1994 in RFC 1633, "Integrated Services in the Internet Architecture: an Overview," the intserv effort grew out of implementation experience with multicast of IETF meetings. According to RFC 1633 authors, real-time applications work poorly across the global Internet "because of variable queueing delays and congestion losses."

In addition to QoS for real-time applications, the intserv model would allow network service providers control over how bandwidth is shared. Allowing all the available bandwidth to be allocated among different classes of traffic even when the network is under a heavy load means that applications can count on having a minimum amount of bandwidth to work with even when the network is congested—instead of being summarily cut off when packets are dropped silently and the hosts on the other end drop the connections.

The ability to control which traffic categories are allowed how much of the available bandwidth is called *controlled link sharing*. The intserv approach defines a service model in which best-effort and *real-time services* (services over which there is some control of end-to-end packet delay) coexist and are facilitated through controlled link sharing.

Whether or not overly influenced by their experiences with multicast, the intserv working group has agreed that any QoS solution would have to support multicast: Real-time applications such as videoconferencing require the ability to handle multiple recipients of the same packets.

15.1.2 RESERVING RESOURCES

QoS generally requires network resources—specifically, network bandwidth and reliable routes—to ensure a uniform quality of service. The process of provisioning circuits, as in ATM and other telecommunication-oriented network protocols, is necessary before any communication can occur between a source and a destination. The *Resource ReSerVation Protocol (RSVP)*, defined in RFC 2205, "Resource ReSerVation Protocol (RSVP)—Version 1 Functional Specification," defines a mechanism by which hosts can, in effect, provision a connection across the connectionless IP Internet. RSVP, a required part of the intserv model, also requires intserv-capable routers in the network over which services are to be provided.

This reservation infrastructure can be dispensed with when services are provided to more general categories of packet, rather than the very specific intserv flows. Diffserv does not specifically require any mechanism on hosts, but vests the responsibility for managing bandwidth with the network itself. Diffserv packets are marked for special treatment by their applications, but the specific way in which those packets are treated is left to routers.

15.1.3 INTSERV IN A NUTSHELL

Central to intserv is the concept of the flow: If packets share source and destination IP addresses as well as source and destination ports, then one can assume that those packets are all part of an application's stream of data flowing between source and destination, with all that entails.

The intserv approach requires that routers keep track of all these flows, examining each packet to determine whether it belongs in a flow and then computing whether there is enough available bandwidth to accept the packet. In other words, intserv requires the following functions.

Admission control   Can the router, or the network at large, provide service to the flow? Can it provide service to the individual packets that comprise the flow? What about other, non-QoS packets?

Packet classification   Every packet that is admitted must be classified. What flow does it belong to? What level of QoS does it get? The three options are to treat the packet "normally" giving it best-effort, *controlled load* for allocating some portion of an uncongested network, and *guaranteed service* for real-time delivery with delays minimized to within preset levels of service.

Packet scheduling   Once a packet is classified, how is it scheduled? Should some packets jump ahead of others? How are packets within a queue treated when the queue exceeds its limits?

Combined with RSVP, intserv tends to be cumbersome to implement and it certainly is not scalable to the global Internet—but it is quite good at managing flows of data within smaller networks.

Ultimately, intserv has proven inadequate to the task of providing a single solution to the QoS problem: The intserv mechanisms are not seen as being scalable to the global Internet, and they can be difficult to implement.

The next pass at the problem became known as *diffserv* to differentiate it from intserv. Cursory examination of the RFCs may not shed much light on the differences between the two, but there are considerable differences. Where intserv is focused on ways of sharing available bandwidth among unique *flows* (series of packets with the same source and destination IP and port addresses), diffserv approached the problem by suggesting that a less granular classification of packets could provide the desired result.

15.1.4 Diffserv in a Nutshell

There is no way that Internet backbone routers could contend with the demands of tracking individual flows in an intserv-enabled global Internet, but network customers and service providers both increasingly demand some form of QoS that can scale well in the global Internet. Differentiated services, diffserv, answers the call by streamlining the process. Diffserv over IP is documented in RFC 2474, "Definition of the Differentiated Services Field (DS Field) in the IPv4 and IPv6 Headers."

Rather than building an elaborate infrastructure for emulating a circuit-based network on top of IP, diffserv allows communicating endpoints to classify their packets into different treatment categories. These categories are identified with a per-hop behavior, or PHB. The PHB is the action that a diffserv routing node can be observed to take when it receives a packet. When a PHB is defined, diffserv routers are supposed to treat packets marked with that value in a certain way.

For example, the Expedited Forwarding (EF) PHB (specified in RFC 2598, "An Expedited Forwarding PHB") is billed as "premium service" and indicates that the packets in that behavior aggregate (BA) should all be processed as they are received, rather than be queued or dropped. Unlike intserv with its traffic flows, the diffserv model calls for the use of BAs at each diffserv router: These are associated with a PHB that indicates how the router will treat the packet.

Aggregates or aggregated flows may also be referred to as classes of packets; routers are configured to respond to these different classes in different (appropriate) ways. Routers may also be configured to break up these classes into subaggregations to be treated slightly differently. For example, a router might be configured to forward premium-service packets from preferred customers over links that are more reliable than premium-service packets coming from customers subscribing to a "budget-premium" service.

Diffserv brings with it the ability to create network service policies specific to a single router, some part of a network, or an entire diffserv routing domain. As long as their policies don't affect the ability to provide guaranteed QoS, network providers can fine-tune their diffserv routers to differentiate how they treat packets.

The diffserv model distributes the task of allocating resources to the routers within a diffserv domain, providing greater flexibility as well as more efficient routing. A backbone router could process diffserv traffic far more easily than it can process intserv traffic: There is no need to negotiate RSVP reservations with all intermediary routers—and no overhead necessarily associated with failure to maintain an RSVP session with one particular router. With diffserv, the PHB mandates how the packet is treated, and different routers can provide the same service without having to maintain state for a particular connection, as with intserv.

15.1.5 Diffserv Versus Intserv?

At first glance, diffserv and intserv may seem to be competing with each other. However, the two models are complementary, with intserv working best within smaller domains, whereas diffserv provides somewhat less precise handling of packets across much larger networks; the two can even be used together, as documented in RFC 2998, "A Framework for Integrated Services Operation over Diffserv Networks."

In this informational document, the authors see intserv, RSVP, and diffserv as "complementary technologies," each of which is intended to achieve end-to-end quality of service. "Together," they write, "these mechanisms can facilitate deployment of applications such as IP-telephony, video-on-demand, and various non-multimedia mission-critical applications. Intserv enables hosts to request per-flow, quantifiable resources, along end-to-end data paths and to obtain feedback regarding admissibility of these requests. Diffserv enables scalability across large networks."

15.2   Differentiated Services and IPv6

The behavior defined for the Differentiated Services field in both IPv4 and IPv6 is the same, so an understanding of diffserv for IPv4 should carry over to diffserv for IPv6. In both protocols, the Differentiated Services field is defined for the six bits following the version in the IP header.[2]

RFC 2474, "Definition of the Differentiated Services Field (DS Field) in the IPv4 and IPv6 Headers," spells out how diffserv works for both protocols. The following are some other RFCs of interest for diffserv.

RFC 2963 "A Rate Adaptive Shaper for Differentiated Services"
RFC 2998 "A Framework for Integrated Services Operation over Diffserv Networks"
RFC 3086 "Definition of Differentiated Services Per Domain Behaviors and Rules for their Specification"
RFC 3260 "New Terminology and Clarifications for Diffserv"
RFC 3290 "An Informal Management Model for Diffserv Routers"
RFC 2430 "A Provider Architecture for Differentiated Services and Traffic Engineering (PASTE)"
RFC 2474 "Definition of the Differentiated Services Field (DS Field) in the IPv4 and IPv6 Headers"
RFC 2475 "An Architecture for Differentiated Service"
RFC 2638 "A Two-bit Differentiated Services Architecture for the Internet"
RFC 2983 "Differentiated Services and Tunnels"

Closely related to the issue of differentiated services is the use of flows in IPv6, as will be seen in the next section.

15.3   IPv6 Flows

The Flow Label field in the IPv6 header was originally designed as a 28-bit field (see notes in RFC 1809), reduced to 24-bits by 1995, and ultimately to 20 bits, as defined in RFC 2460. RFC 2460 states the following.

---

[2]Those bits were originally specified for IPv4 as the Type of Service field in RFC 791 and originally specified as Traffic Class field for IPv6 in RFC 2460.

The 20-bit Flow Label field in the IPv6 header may be used by a source to label sequences of packets for which it requests special handling by the IPv6 routers, such as non-default quality of service or "real-time" service. . . .. Hosts or routers that do not support the functions of the Flow Label field are required to set the field to zero when originating a packet, pass the field on unchanged when forwarding a packet, and ignore the field when receiving a packet.

In an appendix to RFC 2460, a *flow* is defined as "a sequence of packets sent from a particular source to a particular (unicast or multicast) destination for which the source desires special handling by the intervening routers." That "special handling" might be specified by a resource reservation protocol or by some data within the flow packet headers such as a hop-by-hop opction. As to the specifics of the implementation of flows, however, RFC 2460 is silent other than to specify the characteristics of the value of the flow header field.

- Packets that don't belong to flows must have the flow header set to zero.
- Each flow is assigned in a random or pseudo-random manner and (in combination with source address) is uniquely identifiable.
- The flow label is assigned by the source of the flow.
- Packets that belong to the same flow must all originate from the same source address, must be addressed to the same destination, and must be sent with the same value in the flow label header field. Flows are traditionally also identified by the transport layer protocol in use, as with TCP.

As of 1998, the flow label was considered an experimental portion of the IPv6 specification; five years after, the IETF had not yet published the IPv6 flow label specification as a proposed standard RFC. Although still officially a work-in-progress as of mid-2003, publication of an RFC titled "IPv6 Flow Label Specification" may already have occurred by the time this volume is published.

The definition of a flow, meanwhile, has changed.

A flow is a sequence of packets sent from a particular source to a particular unicast, anycast, or multicast destination that the source desires to label as a flow. A flow could consist of all packets in

a specific transport connection or a media stream. However, a flow
is not necessarily 1:1 mapped to a transport connection.

One change from RFC 2460 is that flows can be specified without reference
to the destination address or transport layer protocol type. These values
may not always be available in the IPv6 header, particularly if the packet
is fragmented or encrypted.

The flow label may not be changed from the value assigned by the sender,
unlike the diffserv value, which may be modified to reflect the appropriate
behavior aggregate for a particular router or network as it traverses the
Internet. Routers that don't offer flow-related handling are required to
ignore the flow label and treat the packet as any other.

IPv6 nodes that use flow labeling should assign separate flows for different and unrelated transport layer connections as well as for different
and unrelated application layer data streams. Thus, a multi-user host with
multiple telnet sessions from different users to the same remote host should
assign a separate flow to each of those sessions.

15.4   Explicit Congestion Notification in IPv6

Quality of Service specifications are largely intended to address the problem of how to guarantee a particular level of service for a particular set
of packets. For example, an ISP may want to offer its customers a level
of service that uses only their premium, high-performance networks. To
achieve that level of service, the ISP would need to be able to differentiate
packets coming from subscribers to that service and assign those packets
to a behavior aggregate for which the routing policy is to always route on
the most expensive link.

Network congestion can occur on any link as a result of high-demand
conditions or router malfunctions, and in most cases nodes sending
packets that encounter congestion are only able to detect the condition as a result of some timer—usually in the transport or application
layer protocols—timing out. Explicit Congestion Notification was first
proposed as an experiment for the transport layer in RFC 2481, "A Proposal
to Add Explicit Congestion Notification (ECN) to IP," in 1999, and quickly
moved to the standards track in 2001 when it was published as RFC 3168,
"The Addition of Explicit Congestion Notification (ECN) to IP."

Using ECN and a Congestion Manager implementation, nodes are able to negotiate the use of ECN. The ECN field in the IPv6 (and IPv4 header, as well), consists of the two bits after the Differentiated Services field. Unlike in earlier proposals, the two bits are used together as *codepoints* rather than as separate flag bits. The four different values possible for these two bits—00, 01, 10, and 11—indicate whether the end-nodes (sender and destination) are using an ECN-Capable Transport as well as whether there is congestion at the sender (though not so much congestion that would cause the node to have dropped the packet). These are the four codepoints and their uses.

00   When a node is not using ECN, it puts zeroes in the ECN field.

01/10   These two codepoints are treated in the same way and are also called ECT(0) [for the value 01] and ECT(1) [for the value 10]. These values are set by the sender to indicate that ECN is supported at both ends of the transmission.

11   Routers that are just beginning to experience congestion, or that are experiencing mild congestion, can signal their state by setting the codepoint to 11 in outgoing packets.

The following current RFCs provide more information about Explicit Congestion Notification and congestion control in general.

RFC 2481   "A Proposal to Add Explicit Congestion Notification (ECN) to IP"

RFC 2914   "Congestion Control Principles"

RFC 3124   "The Congestion Manager"

RFC 3168   "The Addition of Explicit Congestion Notification (ECN) to IP"

RFC 2884   "Performance Evaluation of Explicit Congestion Notification (ECN) in IP Networks"

15.5   Summary

Quality of Service, IPv6 Flows, and Explicit Congestion Notification are all related to the quest for better service over an Internet in which, by definition, all packets are supposed to be treated equally. As we've seen in this chapter, Quality of Service is designed to offer consumers of Internet connectivity options for guaranteed levels of service, while IPv6 flows and Explicit Congestion Notification are designed to provide improved routing and connectivity for any nodes on the Internet.

Ultimately, the goal of providing improved performance becomes more important as the network grows larger. An important part of network management that can grow unwieldy in larger networks is the task of configuring nodes. As we'll see in the next chapter, IPv6 provides some new tools as well as improvements on existing tools for configuring and reconfiguring networks and nodes.

16

IPv6 Autoconfiguration

Neighbor Discovery, as discussed in Chapter 13, coupled with the use of local- and site-scoped addresses, makes it possible for IPv6 nodes and networks to use a far wider set of autoconfiguration behaviors than with IPv4. As IPv6 makes it possible to network almost unimaginable numbers of nodes, the need for automated configuration tools becomes ever more important. Anyone who has ever been involved in renumbering an IP network by hand can attest to the difficulty.[1]

In this chapter, we will look at three sets of autoconfiguration tools.

Stateful autoconfiguration (DHCPv6)   The Dynamic Host Configuration Protocol (DHCP) grew out of the Boot Protocol (BOOTP), which allowed nodes (usually diskless nodes) to boot themselves from a network server. DHCP and DHCP for IPv6 (DHCPv6) allow nodes

---

[1]In the early 1990s, the author was one of about a dozen full- and part-time employees at an organization who helped renumber an IP network of about 2000 IP nodes distributed across two buildings and about a dozen subnets. All nodes had to be reconfigured by hand, and the entire project took approximately half a year to complete.

to configure themselves using DHCP servers. The protocols are considered stateful because the DHCP/DHCPv6 servers maintain tables containing the IP addresses and link layer addresses of all the nodes that use their services. The servers use that state to prevent two or more nodes from using the same IP address.

Stateless autoconfiguration   In less formally composed networks, IPv6 allows nodes to configure themselves—that is, assign themselves their own IPv6 addresses—without the aid of a server. There is no central or authoritative repository for IPv6 addresses assigned through stateless autoconfiguration.

Router and network renumbering   The use of locally scoped network addresses means that networks can be shifted from one connectivity provider to another—with new global IPv6 Internet addresses—relatively easily. Internal routing can be achieved using the site-local addresses, while external routing can be accomplished by reconfiguring gateway routers. The process is more easily said than done, as will be seen.

In this chapter, we look at the difference between stateful and stateless autoconfiguration, how DHCPv6 works, how IPv6 stateless autoconfiguration works, and how router and network renumbering can be done in IPv6 networks.

16.1   Stateful and Stateless Autoconfiguration

With the wide deployment of DHCP clients, as well as the inclusion of DHCP server software in virtually every kind of network server, from the simplest home office firewall network appliance on up, it should be safe to say that the vast majority of IP nodes in use today are either configured with DHCP or could be configured with DHCP.

DHCP servers are crucial for any network in which the number of nodes that must be concurrently connected at any given time approaches the number of available IP addresses. The DHCP server can allocate addresses in three ways.

Automatic allocation   DHCP assigns a permanent IP address to a client.

Dynamic allocation   DHCP assigns an IP address to a client for a limited period of time (or until the client explicitly relinquishes the address).

Manual allocation   A client's IP address is assigned by the network administrator, and DHCP is used simply to convey the assigned address to the client.

In all cases, the DHCP server maintains *state* about the clients that use DHCP to configure themselves. ISPs providing broadband services to consumers (and other network providers) may configure their DHCP servers to allocate addresses only to nodes with a particular link layer address to prevent unauthorized use of their service. However, DHCP can be used for ad hoc networking, in which a node not previously known to the DHCP server can be allocated an address.

Stateless autoconfiguration allows nodes to configure themselves completely independently of any central authority because servers to maintain addressing states are unnecessary.

This is not to say that stateful and stateless autoconfiguration are mutually exclusive; quite the reverse is the case, in fact. Neighbor Discovery incorporates features that allow the two types of autoconfiguration to complement each other in an IPv6 network. For example, stateless autoconfiguration is useful because it permits a node to allocate its own IPv6 address that is valid for local-scope network. At the same time, it can query for stateful autoconfiguration services on the local network to allow it to determine its own global IPv6 address, network prefix, and default routers.

16.2   IPv6 Stateful Autoconfiguration: DHCPv6

DHCPv6 is the latest iteration of an autoconfiguration protocol published in RFC 951, "Boot Protocol," in 1985. The following are some RFCs that can provide further information about BOOTP, DHCP, and DHCPv6.

RFC 3397 "Dynamic Host Configuration Protocol (DHCP) Domain Search Option"
RFC 3118 "Authentication for DHCP Messages"
RFC 2132 "DHCP Options and BOOTP Vendor Extensions"
RFC 2131 "Dynamic Host Configuration Protocol"

RFC 1542 "Clarifications and Extensions for the Bootstrap Protocol"
RFC 1534 "Interoperation Between DHCP and BOOTP"
RFC 0951 "Bootstrap Protocol"

The specification for DHCPv6 is still, as of mid-2003, a work-in-progress. Although in many ways quite similar to DHCPv4, DHCPv6 is different enough that the protocol specification does not include specific information about interoperability between the two.

16.2.1 DHCP Messages

DHCP clients and servers communicate by sending DHCP protocol messages using UDP. The client, which (at least to start with) has no valid IP address for itself or for the local DHCP server, sends DHCP requests to the multicast address reserved for DHCP servers in the link scope. These are the two valid addresses for sending DHCPv6 queries.

All_DHCP_Relay_Agents_and_Servers (FF02::1:2)   A link-scoped multicast address used by a client to communicate with neighboring (i.e., on-link) relay agents and servers. All servers and relay agents are members of this multicast group.

All_DHCP_Servers (FF05::1:3)   A site-scoped multicast address used by a relay agent to communicate with servers, either because the relay agent wants to send messages to all servers or because it does not know the unicast addresses of the servers. Note that in order for a relay agent to use this address, it must have an address of sufficient scope to be reachable by the servers. All servers within the site are members of this multicast group.

As long as these addresses are available to the DHCP client, it can configure itself with DHCP.

The client can send UDP messages without an IPv6 address but must provide some link layer address (otherwise, the responses from the servers can't be delivered). The default behavior for DHCP clients is to continue sending all DHCP messages to the multicast addresses reserved for DHCP services rather than directly to a specific DHCP server's unicast address. The reason for this is to allow the use of DHCP relay agents to pass messages from clients to a remote DHCP server; in certain cases, it may be more efficient (faster, less overhead) to allow clients to send unicast messages directly to a DHCP server. In those cases, a client unicast option may be enabled by the server.

Two types of exchanges are defined, those involving two messages and those involving four messages exchanged between the client and the server. These are the DHCPv6 message types.

SOLICIT   Clients send this message to locate a DHCPv6 server.

ADVERTISE   A server sends this message in response to a Solicit message to indicate it is offering DHCP service.

REQUEST   A client sends this message to request configuration parameters, including IP addresses, from a specific server.

CONFIRM   A client sends this message to any available server to determine whether the addresses it was assigned are still appropriate to the link to which the client is connected.

RENEW   A client sends this message to the server that originally provided the client's addresses and configuration parameters to extend the lifetimes on the addresses assigned to the client and to update other configuration parameters.

REBIND   A client sends this message to any available server to extend the lifetimes on the addresses assigned to the client and to update other configuration parameters; this message is sent after a client receives no response to a Renew message.

REPLY   A server sends this message, which contains assigned addresses and configuration parameters, in response to a Solicit, Request, Renew, or Rebind message received from a client. A Reply message with configuration parameters is sent in response to any Information-request message. The server sends this message in response to Confirm messages, confirming or denying that the addresses assigned to the client are appropriate to the link to which the client is connected. A server sends a Reply message to acknowledge receipt of a Release or Decline message.

RELEASE A client sends this message to the server that assigned addresses to the client to indicate that the client will no longer use one or more of the assigned addresses.

DECLINE A client sends this message to a server to indicate that the client has determined that one or more addresses assigned by the server are already in use on the link to which the client is connected.

RECONFIGURE A server sends this message to a client to inform the client that the server has new or updated configuration parameters, and that the client is to initiate a Renew/Reply or Information-request/Reply transaction with the server in order to receive the updated information.

INFORMATION-REQUEST A client sends this message to a server to request configuration parameters without the assignment of any IP addresses to the client.

RELAY-FORW A relay agent sends this message to relay messages to servers, either directly or through another relay agent. The received message, either a client message or a Relay-forward message from another relay agent, is encapsulated in an option in the Relay-forward message.

RELAY-REPL A server sends this message to a relay agent containing a message that the relay agent delivers to a client. The Relay-reply message may be relayed by other relay agents for delivery to the destination relay agent. The server encapsulates the client message as an option in the Relay-reply message, which the relay agent extracts and relays to the client.

16.2.2 CLIENT-SERVER EXCHANGES INVOLVING TWO MESSAGES

A number of DHCP interactions can be completed with the exchange of two messages, a request from the client and a response from the server.

Request for configuration information The simplest interaction occurs when a client does not need an IPv6 address from the server, but just needs some other configuration information (for example, a list of DNS servers). The client sends a DHCP Request message requesting the information it needs to the All_DHCP_Relay_Agents_ and_Servers multicast address; the servers that are listening to that address respond with a DHCP reply that contains the requested information.

Request to extend address lifetime   The client sends a Renew message, and the server sends a Reply message, with the new lifetimes specified so the client can continue using the address.

IPv6 address allocation   Normally, this is a four-message interaction, but it is possible for a client and server to transact an IPv6 address allocation in just two messages when the server already has configuration information assigned to the requesting client and stored in its database. The client can send a DHCP Solicit message to the All_DHCP_Relay_Agents_and_Servers multicast address to request both an address assignment and configuration information, specifying that an immediate Reply message from the server is desired. If there is a server listening to that multicast address that is capable of committing an address in response to that request, it can reply with the address and configuration information.

The more typical IPv6 address allocation process requires four messages, as described next.

16.2.3   CLIENT-SERVER EXCHANGES INVOLVING FOUR MESSAGES

When a node needs to request an IPv6 address as well as configuration information from a DHCP server, the process normally takes an exchange of four messages from client to server, as follows.

Solicit   The client sends a Solicit message to the All_DHCP_Relay_ Agents_and_Servers multicast address to locate available DHCP servers.

Advertise   Any server that is able to respond to the client Solicit does so by sending the Advertise message.

Request   The client sends a Request message to the server it chooses. More than one server may respond to the original Solicit request, so the client may have to choose one server in particular to respond to.

The Request message indicates what configuration parameters the client needs.

Reply   The server responds to the Request message with a Reply message containing the configuration parameters requested by the client.

16.3   IPv6 Stateless Autoconfiguration

Unlike IPv4 nodes, IPv6 nodes are capable of configuring themselves entirely on their own. This is by design and is the result of a considerable amount of thought and effort.

First, the standard method of addressing an IPv6 interface uses the EUI-64 mechanism to uniquely identify the node on the local link; the use of link-local unicast addressing means that all nodes will properly process packets sent to and from the link-local unicast address that a node assigns to itself. However, those packets cannot be forwarded outside the local link.

The use of Neighbor Discovery, however, means that individual nodes that are configured on a link can solicit information about routers and servers on the link. Part of that discovery process can also include identifying the global IPv6 network prefix as well, so the node can, using basic IPv6 protocols, discover all the information it needs to be fully configured without the intervention of a stateful configuration server.

The process of self-configuring includes a number of different steps.

1. Creating a link-local address for the self-configuring node
2. Verifying the uniqueness of the link-local address on the link
3. Determining what information should be autoconfigured and how that information should be obtained

The first and second steps of this process are described in RFC 2462, "IPv6 Stateless Address Autoconfiguration." The third step, that of determining how further configuration information should be acquired, uses mechanisms defined for Neighbor Discovery as well as DHCPv6. RFC 2462 explains it this way.

Stateless autoconfiguration requires no manual configuration of hosts, minimal (if any) configuration of routers, and no additional servers. The stateless mechanism allows a host to generate its own addresses using a combination of locally available information and information advertised by routers. Routers advertise prefixes that identify the subnet(s) associated with a link, while hosts generate an "interface identifier" that uniquely identifies an interface on a subnet. An address is formed by combining the two. In the absence of routers, a host can only generate link-local addresses. However, link-local addresses are sufficient for allowing communication among nodes attached to the same link.

In the stateful autoconfiguration model, hosts obtain interface addresses and/or configuration information and parameters from a server. Servers maintain a database that keeps track of which addresses have been assigned to which hosts. The stateful autoconfiguration protocol allows hosts to obtain addresses, other configuration information, or both, from a server. Stateless and stateful autoconfiguration complement each other. For example, a host can use stateless autoconfiguration to configure its own addresses but use stateful autoconfiguration to obtain other information . . . .

The stateless approach is used when a site is not particularly concerned with the exact addresses hosts use, so long as they are unique and properly routable. The stateful approach is used when a site requires tighter control over exact address assignments. Both stateful and stateless address autoconfiguration may be used simultaneously. The site administrator specifies which type of autoconfiguration to use through the setting of appropriate fields in Router Advertisement messages . . . .

16.3.1 DESIGN GOALS

To some extent, stateless and stateful autoconfiguration can be used to achieve similar results. By looking at the design goals for IPv6 stateless autoconfiguration, as stated in RFC 2462, one can gain a better understanding of the value added by the newer approach.

Eliminate manual configuration prior to connection Individual nodes should not have to be preconfigured before they are connected in order to be able to plug-and-play. An important goal is to provide a mechanism "that allows a host to obtain or create unique addresses for each of its interfaces. Address autoconfiguration assumes that each interface can provide a unique identifier for that interface (i.e., an 'interface identifier'). In the simplest case, an interface identifier consists of the interface's link layer address. An interface identifier can be combined with a prefix to form an address."

Eliminate stateful server/router requirement on small networks
Although DHCP implementations are widely available, small networks consisting of nodes on a single link should not be required
run a "stateful server or router" as a prerequisite to being connected
to an IPv6 internetwork. "Plug-and-play communication is achieved
through the use of link-local addresses. Link-local addresses have a
well-known prefix that identifies the (single) shared link to which a
set of nodes attach. A host forms a link-local address by appending
its interface identifier to the link-local prefix."

**Eliminate stateful address configuration server requirement on large
networks**   Multiple-network sites with multiple routers should not
be requried to maintain a special stateful configuration server unless
they so desire. "In order to generate site-local or global addresses,
hosts must determine the prefixes that identify the subnets to which
they attach. Routers generate periodic Router Advertisements that
include options listing the set of active prefixes on a link."

Facilitate graceful site renumbering   Renumbering a network of any
size should be reasonably simple—for example, when "a site may
wish to renumber all of its nodes when it switches to a new network
service provider. Renumbering is achieved through the leasing of
addresses to interfaces and the assignment of multiple addresses to
the same interface. Lease lifetimes provide the mechanism through
which a site phases out old prefixes. The assignment of multiple
addresses to an interface provides for a transition period during
which both a new address and the one being phased out work
simultaneously."

Control over autoconfiguration method   "System administrators need
the ability to specify whether stateless autoconfiguration, stateful
autoconfiguration, or both, should be used. Router Advertisements
include flags specifying which mechanisms a host should use."

These goals are intended to facilitate the use of IPv6 in networks that
continue to grow in size and scope.

16.3.2   CREATING A LINK-LOCAL ADDRESS

This part of the process of stateless autoconfiguration is simple: The node
simply uses its own network interface link layer address (or other value, if

a link layer address is not appropriate or available) to generate a modified EUI-64 address (see Chapter 8). This value is then concatenated to the well-known link-local prefix (1111 1110 10; see Chapter 8).

Before the node can use this address, however, it must determine that the address it has created is not already in use on the local link; if the address is already being used by another node, there is an address collision and the node must not attempt to use the address.

16.3.3 COLLISION DETECTION

Neighbor Discovery (Chapter 13) becomes important here: The process of checking for nodes already using the desired IPv6 address begins by sending a Neighbor Solicitation message to the address in question. If some other node is using the address, it will respond to the configuring node's solicitation, and the process of autoconfiguration comes to an end. At that point, the node must be configured by hand (presumably, a system administrator will be able to provide an alternate, and unique, value for the link layer address so that the node can autoconfigure without additional assistance).

Once the node determines its proposed IPv6 address is unique on the link, it can configure its network interface with that address. The node can now interoperate with all other nodes on the same link.

16.3.4 ROUTER ADVERTISEMENTS

As noted in Chapter 14, routers are required to periodically announce themselves through advertisement messages. These messages include information about the router sending them as well as about how nodes on the link should configure themselves. In particular, routers advertise to their link whether nodes are required to use stateful or stateless auto-configuration and for what portions of the configuration. For example, routers may specify that nodes are to use stateless autoconfiguration to obtain an IPv6 address but use stateful autoconfiguration (e.g., DHCPv6) to determine other network configuration data.

Although the routers advertise only periodically, a node in the process of autoconfiguring sends Router Solicitation messages to the all-router multicast group. The Router Advertisement response(s) the node gets will indicate how the configuration should be completed. RFC 2462 explains as follows.

> *A "managed address configuration" flag indicates whether hosts should use stateful autoconfiguration to obtain addresses. An "other stateful configuration" flag indicates whether hosts should use stateful autoconfiguration to obtain additional information (excluding addresses).*

If no routers are responding on the local link, the node should attempt to invoke stateful autoconfiguration. The Router Advertisement message may also include network prefix information, in which case the node can statelessly configure its own site-local and global addresses.

16.3.5 PRIVACY ISSUES

The use of IPv6 addresses that are based on the link layer MAC address of a node's network interface results in some interesting side effects.

1. Assuming that the MAC address is a valid Ethernet address (as most end user nodes are likely to be using), then the IPv6 address that is based on that address is likely not only to be unique on the local link but also globally unique across the entire IPv6 Internet. The IEEE MAC addresses are designed to be globally unique, so therefore any address that uses them in their entirety will also be globally unique.

2. Assuming that any given IPv6 address is globally unique, packets sent to and from the interface using that address can be traced unambiguously to a specific host. Unlike in IPv4, where it is not easy to link IP addresses with link layer addresses outside the local link, in IPv6, the link layer address is inseparable from the IP address.

Shortly after the use of modified EUI-64 addresses for IPv6 was decided, microprocessor vendor Intel announced that it would begin shipping CPUs with globally unique identifiers accessible to applications running on those processors. The step was taken for a number of reasons,[2] including the ability to trace stolen CPUs as well as to allow owners of intellectual property (such as software and content) to manage how their content was used

---

[2]Those reasons are unrelated to IPv6.

by linking their licenses to the CPU ID of a single computer. Microsoft has taken similar steps in terms of limiting how their software is installed, even when it is being installed to recover from disk crashes on the originally licensed system.

A constituency of privacy advocates, possibly with reinforcements from anti-IPv6 parties, noted that the same potential for misuse of any static and system-specific identifier, including the modified EUI-64 identifiers used in IPv6, exists.

The resultant uproar, with headlines like "IPv6 Extinguishes Privacy," generated a response in the form of RFC 3041, "Privacy Extensions for Stateless Address Autoconfiguration in IPv6," which suggests an alternate method for generating interface identifiers that don't uniquely and consistently map to the same link layer and global-scope addresses.

The privacy problem stems from the widespread practice of using Web cookies, especially when advertising, and Web tracking exchanges insert seemingly harmless cookies that permit the trackers to connect a single user to some or all of the Web sites she visits. Although it is possible to deny Web sites the ability to set cookies on a system, if the IP address itself is uniquely identifiable with a node, it becomes impossible for a user to stop anyone with access to Web server logs from correlating visits across Web sites.

To avoid the problem, the authors of the RFC suggest two approaches.

1. Use stateful autoconfiguration, by which a node is assigned an address by a central server. The server can be configured to deliver random or pseudo-randomly generated addresses that change periodically.
2. Use stateless autoconfiguration but generate a random/pseudo-random interface ID portion of the address, and periodically change it to a new value. The changed addresses should be selected randomly to prevent attackers from figuring out which addresses belong to the same node over time.

RFC 3041 "proposes the generation of a pseudo-random sequence of interface identifiers via an MD5 hash. Periodically, the next interface identifier in the sequence is generated, a new set of temporary addresses is created, and the previous temporary addresses are deprecated to discourage their further use. The precise pseudo-random sequence depends on both a random component and the globally unique interface identifier (when available), to increase the likelihood that different nodes generate different sequences."

16.4   Renumbering

As we've seen in Part I, the practice of allocating addresses on a permanent or semipermanent basis, especially when allocations are made by ISPs rather than by central authorities, has caused an ongoing explosion in the size of nondefault routing tables. When an ISP allocates a portion of its own allocation, packets addressed to the ISP's customers are easily aggregatable. However, when a customer changes ISPs, the customer must either give up his IPv4 address and renumber their entire network or have his suballocation go with him to the new ISP. In the latter case, backbone routers must now incorporate a separate route for that customer's network, whereas before, packets addressed to the customer's network would be aggregated into the route for the ISP.

Part of the solution in IPv6 is to make renumbering easier, whether renumbering individual nodes, routes, or entire sites. The following protocols have been proposed to simplify the process.

Site renumbering   Discussed as part of IPv6 stateless autoconfiguration in RFC 2462, automatic site renumbering solves the problem of how to keep a lid on the expansion of nondefault routing tables as networks move from one connectivity provider to another as well as the problem of reducing (or even substantially eliminating) the costs of renumbering networks by hand when providers are changed.

DNS support for renumbering   The controversial A6 resource record (see Chapter 18) constitutes an extension to DNS aimed at improving support for renumbering of IPv6 networks. Although it is relatively easy to renumber nodes and routers, the propagation of DNS information that reflects the new IPv6 addresses associated with a domain name poses more of a problem. RFC 2874 "DNS Extensions to Support IPv6 Address Aggregation and Renumbering," although currently considered experimental, proposes one approach to solving the problem. This protocol is discussed in Chapter 18.

Router renumbering   As long as only connectivity within the link-local scope address is required, nodes and routers can function fine without any global IPv6 addresses or prefixes. However, external routing is almost always required, and any support for renumbering of networks must include a mechanism for rapidly updating router prefix configurations at the same time that nodes are renumbered. RFC 2894, "Router Renumbering for IPv6," defines a protocol that allows routers to reconfigure themselves rapidly and with minimal difficulty.

The last part of this section summarizes the approach to network renumbering described in a work-in-progress titled "Procedures for Renumbering an IPv6 Network Without a Flag Day." The term "flag day" is used to refer to the day (or moment) at which some aspect of an entire network (or any other system) is changed. Flag days imply that all changes are made simultaneously because the configuration that works on $F - 1$ will not work on $F + 1$, and vice versa. If your system is not changed prior to the flag day, your system will not work after the flag day; if your system is changed before the flag day, it will not work until after the flag day.

With IPv6 deployment in production networks still far from widespread, the protocols for renumbering are bound to be changed as more experience is gained in using them. For now, however, they offer a good starting point for experimentation.

16.4.1   SITE RENUMBERING

When addresses are leased (meaning, allocated for a discrete time period rather than assigned for all time), sites can be renumbered more easily. At the end of a lease, interfaces must get new addresses at which time they can be given addresses with a new network prefix. The length of time that an address is valid can be specified in router advertisements, so that when a site is about to be renumbered, the routers can be configured to begin advertising the new prefix at the same time specifying that the old prefix is to be deprecated.

As described in RFC 2460, if a node's IP address changes during an interaction with another node, there is no way for the transport layer to handle the change gracefully. TCP circuits cannot survive such a change, and even UDP exchanges usually require using the same IP address throughout.

By differentiating between *preferred* and *deprecated* addresses, upper layers (transport and application protocols) can use the information.

The existence of two classes of addresses can be used to more gracefully deal with addresses that suddenly become invalid; the upper-layer protocols can also use the two classes to choose the preferred address when opening a connection with a remote node.

Further, administrators planning to renumber a network can attempt to schedule the renumbering procedure for a time when the fewest open connections are likely and/or for when the open connections with least impact on organizational function are likely.

16.4.2   ROUTER RENUMBERING FOR IPv6

Renumbering of routers can be relatively simply done as long as there is a way to notify routers of the network prefix for the links to which they are connected. Under IPv4, network prefixes would rarely change—for example, when a network is renumbered or when a router is connected to a different link. Router renumbering in IPv6 networks is expected to occur more frequently, and in order to support such changes, RFC 2894, "Router Renumbering for IPv6," defines a set of ICMPv6 messages for router renumbering.

The set of *Router Renumbering Command* messages containing sequences of *Prefix Control Operations* (PCOs) can be sent to routers to notify them of how to update prefixes. Each PCO contains instructions relating to router prefixes, with the router processing the PCOs to determine whether they refer to any of the router's interfaces and, if so, updating the interface configuration. The RR Commands are ICMP message of type 138; the standard format is shown in Figure 16–1.

Router renumbering requests are multicast to the all-routers scoped address, and routers respond to them with *Router Renumbering Results* messages containing a Match Report (as part of the ICMPv6 message body) for each prefix match with the RR Command. Those replies may indicate that there were no matches with the router's interface prefixes.

RR Commands contain Command Messages, comprised of a Match-Prefix part (the part that indicates what prefix is to be modified by the RR Command), and optionally one or more Use-Prefix parts (to indicate new data to be used for the prefix). Following the Match-Prefix part of the RR Command message, one or more Use-Prefix parts may follow, if appropriate.

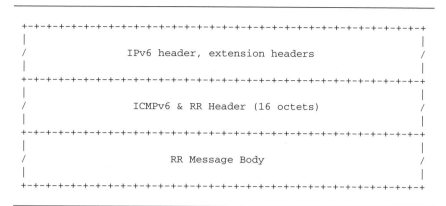

```
+-+-+-+-+-+-+-+-+-+-+-+-+-+-+-+-+-+-+-+-+-+-+-+-+-+-+-+-+-+-+-+-+
|                                                              |
/                  IPv6 header, extension headers              /
|                                                              |
+-+-+-+-+-+-+-+-+-+-+-+-+-+-+-+-+-+-+-+-+-+-+-+-+-+-+-+-+-+-+-+-+
|                                                              |
/                  ICMPv6 & RR Header (16 octets)              /
|                                                              |
+-+-+-+-+-+-+-+-+-+-+-+-+-+-+-+-+-+-+-+-+-+-+-+-+-+-+-+-+-+-+-+-+
|                                                              |
/                        RR Message Body                       /
|                                                              |
+-+-+-+-+-+-+-+-+-+-+-+-+-+-+-+-+-+-+-+-+-+-+-+-+-+-+-+-+-+-+-+-+
```

Figure 16–1: Router Renumbering Command format (from RFC 2894).

16.4.3 RENUMBERING AN IPv6 NETWORK WITHOUT A FLAG DAY

A work-in-progress, "Procedures for Renumbering an IPv6 Network Without a Flag Day," outlines some of the issues involved in renumbering IPv6 networks without disrupting the operation of the networks and without requiring an all-at-once procedure such as are involved with flag day conversions. Rather than defining any specific protocols, the authors of this document suggest a method of evaluating the progress of the process in six different stages, followed by a discussion of the difficulties that may ensue as well as security issues related to network renumbering.

The process of renumbering itself is accomplished using the mechanisms already described to reconfigure router, node, and network. The phases of renumbering are as follows.

1. The network is using the old prefix and is currently stable. Everything works as it should in terms of routing, servers, and all other network nodes.
2. The new prefix is added while the old prefix is still in use. Barring the ability to simultaneously and completely update all nodes with the new prefix, there will be parts of the network that correctly use the new prefix and other parts that will not be able to use the new prefix. Reconfiguring all routing to the new prefixes across all subprefixes (subnets) is estimated to take "a period of time varying from minutes to hours depending on

the size of the network and the degree of automation used in reconfiguration."

3. Once the network has been reconfigured with the new prefix, with all routing stabilized, every interface on the network will have two valid addresses, one for the old and one for the new prefixes. At this point, the old addresses are still being used as the default when opening new network sessions; the new addresses are not yet being used.

4. The process of shutting down the old prefix begins. This includes modifying DNS records to reflect the new prefix and reconfiguring by hand any nodes that still need to be changed to use the new prefix. As the old prefix is taken out of service, the individual nodes should be notified by the various autoconfiguration and neighbor discovery functions that the old prefix should be replaced by the new one for new sessions.

5. The old prefix is removed. As all sessions that still use the old prefix are closed, the old prefix can be removed from each node's configuration.

6. The network is using the new prefix and is currently stable. Everything works as it should in terms of routing, servers, and all other network nodes. Just as at the beginning, when everything was stable, but using the old prefix.

The devil is in the details, of course, and some difficulty, according to the authors of this document, will arise from nodes that are not directly controlled by the network administrator or require manual configuration. These devices are likely to be "unusual" in that they are not typical end-user PCs but rather as follows.

> *VoIP telephones with static configuration of boot or name servers, scanning devices used by manufacturing partners in support of "just in time" purchasing, manufacturing, or shipping activities, the boot servers of routers and switches, and so on. Application designers frequently take short-cuts to save memory or increase responsiveness, and a common short-cut is to use static configuration of IP addresses rather than DNS translation to obtain the same. The downside of such behavior should be apparent; such a poorly designed application cannot even add or replace a server easily, much less change servers or reorganize its address space. The short-cut ultimately becomes very expensive to maintain and very hard to replace.*

In addition to citing security-related problems that can arise when nodes are designed to use network addresses outside of the normal protocols for acquiring addresses (that is, software or hardware that has been hard-coded to use a particular network prefix or address), the authors also describe an attack that is possible during the renumbering process.

> *Attacks are also possible. Suppose, for example, that the new prefix has been presented by a service provider, and the service provider starts advertising the prefix before the customer network is ready. The new prefix might be targeted in a distributed denial of service attack, or a system might be broken into using an application that would not cross the firewall using the old prefix, before the network's defenses have been configured. Clearly, one wants to configure the defenses first and only then accessibility and routing.*

Mostly, though, the authors suggest that while IPv6 network renumbering can be significantly easier than IPv4 network renumbering, it is not child's play, nor should it be undertaken without due consideration of the potential problems that can arise in the process.

16.5   Summary

IPv6 protocols for renumbering networks, nodes, and routers without doing it manually fulfill an important design goal of the next generation protocol. More important is the ability to do renumbering using a small set of standard ICMPv6 messages and the standard tools provided by neighbor discovery, rather than devising any new client-server protocols, as is so often the solution chosen to provide new features or functions within IP networks up to now.

Another important goal, and one that is related in a way to rapid renumbering, has been the ability to network mobile nodes, to be discussed in the next chapter.

17

Mobile IPv6

When an IP node moves from one network to another, as when a notebook computer is used in more than one location, one way to accommodate the changes in the network is to use two or more sets of network configuration to match each location. However, another solution is to use a *mobile IP* protocol to allow the computer to use one IP address for all its communications across any network to which it is attached.

Mobile IP, however, should not be confused with the mechanisms required to allow fast handovers in cellular wireless networks. In that type of network, the handovers are handled at the link layer rather than at the network layer. With a rapidly moving node and a network using small cels, the node would likely remain in the same link layer network even as it moved from one cel to another, thus obviating any need to change IP addresses.

However, mobile IP is most useful for nodes that change location as well as link layer network somewhat less rapidly. At the risk of oversimplifying, an IPv4 mobile node is configured with an IP address on its home network. When the mobile node connects to a network, it listens for a *mobility agent* advertisement to determine whether it is on its home network or some other network. If it is on a foreign network, it requests a *care-of* address from the mobility agent and then notifies a mobility agent on its home network of the care-of address. Communication to and from the mobile node can then be accomplished by tunneling through the remote network using the care-of address.

As we'll see, under IPv4 the process of enabling mobility requires adding special agents and servers, as described in RFC 3344, "IP Mobility Support for IPv4." However, the careful design of IPv6 protocols, especially the use of neighbor discovery functions, means that IPv6 mobility does not require any special infrastructure to be set up to enable mobility.

17.1   IP Mobility

Mobility was from the start an important part of the IPng effort, at least judging by the 1994 publication of RFC 1688, "IPng Mobility Considerations." Here is a list of source documents on mobile IP; IP mobility is still not widespread in part because it can be cumbersome to deploy under IPv4.

RFC 1688 "IPng Mobility Considerations"
RFC 2005 "Applicability Statement for IP Mobility Support"
RFC 2794 "Mobile IP Network Access Identifier Extension for IPv4"
RFC 2977 "Mobile IP Authentication, Authorization, and Accounting Requirements"
RFC 3012 "Mobile IPv4 Challenge/Response Extensions"
RFC 3344 "IP Mobility Support for IPv4"
RFC 3519 "Mobile IP Traversal of Network Address Translation (NAT) Devices"

IPv4 mobility, as defined in RFC 3344, "IP Mobility Support for IPv4," requires three things to work properly.

1. The mobile node must be able to move from one link layer network to another (that is, change link layer network addresses) without having to change its IP address.
2. The mobile node must be able to interoperate with all other IP nodes, without any modifications required to communicate

with a mobile node. In other words, the mobility-enabled node must be backward compatible with the rest of the Internet.

3. The mobile node must be authenticated whenever it tries to update its location. This is to prevent attackers from "impersonating" the mobile node in order to gain access to the mobile node's home network.

IPv4 mobility defines three entities, which exchange mobility information in ICMP messages.

Mobile node   A node (host or router) that can move from one network or subnetwork to another without changing its IP address and that can maintain, without interruption, sessions that were begun while connected on one network after the node is moved to another network (with the assumption that there is no noticeable disruption to the node's connectivity during the shift).

Home agent   A router that acts on behalf of the mobile node on its home network. Packets sent to and from the mobile node when it is away from the home network are tunneled through the home agent. The home agent also keeps track of the mobile node's remote location(s).

Foreign agent   A router that provides routing services to visiting mobile nodes. Mobile nodes must register with the foreign agent when they first connect to the foreign network. The foreign agent router acts as the other end of an IP tunnel for the mobile node, and the foreign agent is recommended for use as the default router for mobile nodes registered on a network.

The IPv4 mobility protocol offers *Agent Discovery* services, with foreign and home agents periodically announcing their presence on a network as well as responding to solicitations for agents sent by mobile nodes in the process of connecting to a network. The protocol also requires the mobile node—when it first connects to a network—to register with its home agent (sometimes directly or sometimes through the foreign agent, depending on how the connection is made).

Figure 17–1 shows how the IPv4 mobility protocol works. Mobility agents periodically transmit advertisements, addressed either to the all-nodes multicast address or the *limited broadcast* address (255.255.255.255, meaning "all nodes on this subnet"). The advertisements include the agents'

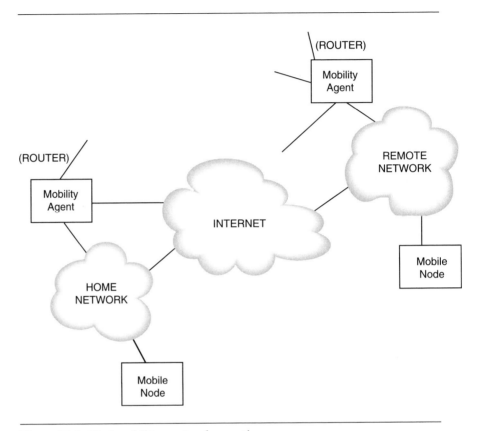

Figure 17–1: IPv4 mobility protocol operation.

IP addresses, so mobile nodes can address packets to the agents. The advertisements also include information about the care-of address(es) that the agent offers, as well as other mobility information such as whether registration is required, how long the registration is valid (lifetime), and whether the agent is accepting new registrations. Optionally, network prefix length information may also be included.

When a mobile node first connects to a new network, it can also solicit advertisements (rather than waiting for the periodic advertisement) by sending out a Router Solicitation ICMP message, with the TTL field set to 1. When it receives a mobility advertisement, the mobile node checks to see whether it is connected on its own home network or not; if it is on a foreign network, it gets a care-of address.

Once the mobile node has its care-of address, it must register that address with its home agent, this time by sending a special mobility message (Registration Request) in a UDP datagram sent to port 434. This message includes the node's home address, home agent, care-of address, and other information; the agent confirms the request with another UDP message (Registration Reply).

The care-of address may either be an address provided by the agent in its advertisement, or it may be acquired on the local network by using some other mechanism such as DHCP to obtain a *co-located care-of address*. In the latter case, the mobile node is configured with an IP address on the foreign network (it must, in order to configure itself with DHCP). When using a co-located care-of address, the mobile node acts as its own tunnel endpoint, unlike in regular care-of addresses, where the tunneling is done through the foreign and home agents. Figure 17–2 shows how the two situations differ; whereas a foreign agent acts as the tunnel endpoint for the transmission of packets to and from the mobile node, when a co-located care-of address is used, the mobile node acts on its own behalf as the tunnel endpoint.

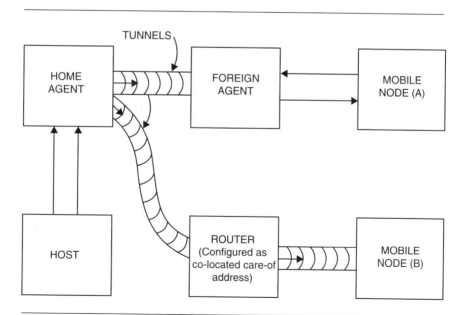

Figure 17–2: Co-located care-of addresses can be used when a mobile node has local connectivity on a foreign network.

This is merely an overview of the IPv4 mobility protocol, and it omits details as well as important aspects of mobility security. It is provided purely as background for discussion of mobility in IPv6.

17.2   Mobility Support in IPv6

As of mid-2003, the specification for mobility support in IPv6 is still a work-in-progress, even though it has been revised almost two dozen times. The objective of mobile IPv6 is still to allow a mobile node to move from link to link while retaining the same, home, IPv6 address. This allows connectivity to the mobile node transparently, no matter where the node is linked to the network.

Unlike in IPv4, where mobility registration uses a separate protocol carried in UDP datagrams, IPv6 mobility is defined as a separate protocol carried in IPv6 extension headers. Although similar to mobility support in IPv4, IPv6 mobility builds on the experiences of IPv4 mobility research as well as new features of IPv6 itself (such as the reliance on extension headers for IP-layer applications like mobility).

The IPv6 approach uses concepts such as binding of a mobile node's home address with its care-of address and more rigorous authorization procedures. The basics of the protocol are described in this section.

17.2.1   IPv6 Mobility Basics

Mobile nodes attached to their home networks send and receive packets just as would any IPv6 node; there is no functional or observable difference between a mobile node on its home network and any other node. When the mobile node moves, however, it needs to acquire one or more care-of addresses at which it can be reached. The care-of address is uniquely linked to the mobile node, but it has the subnet prefix associated with the foreign network to which the mobile node is attached.

As described in Chapter 16, IPv6 nodes of any kind can acquire valid IPv6 addresses when they connect to a new network through standard IPv6 procedures, whether stateful or stateless autoconfiguration. Mobile nodes, therefore, use these procedures to acquire local addresses that they then can use as their care-of addresses.

To use a local address as a care-of address, the mobile node must be able to *bind* its home address and the care-of address together. The mobile node registers its care-of address by sending a *Binding Update* to its home agent, which responds by sending a *Binding Acknowledgment* message.

A big difference between IPv4 and IPv6 mobility occurs by the inclusion of the definition of a *correspondent node*: any node that communicates with a mobile node (the correspondent node may also be a mobile node itself). Mobile IPv6 nodes can notify correspondent nodes of their current locations through a process of *correspondent registration*.

17.2.2   MOBILE/CORRESPONDENT NODE MODES

Two modes for mobility support are provided in the document "Mobility Support in IPv6" for communication between a mobile node and a correspondent node.

Bidirectional tunneling   This mode is available for communication between a mobile node and any IPv6 node, whether or not it has explicit support for IPv6 mobility. In addition, the mobile node does not have to register a binding, either. The mobile node tunnels packets intended for the correspondent node through its home agent; the home agent then intercepts packets addressed to the mobile node's home address and tunnels those packets back to the mobile node via its care-of address.

Route optimization   This mode, so-called because it allows the optimal route between mobile node and correspondent node, works by having the mobile node register its current address binding with the correspondent node. The correspondent node can thus send packets directly to the mobile node's care-of address. In addition to optimizing the path between nodes, this option also reduces the possibility of congestion at the mobile node's home agent (which would otherwise have to mediate all traffic between the two) as well as any risk of connection failure due to circumstances in the mobile node's home network.

Mobile IPv6 can be expected to support additional features such as permitting mobile nodes to use more than one home network.

17.3   Mobile IPv6 Versus Mobile IPv4

These are some important differences between Mobile IPv4 and Mobile IPv6, as cited in the draft specification for IPv6 mobility.

- There is no need for foreign agents; no special local support is necessary to allow a mobile IPv6 node to operate correctly.
- IPv4 mobility defines the default mode of operation through the agency of the mobile node's home network. This tends to stress the mobile node's home agent; the ability to redirect a correspondent node to the mobile node's current address is implemented only as an extension of the IPv4 mobility specifications. IPv6 mobility incorporates route optimization as a fundamental aspect of the protocol.
- Rather than encapsulating packets in tunnels as in IPv4 mobility, most IPv6 packets sent to a mobile node include IPv6 header extensions—a significant difference in terms of processing (no need to encapsulate/decapsulate packets for tunnels).
- Use of IPv6 Neighbor Discovery eliminates the need to rely on ARP or other link layer mechanisms; it also enables functions such as unreachability detection and agent discovery.

Other differences include the way that authentication is accomplished between mobile nodes and their agents or correspondents, as well as how mobile nodes can be accommodated even when they are attached to a network that is behind a firewall or NAT.

17.4   Summary

The early visions for mobile IP included millions of workers connecting their laptop PCs to geographically and organizationally distributed networks, all able to interoperate as if they were still connected to their home networks. Even without mobility, business travelers as well as individuals enjoy relatively simple mobile interoperability, whether they connect via wireless networks in coffee shops or via broadband in hotels.

The greater challenge for mobile IPv6 will undoubtedly prove to be in enabling mobility for non-PC devices, from allowing the use of mobile telephones anywhere to serving Web data from highly mobile platforms. For example, automobile manufacturers might incorporate wireless Web servers to provide access to car diagnostics from anywhere in the world.

Another important aspect of portability is the close correlation between IPv6 and DNS. Where IPv4 nodes could, conceivably, operate without a mechanism for linking domain names to IP addresses, IPv6 insists on applications relying on DNS to translate the applications' domain names to IPv6 addresses, as will be seen in the next chapter.

18

IPv6 and DNS

One of the most pressing challenges facing anyone who wishes to deploy IPv6 is that of deploying Domain Name System (DNS) servers that are able to correctly respond to requests for domain name resolution for both IPv6 and IPv4 nodes. As long as DNS can be relied on to provide accurate linking of IP addresses for domain names, IPv6 nodes can be linked seamlessly and transparently to the application layer and the end user (and, to a great extent, to the transport layer).

DNS is a very distributed database system that defines a variety of different *resource records* (*RRs*) to correspond to different types of data. For example, the A RR contains an address and the MX RR contains mail exchange information. Two different RRs were defined for use with IPv6 addresses: the AAAA and A6 RRs.

In this chapter, we begin with a brief look at how DNS works, followed by an introduction to the two different IPv6 RR types and a discussion of the pros and cons of using each, including a look at the prospects for which of the two is likely to become prevalent in the IPv6 Internet.

18.1   DNS Resource Records

No database can exist without records, and DNS was defined to store name and address information as well as provide the capacity to store other information as well. DNS data is stored in *resource records* (*RRs*). As defined in the internet standard for DNS,[1] "A domain name identifies a node. Each node has a set of resource information, which may be empty. The set of resource information associated with a particular name is composed of separate resource records."

In this section, we look at the basics of DNS RRs, including those originally defined for use with IPv4, how new ones can be added, and the two different RRs that have already been specified for use with IPv6.

Figure 18–1 is a graphical representation of the fields comprising an RR; those fields include the following.

NAME   The domain name where the RR is found; the owner may be implied by the contents of the RR.

TYPE   An encoded 16-bit value specifying what kind of abstract resource is referred to in the RR. RFC 1034 mentions several types, including *A* to indicate a host address, *CNAME* for the *canonical name* of an alias used to simplify access to the resource, *HINFO* for the CPU and OS used by the host, *MX* to identify the resource as a mail exchange for the domain,[2] *NS* to indicate the authoritative nameserver for a domain, *PTR* to indicate a pointer to another part of the domain name space, and *SOA* to indicate the start of a *zone of authority*.

CLASS   Another encoded 16-bit value, the class specifies "a protocol family or instance of a protocol"—for example, the IN class, specifying the Internet system. This value is rarely used.

TTL   The *time to live* of the RR. A 32-bit integer, TTL specifies the number of seconds before the RR should expire. This is used mostly after a resolver has retrieved an RR to indicate how long the cached value should be saved and used before discarding it as out of date.

---

[1]STD 13, which includes RFCs 1034 and 1035.
[2]See Chapter 24 for more about how email works with DNS in IPv6.

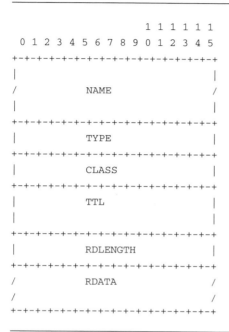

```
                      1 1 1 1 1 1
       0 1 2 3 4 5 6 7 8 9 0 1 2 3 4 5
      +-+-+-+-+-+-+-+-+-+-+-+-+-+-+-+-+
      |                               |
      /              NAME             /
      |                               |
      +-+-+-+-+-+-+-+-+-+-+-+-+-+-+-+-+
      |              TYPE             |
      +-+-+-+-+-+-+-+-+-+-+-+-+-+-+-+-+
      |             CLASS             |
      +-+-+-+-+-+-+-+-+-+-+-+-+-+-+-+-+
      |              TTL              |
      |                               |
      +-+-+-+-+-+-+-+-+-+-+-+-+-+-+-+-+
      |            RDLENGTH           |
      +-+-+-+-+-+-+-+-+-+-+-+-+-+-+-+-+
      /             RDATA             /
      /                               /
      +-+-+-+-+-+-+-+-+-+-+-+-+-+-+-+-+
```

Figure 18–1: Layout of fields within an RR (from RFC 1034).

RDLENGTH   A 16-bit value indicating the length of the resource data, in bytes, limiting the amount of data stored in any RR to no more than 65,535 bytes.

RDATA   The data associated with the RR. The composition and length of this field may vary, depending on the RR type.

Different types of RR have been defined for different purposes, although we'll look here only at the types defined in RFC 1034. Domain nameservers store all their information in these RRs, making the definition of each RR roughly equivalent to a database's design or schema.

Although DNS is most often associated with the process of matching hostnames with IP addresses, DNS makes other data available, for other purposes. One of the most important of these other purposes is making mail exchange (MX) information available. MX records allow Internet mail addressed to one address to be redirected for delivery to some other address for a variety of reasons: to keep private details of an organization's intranet and internal mail systems, to avoid going through a security firewall, or to provide a standard corporate address format (e.g., "firstname.lastname@example.com") while allowing users to receive mail at other addresses.

A number of RRs have been defined for use with DNS security extensions; these include the SIG (security signature), KEY (security key), and NXT (next domain) RRs defined in RFC 2535. Other special purpose RRs include the NAPTR (naming authority pointer) type defined in RFCs 2168 and 2915 and the AAAA and A6 types defined for IPv6 address resolution; there is even an RR defined simply for storing text strings (TXT).

18.2   DNS Extensions for IPv6

IPv6 support under DNS should be straightforward: define a new resource record type for maintaining IPv6 addresses and linking them to domain names. The first specification for DNS support of IPv6 published as RFC 1886, "DNS Extensions to Support IP Version 6," proposes these actions.

Add AAAA Resource Record   The AAAA RR maps a domain name to an IPv6 address. The "quad A" designation is derived from the A RR, which maps a domain name to an IPv4 (32-bit) address; with IPv6 addresses four times the length of IPv4 addresses, the corresponding resource record is four As.

New IPv6 Reverse Lookup Domain   One of the functions of DNS enables reverse lookups, where an IP address is known rather than the domain name. DNS support for this function for IPv6 addresses requires the addition of a similar reverse lookup domain.

Update Query formats   Queries for IPv4 addresses are updated to perform additional processing to recover both IPv4 and IPv6 addresses, if present. The details of the RFC 1886/AAAA proposal are examined in this section.

18.2.1   THE AAAA RESOURCE RECORD

The AAAA resource record stores a single 128-bit IPv6 address in the RDATA field. When a DNS AAAA query is made by a client node, the

DNS server responds with a list of all the AAAA resource records associated with the domain name.

18.2.2 REVERSE LOOKUP DOMAIN

RFC 1886 specifies a reverse-lookup domain at IP6.INT (for looking up the domain associated with a particular address rather than an address for a particular domain name). That domain (IP6.INT) has been deprecated and replaced by the more standard IP6.ARPA, as defined in RFC 3152, "Delegation of IP6.ARPA." The IP4.ARPA domain is used for finding a domain name to match an address, and ARPA is considered an acronym for "Address and Routing Parameters Area";[3] thus, the change for IPv6 is to maintain consistency.

The IPv6 address to be looked up is converted into a name in the IP6.ARPA domain by reversing the order of the hexadecimal digits of the address, separating each digit by a dot ("."), and then adding the suffix "IP6.ARPA" to the end. RFC 1886 provides the example on which this one is based.

```
4321:0:1:2:3:4:567:89ab
```

becomes:

```
b.a.9.8.7.6.5.0.4.0.0.0.3.0.0.0.2.0.0.0.1.0.0.0.0.0.0.1.2.3.4.IP6.ARPA
```

18.2.3 MODIFIED QUERIES

DNS query types, such as name server (NS) and mail exchange (MX) queries, have to be modified to allow them to return both type A and type AAAA results. Doing so allows name servers to send clients all the relevant results for a particular domain name request, including both IPv4 and IPv6 addresses.

---

[3]The acronym ARPA originally derived from the Advanced Research Projects Agency, part of the Department of Defense and an original funding organization of much of the work, including the networks, supporting the original Internet Protocol. The IP4.ARPA domain was originally intended for the use of that agency, but with the release of the program to the public, the domain was already being used, and changing it would have been more complicated than changing the meaning of the acronym.

18.3   DNS and IPv6 Aggregation

Controversy arose from the publication of RFC 2874, "DNS Extensions to Support IPv6 Address Aggregation and Renumbering," as a proposal standard. Apparently, this new specification was to have been considered an alternative to AAAA but in RFC 3363, "Representing Internet Protocol Version 6 (IPv6) Addresses in the Domain Name System (DNS)," the situation was clarified with the A6 proposal (as the protocol defined in RFC 2874 is known) reclassified as experimental.

The A6 resource record solves some problems but also creates other problems as will be made clear in this section. By design, A6 allows the segmentation of host addressing information into multiple A6 records, one of which contains only an IPv6 address, and the other(s) of which specify a domain name for which network prefix information is available.

The result is that any A6 query may require additional lookups: one lookup for the specific host and one or more lookups for domains associated with that host.

By separating the DNS records for node addresses from DNS records for domain names, the A6 proposal makes it possible to more quickly propagate changes in network numbering. If all nodes retain their 64-bit host part addresses and only change the 64 high-order bits of their network addresses when a network is renumbered, then the split makes sense. DNS entries for individual nodes do not need to be changed when the network is renumbered—just the parent domain name entries.

18.3.1   A6 RESOURCE RECORD

The A6 resource record, shown in Figure 18–2 (along with field definitions), can, when combined with other A6 records, carry complete information about the address associated with a particular domain name. The prefix length indicates what portion of the address suffix is contained in the record. If the prefix length is 64, it means that the address suffix field will contain the low-order 8 octets of an address—in other words, the host-part of an IPv6 address. Following the address suffix field, the prefix name field contains a domain name under whose A6 record more addressing information can be found.

```
+-----------+-----------------+-------------------+
|Prefix len.| Address suffix  |   Prefix name     |
| (1 octet) | (0..16 octets)  |  (0..255 octets)  |
+-----------+-----------------+-------------------+
```
```
o  A prefix length, encoded as an 8-bit unsigned integer with
   value between 0 and 128 inclusive.
o  An IPv6 address suffix, encoded in network order (high-order octet
   first).  There MUST be exactly enough octets in this field to
   contain a number of bits equal to 128 minus prefix length, with
   0 to 7 leading pad bits to make this field an integral number of
   octets.  Pad bits, if present, MUST be set to zero when loading
   a zone file and ignored (other than for SIG verification)
   on reception.
o  The name of the prefix, encoded as a domain name....
   this name MUST NOT be compressed.
```

Figure 18–2: A6 resource record format (from RFC 2874).

When the prefix length is zero (meaning that the entire 128-bit address is included in the address suffix field), the prefix name field is not present. In this case, the A6 record looks much like an AAAA record (it consists of a single 128-bit IPv6 address).

When the prefix length is 128 (meaning that the address suffix field would have to be 0 bits long), there is no address suffix field, and there is only a domain name in the resource record.

18.3.2   A6 DOMAIN NAME RESOLUTION

Unlike more typical name resolution with A and AAAA records, A6 name resolution requires the requesting node to compile a chain of A6 records. To illustrate, consider what happens when a DNS client queries a server for the IPv6 address for the domain name.

```
node.example.net
```

The first response might be an A6 record for the node itself, with a prefix value of 8 (64 bits), and the domain name where more information may be acquired.

```
example.net
```

The next step would be to query the DNS for that domain name, in which case the response might be an A6 record containing just an IPv6 network address; that is, the prefix length would be 0, and there would be no domain name at all, and the address itself would be zeroed out in the less-significant 64 bits.

The client making the request could then concatenate the host part of the address (from the first A6 record) with the network part of the address (from the second A6 record), with the result being the proper IPv6 address for the node named node.example.net.

18.3.3   AAAA Versus A6

As already noted, the coexistence of the AAAA and A6 proposals on the standards track was confusing, especially since the AAAA protocol had been the only DNS solution that was widely implemented before A6 came along. The situation was finally clarified with the publication of RFC 3363, "Representing Internet Protocol Version 6 (IPv6) Addresses in the Domain Name System (DNS)," in which the A6 approach was reclassified as experimental. RFC 3364, "Tradeoffs in Domain Name System (DNS) Support for Internet Protocol Version 6 (IPv6)," is a companion document that explains why the choice was made for AAAA over A6, as summarized in the next section.

18.4   Choosing the Next Generation DNS RR

As may be supposed from the two different proposals, the A6 protocol was moved off the standards track at this time because, ultimately, it is too complicated. AAAA records allow simple request/response interactions for DNS clients and servers; the A6 record requires that DNS clients and servers interact more than once for each query, with clients required to collect and verify A6 records as being part of a chain.

RFC 3364, "Tradeoffs in Domain Name System (DNS) Support for Internet Protocol Version 6 (IPv6)," goes into considerably more detail about the trade-offs— including the potential benefits in terms of improved address and domain name aggregation and faster network renumbering with A6. This section lists some of the criteria considered during the debate.

18.4.1 ADVANTAGE: A6

As explained in RFC 3364, A6 has one clear advantage over AAAA.

> *A6 RRs can represent addresses in which a prefix portion of the address can change without any action (or perhaps even knowledge) by the parties controlling the DNS zone containing the terminal portion (least significant bits) of the address. This includes both so-called "rapid renumbering" scenarios (where an entire network's prefix may change very quickly) and [some] routing architectures. . . (where the "routing goop" portion of an address may be subject to change without warning). A6 RRs do not completely remove the need to update leaf zones during all renumbering events (for example, changing ISPs would usually require a change to the upward delegation pointer), but careful use of A6 RRs could keep the number of RRs that need to change during such an event to a minimum.*

Also, an A6 resource record of the zero-length prefix format is identical to an AAAA resource record for the same address. This means that anything you can do with AAAA, you can do with A6. Thus, AAAA shouldn't have any functions that are unavailable to A6, and thus A6 could easily replace AAAA.

18.4.2 ADVANTAGE: AAAA

Although AAAA provides only a subset of the features supported by A6, there are some other considerations to contend with.

- The AAAA resource record differs from the A resource record only in the length of the addresses they contain. Having 15 or more years of experience with what is essentially the same protocol is a considerable advantage for AAAA. A6, by comparison, is an unknown quantity in terms of how it behaves, how it works, and how it fails in the field.
- AAAA resource records are designed for simplicity of data retrieval. The DNS query transaction with AAAA records is simple and straightforward. While A6 records make it easier to update the DNS system with renumbered network data, AAAA records make it easier to retrieve the data.

The RFC includes many other arguments, including less compelling ones in favor of and against each proposal, and discussion of the problems and potential problems inherent in A6. However, ultimately, the choice seems clear: Since data retrieval is a much more frequent task than data update, and since AAAA simplifies retrieval, for the moment the IPv6 Internet will continue to support AAAA as the default resource record for DNS.

18.5   Naming IPv6 Domains

No discussion of IPv6 and DNS would be complete without a brief discussion of the issues of naming IPv6 domains. Depending on how the domains are to be used, decisions must be made regarding how IPv6 domains should be named, particularly in relation to existing IP4 domains.

One option is probably more appropriate if the domains will be IPv6-enabled to allow IPv6 nodes to access the same resources as IPv4 nodes—in other words, if all resources in the example.com domain are to remain accessible both to IPv4 and IPv6 nodes. In those cases, AAAA resource records for the existing domains should be added in parallel to the existing A records for those domains.

The other option is probably more appropriate when the IPv6-enabled domains are to host services and resources that are targeted only at IPv6 nodes. In this case, a set of domains such as ipv6.example.com are set aside for IPv6 use only. The IPv6-only domains would be entered into the DNS with their own AAAA records, while the IPv4-only domains would remain unchanged.

When, and even if, such distinctions are best made will depend on what your networking goals are, as well as on further research into the operation of large IPv6 networks.

18.6   Summary

As often happens, the interoperation of IPv6 and DNS will rest on tried and true results and a straightforward protocol, AAAA, rather than the more feature-full but less-tested alternative, A6. Ultimately, IPv6 relies to a great extent on the use of DNS to eliminate or at least minimize the impact it will have on other protocols.

Although some of these other protocol interactions with IPv6 have been mentioned in previous chapters, the next chapter summarizes the work that has been done to date on integrating IPv6 with the rest of the TCP/IP protocol suite and other related protocols.

19

Next Generation Protocols

Contrary to many expectations, IPv6 will have relatively little impact on other protocols considered to be a part of the TCP/IP network protocol suite. That is by design: It is hard enough to update such a widely deployed protocol as IPv4. Imposing the additional requirement of a whole set of new protocols to work with IPv6 would doom the project from the start.

Although there are over a dozen different specifications related to running IPv6 over [something],[1] those specifications largely explain the approaches implementers should and/or must take when implementing IPv6 over those link layer protocols.

In this chapter, we take a brief look at how IPv6 implementations interoperate with related protocols, including the transport layer protocols, application layer protocols, and link layer protocols. We will also revisit the modifications necessary to infrastructure-related protocols that will be affected by IPv6, especially DNS and routing protocols.

---

[1]For example, "IPv6 over Ethernet," "IPv6 over ATM," and so on.

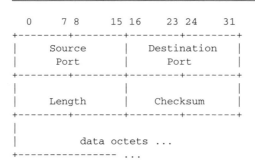

Figure 19–1: UDP headers have no reference to IP version (from RFC 768).

19.1   IPv6 and Transport Layer Protocols

Transport layer protocols need to be made IPv6-aware only to the extent that those protocols must process some or all of the IP headers. For example, UDP and TCP checksums are calculated based on the IP source and destination addresses. Thus, UDP and TCP implementations would need to be patched to allow them to determine the difference between IPv4 and IPv6 packets and the different locations of the addresses in IPv4 and IPv6 packet headers.

For example, the UDP header, from RFC 768, "User Datagram Protocol," is shown in Figure 19–1. Other than the checksum, there is no dependence on an IP version.

The same goes for Transmission Control Protocol (TCP) headers, as shown in Figure 19–2.

The newest transport layer protocol, Stream Control Transmission Protocol (SCTP), is defined in the eponymously titled RFC 2960, and it includes explicit support for initiating streamed sessions with either IPv4 or IPv6 nodes.

19.2   IPv6 and Link Layer Protocols

The following RFCs contain specifications for "IPv6 over X," where X is some type of link layer network. Other specifications that are still

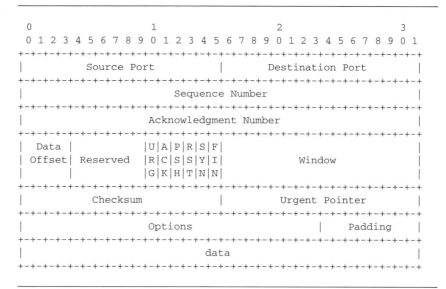

Figure 19–2: The TCP headers contain no direct reference to IP addresses (from RFC 793).

works-in-progress include IPv6 over MAPOS, Mobile IPv4, and Fibre Channel.

RFC 2464 "Transmission of IPv6 Packets over Ethernet Networks"

RFC 2467 "Transmission of IPv6 Packets over FDDI Networks"

RFC 2470 "Transmission of IPv6 Packets over Token Ring Networks"

RFC 2472 "IP Version 6 over PPP"

RFC 2491 "IPv6 over Non-Broadcast Multiple Access (NBMA) Networks"

RFC 2492 "IPv6 over ATM Networks"

RFC 2497 "Transmission of IPv6 Packets over ARCnet Networks"

RFC 2529 "Transmission of IPv6 over IPv4 Domains Without Explicit Tunnels"

RFC 2590 "Transmission of IPv6 Packets over Frame Relay Networks Specification"

RFC 3146 "Transmission of IPv6 Packets over IEEE 1394 Networks"

RFC 3572 "Internet Protocol Version 6 over MAPOS (Multiple Access Protocol Over SONET/SDH)"

In general, these specifications define how IPv6 is expected to work over a specific link layer protocol. Key points include how IPv6 packets are encapsulated in the link layer protocol data unit, how IPv6 multicasts and unicasts are directed on the local link, and how IPv6 interface identifiers (e.g., the 64-bit host part of the IPv6 address) are derived from link layer addresses.

19.3   IPv6-Enabled Applications

As of 2003, most IPv6-enabled applications are still oriented toward the UNIX/Linux/BSD world, although many have been ported to multiple platforms. This section lists applications that have IPv6 support (or have been reported to have IPv6 support).

BitchX (http://www.bitchx.com/)   This popular IRC client has been ported to Windows and Macintosh OSs as well as most popular *NIX platforms.

BIND 9 (http://www.isc.org/products/BIND/bind9.html)   The Internet Software Consortium (ISC) publishes the BIND software for DNS servers and includes support for IPv6 (with A6 RRs) as well as DNSSEC.

Trick or Treat Demon (http://www.vermicelli.pasta.cs.uit.no/ipv6/software.html)   According to the Vermicelli Project (actually, Feico Dillema, its creator), "TOTD is a small DNS proxy nameserver that supports IPv6-only hosts/networks that communicate with the IPv4 world using some translation mechanism."

WWW6to4 (http://www.vermicelli.pasta.cs.uit.no/ipv6/software.html)   This is a lightweight HTTP proxy for use as an IPv4/IPv6 application layer gateway, also created by the Vermicelli Project (Feico Dillema).

IPFilter (http://cheops.anu.edu.au/~avalon/ip-filter.html)   IPFilter is a software package that can be used to provide network address translation (NAT) or firewall services. It can either be used as a loadable kernel module or incorporated into your UNIX kernel;

using it as a loadable kernel module where possible is highly rec-ommended. Scripts are provided to install and patch system files, as required.

LFTP (http://lftp.yar.ru/) A command-line client for file download via FTP and HTTP that supports IPv6.

Quake for IPv6 (http://www.viagenie.qc.ca/en/ipv6/quake/ipv6-quake. shtml) An IPv6-capable Quake client, published by the Canadian research and consulting firm, Viagenie.

FreeS/WAN with IPv6 support (http://www.ipv6.iabg.de/ downloadframe/index.html) IPv6-enabled version of the FreeS/ WAN IPsec-based VPN software for Linux.

Java for IPv6 (https://doc.telin.nl/dscgi/ds.py/View/Collection-188) Code that makes it possible to read and write in IPv6-sockets and IPv6-multicast sockets within Java, as long as you have IPv6 enabled on your Windows (9x/NT) computer.

19.3.1 OTHER APPLICATIONS

Many other applications are being adapted for use with IPv6, including the popular Apache Web server; Mozilla and Lynx browsers; mail agent programs Exim, qmail, Sendmail, and Fetchmail; as well as net-work monitoring and network conferencing programs. A good place to start looking for IPv6-enabled applications is the IPv6 Forum Web site, www.ipv6forum.com. In addition to links to applications, the IPv6 Forum serves as a clearinghouse for information about IPv6 internationally.

19.4 Adding IPv6 Support

KAME is the premier IPv6 implementation (see Chapter 21), written for the FreeBSD operating system, and used by Apple for their OS X server (Jaguar) that supports IPv6. The leader of the KAME project, Jun-ichiro itojun Itoh, is also a prolific developer and writer, and he wrote an excellent guide for programmers who'd like to add IPv6 support to their network applications. The document is available at

http://www.kame.net/newsletter/19980604/. Anyone interested in port-
ing existing applications or writing new ones that support IPv6 should be
required to read this article.

19.5   Summary

To the greatest extent possible, IPv6 interactions with lower- and higher-
layer protocols have been minimized to ease the process of migration to
support for IPv6 in a global Internet. This chapter ends the "protocols"
section of the book. The next chapters elucidate the "practice" of IPv6.

IPv6 Practice

This section provides real-life, hands-on guidance for using IPv6. Starting with a chapter that covers strategies and tactics for planning the transition to an IPv6-enabled network, Part III continues with a chapter offering real-life guidance on enabling IPv6 support on popular network and server operating systems including Windows, Solaris, FreeBSD, and Cisco's IOS. Other chapters offer step-by-step instructions for deploying email and DNS servers under IPv6 and for implementing security through firewalls and IPsec.

The final chapter addresses the issues of the current and future state of the art and science of IPv6 networking.*

---

*Chapter 20 was written by John E. Spence. Chapters 21-24 are adapted from materials published by Zama Networks, Inc., and written by Robert C. Zilbauer, Jr., Grant Furness, Gerald R. Crow, IV, Megan Ewers Roede, Jim Van Gemert, Brian Skeen, and Steve Smith.

20

IPv6 Transition Planning and Strategies

The IETF is putting almost as much effort into developing a smooth transition process as they are into developing the protocol itself, and with good reason. The IPv6-enabled networks of the near future will offer many advantages over today's networks—advantages that are sorely needed as the network platform takes on new applications and millions of new users. But with IPv4 widely deployed and running business-critical operations today, a smooth transition must be assured. Without a good transition tool set, IPv6 networks would not arrive until much later.

This chapter describes a general methodology for transitioning networks to IPv6, after considering many of the "high-level" considerations, and looks at transition tools available to network professionals to get the job done. The chapter ends with a case study of a hypothetical enterprise and its course of action to manage the transition.

Although the case study offers an example, there is no "standard" transition—all enterprises are unique, and each will manage its transition differently. Still, this simple example offers an idea of some of the major steps involved in moving to an IPv6-enabled world. Our hypothetical enterprise is a multinational corporation with 4000 users spread across eight sites in the United States, Asia, and Europe, with a fully deployed IPv4 network. Although the specifics of each network are different, our example should offer something to which almost everyone can relate.

20.1   Start Now

IPv4 will be with us for a long time: The sheer number of IPv4 nodes in the world ensures that we will live in an environment where interoperability is mandatory. Some enterprises will move early to IPv6—typically, those enterprises that can capitalize on the advanced features of IPv6. Other enterprises will wait to let their peers work out the "transition kinks," and they will adopt later in the transition cycle and benefit from the experiences of the early implementers.

Almost without exception, however, regardless of when you plan to transition, today is the right time to start learning about IPv6, training your staff in v6 networking, and reviewing your capital equipment upgrade and service provider plans.

20.1.1   The IPv6 Discovery Lab

It is true that IPv6 is much like IPv4 in many aspects: Routing, routing protocols, and steps for device configuration are logical extensions of well-understood IPv4 concepts. However, in IPv6 the address space is larger, the service set richer, and the on-link autoconfiguration and neighbor discovery processes are different. The ideal place to learn these new concepts is in a test environment.

The first step that any IT department should take toward IPv6 support is building an IPv6 "Discovery" lab modeled on the enterprise's network. Network engineers and IT personnel can learn about the new protocols, the transition tools and techniques, and practice the transition steps utilized in migrating the enterprise's production network.

The important thing is that you get started as soon as possible so you can plan and manage a transition that does not risk major self-inflicted network trouble.

20.1.2 TRANSITION PROJECT MANAGEMENT

Whoever manages the transition to an IPv6-enabled network must keep in mind the following series of goals and objectives.

- Set up a lab at the company's technology headquarters, preferably at the same site where network designers and managers work. Fill the lab with network devices, servers, and clients that are representative of the overall company to create a miniature version of the corporate network.
- Allow the technical staff to learn about IPv6 capabilities and deploy them throughout the lab, use IPv6 transition tools, and stage mock transitions to get hands-on experience with the process of rolling out IPv6 support to corporate resources.
- Distribute IPv6 knowledge to technical staff, and work with them to develop their transition strategy and processes.
- Upgrade DNS to support IPv6 addresses and (if possible) provide DNS resolution over an IPv6 transport.
- Enable IPv6 in the network fabric throughout the enterprise, making sure there is no impact on servers, clients, or current business processes.
- Install dual IPv4/IPv6 stacks on internal servers so they run both protocols, and make sure all applications support IPv6.
- Install dual IPv4/IPv6 stacks on internal clients.
- Deploy IPv6 internally with the aid of DNS records that allow IPv6-capable clients to use IPv6 services. IPv4 will probably still be the most common protocol outside the firewall, so dual-stack IP will continue to be required for external communication.
- Once testing of applications, systems, and networks is complete, begin moving services to the IPv6-enabled infrastructure. As acceptance generally increases, beyond-the-firewall support for IPv6 may also be expected.
- Remove remaining IPv4 configurations, support contracts, and enabling services and run on a pure IPv6 network.

The rest of the chapter provides more detail about the tools, strategies, and processes that will make for a smooth transition within your enterprise.

20.1.3 THE TRANSITION TOOLBOX

The set of tools available for transitioning to IPv6 support continues to expand. Whether intended to solve general transition problems or to enable nodes to communicate in a mixed IPv4/IPv6 environment, these tools can help make the task of supporting IPv6 easier.

- Native IPv6 connectivity
- Tunnel-based IPv6 connectivity
- Automatic tunnels (6to4)
- Intra-site automatic tunnels (ISATAP)

Protocol tunneling has long been used to allow nodes and networks to bypass barriers to interoperability, and IPv6 tunneling is already helping early implementers to use the global IPv4 Internet as a transport for IPv6 packets.

20.1.4   NATIVE IPv6 CONNECTIVITY

This is the simplest and most straightforward way to get IPv6 connectivity: Choose a service provider that offers IPv6 addresses and upstream connectivity. Just as you might be assigned a block of IPv4 addresses with your service, a native IPv6 connectivity provider would assign you a block of IPv6 addresses. Unlike IPv4—under which sufficiently large blocks of addresses are rarely available—IPv6 providers can deliver sufficient IPv6 address space for any foreseeable application.

For example, consider a new enterprise with 400 employees that has been spun off from an established company. The new organization needs to initiate its own connectivity: They could lease a T3 line from a provider, and they still might only get a /24 IPv4 address block (254 addresses).

If that company chooses to enable IPv6 natively, it can get a /48 allocation, the standard for enterprises using IPv6. That allocation is enough to address 2^{16} (65,536) networks, with each network supporting up to 2^{64} (over $1.8 * 10^{19}$) devices.[1] Each of these "/64" networks form the basic network building block since they support autoconfiguration. The block of IPv6 addresses will be "owned" by your ISP. Remember, IPv6 supports only hierarchical route aggregation, but network renumbering in the event of a change in ISP is simplified under IPv6.

---

[1] At this time, there are no networks this large, let alone link layer protocols that could support them. If they are ever built, however, IPv6 will be able to handle them.

With native IPv6 connectivity and continuing IPv4 support, an organization would have direct connectivity for both IP protocols.

20.2   IPv6 Tunneling

As of 2003, most commercial ISPs claiming to offer IPv6 connectivity still do not offer native IPv6 connectivity, so for networks where such service is not available, tunneling offers a next best choice. Tunneling allows isolated IPv6 networks or IPv6 end nodes to communicate with other IPv6 nodes across the IPv4 Internet. There are different types of tunneling, including configured and automatic, but they all work in the same basic way as any tunneling protocol.

IPv6 tunneling is the process of encapsulating an IPv6 packet inside an IPv4 packet and forwarding it across the IPv4 Internet, where it is then decapsulated and forwarded on to its IPv6 destination. Tunneling can also work in reverse to move IPv4 packets across an IPv6 Internet, with an edge gateway encapsulating IPv4 packets inside IPv6 packets and forwarding them across the IPv6 infrastructure. However, given the relative rarity of IPv6 Internets, this type of tunneling is much less common. Tunneling of any form requires dual-stack routers at either end of the tunnel.

20.2.1   Static Tunneling

Consider the scenario shown in Figure 20–1, with two isolated v6 end nodes, two dual-stack routers, a v4 infrastructure, and a tunnel. End nodes A and B, both IPv6 nodes, are separated by an IPv4-only network. For A and B to exchange IPv6 packets, they would require a *6over4 static tunnel* between the dual-stack routers located at either end of the IPv4 network. The term *6over4* refers to the process of tunneling IPv6 packets over an IPv4 infrastructure. Node A could then send IPv6 packets destined for node B to the local dual-stack router, Y, which encapsulates A's IPv6 packets into IPv4 packets. These packets can then be routed across the IPv4 network to router Z, which strips off the IPv4 headers to restore the original IPv6 packets and forward them to their original IPv6 destination (Node B).

Static tunnels require that the dual-stack routers be capable of encapsulating and decapsulating IPv6 packets in IPv4 packets; for tunnels that cross

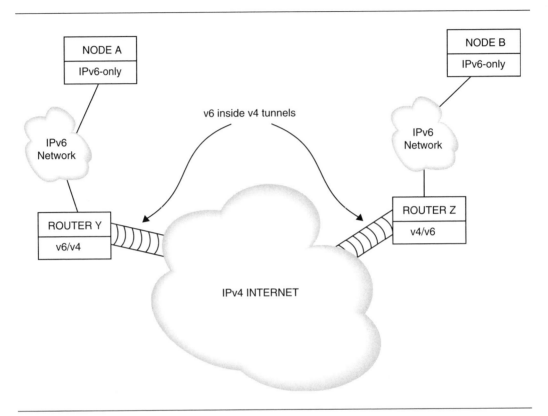

Figure 20–1: Static tunneling of IPv6 across IPv4 infrastructure.

the global IPv4 Internet, each endpoint of the tunnel must be associated with at least one public, globally routable IPv4 address.

Static tunnels are often built between routers under separate administrative control, in which case the administrators of the tunnel endpoint routers can exchange IPv4 and IPv6 tunnel endpoint information and configure their routers appropriately to establish the static tunnel.

Static tunneling can be a valuable mechanism for building bridges allowing IPv6 traffic to flow across IPv4 networks. Static tunnels are easy to configure and require very little administrative overhead, but they do require separate tunnel configurations for each isolated IPv6 network destination. As a result, static tunnels don't scale well. Automatic tunneling solutions are more appropriate for linking more than a handful of IPv6 locations.

20.2.2   AUTOMATIC TUNNELING (6TO4)

Static tunnels require human intervention to record and configure tunnel endpoints. An automatic tunneling solution known as *6to4* allows access to native IPv6-based networks from within an IPv4-only provider network. Any IPv6 node capable of sending and receiving IPv4 packets, and with a globally routable IPv4 address, can use 6to4 to reach IPv6 nodes and networks.

IPv6 nodes can interoperate using 6to4 in two fundamental ways.

6to4 node to 6to4 node   Any standalone 6to4 node (defined as a single machine running IPv6 with 6to4 functionality) can exchange packets with another 6to4 node over an IPv4-only network.

6to4 network to native IPv6 node   6to4 node on an IPv4 network can communicate directly with a node on a native IPv6 connection.

Not only does 6to4 support single node interoperability, but it can also support up to a /48 network behind the node.

Consider again the scenario illustrated in Figure 20–1: two single-node 6to4 islands that wish to exchange IPv6 packets but are connected only by an IPv4 network (see Figure 20–2). Examine the simple network drawing showing nodes "Karlene" and "Alexander."

"Karlene" has an IPv4 address of 200.150.100.30 (please note that this is a real allocated IPv4 address—never use this address yourself), and "Alexander" has the IPv4 address 220.120.80.40 (also a real address). The 6to4 function will "automatically" allocate IPv6 address blocks for these two nodes by using the IPv4 address as the "middle bits" of a new IPv6 address.

An example is the best way to explain. Karlene will autoconfigure the IPv6 address "2002:c896:641e::1."

The "2002" portion of the address is set aside by the IETF specifically for use with 6to4. Every IPv6 packet that starts with the "2002::/16" prefix is, by definition, a 6to4 packet—it contains an IPv4 address. The "c8" is the hex equivalent of "200," the "96" is the equivalent of "150," "64" is the equivalent of "100," and "1e" is the equivalent of "30." The "1" is completely arbitrary but is typically configured as the 6to4 node itself.

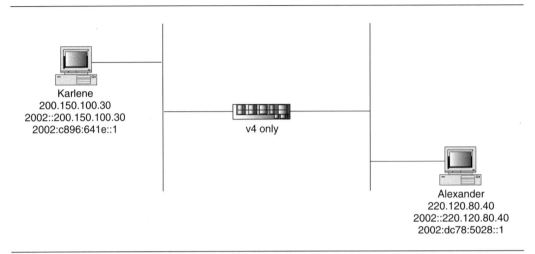

Figure 20–2: Automatic tunneling (6to4).

Essentially, then, each 6to4 packet (that is, any packet that starts with "2002::/16") has an IPv4 address inside. If you look at the address lengths, you see that that the portion of the address space consumed to specify the 6to4 mechanism and the IPv4 address is "2002:c8:96:64:1e::/48."

The v6 address for "Alexander" would be "2002:dc78:5028::1."

Now, both nodes have globally unique, fully routable IPv6 addresses in addition to their routable IPv4 addresses. If Alexander sends a "ping" packet to Karlene, the 6to4 function on Alexander will recognize the "2002::/16" prefix as a 6to4 address and will—knowing the IPv4 addresses that can effect delivery of the packet are inside—automatically tunnel the packet (encapsulate the packet in IPv4) to Karlene at 200.150.100.30. The "packet type" field of the IPv4 packet will specify "IP-in-IP." When the (IPv4) packet arrives at Karlene, the node will, upon finding the IP-in-IP flag, unencapsulate the packet and effect delivery of the IPv6 packet to "2002:c896:641e::1"—Karlene's IPv6 address.

This mechanism will work, automatically, for any number of 6to4 nodes on an extended IPv4 network. The power of the mechanism is the ability to automatically allocate a unique IPv6 address from a unique IPv4 address. The real power, though, is that—since the IPv6 address space is 128 bits

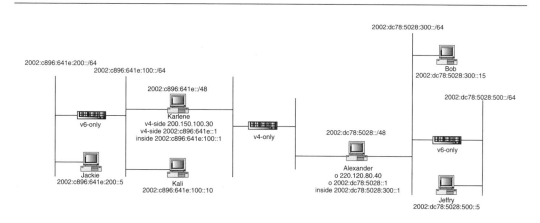

Figure 20–3: 6to4 network to 6to4 network.

where the IPv4 address space is 32 bits—an entire unique IPv6 network can be generated from a single unique IPv4 address.

20.2.3 6TO4 NETWORK TO 6TO4 NETWORK

Recall that the v6 network address derived for Karlene was "2002:c896:641e::1," and recall that only the leftmost 48 bits are required to uniquely describe Karlene as a 6to4 node operating at IPv4 address 200.150.100.30. We could then address an entire network "behind" Karlene, and that network would be represented as "2002:c896:641e::1::/48." Remember that the "/48" specifies how many bits are being used by the prefix, so this leaves a "::/80" for the network. We have, then, actually configured the network "2002:c896:641e::1::/48" as being reachable via Karlene at IPv4 address 200.150.100.30, and we've assigned the IPv6 address "2002:c896:641e::1" to Karlene. The remaining addresses in the block are free to be assigned within a large IPv6 network "behind" Karlene, and Karlene will act as an edge-router to deliver those packets to other 6to4 networks (see Figure 20–3).

This is where the real power in the 6to4 mechanism becomes apparent. Simply allowing two individual nodes—nodes that must, by definition, each have a globally routable (i.e., non-NAT) IPv4 address—to exchange IPv6 packets within a tunnel would not be a worthwhile achievement.

But allowing two "::/48" IPv6 networks to be able to exchange packets via two IPv4 nodes is a powerful transition mechanism. Recall that a "::/80" network implies that each network can be made up of 2^{16} individual networks, where each network can support $2^{64} - 2$ devices.

That's a big network! At the time of this writing, the IETF IPv6 address allocation plan is to allocate a "::/48"-size block to enterprises as a standard allocation. So an enterprise with a single routable IPv4 address can "self-allocate" the same size block for transition as they are likely to hold when they have moved to native v6 addresses.

20.2.4   6TO4 NODE TO NATIVE-IPV6

What about 6to4 nodes or 6to4 networks exchanging packets with native IPv6 nodes? Since native IPv6 nodes do not reside "behind" an IPv4-address and don't use the 6to4-reserved address prefix "2002::/16," how are packets delivered to those nodes? The IETF has designed that capability in the 6to4 mechanism—native IPv6 packet delivery is provided by devices called "6to4 relays" (6to4 relay).

A 6to4 relay is typically a dedicated machine with multiple network interfaces—one on the IPv4 network (where 6to4 nodes and networks would be deployed) and one on the native IPv6 network. The 6to4 relay must implement the 6to4 relay function. Here's how it works.

6to4 relays are located at a well-known IPv4 address—"192.88.99.1" (proposed RFC—3068). We'll see in a moment how this works, but there will be many 6to4 relays operating during the transition. When the IPv6 stack on a 6to4 node (or network—our example uses the simple case) attempts to send a packet to an address beginning with 2002::/16, the previous case is used—the 6to4 function delivers the packet to the IPv4 address encoded in the IPv6 destination address field. If the destination IPv6 address is not in the 2002::/16 network—say the destination address is "2001:2d0:80:ee::6"—the 6to4 node's 6to4 function will recognize that the address is not a 6to4 address, and assume that the address is reachable via a 6to4 relay, and will deliver the packet—encapsulated in IPv4—to the 6to4 relay at 192.88.99.1. The 6to4 relay unencapsulates the packet and sends the v6 packet to the native v6 host.

6to4 relays also provide packet transit from the v6 network to 6to4 nodes and networks located on the v4 network. A native v6 node will send all packets destined for the 2002::/16 network to a nearby 6to4 relay, which will encapsulate the packet in v4 and send it to the IPv4 address encoded within the v6 address.

20.2.5 6TO4 SCALABILITY

There will be many 6to4 relays operating at the intersection of the "old" IPv4 network (the Internet) and the "new" IPv6 network (let's call it the "v6net"). If a 6to4 node on the Internet wishes to deliver a packet to a node on the v6net, there will be multiple 6to4 relays that could be used to effect transit. Likewise, any v6net node sending a packet to a 6to4 node (i.e., 2002::/16) can use the services of a number of 6to4 relays. The nodes choose the "best" 6to4 relay, using exterior routing protocols that determine the best path between networks.

We'll just touch on this—this is standard BGP network routing. Each 6to4 relay will advertise a route to the entire 2002::/16 network into the v6net. BGP optimization will determine, for each node or network, the logically closest 6to4 relay to deliver packets to that network. Similarly, each 6to4 relay will advertise the well-known network address 192.88.99.0 (mask 255.255.255.0) into the Internet, and 6to4 nodes will choose the logically closest 6to4 relay to deliver their packets to the v6net.

Each network looks like a large multihomed network to the peer network (i.e., the v6net looks like a multihomed network to the Internet, and vice versa).

Two last important points: 6to4 relays are stateless—they don't track sessions to streams of packets, they provide delivery on a packet-by-packet basis, and each packet contains all the information the relay needs to effect delivery. This is important because the multirelay environment implies that as the networks change over time (including in real-time, during a internetwork session) different 6to4 relays can be used in a given session. In fact, if you consider the complex topologies of these networks, it is very likely that two machines exchanging packets across the v6net-Internet boundary will use the services of different 6to4 relays. As an example, a packet originating from nodeA on the Internet bound for nodeB on the v6net will transit via relayQ. Packets flowing in the other direction will use the services of relayU. In midsession, if there are changes to the BGP+ routing environment within the v6net, packets may shift to transit via relayV (Figure 20–4).

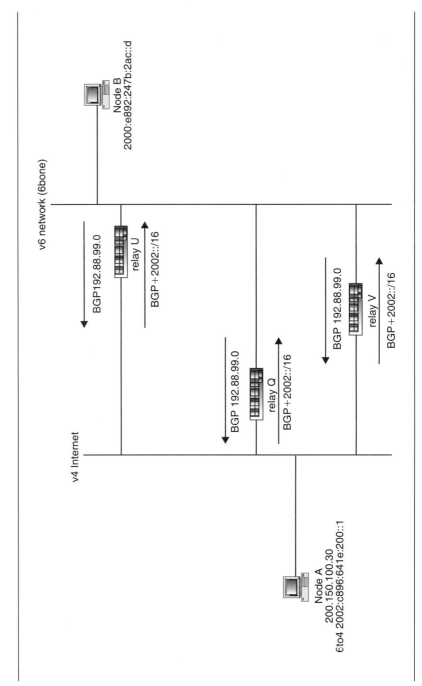

Figure 20–4: 6to4 coping with changing topologies.

The last important point is we assume that the Internet and v6nets are both "fully meshed." In other words, we assume that any 6to4 relay has connectivity to every 6to4 node and native v6net node. This is a requirement (and not a bad assumption) if we are to allow multiple 6to4 relays to advertise reachability to the entirety of both networks.

20.3   ISATAP

Intra-Site Automatic Tunnel Addressing Protocol (ISATAP) is a complementary transition tool to 6to4. Whereas 6to4 provides a mechanism for v6-capable nodes or networks existing within a larger IPv4-only network to gain access to other IPv6 networks, ISATAP provides v6 connectivity within an enterprise where the internal network fabric is not entirely IPv6-capable. ISATAP is another form of "automatic tunnel."

ISATAP is currently an IETF draft, so there may still be changes in how the mechanism works.

Let's look at an example. Figure 20–5 shows an enterprise that has obtained a ::/48 network prefix (3ffe:80f0:0004::/48). We see that there are three internal routers and five hosts shown. We see that HostE has a native v6-address. RTRz (Router Z) is v6-enabled, so HostD has a native v6-address. We see that RTRy and RTRx are v4-only routers—for whatever reason they are not deployed with a v6 capability. ISATAP allows us to extend a global v6 address and global v6-capability to HostC, HostA, and HostB. Addresses and other notes on the diagram will be used throughout the example.

As you recall, 6to4 allows a node with a globally routable v4 address to construct a globally routable v6 network—the v4 address of the 6to4 node (or edge-node) makes up the low-order 32 bits of the 48-bit 6to4 prefix (2002::/16 making up the highest-order 16 bits). The remaining address bits—the lowest 80 bits—are used for v6 addressing inside the 6to4 site.

For ISATAP, the high-order 48-bits are obtained as a globally routable v6-address block for the enterprise, and ISATAP uses the lower 80 bits to construct addresses inside the enterprise. In fact, the IPv4 addresses of the ISATAP hosts are used to construct the lowest 32 bits of the ISATAP address.

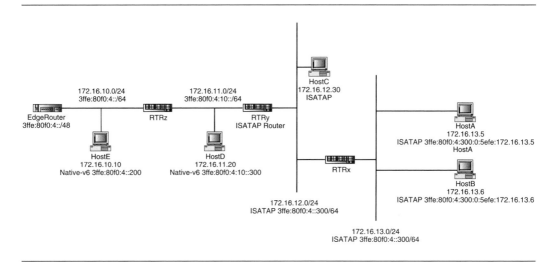

Figure 20–5: Deploying ISATAP.

The ISATAP host uses the services of an "ISATAP router"—typically a router that has a native v6-interface and a v4-only interface designated as the ISATAP interface. The network administrator assigns an "ISATAP prefix" to the router (in our case 3ffe:80f0:4:300::/64). The IPv4 address of the router is also added to the enterprise DNS under the well-known name "ISATAP." The ISATAP router will then forward v6-packets onto the native v6 network from ISATAP hosts using the router as its ISATAP tunnel-endpoint.

Here's how it works. HostA is configured with an IPv4-address (you can see that does not need to be routable) to run the ISATAP mechanism. When HostA enables its network link, seeing that it is an ISATAP host, it asks the DNS for the address of "ISATAP." The DNS replies with the v4-address of RTRy. Next, HostA tunnels a router discovery packet (IPv6-in-IPv4) to RTRy, and RTRy responds with a router advertisement (including the network prefix for HostA to use—3ffe:80f0:4:300::/64). Upon receipt of the prefix, HostA constructs its globally unique IPv6 address, 3ffe:80f0:4:300:0:5efe:172.16.13.5 (the "0:5efe" in the address is a reserved value that specifies an ISATAP address). At this point, HostA has obtained full IPv6 capability via the services provided by the ISATAP router RTRy.

The ISATAP specification makes arrangements for the graceful transition to native v6 capability. Only ISATAP nodes that do not receive multicast router advertisements (RA) for IPv6 will configure and use ISATAP interfaces. When an ISATAP machine receives its first unsolicited native RA, it will deprecate the ISATAP interface in favor of its newly acquired native v6 interface. In this fashion, ISATAP traffic will automatically give way to native v6 traffic as additional enterprise routers are configured with v6.

Our example is for a simple enterprise network where all ISATAP hosts use the same ISATAP router. In a larger enterprise, multiple ISATAP routers can be deployed, and some scheme of load-balancing DNS can direct different hosts to different ISATAP routers. One possibility would be simple round-robin DNS processing, where the load would be balanced between however many ISATAP routers were configured on the network and in the DNS. More effective techniques to distribute traffic between multiple ISATAP routers may be introduced.

20.4   Preparing for Transition

The first steps to a successful transition is to make sure your staff is well trained and that the enterprise has a place to test out equipment and concepts. A little training will go a long way for IPv4-savvy engineers.

20.4.1   IPv6 Training

IPv6 and IPv4 are alike in many ways, and learning IPv6 concepts normally comes easily to current network practitioners. Conceptually, packet generation and formatting, routing, and packet handling are similar but not identical.

It is time consuming, however, for network practitioners to make the leap to IPv6 without some formal training. New concepts, like autoconfiguration, neighbor discovery, address planning and subnetting, and the extensions to the routing protocol are unfamiliar at first but are easily mastered when explained by an experienced IPv6 engineer. Reinforcing these concepts in a lab setting is critical, and having a "sandbox" environment to experiment in back at the students home-enterprise is also important.

Training should span a number of different disciplines. Network engineers that will be designing the IPv6 network need to understand it at all levels. This includes a general overview of the protocol, transition strategies and methods, and any areas of specialty instruction appropriate for that engineer (i.e., routing protocols, DNS, address architecture). Like the network engineer, network administrators will need general knowledge of IPv6m but also hands-on experience with network devices' (routers, switches, firewalls, servers, etc.) configuration and support procedures.

So whereas it is important that your network staff receive structured IPv6 training, it is important not to overlook the large base of common ground upon which your existing engineers can build. They will quickly master the new protocol with some training and time to experiment.

20.4.2   THE LEARNING LAB

There are a number of things to consider when designing your *IPv6 Learning Lab*. First and foremost is the requirement of knowing your own business and building the lab to help your people understand the components and architectures you'll be dealing with most often. If your organization will be buying IPv6 technology and deploying it internally, your lab should reflect the products and services you will be purchasing as well as the internal network environment; if your organization will be reselling IPv6 technologies, your lab should incorporate the products and services you intend to sell as well as the environments into which you will be selling.

Here are some other suggestions for designing and building a learning lab.

Flexibility   Build independent areas in the lab so different types of testing, on different components or software versions, can take place at the same time. Some projects will be long lived, so make sure you don't have to disrupt tests-in-progress for "right now" exercises.

Isolation   The lab should always be separate from any production environment. Your lab is an environment for learning, and that means being able to change configurations and try things that might not work. Isolating the lab environment ensures that experiments will not produce any problems on your organization's production network, and vice versa.

Partnerships   You can leverage your lab investment by offering to do testing for companies with whom you have relationships, whether they be customers or suppliers. This is a great way to build a win-win relationship with a key provider and gives you the benefit of early insight into their products and experience for your staff while giving them early feedback on their products.

Interoperability   IPv6 is a feature-rich protocol, and you'll want to ensure that all the components, particularly components from different vendors, all work smoothly together. Vendors tend to concentrate on interoperability within their own product lines, so it is important to stock the same components that your organizational network uses so you can test in your own lab.

The learning lab should incorporate testing facilities for three major areas.

Network Infrastructure   The lab should, at a minimum, include core and edge routers, switches, firewalls, and other relevant devices. At the very least, you should have one core router, one edge router, two or three multilayer switches, and one v6-capable firewall.

Network Operating Systems   In addition to the operating systems already in use in your network environment, you may want to consider adding other OSes to test for interoperability. A great deal of experimentation with IPv6 has been done with various flavors of BSD and Linux; Microsoft's IPv6 support under the latest versions of Windows will undoubtedly be superior to that of earlier versions.

Network Services   In addition to any network services DNS (Static and Dynamic), DHCPv6 (HP-UX11i, W2K2), HTTP (Apache), Security (IPF, Checkpoint, Router ACL), Printing, Network Management (HPOV), and so on.

The key thing is to build a learning lab that fits your business needs.

20.5   Planning

Planning is critical for a trouble-free transition. There are many variables, but two are particularly important. One is planning for long-lived physical and software assets that will affect the pace of transition, and the other is an architectural decision about traffic flows in your transitioning network.

20.5.1 PLAN CAPITAL PURCHASES

Many network component providers are planning their IPv6 product line, and some are deploying products today that support IPv6—either beta or true production-ready versions. Several of these vendors (Cisco, for example) have published "product roadmaps" that lay out their plans for IPv6 support. Some products will be "dead-ended" before v6 support is added.

So an enterprise needs to carefully plan its network and system capital purchases to avoid a situation where a new component has been purchased (i.e., a core router) that has significant depreciable life left but does not support IPv6 when the enterprise is ready to transition.

These types of costly mistakes are easily avoided. Talk to your network vendors, and ask to see their roadmaps, or be briefed by their product development people on their plans. Get firm commitments for product plans and milestone dates. The transition to IPv6 provides an excellent opportunity to review your network plans—and change strategies or your favored vendor providers—if that works to your advantage.

20.5.2 TRANSLATION

Whether or not an enterprise plans to use packet translation during the transition has a major impact on how the new network is deployed.

A firm can choose to not use translation—you simply lose the ability for v4-only and v6-only nodes to talk to each other. If the network fabric is v6/v4 enabled, and the network servers (i.e., any machine that multiple clients exchange packets with) are v4/v6 enabled (i.e., running "dual stack"), then new computer clients can be deployed with only v6 connectivity, while "old" systems can continue to run IPv4. In this manner, no protocol translation is needed—systems exchange packets via the "highest common denominator" protocol, choosing v6 if they both support it, and v4 if one endpoint is not v6-ready.

Alternatively, all new client systems can be deployed dual-stack. This gives complete backward-compatibility with deployed systems that can only support v4, and yet new applications that can take advantage of v6 can use v6 when communicating with newly deployed systems. Typically, in environments where clients greatly outnumber servers, deploying both protocols on clients is not the best strategy.

The enterprise can also install a translator. Translators provide the most complete interoperability for the network. Any machine can talk to any other, and as more and more network nodes become v6-enabled, traffic migrates to an all-v6 base. This is a good implementation choice for environments that are more peer-to-peer oriented than client-server oriented. The problem with translation is that it is slow (translation—especially software translation takes time) and can create a bottleneck in the network for translation traffic. Yet, the delay caused by translation may be offset by the ability to access content or services that exist only in the v4 world.

Translation devices are not yet widely available, so it is hard to quantify the network efficiency affects of translation on a network. Nonetheless, it is an important consideration you will need to evaluate when your enterprise makes the migration to v6.

20.5.3 APPLICATIONS

Applications must be v6-capable to support the enterprise transition. Although most v6 changes are isolated at the network layer, many applications that use network services do validation checking on inputs (i.e., when a node rejects an IPv6 address because the node has been configured to allow only valid IPv4 addresses) or results from DNS.

At the least, any network application will need to be recompiled using the v6-capable link libraries. For purchased applications, make sure the vendor verifies v6-support before you buy.

20.5.4 PUBLIC INTERNET SITES WILL LAG

Commerce and nontechnology sites on the Internet will likely be midphase adopters of IPv6. Much in the way that Web site builders optimize their designs for the "middle" of the market in terms of browser compatibility and bandwidth requirements, Internet sites that have a mass market appeal will not support IPv6 until there is a critical mass in the user community—especially if translation becomes a commonly deployed transition tool. Once critical mass is achieved, or as the volume of IPv4 packets diminish in favor of an accelerating IPv6 packet count, network service providers will move into the v6 environment in an effort to "chase the money."

For these reasons, an enterprise may choose to deploy translation—not inside the network (which we described before as an option) but at the network edge—to provide v4-capability for workstations to communicate with lagging Internet-based systems. Proxy services, where your internal clients talk to the proxy via v6, but the proxy talks to the Internet site via v4, may also become available.

20.5.5   IPv6 Routing

While IPv6 has been under development for many years, it is only in the recent few that support for v6 has been incorporated into the equipment that comprises the Internet's infrastructure. Currently, IPv6 packet forwarding (routing) is being handled in two ways. The first, and most common, is via "software-based forwarding." In a software-based system, the network engineer or administrator downloads and installs a new image (operating system) onto the existing router (IPv4-only) that identifies how to handle IPv6 packets. When packets (IPv6) come through the router that cannot be handled by the hardware, they are passed along to the operating system and processed.

The second method is by hardware-based forwarding. Unlike software-based forwarding, the instructions for handling IPv6 packets are "hard coded" into the chip sets on the routers (much like the CMOS on a PC). Almost all routers today do hardware-based forwarding for IPv4 packets. Hardware-based forwarding is very efficient and generally trouble free.

The significant difference between the two methods is in performance. In a software-based implementation, every IPv6 packet must be handled by the operating system, which requires additional time. While that time may be relatively small on a per-packet basis, it makes a dramatic difference in a production network. Production network routers may handle billions of packets per day, making software-based forwarding inefficient for practical purposes. Unfortunately, many of today's routers cannot be "upgraded" to handle IPv6 in the hardware and must be replaced to support IPv6.

Additionally, there are other factors that will affect the performance and efficiency of IPv6 routing. As previously mentioned, two IPv6-enabled routers can pass packets through an IPv4 cloud by utilizing tunnels. However, the process of encapsulation and decapsulation increases the amount of time it takes to handle each packet. And by encapsulating the packet within an IPv4 packet, many of the improvements and benefits of IPv6 are lost.

The actual protocols utilized to provide IPv6 packet routing are very similar to those available today for IPv4. Routing protocols, such as RIP and OSPF, are available, and at the time of this writing the following routing protocols have been enhanced or developed for IPv6: RIPv2 to RIPng, OSPFv2 to OSPFv3, BGP4 to BGP4+, and ISIS. Other protocols, such EIGRP, may be enhanced to support IPv6 in the future.

Of course, one of the most important aspects of the transition process is that each piece of equipment handles the IPv6 packet uniformly. The IETF and the IPv6 working groups have spent a great deal of time and energy standardizing IPv6. However, not all equipment manufacturers will support every aspect of IPv6 at the same time. Many of today's IPv6-enabled router manufacturers support IPv6 at some level but don't necessarily support all of the more advanced features or routing protocols. As IPv6 matures the level of interoperability between vendors will increase.

20.5.6 OBTAINING AND PLANNING FOR IPv6 ADDRESSES

Planning for IPv6 addressing is largely a matter of allocating addresses wisely throughout your enterprise. v6 addresses are made to summarize well—that is, to be hierarchical. If your address blocks are well planned for summarization, your network will be more efficient, easier to manage, and cheaper to implement.

Plan for the future. Leave plenty of "reserved" space in your addressing scheme to account for future growth. In this way you avoid having to add noncontiguous blocks of addresses throughout the network as it grows.

Use address scoping (link-local, site-local, global) where feasible. For example, for a directly connected Ethernet link between two routers, use only the link-local addresses of the routers. Or for an isolated v6 network that does not need to route outside the "site," utilize site-local addressing only.

Most enterprises will obtain v6 allocations from your current v6 ISP (ISP would provide a block from their current v6 allocation). Unlike IPv4 allocations, where enterprises can "own" their own addresses and move them from ISP to ISP, v6 addressing—since it is designed to be hierarchical—works differently. Large ISPs receive large IPv6 address blocks and allocate them to smaller ISPs and large enterprises. Your v6 addresses will almost always be part of a larger block allocated to your ISP.

You can also get a block for your enterprise from a test allocation. The 6Bone (www.6bone.com—addresses in the 3ffe::/16 range) will provide addresses to most any enterprise wanting to gain early experience with IPv6. This is, however, very much a "do-it-yourself" project, and it is a much larger project recommended only for companies who want to be a bit ahead of the leading edge.

Last, if your enterprise is going to be an ISP, after you've managed your business well with a test allocation from the 6Bone, you can seek a large block of production addresses from a public Internet registry like IANA, ARIN, or APNIC for production v6 address blocks.

20.6   Migration

At this point the enterprise is ready to begin the gradual transition to an all-IPv6 network. The goal is to migrate the network to IPv6 with no disruption to current v4 operations. The following steps form a logical process of enabling the base infrastructure, network fabric, and finally, the server and client nodes on the network.

20.6.1   UPGRADE YOUR DNS ENVIRONMENT

Two important distinctions on v6 DNS functionality need to be made up-front. Some newer DNS implementations provide support for v6 address records (AAAA and A6 records) but do not answer DNS queries via the IPv6 protocol. Other implementations provide both—the v6 records and the ability to respond to queries via IPv6. We will not discuss DNS configuration in detail here.

A properly configured DNS can contain both v4 and v6 records for a given hostname. For example, the host "bob.pretend.dog" (note that "dog" is not a real domain) can be resolved by the DNS as either 10.20.30.40 or 3ffe:4b0::2. In fact, if both records are available, both are returned to the DNS client. The client then chooses which address to use, based on the protocols available on the client.

You see that this is an ideal situation for transition. IPv6-capable clients, seeking access to IPv6-capable applications on the network will use the v6 address returned by the DNS (we assume that the server in this example is dual-stacked). As long as there is also an IPv4 address associated with the server, IPv4-only clients will access the application via IPv4—using the v4 address returned by the DNS. As the transition progresses and more network services move to dual-stack (and more clients move to dual-stack), traffic will migrate to IPv6. Complete transition will be marked by the removal of all v4 address records from the DNS.

20.6.2 UPGRADE THE NETWORK FABRIC

At this point, all the components that make up the fabric of your network must be upgraded to be IPv6 compatible—as well as IPv4 capable, since there will be a transition period during which both protocols will be active on the network. The upgrade task can be divided into three steps.

1. Determine specifically how each component needs to be upgraded, and outline a detailed transition plan—including a recovery/backout procedure.
2. Obtain the hardware and software components needed, and test them together in a nonproduction environment.
3. Complete the transition plan.

20.6.3 OUTLINE THE PLAN

Begin by outlining the transition plan. Consider the specific components that will be upgraded, and consult the vendor on the proper procedures. Make sure a backout plan exists for each component in the network and for the transition plan as a whole.

Consider the following for each component.

• Do the network routers support hardware- or software-based IPv6 packet handling?

- If IPv6 is handled in software, what device image is required for IPv6 support?
- Are there additional hardware requirements to support IPv6—or the new software image—like additional memory or storage?
- If this is a multivendor network, carefully compare the components for hardware support capabilities (i.e., one vendor may support gigabit Ethernet for IPv6, whereas another vendor will not).
- Verify that the routing scheme used on the network will support IPv6. Verify that the layer 3 switches in the network support IPv6.
- Layer 2 switches, since they do not examine or act upon IP headers, should support IPv6 without any modification.
- Examine the network edge devices like firewalls and intrusion detection systems to ensure they support IPv6, and plan for their upgrade.

20.6.4 OBTAIN UPGRADE COMPONENTS

Once the plan is in place, collect the hardware components and software images needed to begin the transition. In some cases, this will be as simple as downloading a new device image from your vendor. In other cases, a complete "forklift upgrade" will be required.

Test everything in a nonproduction environment. The learning lab should easily adapt to this new level of testing. Conduct a system—not component—test before beginning the transition. Be systematic in testing, and remember to test for performance as well as for functionality and interoperability. Make changes to the network under test as you would in your production environment to ensure that the operational procedures in place are also sufficient to support the new IPv6-capable network.

20.7 Transition

At this point, the network is ready to transition to dual-protocol capability. Plan the specific upgrades by scheduling network outages, and leave yourself plenty of time to handle the unforeseen problems that inevitably arise. If too many problems arise to complete the transition successfully, use the backout plan.

20.7.1   DUAL-STACK THE SERVERS

Once you have completed these steps, you are ready to enable server platforms with IPv6 in addition to IPv4. The applications available at the server must also be IPv6 compatible and configured properly.

In a typical enterprise, servers should be given assigned IPv6 addresses. Clients should autoconfigure—that feature is one of the great strengths of IPv6. When the addressing scheme is developed, provisions should be made to reserve consistent blocks for servers (i.e., in each ::/64 network use the addresses 200 to 2000 for servers).

The process, then, is simple. Configure IPv6 on each server, using a static address from the block set aside for that purpose, and add that v6 address to the DNS—in addition to the IPv4 address already associated with the server name.

20.7.2   DEPLOY IPv6-CAPABLE CLIENTS

At this point, new client workstations can be deployed with v6-support only. v6-capable workstations will self-select v6 connectivity to v6-capable hosts in your network by choosing the v6-address returned by the DNS, while older v4-only workstations will continue to use IPv4 (assuming that the specific host has both IPv4 and IPv6 entries in the DNS).

20.7.3   PHASE OUT IPv4

Over time, as older workstations are retired, the enterprise will complete its transition to IPv6. Network engineers monitoring the network will detect when IPv4 traffic is gone. At that time, new servers can be deployed as v6-only systems. Eventually, v4 support can be dropped at every point in the network—servers, network devices, ISP upstream—everywhere.

20.8   Summary

The keys to a successful migration are preparing your staff, planning ahead, starting early, and being patient. The transition for large enterprises will take years, since new capital equipment purchases supplant older systems, new application development and deployment takes place, and critical-but-not-upgradeable applications and systems are replaced.

IPv6 transition will follow the adoption path of network-effect systems. It will be slow at first, since there are few IPv6-enabled peer machines to talk to, but then, as the number of v6-capable machines increases, deployment plans will "turn the corner" and proceed rapidly toward an all-IPv6 system. You don't want your enterprise to be caught off guard.

21

Configuring IPv6 on Server Operating Systems

This chapter includes step-by-step instructions for configuring IPv6 on the Windows NT, FreeBSD, and Solaris operating systems.

21.1   Configuring IPv6 on Windows NT*

This section provides step-by-step instructions for configuring IPv6 on Windows NT (versions 4.0, 5.0/2000, and 5.1/XP).

21.1.1   MICROSOFT SUPPORT

Microsoft first publicly released a technical preview IPv6 stack for development purposes in March 2000 to work with Windows NT 4.0 and

---

*This section is adapted from a document written by Jim Van Gemert, © Zama Networks.

Windows 2000. Microsoft did not publish Windows 9x support and later acknowledged it will only develop and support IPv6 for Windows NT releases.

Microsoft has released three versions of IPv6 for Windows NT including "Research IPv6 Protocol," "IPv6 Technology Preview," and "IPv6 Developer Edition." Research IPv6 Protocol installs and works on Windows NT 4.0 and 5.0. IPv6 Technology Preview installs and works only on Windows NT 5.0 (2000). IPv6 Developer Edition is integrated with Windows NT 5.1 (XP) but not activated by default after install.

Microsoft has published a number of documents introducing IPv6 to Windows developers and early adopters, available at their IPv6 Web sites.

21.1.2 MICROSOFT IPv6 TECHNOLOGY PREVIEW

Microsoft's IPv6 Technology Preview[1] can be obtained from msdn. microsoft.com/downloads/sdks/platform/tpipv6/download.asp.

System Requirements

- Windows 2000 SP1
- Ethernet network adapter (any Ethernet adapter supported by Windows 2000 should work with the IPv6 Technology Preview)
- IPv4 protocol (the Internet Protocol [TCP/IP] supplied with Windows 2000 must be installed)

Installing the IPv6 Technology Preview for Windows 2000

1. Log on to the Windows 2000 computer with a user account that has local administrator privileges.
2. Using Windows Explorer, run the Setup.exe program from the location where you extracted the IPv6 Technology Preview files.

---

[1]As of 2003, Microsoft incorporates IPv6 support in its Windows Server 2003 family, Windows XP, and Windows CE.NET version 4.1 operating systems. IPv6 support in Windows XP is a developer release version, whereas a production-quality version is incorporated into Windows XP Service Pack 1 (SP1).

3. From the Windows 2000 desktop, click Start, point to Settings, and then click Network and Dial-up Connections. As an alternative, you can right-click My Network Places, and then click Properties.
4. Right-click the Ethernet-based connection to which you want to add the IPv6 protocol, and then click Properties. Typically, this connection is named Local Area Connection.
5. Click Install.
6. In the Select Network Component Type dialog box, click Protocol, and then click Add.
7. In the Select Network Protocol dialog box, click Microsoft IPv6 Protocol, and then click OK.
8. Click Close to close the Local Area Connection Properties dialog box.

The Microsoft IPv6 Protocol is automatically added to all Ethernet interfaces on your computer.

21.1.3 Microsoft Windows Integrated IPv6 Release

Support for IPv6 was first incorporated into a production Microsoft product in Windows XP. To enable IPv6, the operating system must first be installed normally, with IPv6 support; then install the IPv6 Developer Edition from the Network Configuration, as follows.

1. Log on to the Windows XP computer with a user account that has local administrator privileges.
2. From the Windows XP desktop, click Start, point to Settings, and then click Network and Dial-up Connections. As an alternative, you can right-click My Network Places, and then click Properties.
3. Right-click the Ethernet-based connection to which you want to add the IPv6 protocol, and then click Properties. Typically, this connection is named Local Area Connection.
4. Click Install.
5. In the Select Network Component Type dialog box, click Protocol, and then click Add.
6. In the Select Network Protocol dialog box, click Microsoft IPv6 Developer Edition Protocol, and then click OK.
7. Click Close to close the Local Area Connection Properties dialog box.

The Microsoft IPv6 Protocol is automatically added to all Ethernet interfaces on your computer.

21.1.4 INSTALLER COMMENTS

At a command line enter IPv6 if to determine your IPv6 address. Sample output from the IPv6 if command is shown in Table 16–1. Interface #1 is a pseudo-interface used for loopback. Interface #2 is a pseudo-interface used for configured tunneling, automatic tunneling, and 6to4 tunneling. Other interfaces are numbered sequentially in the order in which they are created. The number on your IPv6 network interface is not static and can be any number above 2.

A key indicator is the link-level address of your NIC, with a MAC address like 00-01-02-e8-ec-31. In Table 21–1, Interface 3 is connected to an IPv6 network. It has the preferred address 3ffe:80f0:10:2:201:2ff:fee8:ec31, a combination of site information (3ffe:80f0:10:2) and local information (201:2ff:fee8:ec31). If only one preferred address is supplied, your NIC has not received site broadcast information, and the preferred address will be still set to default (fe80::201:2ff:fee8:ec31).

Internet Protocol (IPv4) is needed for name resolution even if an IPv6 DNS address can be supplied. (I have tested Internet Explorer 5.0 with SP1, 5.5, and 6.0 Beta release on Windows 2000. I have also tested IE 5.6 on Windows XP Beta 1.) If Internet Explorer is updated, the Microsoft stack must be reinstalled to access IPv6 sites.

21.2   Configuring IPv6 on FreeBSD**

This section provides step-by-step instructions for configuring IPv6 on the FreeBSD operating system. Here's a brief list of what you'll need for this project.

- An Intel-based machine with network connectivity. My recommendation on bare minimum requirements would be a Pentium machine with 1GHz hard drive space and 64MB of RAM.

**This section is adapted from a document written by Gerald R. Crow IV, © Zama Networks.

```
Interface 3 (site 1): Local Area Connection
  uses Neighbor Discovery
    link-level address: 00-01-02-e8-ec-31
      preferred address 3ffe:80f0:10:2:201:2ff:fee8:ec31,
      2591896s/604696s (addrconf)
      preferred address fe80::201:2ff:fee8:ec31,
      infinite/infinite
      multicast address ff02::1, 1 refs, not reportable
      multicast address ff02::1:ffe8:ec31, 2 refs,
      last reporter
    link MTU 1500 (true link MTU 1500)
    current hop limit 128
    reachable time 23500ms (base 30000ms)
    retransmission interval 2000ms
    DAD transmits 1
Interface 2 (site 0): Tunnel Pseudo-Interface
  does not use Neighbor Discovery
    link-level address: 0.0.0.0
      preferred address ::172.16.12.183,
      infinite/infinite
    link MTU 1280 (true link MTU 65515)
    current hop limit 128
    reachable time 0ms (base 0ms)
    retransmission interval 0ms
    DAD transmits 0
Interface 1 (site 0): Loopback Pseudo-Interface
  does not use Neighbor Discovery
    link-level address:
      preferred address ::1, infinite/infinite
    link MTU 1500 (true link MTU 1500)
    current hop limit 1
    reachable time 0ms (base 0ms)
    retransmission interval 0ms
    DAD transmits 0
```

Table 21–1: Sample output from Microsoft Windows command, ipv6 if.

- If a static address is being used, you should have the gateway address, netmask, and IPv6 address (obtain this from the Network Administrator or your IPv6 ISP).
- The FreeBSD 4.2 software. FreeBSD can be downloaded free from ftp://ftp.freebsd.org/, or the CDs can be purchased from Walnut Creek (http://www.osd.bsdi.com) for $40.

21.2.1 KERNEL CONFIGURATION

Thanks to the KAME Project (http://www.kame.net), FreeBSD's default installation comes with IPv6 support built into the kernel. If someone has changed the kernel on your machine or you would like to enable more options, here is a list of IPv6-related kernel entries (all kernel options can be found in /sys/i386/conf/LINT).

```
...
options          INET6            # IPv6 communications protocols
...
pseudo-device    gif      4       # IPv6 and IPv4 tunneling
pseudo-device    faith    1       # IPv6-to-IPv4 relaying (translation0
pseudo-device    stf      1       # 6to4 IPV6 over IPv4 encapsulation
...
```

The default kernel configuration file is /sys/i386/conf/GENERIC and by default is configured with all the preceding options except 6to4 encapsulation. For documentation on building a FreeBSD kernel, go to http://www.freebsd.org/handbook.

The first thing you need to decide is how to assign the IPv6 IP address. Static requires a little more configuration but will ensure our address information never changes. The automatic configuration is quite painless but should only be done on a host machine where a change of IP address will not be catastrophic.

21.2.2 AUTO-CONFIGURATION

To obtain the IPv6 IP address through Auto-Configuration, merely follow this simple three-step procedure.

The first step will be to put an entry into the /etc/rc.conf file so FreeBSD knows at boot time to be on an IPv6 network. Make the following entry with your favorite text editor into the /etc/rc.conf file.

```
ipv6_enable="YES"
```

Step number 2 will be to insert any outside (if not using DNS) and local host information. The /etc/hosts file is still being used for both IPv4/IPv6 host resolution and should look similar to the following example. At a bare minimum you should make an entry for the IPv6 loopback address. (Comments are noted with a #.)

```
127.0.0.1          localhost.mydomain.com localhost # IPv4 loop back address
192.168.25.5       myhost.mydomain.com myhost       # IPv4 local host IP address
::1                localhost                         # IPv6 loop back address
3ffe:80f0:1:1:201:2ff:fe00:2112  ahost              # entry for an outside host
```

Finally, reboot the machine. When the machine comes back up, it should obtain an IPv6 address using neighbor discovery. To make sure it obtained an IPv6 address, run the command ifconfig <interface>. You should see two INET6 lines under the interface name that look similar to the following. (Comment noted with a #.)

```
>ifconfig xl0

xl0: flags=8843<UP,BROADCAST,RUNNING,SIMPLEX,MULTICAST> mtu 1500

   inet 192.168.25.5 netmask 0xffffffe0 broadcast 192.168.25.31

   inet6 fe80::201:2ff:fe3b:a30%xl0 prefixlen 64 scopeid 0x2

   inet6 3ffe:80f0:1:1:201:2ff:fe3b:a30 prefixlen 64  # IPv6 Network information

   ether00:01:02:3b:0a:30
```

Now, using the ping6 command and the IPv6 address of a machine on your network, test the machine's IPv6 connectivity. If your results look similar to the following example, then IPv6 is configured and working properly on your FreeBSD 4.2.

```
>ping6 3ffe:80f0:1:1:201:2ff:fe00:2112

PING6(56=40+8+8 bytes) 3ffe:80f0:1:1:201:2ff:fe3b:a30 -->

3ffe:80f0:1:1:201:2ff:fe00:2112

16 bytes from 3ffe:80f0:1:1:201:2ff:fe00:2112, icmp_seq=0 hlim=255 time=0.495 ms

16 bytes from 3ffe:80f0:1:1:201:2ff:fe00:2112, icmp_seq=1 hlim=255 time=0.335 ms

16 bytes from 3ffe:80f0:1:1:201:2ff:fe00:2112, icmp_seq=2 hlim=255 time=0.321 ms

16 bytes from 3ffe:80f0:1:1:201:2ff:fe00:2112, icmp_seq=3 hlim=255 time=0.338 ms

16 bytes from 3ffe:80f0:1:1:201:2ff:fe00:2112, icmp_seq=4 hlim=255 time=0.303 ms
```

```
--- 3ffe:80f0:1:1:201:2ff:fe00:2112 ping6 statistics ---

5 packets transmitted, 5 packets received, 0% packet loss

round-trip min/avg/max = 0.303/0.358/0.495 ms
```

If connected to the Internet with IPv6 capability, you need to test the connectivity and routing to the outside world. This can be done using the ping6 command on a known working IPv6 address out on the Internet, such as the following.

```
>ping6 3ffe:80f0:1:1:201:2ff:fee8:efa1

PING6(56=40+8+8 bytes) 3ffe:80f0:1:1:201:2ff:fe3b:a30 -->

3ffe:80f0:1:1:201:2ff:fee8:efa1

16 bytes from 3ffe:80f0:1:1:201:2ff:fee8:efa1, icmp_seq=0 hlim=255 time=0.476 ms

16 bytes from 3ffe:80f0:1:1:201:2ff:fee8:efa1, icmp_seq=1 hlim=255 time=0.455 ms

16 bytes from 3ffe:80f0:1:1:201:2ff:fee8:efa1, icmp_seq=2 hlim=255 time=0.379 ms

16 bytes from 3ffe:80f0:1:1:201:2ff:fee8:efa1, icmp_seq=3 hlim=255 time=0.343 ms

16 bytes from 3ffe:80f0:1:1:201:2ff:fee8:efa1, icmp_seq=4 hlim=255 time=0.359 ms

--- 3ffe:80f0:1:1:201:2ff:fee8:efa1 ping6 statistics ---

5 packets transmitted, 5 packets received, 0% packet loss

round-trip min/avg/max = 0.343/0.402/0.476 ms
```

21.2.3 STATIC CONFIGURATION

If a static address is what you're after, then configuration will be similar, and it is still a three-step procedure. Before continuing make sure you have obtained an IPv6 static IP, netmask, and default route from your network administrator or IPv6 ISP.

The first step is to make the appropriate IPv6 entries in the /etc/rc.conf file with your favorite text editor. Make sure that these entries are in the listed order, or there will be problems (comments noted with a #).

```
ipv6_enable="YES"

Ipv6_network_interfaces="xl0"   # xl0 is interface name
```

```
ipv6_ifconfig_xl0="3ffe:80f0:1:1:201:2ff:
   fe00:2113 prefixlen 64"                         # IPv6 address and netmask
ipv6_defaultrouter="fe80::204:28ff:febf:
   b000%xl0"                                       # IPv6 router address/interface
```

Step number 2 is to insert any outside (if not using DNS) and local host information. The /etc/hosts file is still being used for both IPv4/IPv6 host resolution and should look similar to the following (comments noted with a #).

```
127.0.0.1      localhost.mydomain.com localhost   # IPv4 loopback address
192.168.25.5   myhost.mydomain.com myhost         # IPv4 local host address
::1            localhost                           # IPv6 loopback address 3ffe:80f0:
                                                     1:1:201:2ff:fe00:2113
                                                   my6host.mydomain.com my6host
                                                   # IPv6 local IP address
                                                   3ffe:80f0:1:1:201:2ff:fe00:2112
                                                   ahost   # entry for outside host
```

Finally, reboot the machine. When the machine comes back up, it should configure the IPv6 network connection from the /etc/rc.conf. To make sure everything went as planned, take a look at your interface configuration using the ifconfig <interface> command. You should see the second occurrence of inet6 with the value of the static IP (comments noted with a #).

```
>ifconfig xl0
xl0: flags=8843<UP,BROADCAST,RUNNING,SIMPLEX,MULTICAST> mtu 1500
inet 192.168.25.5 netmask 0xffffffe0 broadcast 192.168.25..31
inet6 fe80::201:2ff:fe3b:a30%xl0 prefixlen 64 scopeid 0x2
inet6 3ffe:80f0:1:1:201:2ff:fe00:2113 prefixlen 64      # static address
ether 00:01:02:3b:0a:30
media: autoselect (10baseT/UTP) status: active
supported media: autoselect 100baseTX <full-duplex> 100baseTX 10baseT/UTP
            <full-duplex> 10baseT/UTP 100baseTX <hw-loopback>
```

Next, make sure that the default route was configured correctly using the netstat rn command. There will be much more information, but the IPv6 default setting is all you should be concerned with.

```
>netstat -rn

Internet6:

Destination      Gateway                              Flags     Netif

default          fe80::204:28ff:febf:b000%xl0         UGSc      xl0
```

As a final test ping a remote machine that you know to be up and running with the ping6 command. If the output from the command looks similar to the following, IPv6 is configured and working properly.

```
>ping6 3ffe:80f0:1:1:201:2ff:fe00:2112

PING6(56=40+8+8 bytes) 3ffe:80f0:1:1:201:2ff:fe00:2113 -->

3ffe:80f0:1:1:201:2ff:fe00:2112

16 bytes from 3ffe:80f0:1:1:201:2ff:fe00:2112, icmp_seq=0 hlim=255 time=0.461 ms

16 bytes from 3ffe:80f0:1:1:201:2ff:fe00:2112, icmp_seq=1 hlim=255 time=0.357 ms

16 bytes from 3ffe:80f0:1:1:201:2ff:fe00:2112, icmp_seq=2 hlim=255 time=0.319 ms

16 bytes from 3ffe:80f0:1:1:201:2ff:fe00:2112, icmp_seq=3 hlim=255 time=0.478 ms

16 bytes from 3ffe:80f0:1:1:201:2ff:fe00:2112, icmp_seq=4 hlim=255 time=0.368 ms

--- 3ffe:80f0:1:1:201:2ff:fe00:2112 ping6 statistics ---

5 packets transmitted, 5 packets received, 0% packet loss round-trip

min/avg/max = 0.319/0.396/0.478 ms
```

If connected to the Internet with IPv6 capability, you need to test the connectivity and routing to the outside world. This can be done using the ping6 command on a known working IPv6 address out on the internet, such as the following.

```
>ping6 3ffe:80f0:1:1:201:2ff:fee8:efa1

PING6(56=40+8+8 bytes) 3ffe:80f0:1:1:201:2ff:fe00:2113 -->

3ffe:80f0:1:1:201:2ff:fee8:efa1

16 bytes from 3ffe:80f0:1:1:201:2ff:fee8:efa1, icmp_seq=0 hlim=255 time=0.483 ms

16 bytes from 3ffe:80f0:1:1:201:2ff:fee8:efa1, icmp_seq=1 hlim=255 time=0.356 ms
```

```
16 bytes from 3ffe:80f0:1:1:201:2ff:fee8:efa1, icmp_seq=2 hlim=255 time=0.362 ms

16 bytes from 3ffe:80f0:1:1:201:2ff:fee8:efa1, icmp_seq=3 hlim=255 time=0.483 ms

16 bytes from 3ffe:80f0:1:1:201:2ff:fee8:efa1, icmp_seq=4 hlim=255 time=0.352 ms

--- 3ffe:80f0:1:1:201:2ff:fee8:efa1 ping6 statistics ---

5 packets transmitted, 5 packets received, 0% packet loss

round-trip min/avg/max = 0.352/0.407/0.483 ms
```

21.2.4   DNS CONFIGURATION

Configuration for DNS is still located in /etc/resolv.conf, with the added bonus of using IPv6 addresses instead of IPv4 address if need be. The following is the configuration for /etc/resolv.conf to make the request over IPv6 for the primary DNS server and over IPv4 for the secondary DNS server.

```
domain          mydomain.com
nameserver      3ffe:80f0:1:1:201:2ff:fe00:2112
nameserver      192.168.25.254
```

21.2.5   TROUBLESHOOTING

If any of the preceding configurations and/or tests do not work for you, here are some things to check.

- Make sure that all IPv6 IP addresses have colons (:) and not semicolons (;).
- Make sure the addresses we are using for configuration and ping testing are correct.
- Make sure the network you're connected to is IPv6-capable.

21.3   Configuring Solaris 8 for IPv6[†]

This section provides step-by-step instructions for configuring IPv6 on the Solaris 8 operating system. Here is what you'll need for this project.

[†]This section is adapted from a document written by Robert C. Zilbauer Jr., © Zama Networks.

- A platform capable of supporting Solaris 8. A Sun Sparc-based system would work quite well. Also, most modern Intel or Intel-compatible systems will fit the bill. I'd recommend at least 1.5GHz of disk space (for a comfortable OS install plus any third-party niceties you may want) and at least 128MB of RAM. Of course, in the case of disk space and RAM, more is always better.
- Network information such as gateway address, netmask, and the IPv6 address assigned to your new system (if a static address is desired), and so forth.
- Sun Solaris 8, available for download from Sun Microsystems for free (http://www.sun.com/software/solaris/binaries/get.html), or can be purchased for a media fee of $75 (as of this writing).
- Solaris 8 system correctly configured for use with IPv4.

At this point, we'll assume you have Solaris 8 installed, you chose to enable the IPv6 stack during the OS installation, and your IPv4 network connectivity is configured and working.

The first thing you'll need to decide is how you want your IPv6 address defined. You have two choices: You can either have it automatically configured via the Neighbor Discovery protocol or you can define your IPv6 address statically. We'll describe the automatic configuration method first, since that's the easiest.

21.3.1 AUTOCONFIGURATION

On the Solaris side of things, this is the easiest way to configure your IPv6 address. Of course, this presupposes that there's a router on your network running the Neighbor Discovery protocol and advertising the correct IPv6 address prefix. Assuming you have such a beast available, automatic configuration of your IP address is as simple as using the touch command.

You'll need to know the name of the interface over which you want to use IPv6. The primary interface on a Sun machine is often hme0. On an Intel-based machine it is often elxl0. However, if you don't know, you can usually use the ifconfig -a command to check. The output of that command will look something like this.

```
lo0:   flags=1000849<UP,LOOPBACK,RUNNING,MULTICAST,IPv4> mtu 8232 index 1
       inet 127.0.0.1 netmask ff000000
hme0:  flags=1000843<UP,BROADCAST,RUNNING,MULTICAST,IPv4> mtu 1500 index 2
       inet 192.168.25.5 netmask ffffff00 broadcast 192.168.25.255
znb0:  flags=1000843<UP,BROADCAST,RUNNING,MULTICAST,IPv4> mtu 1500 index 3
       inet 192.168.0.2 netmask ffffff00 broadcast 192.168.0.255
```

This example is from a Sun machine with two Ethernet interfaces. The first entry, lo0, is the loopback interface. The second entry is the primary interface, hme0, and the third entry is an additional interface, znb0. In our case, we'll be using the primary interface for our IPv6 traffic, but the same steps would apply to any other interface on the machine. You'd just use the name of your chosen interface wherever hme0 is referenced in this paper.

Now that we know the name of the interface we want to use, setting up autoconfiguration of your IPv6 address is simple. Just create an empty file called /etc/hostname6.<interface name>, and you're done. The easiest way to do this is by using the touch command. In our case, we'd do the following.

```
flotsam# touch /etc/hostname6.hme0
```

Then reboot. The "neighbor discovery protocol daemon" (see the in.ndpd(1m) man page for more information) will get the IPv6 prefix from your router, tack on your machine's 64-bit Extended Unique Identifier (EUI-64) address, and set the resulting address as the IPv6 address for the interface you specified.

21.3.2 DEFINING A STATIC IPv6 ADDRESS

If a static address is what you're after, don't go anywhere just yet. You've still got some work to do. As with automatic configuration, you still need an /etc/hostname6.<interface> file. However, when using a static address, this file is not empty.

In keeping with our example (using hme0 as our IPv6 interface), you'd need your /etc/hostname6.hme0 to contain one line with the following format.

```
addif host.name.domain/mask up
```

In our case, we want our new machine, flotsam.mydomain.com, to come up with the IPv6 address 3ffe:80f0:1:3:a00:20ff::5. To do this we would edit /etc/hostname6.hme0 and give it the following contents.

```
addif flotsam.mydomain.com/64 up
```

Then, in /etc/inet/ipnodes, we would add an entry for the static IP we want our machine to be known by.

```
3ffe:80f0:1:3:a00:20ff::5   flotsam.mydomain.com      flotsam
```

(Note: If you're familiar with configuring an IPv4 interface, you'll notice that the relationship between /etc/hostname6.hme0 and /etc/inet/ipnodes is very similar to their IPv4 counterparts: /etc/hostname.hme0 and /etc/hosts.)

Where your IPv6 default route is concerned, you should be fine with the autoconfigured value. Even though you have your IP address defined statically, the Neighbor Discovery process should retrieve a valid IPv6 default route from your properly configured router.

Finally, reboot the machine. When it comes up, you should have both your IPv4 and your IPv6 interfaces configured. When you take a look at your interface configuration using `ifconfig -a`, you should see something similar to the following.

```
lo0:  flags=1000849<UP,LOOPBACK,RUNNING,MULTICAST,IPv4> mtu 8232 index 1
         inet 127.0.0.1 netmask ff000000
hme0: flags=1000843<UP,BROADCAST,RUNNING,MULTICAST,IPv4> mtu 1500 index 2
         inet 192.168.25.5 netmask ffffff00 broadcast 192.168.25.255
         ether 0:1:2:c4:d:ee
lo0:  flags=2000849<UP,LOOPBACK,RUNNING,MULTICAST,IPv6> mtu 8252 index 1
         inet6 ::1/128
hme0: flags=2000841<UP,RUNNING,MULTICAST,IPv6> mtu 1500 index 2
         ether 0:1:2:c4:d:ee
         inet6 fe80::201:2ff:fec4:dee/10
hme0:1: flags=2000841<UP,RUNNING,MULTICAST,IPv6> mtu 1500 index 2
         inet6 3ffe:80f0:1:3:a00:20ff::5/64
```

In addition, you should use the `netstat -rn` command to verify that your routing tables are configured correctly. They should look something like this.

```
flotsam# netstat -rn

Routing Table: IPv4

Destination      Gateway         Flags Ref Use Interface

--------------   --------------  ----- --- --- ---------

192.168.25.0     192.168.25.5    U      1   172  hme0

224.0.0.0        192.168.25.5    U      1    0   hme0

default          192.168.25.1    UG     1   545

127.0.0.1        127.0.0.1       UH     3   12   lo0

Routing Table: IPv6

Destination/Mask       Gateway                       Flags Ref Use If

--------------------   ------------------------      ----- ----- --- --- -------

3ffe:80f0:1:3::/64     3ffe:80f0:1:3:a00:20ff::5       U     1    0  elxl0:1

fe80::/10              fe80::a00:20ff:fec5:6fa0        U     1    0  hme0

ff00::/8               fe80::a00:20ff:fec5:6fa0        U     1    0  hme0

default                fe80::a00:20ff:fec5:6fa0        U     1    0  hme0

::1                    ::1                            UH     1    0  lo0
```

Now, make sure your IPv6 connectivity is working. Ideally, you have another machine on your network configured for IPv6 to test against. Try to ping that other machine's IPv6 address (assuming that you know it will return a ping). If that works, then you've got IPv6 properly configured for your interface.

21.3.3   DNS Configuration

One more step to take is to configure your new machine to use DNS to look up IPv6 hosts on the network. This step is not required for network connectivity, but it does make life easier. You'll need to edit your /etc/nsswitch.conf file to do this.

Just like with IPv4 and the hosts entry, you should add dns to the ipnodes entry to allow DNS lookups for IPv6 addresses. After making that change, your hosts and ipnodes lines in /etc/nsswitch.conf will look like this.

```
hosts:          files dns
ipnodes:        files dns
```

You've just completed the configuration for an IPv6 interface on a Solaris 8 machine.

21.4 Other Resources

Increasingly, commercial operating systems ship with IPv6 support. Users of Linux can find information about using IPv6 in the IPv6 HOWTO document at http://www.tldp.org/HOWTO/Linux+IPv6-HOWTO/. The Apple Macintosh OS X 10.2 server OS incorporates the KAME IPv6 stack as well.

21.5 Summary

Configuring an operating system for IPv6 support is just the first step in building an IPv6 network. The next step, described in the next chapter, is to configure IPv6 routers to enable your network to connect to other IPv6 networks.

22

Configuring IPv6 Routers

This chapter includes step-by-step instructions for configuring IPv6 on Cisco, Hitachi, and NEC routers.

22.1 Configuring a Cisco 2611 Router for IPv4/v6*

Cisco Systems is shipping IPv6-capable IOS versions, and now is the time to get yourself an inexpensive Cisco router (such as a 2611) and learn the configuration techniques you'll be using soon on your production routers.

This section describes the beta version of Cisco IPv6 support. Check with Cisco for more current releases. You need to be a Cisco customer and have access to "Cisco Connection Online" (CCO) to obtain the IOS images.

---

*This section is adapted from a document written by John E. Spence, © Zama Networks.

This section provides instructions to configure a Cisco 2611 router, running IOS "Version 12.2(0.5)T." Our topology is fairly simple, but not trivial—about what one would expect for a medium- to large-size enterprise. We assume that you'll have an upstream connection from your router to the IPv4/IPv6 world, a small network directly connected to an internal firewall device, and a network (this might be a number of networks) that is inside your firewall device (which is acting as a smart router). We use static routes in this example, and we focus on IPv6-related issues.

22.1.1 GATHERING THE PIECES

To complete this configuration, you'll need a Cisco 2611 (or similar) router with at least two network interfaces, access to Cisco "beta" IOS images, a terminal for configuration, and a network into which to drop your router. One network is your "upstream" connection to an IPv6-capable device. Another network is the connection between your 2611 and your firewall (if you want to really emulate an enterprise network, you should implement an IPv6-enabled firewall, discussed in [ZAMAFW]). The last network is a "downstream" network—on the inside of your firewall (and therefore not connected directly to your 2611) with an IPv6-capable device connected, from which you can test your router configuration.

The early images are pretty big. For the image we'll use you need 16MB of "flash" memory (static memory that stores the image) and at least 32MB of "main" memory (in which to run the image). Many 2611s come with less memory than you'll need.

You'll need some specifics about the network topology you are going to build, as well as the topology you'll be meshing with. Here's what you need to plan for ahead of time, starting with general network information.

- A physical connection to an upstream IPv6- and IPv4-capable device (router or switch) that is routing IPv6 and IPv4 packets your way.
- Primary and secondary DNS that serves IPv4 and IPv6 records. Assume we're getting this service from our provider, and they've specified 192.168.201.4 and 192.168.201.5 as primary and secondary, respectively. Initially, you'll want this service, but later you'll want to experiment with building and running your own.

- (Optional) primary and secondary NTP servers, also from your ISP.

You'll also need IPv6 network configuration information.

- An IPv6 network to use behind your router. We'll use 3ffe:80f0:10::/48, which was allocated to us by our ISP. This is the recommended enterprise allocation, according to ARIN. We'll subnet this in a moment for use for the connector-network with the firewall as well as behind the firewall.
- An IPv6 address to use at the outside interface of the router (the provider will route all your v6 traffic via this address). Your ISP will specify this as well; we'll use 3ffe:80f0:1:2::101/64.
- An IPv6-address that will be your router's default route, also from your ISP. We'll use 3ffe:80f0:1:2::1/64.

And you'll need IPv4 network configuration information.

- Two IPv4 networks—both allocated by your ISP. First, a network to use behind your firewall. We'll use 192.168.200.32/27 (that's mask 255.255.255.224—32 addresses). Let's also assume we've been given network 192.168.200.252/30 (mask 255.255.255.252) to use. You'll see these again shortly. You'll notice that your ISP will allocate you quite a large number of IPv6 addresses but not many IPv4 addresses.
- An IPv4 address to use at your router's outside interface (as with IPv6, your provider will send all your v4 traffic via this IP address). We'll use 192.168.200.2/27.
- An IPv4 address that will be your router's default route. We'll use 192.168.200.1/27.

22.1.2 PLANNING YOUR NETWORK

Now that you've got the information you need from your IPv6-capable ISP, we can plan your network. Here, we'll plan on having a network segment "downstream" from our router, directly attached, that connects to another device (this would be, typically, either a "core router" for your enterprise or an IPv6-capable firewall). So both sides of the Cisco 2611 will be point-to-point networks. Beyond the firewall (I'm going to make that assumption) we'll have an IPv6 network and an IPv4 network. The topology used for this example is shown in Figure 22–1.

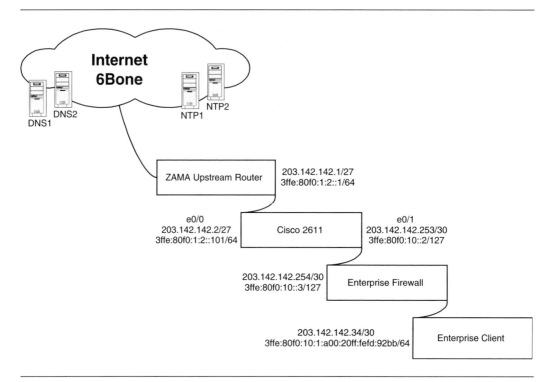

Figure 22–1: Network and system topology and interfaces for Cisco 2611 IPv6 configuration.

For our router, let's choose the interface addresses. First, we'll do IPv4. We'll use the address we got from our provider for our "outside" address (we use interface "e0/0"), and that's 192.168.200.2, mask 255.255.255.224.

For our "connector network" (that's the two-node network connecting our routers "inside" interface to the firewall), let's use the little network we got from our ISP: 192.168.200.252/30 (that's mask 255.255.255.252). We'll use 192.168.200.253/30 for our router's "inside" interface (we use "e0/1"). For the firewall interface on this network (we won't configure the firewall, but we need to choose that address), let's choose 192.168.200.254/30.

The network behind the firewall inside our network, will use the 32-address network we got from our provider—192.168.200.32/27.

Now, let's design the IPv6 network, which, of course, has the same physical topology as the IPv4 network. In the case of our IPv6 addresses, we received a single "/48" block from our provider.

Our "outside" interface is set by our provider. We'll be using 3ffe:80f0:1:2::101/64 on e0/0 (static, since we don't want to have to change the routes in the upstream router if we change our hardware).

Inside, we need to think about that "connector network." The analogous IPv6 network would be 3ffe:80f0:10::2/127. Our e0/1 interface will be 3ffe:80f0:10::2/127, and the same network interface at the firewall would be 3ffe:80f0:10::3/127. Behind the firewall, we'll assume we've allocated part of our huge /48 network—let's say 3ffe:80f0:10:1::/64 (just perfect for a single network supporting IPv6 autoconfiguration).

22.1.3   INSTALLING THE IOS IMAGE

The first step is to get the IOS image. Connect to http://www.cisco.com/warp/public/732/ipv6/index.html, and click on "Obtain IOS IPv6 Beta Software." Find the right image for your router—we'll use "c2600-is-mz.122-0.5.T." Click on the image name, review and approve the license agreement, and download the image. Put the image onto a TFYP server you can access from the current location of the 2611.

Assuming that you are bringing your 2611 to life from an unused state, you'll need to use the "tftpdnld" facility to get the image onto the machine from your TFTP server. This is nothing special; it is very well covered in the Cisco 2600 documentation. You can also use the image that comes installed on the device, put it on the network, and tftp the IPv6-capable image to the machine.

22.1.4   CONFIGURING THE ROUTER

When you've got the image loaded on your router, you'll finish up by doing a "reload." The router will ask you to confirm that you really want to do that. Say "Yes." The router will reload and come up with the basic dialog. This is where you answer basic questions about your router's name, IP-address, netmask, and a couple of other things. This is a very standard Cisco dialog, so we won't go into it here.

Once you've run through the basic setup, get into the routers privileged level and run these commands. These are "best practice" settings for an early experience IPv6 router under test. You can review these commands using the "Cisco Command Lookup Tool"; the output should look something like this.

```
service timestamps debug uptime
service timestamps log datetime msec localtime
service password-encryption
logging buffered 16384 debugging
logging rate-limit console 10 except errors
logging console informational
clock timezone PDT -8
clock summer-time PDT recurring
no ip bootp server
no ip dhcp-client network-discovery
no ip finger
no ip http server
ip subnet-zero
no ip source-route
ip classless
```

The next step is to configure the interfaces. We've got two interfaces to configure on our router: the outside interface (e0/0) and the inside interface (e0/1).

First, assign an IPv4 address to the outside interface, e0/0, by going into configuration mode, accessing the interface, and entering the command to assign the v4 address.

```
cisco2611# config terminal
cisco2611 (config)# interface Ethernet0/0
cisco2611(config-if)# ip address 192.168.200.2
   255.255.255.224
```

The Cisco 2611 only supports 10Mbit interfaces, but it can run at half-duplex or full-duplex. In our case, we were seeing errors on the interface, so we forced both sides (our router and the upstream ISP's router) to half-duplex and eliminated IP-redirects with these commands.

```
cisco2611(config-if)# half-duplex
cisco2611(config-if)# no ip redirects
```

Now we'll configure the IPv6 capability and address, like this.

```
cisco2611(config-if)# ipv6 enable
cisco2611(config-if)# ipv6 address 3ffe:80f0:1:2::101/64
```

Exit this configuration level with the exit command.

```
cisco2611(config-if)# exit
```

Finally, copy the changes you've made to the startup configuration.

```
copy running-config startup-config
```

The external interface configuration is now complete, and the internal interface can be configured. Configuring the internal interface is different from the external configuration in two ways.

- The config command is unnecessary (the system is already in configuration mode, so we omit that command).
- The internal interface does accept "IP redirects," so that configuration command can be omitted.

The configuration session for interface e0/1, including saving and exiting the configuration session, is as follows.

```
cisco2611 (config)# interface Ethernet0/1
cisco2611(config-if)# ip address 192.168.200.253
  255.255.255.252
cisco2611(config-if)# ipv6 enable
  cisco2611(config-if)# ipv6 address 3ffe:80f0:10::2/127
cisco2611(config-if)# exit
cisco2611 (config)# exit
cisco2611# copy running-config startup-config
```

22.1.5 SITE-SPECIFIC AND IPv6-SPECIFIC ROUTER CONFIGURATION

Let's configure the site-specific parameters. You'll need to specify your domain name.

```
ip domain-name zama6.com
```

You'll need to specify your nameservers. These should return both IPv4 and IPv6 records, although you'll note that you must specify an IPv4 address for the DNS servers at this time (with this version of IOS).

```
ip name-server 192.168.201.5
ip name-server 192.168.201.4
```

You need to enable unicast-routing for IPv6—this enables IPv6 routing.

```
ipv6 unicast-routing
```

As with any router, you need to specify your default route—or "route of last resort" for the router. This is where any traffic for which the router has no explicit routing information will be forwarded. Specify IPv4 and IPv6 default routes.

```
ip route 0.0.0.0 0.0.0.0 192.168.200.1
ipv6 route ::/0 3FFE:80F0:1:2::1
```

You also need to specify the static route for the network behind your firewall, both IPv4 and IPv6.

```
ip route 192.168.200.32 255.255.255.224 192.168.200.254
ipv6 route 3FFE:80F0:10:1::/64 3FFE:80F0:10::3
```

Set your NTP servers. Set two; the router will use the first one that works. This is the only way to get time synchronized to the accuracy needed to troubleshoot networking issues.

```
ntp server 192.168.202.5
ntp server 192.168.202.4
```

22.1.6 Testing Connectivity

Let's make sure we can "ping" (IPv4 and IPv6) our upstream default route and a known IPv6 address on the 6Bone—then our downstream explicit route. You see we use "ping ip." You can just say "ping" on a Cisco router, and it will assume you mean IPv4, but I'm explicitly telling the IOS I want

373

an IPv4 ping. The IPv6 ping uses the parameter "ping ipv6." From the 2611, these should look like this.

```
----- ping IPv4 of upstream default interface
   (by IP-address) ------
ent-firewall# ping ip 192.168.200.1
Type escape sequence to abort.
Sending 5, 100-byte ICMP Echos to 192.168.200.1,
   timeout is 2 seconds:
!!!!!
Success rate is 100 percent (5/5),
   round-trip min/avg/max = 1/2/4 ms
----- ping IPv6 of upstream default interface
   (by IP-address) ------
ent-firewall#ping ipv6 3ffe:80f0:1:2::1
Type escape sequence to abort.
Sending 5, 100-byte ICMP Echos to 3FFE:80F0:1:2::1,
   timeout is 2 seconds:
!!!!!
Success rate is 100 percent (5/5),
   round-trip min/avg/max = 1/2/4 ms
```

You get the idea. I'll just show the IPv6 pings for the other interfaces.

```
----- ping IPv6 of www.zama6.net (by IP-address) ------
ent-firewall#ping ipv6 3ffe:80f0:1:1:b0c:20ff:fed9:1dd2
Type escape sequence to abort.
Sending 5, 100-byte ICMP Echos to
   3FFE:80F0:1:1:b0c:20FF:FED9:1DD2, timeout is 2 seconds:
!!!!!
Success rate is 100 percent (5/5),
   round-trip min/avg/max = 1/1/4 ms
----- ping IPv6 of downstream interface (by IP-address) ------
ent-firewall#ping ipv6 3ffe:80f0:10::3
Type escape sequence to abort.
```

```
Sending 5, 100-byte ICMP Echos to 3FFE:80F0:10::3,
  timeout is 2 seconds:
!!!!!
Success rate is 100 percent (5/5),
  round-trip min/avg/max = 1/2/4 ms
```

22.1.7 TESTING DNS OPERATION

Let's make sure the DNS is working right—especially for IPv6 records.

```
----- ping IPv4 of www.zama6.net (by name) ------
ent-firewall#ping ip www.zama6.net
Translating "www.zama6.net"...
domain server (192.168.201.5)
[OK]
Type escape sequence to abort.
Sending 5, 100-byte ICMP Echos to 192.168.201.10,
  timeout is 2 seconds:
!!!!!
Success rate is 100 percent (5/5),
  round-trip min/avg/max = 1/2/4 ms
----- ping IPv6 of www.zama6.net (by name) ------
ent-firewall#ping ipv6 www.zama6.net
Translating "www.zama6.net"...
domain server (192.168.201.5)
[OK]
Type escape sequence to abort.
Sending 5, 100-byte ICMP Echos to
  3FFE:80F0:1:1:b0c:20FF:FED9:1DD2,
  timeout is 2  seconds:
!!!!!
Success rate is 100 percent (5/5),
  round-trip min/avg/max = 1/2/4 ms
```

22.1.8 TESTS FROM INSIDE YOUR NETWORK

Let's put the machine inside our network to work—ent-client. Ideally, this machine will be a full-function IPv4/IPv6 machine. ZAMA has written a HOWTO for setting up an IPv6-enabled Sun Solaris 8 system that would be ideal [ZAMASOL8].

Let's do a traceroute through our 2611 to www.kame.net—well outside our network. This will show that our router is correctly configured and passing traffic, since we'll do DNS via IPv4 and "traceroute" via IPv6 (both through the 2611). Note the "-A inet6" qualifier on the "traceroute" command. This is a common (but not consistent) flag for Solaris network commands for "use the IPv6 stack."

```
---------- traceroute ---------
ent-client# traceroute -A inet6 www.kame.net
traceroute: Warning: kame212.kame.net has multiple addresses; using
     3ffe:501:4819:2000:5054:ff:fedc:50d2
traceroute: Warning: Multiple interfaces found;
     using 3ffe:80f0:10:1:b0c:20ff:fefd:92bb @ hme0:1
traceroute to kame212.kame.net
     (3ffe:501:4819:2000:5054:ff:fedc:50d2),
     30 hops max, 60 byte packets
1    slate1.zama6.com (3ffe:80f0:10:1::1)  0.841 ms    0.450 ms    0.379 ms
2    3ffe:80f0:10::2      1.380 ms *      1.677 ms
3    3ffe:80f0:1:2::1      2.496 ms *      2.805 ms
4    3ffe:c00:e:13::1      29.772 ms      28.332 ms *
5    3ffe:401:0:1::16:2    209.622 ms      206.875 ms      204.944 ms
6    3ffe:8000:ffff:5::2    439.288 ms      458.564 ms      434.740 ms
7    3ffe:501:0:1802:2e0:18ff:fe98:a28d 426.839 ms   434.244 ms   426.978 ms
8    pc2.fujisawa.wide.ad.jp(2001:200:0:1001:2a0:24ff:fe83:8b33)
     436.466 ms      432.816 ms      439.956 ms
9    paradise.v6.kame.net (3ffe:501:4819:2000:2e0:18ff:fe98:f19d)
     435.030 ms      440.840 ms      436.413 ms
10   pine.v6.kame.net (3ffe:501:4819:2000:5054:ff:fedc:50d2)
      436.626 ms    434.037 ms 434.600 ms
--- end ----
```

22.1.9 Closing Topics

That's about it. We've built an IPv6-capable Cisco 2611 from the ground up and tested IPv4 and IPv6 functionality. It won't be fast—yet—but now you can get to work trying other IPv6 applications and utilities. The testbed is ready.

Warning: Until you understand the various support protocols for IPv6 (i.e., ndpd.conf), be careful about configuring ACL or firewalls. It is suggested you start with relatively "open" rules and watch how the system communicates using tools like "snoop" (Solaris) or "tcpdump," then tighten down your security stance.

22.2 Configuring a Cisco 7200 Router**

This section describes in detail how to configure the Cisco 7200 Series Routers for Native IPv6 and IPv6 tunneling.

22.2.1 Gathering the Pieces

Here's a brief list of what you'll need for this project.

- Cisco 7200 Series Router
- Cisco IOS 12.1
- IPv6 address space from your Internet Service Provider, native or tunnel.

To run IPv6, either at the Enterprise or backbone level, it is necessary to have IPV6-capable routers. Many organizations working with IPv6 are using software-based routers built on the Solaris or BSDI UNIX Operating Systems. While this is a workable solution for small networks, it is not a scalable solution that will grow with the users' needs.

Cisco currently has production and beta IPv6 images for their 7200 series routers, as well as several others. The 7200 is simple to configure for

---

**This section is adapted from a document written by Grant Furness and Brian Skeen, © Zama Networks.

IPv6, particularly if one is already familiar with the Cisco product line and command line interface.

The Cisco IOS 12.1 image, which can be downloaded from Cisco Connection Online, is required to run IPv6. Several images can be found at http://www.cisco.com/ipv6/. If you have any questions regarding the proper selection of an image or downloading the newest image, contact ipv6-support@cisco.com. We are using the 12.1(20001029) beta image. This release is stable, sitting in front of our production IPv6 network. We have not experienced any serious problems with routing or subnetting issues.

22.2.2 AUTOCONFIGURATION

IPv6 is simple to configure on the 7200, particularly if you are familiar with the Cisco Command Line Interface. First, you must be in enable mode and then configure terminal mode.

IPv6 on the Cisco product line is run at an interface level, meaning that you must enable IPv6 on each interface you wish to operate an IPv6 network. From the command line, enter this interface to configure its address and network information, and enter the command ipv6 enable to turn IPv6 on. The command ipv6 unicast-routing will enable IPv6 routing.

Once IPv6 is enabled, you can assign the interface's address. Probably the simplest way to do this is to assign the network portion that the router will broadcast, followed by ::1. In the following example, the network portion of the address is 3FFE:80F0:1:1::/64. Simply place a value after the double colon (::) and before the /64 in the address assignment, and you now have an IPv6 address assigned to your interface.

```
ipv6 address 3FFE:80F0:1:1::1/64
```

With the address assigned, you can now configure the router discovery protocol information for the router to advertise to its clients. The following command gives the router all the information it needs to broadcast network information to the clients under it.

```
ipv6 nd prefix-advertisement 3FFE:80F0:1:1::/64
  86400 86400 onlink autoconfig
```

The ipv6 nd prefix-advertisement is defining the function of the command as broadcasting the network prefix information, 3FFE:80F0:1:1::/64. Note that the network address being broadcast is a /64, which comprises half of the 128-bit IPv6 address. The number following the / in a network address broadcast refers to the number of bits in the network portion of the address, in this case 64 bits. The other half is composed of the client's MAC address. This idea is analogous to 192.168.12 being the network portion of a private Class C address space.

The next two fields indicate when the client is to check back for the network information in case it has changed. The first is valid lifetime in seconds, here 86400, which is 24 hours. The client must check back with the router within the timeframe to verify its network information. The second is preferred lifetime, or when the router prefers that the clients check back to verify network information. This is also set to 86400 seconds, as indicated by Cisco documentation.

According to RFC 2462, when the preferred lifetime of an IPv6 address is expired, that address is deprecated, and "should not be used in any new communications if an alternate (nondeprecated) address is available and has sufficient scope." However, the client should continue to use the deprecated address for communications already under way. In no case can the address be used for either outgoing or incoming new communications after the valid lifetime is expired.

The onlink designation says that the IPv6 address allocation will only occur on nodes attached to that particular network link.

The autoconfig command tells the clients that their addresses are to be automatically configured. The network portion of the address is to be taken explicitly from the router, as just outlined. The host portion of the address will be derived from the MAC address.

The entire configuration looks like this.

```
cisco-router> enable
cisco-router# configure terminal
cisco-router# interface e2/1
cisco-router# ipv6 enable
cisco-router# ipv6 address 3FFE:80F0:1:1::1/64
```

```
cisco-router# ipv6 nd prefix-advertisement
              3FFE:80F0:1:1::/64 86400 86400
              onlink autoconfig
```

22.2.3 TUNNEL CONFIGURATION

Cisco IOS 12.1 can also connect IPv6 devices via tunnels through IPv4. The information required to configure a static tunnel is different from the information required for a static network autoconfiguration. The administrator will need to know the destination router's IPv6 address and IPv4 address, the client's IPv4 address, and the tunnel mode.

Do not assign an IPv4 address directly to the interface for tunneled IPv6 traffic. Instead, assign the IPv4 address to the tunnel endpoint, which is tied to the interface.

As in the static network configuration, enable IPv6 on the tunnel interface.

```
cisco-router#    int Tunnel10
cisco-router#    ipv6 enable
cisco-router#    ipv6 address 3FFE:80F0:2::8/126
```

Note that the address assignment being made here is a /126, meaning that the network portion of this address is comprised of 126 of the 128 bits of the address. The reason for this is that the tunnel is a PPP link, and only two addresses are needed to form the link, and one is reserved for the anycast address. The IPv4 waste of two addresses, one for the network and one for the broadcast, are no longer necessary with IPv6.

The addresses for both sides of the tunnel are statically configured, not automatic. The router administrator will need to set aside the address space of this network to ensure that the tunnel recipient will have globally unique addresses.

Now that the IPv6 information is configured in the Tunnel interface, the tunnel requires the IPv4 information. The tunnel will need to know its source and destination addresses. From the viewpoint of the router, the source address will be applied to the router side of the tunnel and the destination address will be applied to the client side of the tunnel. It is

also necessary to dictate what type of tunnel the interface is—ipv6ip in
this case.

```
cisco-router#      tunnel source 192.142.129.2
cisco-router#      tunnel destination 192.31.7.104
cisco-router#      tunnel mode ipv6ip
```

The complete IPv6 through IPv4 tunnel configuration looks like the
following example.

```
interface Tunnel10
description connection to client's side of tunnel
  3ffe:80f0:f:4::/64
no ip address
ipv6 enable
ipv6 address 3FFE:80F0:2::8/127
tunnel source 192.142.129.2
tunnel destination 192.31.7.104
tunnel mode ipv6ip
```

The client side of the tunnel will need to be given an address range,
preferably in the form of a network address assignment. In the preceding
example, the client's network is 3ffe:80f0:f:4::/64. If the client side of the
tunnel is a router or a UNIX computer, it can be configured to broadcast this
address range to the machines on his LAN, just as in the first section of this
document—exceptions being made for platform differences, of course. It is
important to keep record of this address assignment to ensure the global
uniqueness of each address on that network (description connection to
client's side of tunnel 3ffe:80f0:f:4::/64).

22.2.4   BGP4+

One of the more common ways to perform routing on the external side of
the router is by using BGP with IPv6, or BGP4+. The first step is to identify
that BGP will be working on IPv6 with the command: no bgp default ipv4-
unicast. Then, simply identify your AS number and your BGP neighbors'
IPv6 addresses and AS numbers.

```
router bgp <your as number>
neighbor <neighbor's IPv6 address> <neighbor's as number>
```

Here is an example of a BGP4+ configuration.

```
router bgp 9340
neighbor 3FFE:82E1:8000::12 remote-as 8102
```

This configuration shows one BGP entry, but having multiple entries is simply a matter of adding more entries to the configuration. You can also log all BGP neighbor changes with this command.

```
bgp log-neighbor-changes
```

22.2.5   STATIC ROUTING

The addition of static routes in IPv6 is as simple as in IPv4. This is the command.

```
ipv6 route <destination IPv6 network><IPv6 interface>
```

Here is an example from my routing table.

```
ipv6 route 3FFE:80F3:1:4::/64 3FFE:80F3:1:2:A01:20ff:FED9:52B4
```

Routing your tunnel clients' networks is the same, only you need to direct all traffic bound for the network through your end of the tunnel interface, which can be done by simply referring to the name of the tunnel.

```
ipv6 route 3FFE:80F0:F:4::/64 Tunnel10
```

Since we are connected to the 6Bone via a tunnel, we need a command to direct all IPv6 traffic out through our end of the tunnel interface to our upstream provider. This is done via the same static route command.

```
ipv6 route 3FFE::/16 Tunnel10 120
```

The number at the end of the command—120 in this case—is the Administrative Distance. The Administrative Distance is the level of trust that can be placed on the source of routing information in the BGP and OSPF routing protocols. The value is an integer between 1 and 255. The higher the value, the lower the trust level to be placed on that source. A value of 255 means the source should be ignored.

The preceding information is all that is necessary to configure a Cisco 7200 router for IPv6. The configurations shown will enable users to communicate with both Native IPv6 and Tunneled IPv6.

22.3   Configuring IPv6 on Hitachi GR2000 Series Routers[†]

This section describes the necessary steps for configuring a Hitachi GR2000 series router to communicate over IPv6. Many of the commonly used features of IPv6, including Static Neighbor Discovery (NDP) configuration, Address Auto-configuration, Ripng, BGP4+, and 6over4 tunneling, are included to provide configuration and command reference.

22.3.1   GATHERING THE PIECES

Here's a brief list of what you'll need for this project.

- Hitachi GR2000 Series Routers
- Hitachi OS 05-00-AA/OS6
- IPv6 address space from your Internet Service Provider, native or tunnel.

22.3.2   BACKGROUND

To run IPv6 either at the Enterprise or Backbone level, it is necessary to have IPv6-capable routers. The Hitachi GR2000 Series Router, built on the BSDI UNIX Operating Systems, currently supports software-based forwarding of all IPv6 packets. The procedures listed in this document were tested using Fast Ethernet and Gigabit Ethernet interfaces, but Hitachi does currently offer IPv6 support on their ATM and Packet Over Sonet (POS) line cards as well.

This router has a three-tier user interface to provide different levels of administrative security: Command, Admin, and Config. The Command- and Admin-level interfaces have read-only permission and are used for command verification and low-level troubleshooting. The Config-level

[†]This section is adapted from a document written by Brian Skeen, © 2001 Zama Networks.

interface has read-write permission and is used to perform all router configuration commands.

22.3.3 REQUIRED IOS IMAGE

The procedures listed here were tested on Hitachi OS release, 05-00-AA/OS6, which at the time of this writing, is the most current beta image available for testing. We have found this release to be stable and have not experienced any serious routing or subnetting issues related to the current OS revision.

22.3.4 DEFINING THE ETHERNET LINE

Before any configuration can be assigned to a router interface, you must first create the interface line configuration for the physical port to be used.

The following example shows how to define a 100MB, full-duplex Ethernet line named to_gr2000b. Note that you must first access the Config-level interface and open the configuration file prior to issuing the first configuration command.

```
*** Welcome to the Router ***
GR2000A/command: admin
GR2000A/admin: config
GR2000A/config: open
GR2000A/config: set line to_gr2000b ethernet 1/2
GR2000A/config> line to_gr2000b ethernet 1/2 type 100m_full_duplex
GR2000A/config>apply
GR2000A/config>save
```

To verify the previous line configuration, the show line <linename> command is used as follows.

```
GR2000A/config: show line to_gr2000b
line to_gr2000b ethernet 1/2 {
        type 100m_full_duplex;
};
```

22.3.5 DEFINING A STATIC IPv6 ADDRESS TO THE LINE

Now that the line configuration has been completed, the IP command can be used to set an IPv6 address on the configured line. Once IPv6 has been configured on the line, the router will also generate a link-local Unicast address on the line by prepending the predefined fe80::2 prefix with the interface's 64-bit interface identifier.

The following example shows how to define a static Unicast address with a 64-bit prefix length to the line to_gr2000b.

```
GR2000A/config: ip to_gr2000b 3ffe:80f0:3:3000::1 -prefixlen 64
GR2000A/config>apply
GR2000A/config>save
```

To verify the previous ip configuration, the show ip <linename> command is used as follows.

```
GR2000A/config: show ip to_gr2000b
        ip to_gr2000b {
                3ffe:80f0:3:3000::1 prefixlen 64;
        };
```

To verify the entire IPv6 interface configuration, the interface <linename> command is used at the Admin-level interface as follows.

```
GR2000A/admin: interface to_gr2000b
        to_gr2000b:
        flags=80e3<UP,BROADCAST,NOTRAILERS,RUNNING,NOARP,MULTICAST>
         mtu 1500
         inet6 3ffe:80f0:3:3000::1/64
         inet6 fe80::240:66ff:fe10:8931%to_gr2000b/64
         NIF1/Line2: UP media 100BASE-TX full 00:40:66:10:89:31
         Time-since-last-status-change: 2,04:44:52
         Last down at: 04/28 04:39:25
```

To verify that the interface is up and configured, the ping6 <IPv6 address> command can be used as follows.

```
GR2000A/admin: ping6 3ffe:80f0:3:3000::1
```

```
PING6(56=40+8+8 bytes) 3ffe:80f0:3:3000::1 --> 3ffe:80f0:3:3000::1

16 bytes from 3ffe:80f0:3:3000::1, icmp_seq=0 hlim=64 time=0.42 ms

16 bytes from 3ffe:80f0:3:3000::1, icmp_seq=1 hlim=64 time=0.343 ms

^C

--- 3ffe:80f0:3:3000::1 ping6 statistics ---

2 packets transmitted, 2 packets received, 0% packet loss

round-trip min/avg/max = 0.343/0.381/0.42 ms
```

22.3.6 DEFINING AN IPv6 STATIC ROUTE

The static command is used to define a static IPv6 route on the GR2000 series router. Static routes can be used instead of, or in addition to, a dynamic routing protocol to specify the path to a destination network.

The following example shows how to define an IPv6 default route using a next-hop gateway address of 3ffe:80f0:3:3000::2.

```
GR2000A/admin:config

GR2000A/config: static :: prefixlen 0 gateway
   3ffe:80f0:3:3000::2

GR2000A/config>apply

GR2000A/config>save
```

To verify the previous IPv6 Static Route configuration, the show static command is used as follows.

```
GR2000A/config: show static
             static {
                     :: prefixlen 0 gateway  3ffe:80f0:3:3000::2;
             };
```

22.3.7 DEFINING A STATIC NEIGHBOR DISCOVERY ENTRY

The NDP command is used to define a static Neighbor Discovery (ND) entry in the router's IPv6 neighbor cache table. The Neighbor Discovery protocol is used by nodes (hosts and routers) to determine the link layer addresses for neighbors known to reside on attached links, to quickly purge cached values that become invalid, to actively keep track of which neighbors are reachable, and to detect changed link layer addresses within the network.

In most cases, the process of defining a static Neighbor Discovery entry will not be required, but it has been included here as reference. Defining a static ND entry in IPv6 is similar to defining a static ARP entry in IPv4 and may be useful if you needed to create a virtual IPv6 address to virtual MAC address mapping that could not otherwise be negotiated dynamically by the router.

The following example shows how to define a permanent static entry that maps IPv6 address 3ffe:80f0:3:3000::3 to MAC address 00:0b:0c:0d:0e:03 on line to_gr2000b.

```
GR2000A/config: ndp 3ffe:80f0:3:3000::3 to_gr2000b
  -mac_address 00:0b:0c:0d:0e:03
GR2000A/config>apply
GR2000A/config>save
```

To verify the Static NDP Entry configuration, the ndp -a command is used as follows.

```
GR2000A/admin: ndp -a

Neighbor                Link layer Addr  Netif       Expire      S Flgs P
3ffe:80f0:3:3000::3 0:b:c:d:e:3         to_gr2000b permanent  R   S
```

22.3.8 Defining an IPv6 Router Advertisement

The RA command is used to define specific Router Advertisement parameters on a given interface. Router Advertisements (RA) can be configured to provide on-link prefix information to be used by local hosts for Address Autoconfiguration and may also be used to define the amount of time, in seconds, that information on the reachability of adjacent nodes is valid.

The following example shows how to define a 64-bit prefix with lifetime values of 24 hours on interface gr_2000b. The valid-lifetime value specifies the length of time (in seconds) that the configured address remains in the valid state. The preferred-lifetime value specifies the length of time (in seconds) that the configured address is preferred, or the time until deprecation. The valid lifetime value must be greater than or equal to the preferred lifetime value.

```
GR2000A/config: ra interface to_gr2000b enable
GR2000A/config> ra interface to_gr2000b prefix 3FFE:80F0:3:3000::
prefixlen 64 valid-lifetime 86400 preferred-lifetime 86400
GR2000A/config>apply
GR2000A/config>save
```

To verify the Router Advertisement configuration, the show ra command is used as follows.

```
GR2000A/config: show ra
ra yes {
        interface to_gr2000b enable {
                prefix {
                    3ffe:80f0:3:3000:: prefixlen 64 valid-lifetime 86400
                       preferred-lifetime 86400;
            };
                reachable-time 1800;
        };
};
```

22.3.9 DEFINING A CONFIGURED 6OVER4 TUNNEL INTERFACE

Configured 6over4 tunneling is a transition mechanism that provides a method for isolated IPv6 hosts to communicate across an IPv4 transport network. With 6over4 tunneling, an IPv6 packet originating at one end of the tunnel is encapsulated within an IPv4 packet and transmitted across the IPv4 network, where it is then decapsulated back to an IPv6 packet and forwarded to its IPv6 destination. A dual-stack router, one that can communicate both via IPv4 and IPv6, is required at each end of the tunnel to perform the encapsulation process.

The following example shows the router configuration steps required at both ends of the tunnel to define a 6over4 tunnel named test-6over4 (Figure 22–2). An IPv4 address must first be assigned to the encapsulating interface on each router. A static route is also defined using a next-hop address of the remote tunnel endpoint.

```
************** ON GR2000A*************
GR2000A/config: ip to_gr2000b 172.16.16.2  mask 255.255.255.252
GR2000A/config> tunnel test-6over4 172.16.16.2 remote 172.16.16.1
GR2000A/config> ip test-6over4 3ffe:80f0:3:5000::2
  destination_ip_address 3ffe:80f0:3:5000::1
GR2000A/config> static :: prefixlen 0 gateway 3ffe:80f0:3:5000::1
GR2000A/config> apply
GR2000A/config> save
************** ON GR2000B *************
GR2000B/config: ip to_gr2000a 172.16.16.1  mask 255.255.255.252
GR2000B/config> tunnel test-6over4 172.16.16.1 remote 172.16.16.2
GR2000B/config> ip test-6over4 3ffe:80f0:3:5000::1
  destination_ip_address 3ffe:80f0:3:5000::2
GR2000B/config> static :: prefixlen 0 gateway 3ffe:80f0:3:5000::2
GR2000B/config> apply
GR2000B/config> save
```

To verify the 6over4 Tunnel Configuration on router GR2000A, the config show tunnel and config show ip <tunnel name> commands are used as follows.

```
GR2000A/admin: config show tunnel

  tunnel test-6over4 {
     172.16.16.2 remote 172.16.16.1;
  };

GR2000A/admin: config show ip test-6over4

  ip test-6over4 {
     3ffe:80f0:3:5000::2 destination_ip_address 3ffe:80f0:3:5000::1;
  };
```

To verify that the tunnel interface is up and configured, the ping6 <IPv6 address> command can be used as follows.

```
GR2000A/admin: ping6 3ffe:80f0:3:5000::1
PING6(56=40+8+8 bytes) 3ffe:80f0:3:5000::1 --> 3ffe:80f0:3:5000::1
16 bytes from 3ffe:80f0:3:5000::1, icmp_seq=0 hlim=64 time=3.052 ms
```

```
16 bytes from 3ffe:80f0:3:5000::1, icmp_seq=1 hlim=64 time=2.894 ms
^C
--- 3ffe:80f0:3:5000::1 ping6 statistics ---
2 packets transmitted, 2 packets received, 0% packet loss
round-trip min/avg/max = 2.894/2.973/3.052 ms
```

22.3.10   ENABLING THE RIPNG PROTOCOL

RIPng is an Interior Gateway routing protocol supported in IPv6 on the GR2000 series router. RIPng uses a hop count metric to determine the best route to a particular destination network.

The following example shows how to enable RIPng on the GR2000 router and how to define RIPng routing updates to be sent and received on interface to_gr2000b.

```
GR2000A/config: ripng yes
GR2000A/config> ripng interface to_gr2000b ripin ripout
GR2000A/config>apply
GR2000A/config>save
```

To verify the RIPng configuration, the show ripng command is used as follows:

```
GR2000A/config: show ripng
ripng yes {
        1 interface to_gr2000b ripin ripout;
};
```

22.3.11   ENABLING THE BGP4+ PROTOCOL

BGP4+ is an Exterior Gateway Routing Protocol supported in IPv6 on the GR2000 series router. BGP4+ is used to exchange loop-free routing table information between routers located on different autonomous systems.

The following example shows how to enable BGP4+ on the router, how to set up a BGP4+ peering relationship with a remote router located in AS 65002, and how to export (advertise) all directly connected routes to AS 65001 via the BGP4+ protocol. Prior to BGP4+ configuration, the autonomous system number and router-id for the local router must be specified. Note that the configuration file is closed after the final configuration command has been entered.

```
GR2000A/config: autonomoussystem 65001
GR2000A/config>routerid 203.142.143.45
GR2000A/config> bgp4+ yes
GR2000A/config> bgp4+ externalpeeras 65002 peer 3ffe:80f0:3:4000::1
GR2000A/config>export proto bgp4+ as 65001 proto direct
GR2000A/config>apply
GR2000A/config>save
GR2000A/config:close
```

To verify the BGP4+ Configuration, the show bgp4+ and show export commands are used as follows.

```
GR2000A/config> show bgp4+
bgp4+ yes {
1 group type external peeras 65001 {
    peer 3ffe:80f0:3:4000::1;
    };
};
GR2000A/config> show export
export proto bgp4+ as 65001 {
    proto direct;
};
```

The preceding information is all that is necessary to configure a Hitachi GR2000 series router for IPv6. The configurations shown will enable users to communicate with both Native IPv6 and Tunneled IPv6.

22.4   Configuring NEC IX5010 Series Routers for IPv6‡

This section describes the necessary steps for configuring a NEC IX5010 series router to communicate over IPv6. Many of the commonly used

‡This section is adapted from a document written by Brian Skeen and Steve Smith, © Zama Networks.

features of IPv6, including Static Neighbor Discovery configuration, Address Autoconfiguration, Configured 6over4 tunneling, RIPng, and BGP4, are included to provide configuration and command reference.

22.4.1 GATHERING THE PIECES

Here's a brief list of what you'll need for this project.

- NEC IX5010 Routers
- NEC OS 5.1.07
- IPv6 address space from your Internet Service Provider, native or tunnel.

22.4.2 BACKGROUND

To run IPv6 at the Enterprise or Backbone level, it is necessary to have IPv6-capable routers. The NEC IX5010 Router currently supports hardware-based forwarding of all IPv6 packets. The procedures listed in this document were tested using Fast Ethernet interfaces, but NEC does currently offer IPv6 support on their Gigabit Ethernet, ATM, and Packet Over Sonet (POS) line cards as well.

This NEC router has a two-tier user interface to provide different levels of administrative security: operator-mode and supervisor-mode. The operator mode has read-only permission and is used for command verification and low-level troubleshooting. The supervisor mode has read-write permission and is used to perform all router configuration commands.

The procedures listed here were tested on NEC OS release 5.1.07, which at the time of this writing is the most current beta image available for testing. We have found this release to be stable and have not experienced any serious routing or subnetting issues related to the current OS revision.

22.4.3 DEFINING VLAN CONFIGURATION

Before any IPv6 configuration can be assigned to a router interface, you must first configure the VLAN parameters for the specific port(s) to be used. By default, all ports on the NEC IX5010 router are assigned to a default VLAN—in this case, VLAN 2. In order to assign a port currently in the default VLAN to a new VLAN, it must first be removed from the default VLAN.

On the IX5010 router, there are two VLAN modes that allow you to change and activate VLAN configuration parameters. The command vlan-mode change is used to change the VLAN status to permit configuration changes. Once configuration data has been changed, the command vlan-mode active is used to activate the newly registered VLAN data.

The following example shows the necessary steps to define a new VLAN (VLAN-ID 200) named NEC1-to-NEC2; assign port 25 to the new VLAN, and then activate the VLAN for use. Note that you must first access the supervisor mode prior to issuing the first configuration command. Also note that port 25 must be removed from the default VLAN (VLAN-ID 2) before it can be assigned to VLAN 200. The session should appear as follows.

```
*** Welcome to the Router ***
•    nec1> supervisor
•    Password: **********
•    nec1# vlan-mode change
•    nec1# no vlan port 2 25
•    nec1# vlan register 200 NEC1-to-NEC2 25
•    nec1# vlan-mode active
•    nec1# save configall
```

To verify the previous VLAN configuration, the show vlan register command is used as follows.

```
•    nec1# show vlan reg
VLAN ID                              : 200
VLAN Name                            : NEC1-to-NEC2
Ethernet Port                        : 25
LEC ID                               :
PPP ID                               :
```

22.4.4   ENABLING IPv6 ON A CONFIGURED VLAN

Once the VLAN configuration has been completed, the IPv6 command must be used to enable IPv6 functionality on the configured

VLAN. By default, once IPv6 has been enabled on the VLAN, the router will also generate a link-local Unicast address on the interface by prepending the predefined fe80::2 prefix with the interface's 64-bit interface identifier.

The following example shows how to enable IPv6 on the configured VLAN 200.

- `nec1# ipv6 interface enable vlan 200`
- `nec1# ipv6 interface status vlan 200 up`

To verify the previous IPv6 configuration, the show `ipv6 interface vlan <ID>` command is used as follows.

```
· nec1# show ipv6 interface vlan 200
vlan_200 (default_site)
LowerLayer                : vlan_200
Mtu Size                  : 1500
   Reassemble Size        : 65535
Frame Type                : dix
Interface ID              : 02:00:4c:ff:fe:94:9b:55
Phys. Address             : 00:00:4c:94:9b:55
Admin. Status             : up Operation Status : up
Last Change time          : 3 Days 15 Hours 15 Min. 5 Sec.
```

22.4.5 Defining a Static IPv6 Address to the Interface

Now that IPv6 functionality has been enabled on VLAN 200, the IPv6 address-table command can be used to set an IPv6 address on the configured VLAN.

The following example shows how to define a static Unicast address with a 64-bit prefix length to VLAN 200.

`· nec1# ipv6 address-table vlan 200 3ffe:80f0:3:e::1 64`

To verify the previous IPv6 configuration, the show ipv6 address-table command is used as follows.

```
·  nec1# show ipv6 address-table
3ffe:80f0:3:e::@vlan_200 64
              Anycast    Stateful    Preferred
3ffe:80f0:3:e::1@vlan_200 64
              Unicast    Stateful    Preferred
fe80::200:4cff:fe94:9b55@vlan_200 64
              Auto    Stateful    Preferred
```

To verify that the VLAN interface is up and configured correctly, the ping6 <IPv6 address> command can be used as follows.

```
·    nec1# ping6 3ffe:80f0:3:e::1
Pinging 3ffe:80f0:3:e::1 with 56 bytes data
·
O
----ping statistics----
1 packets transmitted, 1 packets received, 0% packet loss
round-trip (ms) min/avg/max = 2/2/2
```

22.4.6 DEFINING AN IPv6 STATIC ROUTE

The ipv6 routing-table command is used to define static IPv6 routes on the NEC IX5010 router. Static routes can be used instead of, or in addition to, a dynamic routing protocol to specify the path to a destination network.

The following example shows how to define an IPv6 default route using a next-hop gateway address of 3ffe:80f0:3:e::2.

```
· nec1# ipv6 routing-table :: 0 3ffe:80f0:3:e::2
```

To verify the previous IPv6 Static Route configuration, the show ipv6 routing-table command is used as follows.

```
· nec1# show ipv6 routing-table
  5 routing entries in tables.
  Static 3ffe:80f0:3:e::/64 [1]     never_aged
       via 3ffe:80f0:3:e::2@vlan_200
  Direct 3ffe:80f0:3:e::/128 [1]     never_aged
```

```
                           via ::1@loopback_0
          Direct 3ffe:80f0:3:e::1/128 [1]     never_aged
```

22.4.7 DEFINING A STATIC NEIGHBOR DISCOVERY ENTRY

The ipv6 nd and vlan mac-table commands are used to define a static
Neighbor Discovery (ND) entry in the router's IPv6 neighbor cache table.
The Neighbor Discovery protocol is used by nodes (hosts and routers)
to determine the link layer addresses for neighbors known to reside on
attached links, to quickly purge cached values that become invalid, to
actively keep track of which neighbors are reachable, and to detect changed
link layer addresses within the network.

In most cases, the process of defining a static Neighbor Discovery entry will
not be required, but it has been included here as reference. This process of
defining a static ND entry in IPv6 is similar to defining a static ARP entry
in IPv4 and may be useful if you need to create a virtual IPv6 address
to virtual MAC address mapping that could not otherwise be negotiated
dynamically by the router.

The following example shows how to define a permanent static entry that
maps IPv6 address 3ffe:80f0:3:e::3 to the MAC address 0a:0b:0c:0d:0e:0f on
VLAN 200.

- `nec1# ipv6 nd cache register vlan 200 3ffe:80f0:3:e::3`
  `0a:0b:0c:0d:0e:0f`
- `nec1# vlan-mode change`
- `nec1# vlan mac-table 2 0a:0b:0c:0d:0e:0f ether 25`
- `nec1# vlan-mode active`
- `nec1# save configall`

To verify the Static ND entry configuration, the `show ipv6 nd cache
status` command is used as follows.

- `nec1# show ipv6 nd cache status`

```
Interface : vlan 200
Ipv6 Address         status      Expire type Link Layer Address
3ffe:80f0:3:e::2    REACHABLE    3773    D     00:00:4C:94:A1:DB
3ffe:80f0:3:e::3    REACHABLE    0       R     0A:0B:0C:0D:0E:0F
```

22.4.8   DEFINING AN IPv6 ROUTER ADVERTISEMENT

The nd ra command is used to define specific Router Advertisement parameters on a given interface. Router Advertisements (RA) can be configured to provide on-link prefix information to be used by local hosts for Address Autoconfiguration and may also be used to define the amount of time, in seconds, that information on the reachability of adjacent nodes is valid.

The following example shows how to define a 64-bit prefix with lifetime values of 24 hours on VLAN 200. The valid-lifetime value (86400) specifies the length of time (in seconds) that the configured address on the host should remain in the valid state. The preferred-lifetime value (86400) specifies the length of time (in seconds) that the configured address on the host is preferred, or the time until deprecation. The valid lifetime must be greater than or equal to the preferred lifetime value.

```
· nec1# ipv6 nd ra prefix vlan 200 3ffe:80f0:3:e::
  64 86400 86400
· nec1# ipv6 nd ra send vlan 200
```

To verify the Router Advertisement configuration, the show ipv6 nd ra command is used as follows.

```
· nec1# show ipv6 nd ra
Interface : vlan 200
Send Router Advertisement : yes
Max RA Interval       : 600    Min RA Interval    : 198
Managed Config Flag   : off    Other Config Flag  : off
Reachable Time        : 0      NS Interval        : 0
RA Lifetime           : 1800   Hop Limit          : 64
Link MTU              : 1500
Link Layer Address    : 00:00:4C:94:9B:55
Prefix                : 3ffe:80f0:3:e::/64
Site Prefix Length    : 0
Valid Lifetime        : 86400 Valid Lifetime Mode     : fix
Preferred Lifetime    : 86400 Preferred Lifetime Mode : fix
OnLink Flag           : on Autonomous Flag            : on
```

22.4.9 DEFINING A CONFIGURED 6OVER4 TUNNEL INTERFACE

Configured 6over4 tunneling is a transition mechanism that provides a method for isolated IPv6 hosts to communicate across an IPv4 transport network. With configured 6over4 tunneling, an IPv6 packet originating at one end of the tunnel is encapsulated within an IPv4 packet and transmitted across the IPv4 network, where it is then decapsulated back to an IPv6 packet and forwarded to its IPv6 destination. A dual-stack router, one that can communicate both via IPv4 and IPv6, is required at each end of the tunnel to perform the encapsulation process.

The following example shows the router configuration steps required at both ends of the tunnel to define a configured 6over4 tunnel with tunnel-ID 1 (Figure 22–2). Note that an IPv4 address must first be assigned to the encapsulating interface on each router.

```
************* ON NEC1*************
· nec1# ip address-table vlan 200 192.168.0.1 255.255.255.252
· nec1# tunnel register tun64 1 192.168.0.1 192.168.0.2
· nec1# ipv6 interface enable tun64 1
```

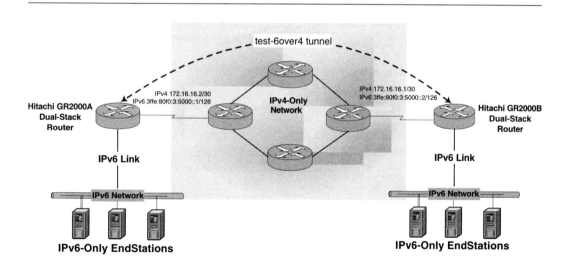

Figure 22–2: Defining a 6over4 tunnel.

- nec1# ipv6 interface status tun64 1 up
- nec1# ipv6 address-table tun64 1 3ffe:80f0:3:f::1 126

************* ON NEC2 *************
- nec2# ip address-table vlan 200 192.168.0.2 255.255.255.252
- nec2# tunnel register tun64 1 192.168.0.2 192.168.0.1
- nec2# ipv6 interface enable tun64 1
- nec2# ipv6 interface status tun64 1 up
- nec2# ipv6 address-table tun64 1 3ffe:80f0:3:f::2 126

To verify the 6over4 tunnel configuration on router NEC1, the show tunnel register command is used as follows.

```
·    nec1# show tunnel register
     tun64_1
       IPsec        : off        MTU size : 1480
       Eventlog     : disable    Reachability-monitor : enable
       lowerlayer   : vlan_200
       ope status   : UP
       src addr     : 192.168.0.1
       dst addr     : 192.168.0.2
```

To verify that the tunnel interface is up and configured, the ping6 <IPv6 address> command can be used as follows.

```
·    nec1# ping6 3ffe:80f0:3:f::2
Pinging 3ffe:80f0:3:f::2 with 56 bytes data .
o
----ping statistics----
1 packets transmitted, 1 packets received, 0% packet loss
round-trip (ms) min/avg/max = 8/8/8
```

22.4.10 ENABLING THE RIPNG PROTOCOL

RIPng is an interior gateway routing protocol supported in IPv6 on the IX5010 router. RIPng uses a hop count metric to dynamically determine the best route to a particular destination network.

The following example shows how to register (enable) RIPng on VLAN 200, how to enable RIPng routing updates to be sent and received on VLAN 200, and how to specify a default route to be sent from the VLAN 200 interface. Note that the receive default route parameter is disabled by default.

- `nec1# ipv6 ripng register vlan 200 enable enable`
- `nec1# ipv6 ripng send default-route vlan 200`

To verify the RIPng configuration, the show ipv6 ripng register command is used as follows.

```
· nec1# show ipv6 ripng register
  Interface                  : vlan 200
  Send Config                : Enable
  Receive Config             : Enable
  Split Horizon Mode      •  : Enable
  Poisoned Reverse Mode      : Enable
  Send Metric Offset         : 0
  Receive Metric Offset      : 1
  Send Default Route         : Enable
  Receive Default Route      : Disable
  Default Route Nexthop      : localhost
  Inbound Distribute List    : Not Set
  Outbound Distribute List   : Not Set
  [Security Config]
  Transport                  : (AH)None    (ESP)None
  Tunnel                     : (AH)None    (ESP)None
```

22.4.11 ENABLING THE BGP4+ PROTOCOL

BGP4+ is an exterior gateway routing protocol supported in IPv6 on the IX5010 router. BGP4+ is used to exchange loop-free routing table information between routers located in different autonomous systems.

The following example shows the basic steps to enable BGP4+ on the IX5010 router, to set a BGP4+ neighbor peering relationship with a remote router located in AS 65002, to advertise a specific network using BGP4+, and finally, to advertise an IPv6 default route to a specific neighboring router. Note that the BGP4+ peering session is shut down and reset after finishing the configuration to initialize BGP4+ routing.

- · nec1# ipv6 bgp enable 65001 192.168.0.1
- · nec1# ipv6 bgp neighbor remote-as 3ffe:80f0:3:e::2 65002
- · nec1# ipv6 bgp network 2001:2d0::/35
- · nec1# ipv6 bgp originate default 3ffe:80f0:3:e::2

Reset and shut down BGP sessions with a specific neighbor.

- · nec1# ipv6 bgp neighbor shutdown 3ffe:80f0:3:e::2
- · nec1# ipv6 bgp neighbor reset 3ffe:80f0:3:e::2

To verify the BGP4+ configuration, the show ipv6 bgp neighbor, show ipv6 bgp speaker and show ipv6 bgp network commands are used as follows.

```
· nec1# show ipv6 bgp neighbor
Address            State         AS       BGP-ID        Up Time
3ffe:80f0:3:e::2   Established   65002    192.168.0.2   000-00:01:59
· nec1# show ipv6 bgp speaker
BGP Protocol: Enabled
AS Number: 65001
BGP Identifier: 192.168.0.1
TCP-Segment Size: 1024
BGP load-sharing: Disabled
Synchronization: Yes
Export-Internal: No
Default Local Preference: 100
Ignore AS-Path: No
Always-Compare-MED: No
Import routes: None
· nec1# show ipv6 bgp network
Network:
Index Network/Prefixlen
1     2001:2d0::/35
```

22.4.12 CONCLUSION

The preceding information includes all the basic steps necessary to configure an NEC IX5010 router for IPv6. The configurations shown will enable users to communicate with both native IPv6 and tunneled IPv6 hosts.

22.5 Summary

Although your router of choice may not have been included in this chapter, having configured several different routers for use with IPv6 you should be able to extend the lessons to any other router that supports IPv6. In the next chapter, we look at some practical solutions to security problems applied to IPv6 networks.

23

Practical IPv6 Security Solutions

This chapter includes step-by-step instructions for setting up an IP firewall, IPsec, and TCP wrappers for Solaris IPv6 systems. Pointers to other IPv6 security resources are included at the end of the chapter.

23.1   IPv6/v4 IP Filtering Firewall on Solaris 8*

Commercial firewalls protecting network assets of companies and institutions around the world are commonplace. In fact, few "interesting" network systems are not behind a firewall. Currently, there are no (at least none we could find) commercial firewalls that provide IPv6 support. This leaves an interesting dilemma; deploy systems undefended or restrict your IPv6 test-and-deployment efforts to isolated internal test networks. In today's connected world, neither of these options is acceptable.

---

*This section is adapted from a document written by John E. Spence, © Zama Networks.

This section describes in detail how to obtain, build, install, configure, and operate an IPF-based IPv6-capable firewall on Sun Solaris 8 (SPARC architecture). IPv4 is also configured (routable IPv4 addresses have been changed to nonroutable addresses). As this machine will act as a "smart router," IPv6 router concepts are discussed as well. With an IPF firewall deployed, your enterprise will be enabled to join IPv6 networks (like the 6bone).

23.1.1 Components You'll Need

You'll need a modern Sun Sparc-based system with at least two network interfaces. You'll need information about your network and upstream connections.

- Routable IPv4 addresses for behind your IPF firewall. Alternatively, you can use nonroutable devices and use IPF NAT, but you won't be able to connect into the network for services (i.e., SSH to a specific address). You can skip IPv4 support entirely if you wish.
- An IPv6 network for behind your firewall. In order to allow machines inside your firewall to use the autoconfigure feature to obtain their IPv6 addresses, this must be at least a /64 network (more information on this follows). The point at which you'll connect your firewall's outside interface— whatever is "upstream" from your device—will supply this block of addresses.
- Obtain the IPv4 and IPv6 addresses for your outside (unprotected) interface. I'm assuming that you'll have a static IPv4 address and that you'll autoconfigure the IPv6 address of your outside interface. This means that your upstream router must be running the "neighbor discovery" protocol and providing your firewall with the IPv6 prefix to use for autoconfiguration.
- Obtain the IPv4 and IPv6 (if available) DNS information for your network—your upstream provider usually supplies this.

You'll need the Sun Solaris C compiler. The gcc compiler won't work. You must obtain and license the real Sun C compiler. You'll also need the gzip program.

23.1.2 CONFIGURING IPv6/IPv4 INTERFACES

Sun Solaris 8 has native IPv6 support—you just have to select that "Install IP Version 6 Support" feature at install time. If Solaris 8 is already installed, you can enable IPv6 support by creating the /etc/hostname6.<interface index> file by using "touch /etc/hostname6.<interface index>." When the machine is rebooted, it will boot up with IPv6 support enabled.

To install from scratch, load Sun Solaris 8 with IPv6 support enabled. Partway through the installation of Solaris, after you've entered some of your IPv4 information, the program will ask if you want IPv6 support. After installation completes, run the command "netstat -rn." You should have two routing tables—one for IPv4 and one for IPv6. If you do, you've got IPv6 support successfully installed.

Let's enable the IPv6 interface and check the IPv4 interface. You need to know the names of your two interfaces. Let's assume that the inside interface is called "hme1" and the outside interface is called "hme0." Create four files.

```
"/etc/hostname.hme0"
ipfw-o
```

(That is, filename "/etc/hostname.hme0," with the single line in it "ipfw-o".)

```
"/etc/hostname.hme1"
ipfw-i
"/etc/hostname6.hme0"                    (empty file)
"/etc/hostname6.hme1"                    (empty file)
```

Now check the entries you have in your "/etc/hosts" file. You should have an entry for each of the lines that appear in your "/etc/hostname.hmeX" files—like this.

```
192.168.140.48   ipfw-o.zama6.net   ipfw-o   loghost
192.168.200.1    ipfw-i.zama6.net   ipfw-i
```

Note that nonroutable addresses have been substituted for the public-side routable addresses.

This is what will tell your two interfaces how to configure themselves for IPv4. The empty "/etc/hostname6.hmeX" files tell your two interfaces to autoconfigure from the neighbor discovery announcements from the routers.

Make sure you've got the right entries in your "/etc/netmask" file. They ensure that the new interfaces have the right netmasks.

```
"/etc/netmasks"
192.168.200.0    255.255.255.0
192.168.140.32   255.255.255.224
```

At this point, reboot to have the interfaces configured for IPv4.

Make sure IPv4 is happy. Ideally, you have a machine on the inside of your new network configured for IPv4 to test against. If you don't, set up one now. Try to "ping" a machine outside your interface that you know will return a ping. If that works, then you've got IPv4 properly configured for your external interface (my ipfw-o interface). If you can ping internally, then that interface is properly configured (my ipfw-i interface).

23.1.3 CONFIGURE NEIGHBOR DISCOVERY ADVERTISEMENTS FOR THE INTERNAL INTERFACE

Your firewall is acting as a smart router, and it must be running the Neighbor Discovery protocol—and advertising the right IPv6 address prefix—to allow machines inside the firewall to autoconfigure their interfaces. Edit the "/etc/inet/ndpd.conf" file as shown.

```
ifdefault AdvReachableTime 30000 AdvRetransTimer 2000
if hme1 AdvSendAdvertisements on
prefix 3ffe:80f0:1:5::/64 hme1
```

This shows that our inside network is "3ffe:80f0:1:5::/64" on the "hme1" interface. That leaves 64 bits of the address for machines to autoconfigure their interfaces. So all machines inside this firewall will have addresses like "3ffe:80f0:1:5:a00:20ff:fed9:21ea/64," which is the prefix we are advertising plus the EUI-64 address based on the 48-bit MAC address of the host's Ethernet card.

amazon.co.uk

Thank you for shopping at Amazon.co.uk!

Invoice for
Your order of 7 August, 2012
Order ID 203-4608160-6064364
Invoice number EUVIN51-OFS-GB-36050166
Invoice date 8 August, 2012

Billing Address
Ian Tomkins
38 Pennington Close
Colden Common
WINCHESTER, Hants SO21 1UR
United Kingdom

Shipping Address
Ian Tomkins
38 Pennington Close
Colden Common
WINCHESTER, Hants SO21 1UR
United Kingdom

Qty.	Item	Our Price (excl. VAT)	VAT Rate	Total Price
1	**Samsung UE40EH5000 40-inch Widescreen Full HD 1080p LED TV with Freeview HD (New for 2012)** Electronics. B007IHYP5Y : 8806071786315 (** P-1-F260A360 **)	£298.88	20%	£358.66
	Shipping charges	£0.00		£0.00

Subtotal (excl. VAT) 0%
Subtotal (excl. VAT) 20%
VAT at 20%
Total VAT
Total

£0.00
£298.88
£59.78
£59.78
£358.66

Conversion rate - £1.00 : EUR 1.27

This shipment completes your order.

You can always check the status of your orders or change your account details from the "Your Account" link at the top of each page on our site.

Thinking of returning an item? PLEASE USE OUR ON-LINE RETURNS SUPPORT CENTRE.
Our Returns Support Centre (www.amazon.co.uk/returns-support) will guide you through our Returns Policy and provide you with a printable personalised
return label. Please have your order number ready (you can find it next to your order summary, above). Our Returns Policy does not affect your statutory rights.

Amazon EU S.a.r.L, 5 Rue Plaetis, L-2338, Luxembourg
VAT number : GB727255821

Please note - this is not a returns address - for returns - please see above for details of our online returns centre

21/D17JJ5qR/-1 of 1-//1N/econ-uk/7771201/0809-18:00/0809-13:23 Pack Type : OWN

Reboot one more time. When the machine comes up, you should have all your interfaces configured. The IPv4 addresses are configured via the static addresses we assigned to them. The IPv6 interfaces should both autoconfigure—the outside interface using the Neighbor Discovery prefix advertised by the upstream router and the inside interface (hme1) by the Neighbor Discovery prefix the firewall is advertising.

Your interfaces should look something like this.

```
ipfw-o# ifconfig -a
lo0:    flags=1000849<UP,LOOPBACK,RUNNING,MULTICAST,IPv4> mtu 8232 index 1
        inet 127.0.0.1 netmask ff000000
hme0:   flags=1000843<UP,BROADCAST,RUNNING,MULTICAST,IPv4> mtu 1500 index 2
        inet 192.168.140.48 netmask fffffffe0 broadcast 192.168.140.63
        ether 8:0:20:d9:21:ea
hme1:   flags=1000843<UP,BROADCAST,RUNNING,MULTICAST,IPv4> mtu 1500 index 3
        inet 192.168.200.1 netmask ffffff00 broadcast 192.168.200.255
        ether 8:0:20:d9:21:ea
lo0:    flags=2000849<UP,LOOPBACK,RUNNING,MULTICAST,IPv6> mtu 8252 index 1
        inet6 ::1/128
hme0:   flags=2000841<UP,RUNNING,MULTICAST,IPv6> mtu 1500 index 2
        ether 8:0:20:d9:21:ea
        inet6 fe80::a00:20ff:fed9:21ea/10
hme0:1: flags=2080841<UP,RUNNING,MULTICAST,ADDRCONF,IPv6> mtu 1500 index 2
        inet6 3ffe:80f0:1:2:a00:20ff:fed9:21ea/64
hme1:   flags=2100841<UP,RUNNING,MULTICAST,ROUTER,IPv6> mtu 1500 index 3
        ether 8:0:20:d9:21:ea
        inet6 fe80::a00:20ff:fed9:21ea/10
hme1:1: flags=2080841<UP,RUNNING,MULTICAST,ADDRCONF,IPv6> mtu 1500 index 3
        inet6 3ffe:80f0:1:5:a00:20ff:fed9:21ea/64
```

Your routing table should look like this.

```
ipfw-o# netstat -rn
Routing Table: IPv4
```

```
Destination           Gateway           Flags  Ref   Use   Interface
------------------    --------------    -----  ---   ----  ---------
192.168.140.32        192.168.140.48    U      1     495   hme0
192.168.200.0         192.168.200.1     U      1     1027  hme1
224.0.0.0             192.168.140.48    U      1     0     hme0
default               192.168.140.33    UG     1     2017
127.0.0.1             127.0.0.1         UH     2     474   lo0
Routing Table: IPv6
Destination/Mask      Gateway                       Flags  Ref  Use    If
-------------------   -------------------------     -----  ---  -----  -------
3ffe:80f0:1:5::/64    3ffe:80f0:1:5:a00:20ff:fed9:21ea  U  1    9      hme1:1
3ffe:80f0:1:2::/64    3ffe:80f0:1:2:a00:20ff:fed9:21ea  U  1    4      hme0:1
fe80::/10             fe80::a00:20ff:fed9:21ea      U      1    3      hme1
fe80::/10             fe80::a00:20ff:fed9:21ea      U      1    1      hme0
ff00::/8              fe80::a00:20ff:fed9:21ea      U      1    0      hme0
default               fe80::290:92ff:fe5c:223f      UG     1    10     hme0
::1                   ::1                           UH     1    0      lo0
```

Test these interfaces for IPv6. You should be able to ping IPv6 machines
on both sides of your soon-to-be-firewall, like this.

```
ipfw-o# ping -I 1 -A inet6 3ffe:80f0:1:1:a00:20ff:fed9:da43
PING 3ffe:80f0:1:1:a00:20ff:fed9:da43: 56 data bytes
64 bytes from catera.zama6.net (3ffe:80f0:1:1:a00:20ff:fed9:da43):
  icmp_seq=0. time=1. ms
64 bytes from catera.zama6.net (3ffe:80f0:1:1:a00:20ff:fed9:da43):
  icmp_seq=1. time=1. ms
```

(You can see this machine is on the public side of our firewall.)

```
ipfw-o# ping -I 1 -A inet6 3ffe:80f0:1:5:2e0:18ff:fed8:45ab
PING 3ffe:80f0:1:5:2e0:18ff:fed8:45ab: 56 data bytes
64 bytes from mach1 (3ffe:80f0:1:5:2e0:18ff:fed8:45ab):
  icmp_seq=0. time=1. ms
```

```
64 bytes from mach1 (3ffe:80f0:1:5:2e0:18ff:fed8:45ab):
  icmp_seq=1. time=0. ms
```

(You can see this machine is inside our network—by the "3ffe:80f0:1:5" part of the address.)

23.1.4 MAKE SURE THE MACHINE IS ROUTING PACKETS

The Sun machine may or may not think it is a router, and it should forward packets not addressed to itself. It's supposed to make itself a router, by default, if it detects that it has multiple network interfaces. Mine didn't, but you can check—and then make it. Use these commands to check the status of these settings.

```
ipfw-o# ndd -get /dev/ip ip6_forwarding
1
ipfw-o# ndd -get /dev/ip ip_forwarding
1
```

In each case, these are set to 1, which means "on." If they had returned "0" they would have been off. To turn them on if they are off, use the command (use the similar form of the command for the other two settings).

```
ipfw-o# ndd -set /dev/ip ip6_forwarding 1
```

Now you should be routing. Go to the machine inside your network and see if you can "ping" (or otherwise connect) to a machine outside your firewall, using IPv4 and IPv6. Here are my traceroutes.

```
mach1# traceroute -A inet6 www6.zama6.net
traceroute: Warning: Multiple interfaces found;
  using 3ffe:80f0:1:5:2e0:18ff:fed8:45ab @ iprb0:1
traceroute to www6.zama6.net (3ffe:80f0:1:1:a00:20ff:fed9:da43), 30 hops max,
  60 byte packets
1 3ffe:80f0:1:5:a00:20ff:fed9:21ea 0.681 ms 0.487 ms 0.374 ms
2 3ffe:80f0:1:2::1 0.987 ms * 1.678 ms
3 catera.zama6.net (3ffe:80f0:1:1:a00:20ff:fed9:da43) 1.943 ms 2.552 ms 1.916 ms
```

```
mach1# traceroute -A inet www.zama6.net
traceroute to catera.zama6.net (192.168.170.10), 30 hops max, 40 byte packets
1 192.168.200.1 (192.168.200.1) 0.535 ms 0.398 ms 0.310 ms
2 192.168.140.33 (192.168.140.33) 0.759 ms 0.781 ms 0.708 ms
3 catera.zama6.net (192.168.170.10) 1.207 ms 1.166 ms 1.069 ms
```

The system can now function as a router; the next step is to turn it into a firewall.

23.1.5 OBTAINING, BUILDING, AND INSTALLING IPF

Get the IPF package. Our firewall is built using IPF v3.4.16. The best place to get the source code (yep—no precompiled binaries—we're going to build this from scratch) is from the genius that wrote (and still actively manages) the IPF effort: Darren Reed. Start with this page, and download the most recent software from http://coombs.anu.edu.au/~avalon/.

Once you have the software, uncompress it using the "gzip" utility, and then use the "tar" utility to expand the archive and make the directories.

```
gunzip ip-fil3.4.16.tar.gz
tar -xvf *.tar
```

To support IPv6, you must un-comment the line in the Makefile that reads the following.

```
#INET6=-DUSE_INET6
```

Then make the software according to the directions in "INSTALL.Sol2." Essentially, you run the "configure" script, then run "make solaris," then "cd SunOS5," then run "make package" (as root). This will end with an installation of the software.

```
make solaris cd SunOS5 make package
```

For me it worked very smoothly once I had the Solaris compiler. When you are done, check to make sure it's really there.

```
ipfw-o# pkginfo | grep ipf
```

```
system   ipf    IP Filter
system   ipfx   IP Filter (64-bit)
```

Most of the good stuff is installed into /usr/sbin, so make sure that is on your PATH. Other components are installed into "/etc/rc2.d"; you'll want to check those.

23.1.6 CONFIGURING IPF RULES FOR IPv4 AND IPv6

Now you need some rules. This is very well covered on a number of Internet sites, starting with the preceding URL to "coombs" in Australia. Rules can be quite complex. Our setup is fairly simple, but it provides a nice start. I've created my files in the "/etc/opt/ipf" directory. Review my rules, including the comments. You'll see I'm logging almost everything (we'll talk more about logging later), which is a good way to start. The level of logging can be reduced as you put your firewall into production.

```
------- IPv4 ruleset (/etc/opt/ipf/ipf.conf) -------
ipfw-o# cat ipf.conf
# hme0 is unprotected side
# hme1 is private side
# by default block all outside traffic
block in log level local4.info on hme0 all
# eliminate frags and shorts
block in log level local4.info quick on hme0 from any to any with short frag
block in log level local4.info quick on hme0 proto tcp all with short
# by default pass all traffic coming from the inside interface to the firewall
pass in on hme1 all
# block all inbound non-routable IPv4 addresses at the outside interface
block in log level local4.info quick on hme0 from 192.168.0.0/16 to any
block in log level local4.info quick on hme0 from 172.16.0.0/12 to any
block in log level local4.info quick on hme0 from 10.0.0.0/8 to any
block in log level local4.info quick on hme0 from 127.0.0.0/8 to any
# block all non-routable (except 192.168 - ours) IPv4 addresses on the
   inside interface
block in log level local4.info quick on hme1 from 172.16.0.0/12 to any
block in log level local4.info quick on hme1 from 10.0.0.0/8 to any
block in log level local4.info quick on hme1 from 127.0.0.0/8 to any
# allow all outbound tcp, udp, and icmp traffic using KEEP STATE ...
```

```
pass out quick on hme0 proto tcp/udp from any to any keep state
pass out quick on hme0 proto icmp from any to any keep state
# allow inbound from the world these services - telnet, ssh, and ftp
pass in log level local4.info quick proto tcp from any to any port = 22
pass in log level local4.info quick proto tcp from any to any port = 23
pass in log level local4.info quick proto tcp from any to any port
  = 21 flags S keep state
pass out log level local4.info quick proto tcp from any to any port
  = 21 flags S keep state
------- end IPv4 ruleset -------
------- IPv6 ruleset (/etc/opt/ipf/ipf6.conf)-------
ipfw-o# cat ipf6.conf
# hme0 is outside
# hme1 is inside
block in log level local6.info on hme0 all
pass in log level local6.info on hme1 all
# anti-spoofing v6 style
block in log level local6.info quick on hme0 from 3ffe:80f0:1:5::/64 to any
# outbound - very permissive - use KEEP STATE
pass out log level local6.info quick on hme0 proto tcp from any to any keep state
pass out log level local6.info quick on hme0 proto udp from any to any keep state
pass out quick on hme0 proto icmp from any to any keep state
pass out quick on hme0 proto ipv6-icmp from any to any keep state
pass in quick on hme1 proto ipv6-icmp from any to any
# need rule below to make outbound IPv6 pings work - I think you should not need it
pass in quick on hme0 proto ipv6-icmp from any to any
# allow SSH and telnet
pass in log level local6.info quick proto tcp from any to any port = 22
pass in log level local6.info quick proto tcp from any to any port = 23
------- end IPv6 ruleset -------
```

23.1.7   Configuring IPF NAT for IPv4

We want this to be an IPv4/IPv6 firewall, so we've configured both interfaces for both protocols. I've configured IPv4 NAT (IPv6 NAT will rarely,
if ever, be used—think about it) to support "one-to-many" NAT. You need
this if you want people inside your protected network to be able to get to
sites on the public side. Your internal system (perhaps at 192.168.200.10)
will hit Web sites on the Internet looking like it came from the outside IPv4
address of your firewall (192.168.140.48).

If you want to be able to run an IPv4 Web site, internally, you have to configure "one-to-one" NAT. Then a machine outside your firewall (say on the Internet) can make connections into your protected network. The address you use to represent the internal device (say a Web server) must be a routable address. Here's what this looks like.

```
------- IPv4 NAT (/etc/opt/ipf/ipnat.conf) ---------
# this line is required to support active ftp's
map hme0 0/0 -> 0/32 proxy port 21 ftp/tcp
# provides one-to-many internal NATing for inside -to-outside connections
map hme0 192.168.200.0/24 -> 0/32
# allow outside systems to make connections into our 192.168.200.10 system
bimap hme0 192.168.200.10/32 -> 192.168.140.169/32
------- end IPv4 NAT (/etc/opt/ipf/ipnat.conf) ---------
```

Loading and Verifying that IPF Is Active Again

The best documentation for this topic is at the IPF site at http://www.obfuscation.org/ipf/ipf-howto.html#TOC_29. You may want to do this at the system console—or at least make sure you have access to the system console. In brief, you manipulate your IPF rules with the "ipf" and "ipnat" commands. The simple method is to explicitly load the rules you want to use. Here are the commands I use (for IPv4, IPv6, and NAT).

```
ipf -Ef /etc/opt/ipf/ipf.conf
ipf -6 -Ef /etc/opt/ipf/ipf6.conf
ipnat -CF -f /etc/opt/ipf/ipnat.conf
```

The "-6" option, in the second command, specifies that you are working with the IPv6 ruleset. To see if you have IPF loaded properly, use the "ipfstat" commands. Here's what I show when I check my rules (this is the same as "ipfstat 6").

```
ipfw-o# ipfstat
dropped packets:              in 0   out 0
non-data packets:             in 0   out 0
no-data packets:              in 0   out 0
non-ip packets:               in 0   out 0
```

```
bad packets:                        in 0  out 0
copied messages:                    in 0  out 3520
IPv6 packets:                       in 1468 out 1154
input packets:                      blocked 139 passed 165017 nomatch 36 counted 0
                                        short 446
output packets:                     blocked 0 passed 162826 nomatch 386 counted 0
                                        short 360
input packets logged:               blocked 139 passed 5917
output packets logged:              blocked 0 passed 5874
packets logged:                     input 0 output 0
log failures:                       input 42 output 49
fragment state(in):                 kept 0 lost 0
fragment state(out):                kept 0 lost 0
packet state(in):                   kept 167        lost 0
packet state(out):                  kept 2062       lost 128
ICMP replies:                       0
TCP RSTs sent: 0 Invalid source(in):        0
Result cache hits(in):              753    (out): 293
IN Pullups succeeded:               0      failed: 0
OUT Pullups succeeded:              5      failed: 0
Fastroute successes:                0      failures:    0
TCP cksum fails(in):                0      (out): 0
Packet log flags set:               (0)    none
```

23.1.8   Testing IPv6 Rules

The best testing method is to get on your internal machine and work on the Internet. See if you can still "ping," ftp, and make telnet and Web connections to external hosts. See if you can make TCP connections from machines (i.e., see if you can hit a Web site) outside your firewall to internal machines. Check the logfiles. Do all the tests for IPv4 and IPv6.

You can monitor the traffic to your site interactively by running the "ipmon" command. This command shows you traffic transiting the firewall. You can also set up ipmon to run in the background and capture packets using the UNIX syslog facility, and that's what I have done.

My logging is done to two files—one for IPv4 packets and one for IPv6 packets. This is accomplished by configuring the rule files with "log level" clauses, creating the target logfiles, and configuring the syslog configuration files. Specifically, follow these steps.

Make sure your "/etc/opt/ipf/ipf.conf" and "/etc/opt/ipf/ipf6.conf" rule files contain log statements that specify the log level and facility you will use. Look back in this paper to the rule files. A typical statement looks like this (IPv6).

```
pass in log level local6.info quick proto tcp from any to 3ffe:80f0:1:5:
  2e0:18ff:fed8:45ab port = 80
```

This statement says "log this traffic using local6.info as the syslog facility."

Next, decide where you want the IPF logfiles to live (mine are in "/var/log/ipfw"). Use the "touch" command to create the files.

```
"touch /var/log/ipfw/ipfw4.log", then "touch /var/log/ipfw/ipfw6.log"
```

Now configure "/etc/syslog.conf." This file can be pretty tricky; just copy what I have here. Make sure you use TAB, not SPACE, between the fields, or it won't work. The relevant part of my file is as follows. (You can put these lines anywhere. Mine are in the middle.)

```
local4.info
/var/log/ipfw/ipfw4.log local6.info
/var/log/ipfw/ipfw6.log
```

We're getting close. Now restart syslog. I just use the scripts already in "/etc/rc2.d." Run these commands.

```
"/etc/rc2.d/S74syslog stop", then "/etc/rc2.d/S74syslog start"
```

Now you need to start ipmon. I use the command "ipmon s."

That should do it. Send some packets (for which you are logging) through the firewall, and check the files we set up. They should have lines in them.

Examining the IPF logfiles

The logfiles are pretty straightforward. Here are a few lines from each of my IPv4 and IPv6 files.

```
------ IPv4 --------
Jan 18 09:44:06 ipfw-o ipmon[18509]: [ID 702911 local4.info] 09:44:06.328225
   hme0 @0:16 p 192.168.130.74 -> 192.168.200.10 PR icmp len 20 60 icmp 8/0 IN
Jan 18 09:44:06 ipfw-o ipmon[18509]: [ID 702911 local4.info] 09:44:06.328225
   hme0 @0:16 p 192.168.130.74 -> 192.168.200.10 PR icmp len 20 60 icmp 8/0 IN
Jan 18 09:44:09 ipfw-o ipmon[18509]: [ID 702911 local4.info] 09:44:09.451586
   hme0 @0:15 p 192.168.130.74,1916 -> 192.168.200.10,80 PR tcp len 20 48 -S IN
Jan 18 09:44:09 ipfw-o ipmon[18509]: [ID 702911 local4.info] 09:44:09.474124
   hme0 @0:15 p 192.168.130.74,1916 -> 192.168.200.10,80 PR tcp len 20 234 -AP IN
------- end IPv4 ------------
```

This segment shows four packets. The first two are ICMP pings from outside the network through to the internal Web server, for which we have set up static NAT (routable 192.168.140.169 is nonroutable 192.168.200.10). The next two packets are HTTP connections from the same external IPv4-address to the internal Web server. The entire portion shown here is from syslog itself—not IPF.

```
Jan 18 09:44:09 ipfw-o ipmon[18509]: [ID 702911 local4.info]
```

The IP portion of that same line is as follows.

```
09:44:09.474124 hme0 @0:15 p 192.168.130.74,1916 ->
   192.168.200.10,80 PR tcp len 20 234 -AP IN
```

The logfile format is as follows.

```
time packet received
interface packets processed on
group and rule number (I'm not using groups, so this is rule 15)
action ("p" for passed, "b" for blocked)
source address and port, arrow symbol, and destination address and port
"PR tcp" means that the protocol is TCP
```

```
"len 20 234" means that the packet header length is 20 bytes, and total packet
   length is 234 bytes
"-AP" are flags set on the rule (A says this was an "ACK" packet)
"IN" means the packet was inbound on the interface
-------- IPv6 ------------
Jan 14 06:28:44 ipfw-o ipmon[16863]: [ID 702911 local6.info] 06:28:43.390833
   hme0 @0:4 p fe80::290:92ff:fe5c:223f -> ff02::1 PR ipv6-icmp len 40 (56) IN
Jan 14 06:28:44 ipfw-o ipmon[16863]: [ID 702911 local6.info] 06:28:43.390833
   hme0 @0:4 p fe80::290:92ff:fe5c:223f -> ff02::1 PR ipv6-icmp len 40 (56) IN
Jan 9 08:22:35 ipfw-o ipmon[16598]: [ID 702911 local6.info] 08:22:35.153816
   hme1 @65535:0 p 3ffe:80f0:1:1:a00:20ff:fed9:da43,telnet ->
   3ffe:80f0:1:5:2e0:18ff:fed8:45ab,32835 PR tcp len 40 20 -A K-S OUT
-------- end IPv6 ---------
```

Here we see three packets—two ICMP packets and a "telnet" packet. Except for the address format and length, the format is identical. Note the "-A K-S OUT" ending. This was an ACK packet, for which we were keeping state (via "keep state") and was outbound on the interface.

23.1.9 CLOSING TOPICS

That pretty much completes your firewall build. There are a few more housekeeping things to do, but just a few. The most important thing is to make sure that your firewall will restart upon reboot, and you should test that now. First, consider some new "/etc/rc2.d" files that will run these commands upon startup, or consider putting them into "/etc/rc2.d/S69inet."

```
ndd -set /dev/ip ip_forwarding 1
ndd -set /dev/ip ip6_forwarding 1
ndd -set /dev/ip ip_forward_directed_broadcasts 0
ndd -set /dev/ip ip_forward_src_routed 0
ndd -set /dev/ip ip_respond_to_echo_broadcast 0
```

Check the "/etc/rc2.d/S65ipfboot" file to make sure it points to your ruleset and that it does all the things you want it to do.

Play around with the ipfstat commands, using these parameters, to get useful information.

```
ipfstat -6
ipfstat  i -n
ipfstat  6  i -n
ipfstat  o -n
ipfstat  6  o   n
ipfstat  i  h
ipfstat  6  i    h
ipfstat  o - h
ipfstat  6  o -h
ipfstat  s
```

23.2   IPv6/v4 IP Filtering Firewall on FreeBSD**

This section provides step-by-step instructions for setting up a firewall using a system running FreeBSD 4.2.

23.2.1   GATHERING THE PIECES

Here's a brief list of what you'll need for this project.

- An Intel-based machine running FreeBSD 4.2 configured and running with IPv4 and IPv6 network connectivity. (Refer to ZamaDoc #1012 for configuration.)
- The GNU gcc compiler and gzip, which should have been installed with FreeBSD 4.2
- IPF 3.4.16 package, which can be obtained at ftp://coombs.anu.edu.au/pub/net/ip-filter/ip-fil3.4.16.tar.gz.

You can also download it from the Zama ftp site at ftp://203.142.143.7/pub/ipv6/src/.

**This section is adapted from a document written by Gerald R. Crow IV, © Zama Networks.

23.2.2   BUILDING AND INSTALLING IPF

Like most source packages, ipf comes compressed and bundled into a tar file. If you're using the GNU version of tar, you can un-tar the package at the same time that you're uncompressing it. The following command will accomplish this.

```
>tar xvfz ip-fil3.4.16.tar.gz
```

Otherwise, change to the directory where you have placed the file ip-fil3.4.16.tar.gz and unzip it using the gzip command.

```
>gzip  d ip-fil3.4.16.tar.gz
```

Use the tar command on the file ip-fil3.4.16.tar.

```
>tar xvf ip-fil3.4.16.tar
```

Change the directory to ./ip_fil3.4.16, and use your favorite text editor to uncomment this line from the Makefile.

```
#INET6=-DUSE_INET6
```

Within the ./ip_fil3.4.16 directory, run these commands as root.

```
>make freebsd4 >make install-bsd
```

Change the directory to ./ip_fil3.4.16/FreeBSD-4.0/, and use the cp command to copy the file ipv6-patch-4.1 to ipv6-patch-4.2. Even though the patch in the following step is written for FreeBSD 4.1, there should be no issues using it for 4.2. What it does is patch the files ip6_input.c and ip6_output.c.

```
>cd ./FreeBSD-4.0 >cp ipv6-patch-4.1 ipv6-patch-4.2
```

Now run the kinstall script in the current directory to apply the patch and update your kernel with IPF options. Substitute your kernel name for GENERIC if needed.

```
>./kinstall

Installing ip_fil.c ip_fil.h ip_nat.c ip_nat.h ip_frag.c ip_frag.h ip_state.c
```

```
    ip_state.h fil.c
ip_proxy.c ip_proxy.h ip_ftp_pxy.c ip_rcmd_pxy.c ip_raudio_pxy.c mlf_ipl.c
    mlfk_ipl.c ipl.h ip_compat.h
ip_auth.c ip_auth.h ip_log.c Linking /usr/include/osreldate.h to /sys/sys/
    osreldate.h
Patching ip6_input.c and ip6_output.c Hmm...
Looks like a new-style context diff to me...
The text leading up to this was:
--------------------------
|*** ip6_input.c.orig
        Sat Jul 15 07:14:34 2000
|--- ip6_input.c
            Thu Oct 19 17:14:37 2000
                        4.2

--------------------------
Patching file ip6_input.c using Plan A...
Hunk #1 succeeded at 118 (offset -2 lines).
Hunk #2 succeeded at 287 (offset -4 lines).
Hmm...
The next patch looks like a new-style context diff to me...
The text leading up to this was:
--------------------------
| |*** ip6_output.c.orig      Sat Jul 15 07:14:35 2000
|--- ip6_output.c            Thu Oct 19 17:13:53 2000

--------------------------
Patching file ip6_output.c using Plan A...
Hunk #1 succeeded at 104 with fuzz 2 (offset -2 lines).
Hunk #2 succeeded at 787 with fuzz 1 (offset -2 lines).
Done
Kernel configuration to update [GENERIC] Rewriting GENERIC...
You will now need to run config on GENERIC and build a new kernel.
```

This script will copy your current running kernel configuration file in the /sys/i386/conf directory to the same name with a .bak extension before any editing takes place. For example, GENERIC will be copied over to GENERIC.bak.

Now we need to copy the file osreldate.h to a place where IPF's kernel code can find it.

```
>cp /usr/include/osreldate.h /usr/src/include
```

Since FreeBSD 4.2 comes with an IPv4-only version of ipmon in the /sbin directory, we need to copy the new IPv6 enabled binary there from the /usr/sbin directory.

```
>cp /usr/sbin/ipmon /sbin
```

Installation of IPF is complete, and you now need to rebuild the kernel to implement your changes.

23.2.3   REBUILDING A KERNEL WITH IPF

The following are the steps needed to rebuild a kernel with the IPF options enabled. If for any reason you have changed the name of your kernel, substitute your kernel's name for GENERIC in the following steps.

Change directories to where the kernel configuration file is located and execute the following commands.

```
>cd /sys/i386/conf
>config GENERIC
```

Now execute the following commands in this order to compile and install the kernel.

```
>cd ../../compile/GENERIC
>make depend
>make
>make install
```

Reboot the machine, and the kernel will come up with IPF enabled.

23.2.4   CONFIGURE IPF RULES

Now that the machine is up and running with IPF enabled, your next step will be to create the configuration files. A firewall is only as secure as you configure it, so if you have never configured your own firewall, good resources can be found at http://coombs.anu.edu.au/~avalon/ and in Zama Doc #1008.

You need to create separate IPv4 and IPv6 configuration files for the two firewalls to coexist. The following example is for a FreeBSD 4.2 machine with one interface. This configuration will only allow SSH connections and ICMP traffic from the outside world (comments noted with #s).

```
-----IPv4 rule set (/etc/ipf.rules)-----
# Block all by default.
block in log level local4.info all
# Eliminate frags and shorts
block in log level local4.info quick from any to any with short frag
block in log level local4.info quick proto tcp all with short
# Allow the following in through the filter: SSH and ICMP.
pass in proto tcp/udp from any to any port = 22 keep state
pass in proto icmp from any to any
# Allow all outbound TCP, UDP, and ICMP traffic.
pass out quick proto tcp/udp from any to any keep state
pass out quick proto icmp from any to any keep state
-----End of IPv4 rule set-----
-----IPv6 rule set (/etc/ipf6.rules)-----
# Block all by default.
block in log level local6.info on xl0 all
# Allow the following through the filter: SSH and ICMP.
pass in on xl0 proto tcp from any to any port = 22 keep state
pass in on xl0 proto ipv6-icmp from any to any
# Allow all outbound TCP, UDP, and ICMP traffic
pass out quick on xl0 proto tcp from any to any keep state
pass out quick on xl0 proto udp from any to any keep state
pass out quick on xl0 proto icmp from any to any keep state
-----End of IPv6 rule set-----
```

23.2.5 CONFIGURING SYSLOG FOR IPF LOGGING

Using the ipmon command, you can specify where you would like IPF to log activity. If you would like to use syslog to do all IPF logging, follow these steps.

Open /etc/syslog.conf with your favorite text editor and insert the following just above the line that says "!startslip." Make sure all white spaces are tabs or syslog will not work.

```
# IPv4 IPF log local4.info
                                            /var/log/ipf4.log
# IPv6 IPF log local6.info
                                            /var/log/ipf6.log
```

Now that we have configured IPF logging to use syslog, all we have to do is create the log files we will be using by running the following commands.

```
>touch /var/log/ipf4.log
>touch /var/log/ipf6.log
```

Restart the syslog process so it will reload the syslog.conf file.

23.2.6 START AND TEST IPF

The ipf command works with the same switches, except you need to use a "-6" before any commands that are pertaining to the IPv6 configuration. Now that everything is configured correctly, run the following commands to start IPF with the IPv4 and IPv6 rules.

```
>ipf  f /etc/ipf.rules
>ipf  6f /etc/ipf6.rules
```

Now we need to start IPF's logging utility, ipmon. The D option tells it to run as a daemon, and the s option tells it to use syslog for logging.

```
>ipmon  Ds
```

To make sure that the rules were loaded, run the following commands. I have included my machine's output in the following examples.

```
>ipfstat  io
-----IPv4 running rules output-----
pass out quick proto tcp/udp from any to any keep state
pass out quick proto icmp from any to any keep state
block in log level local4.info from any to any
block in log level local4.info quick from any to any with short frag
block in log level local4.info quick proto tcp from any to any with short
pass in proto tcp/udp from any to any port = ssh keep state
pass in proto icmp from any to any
>ipfstat  6io
-----IPv6 running rules output-----
pass out quick on xl0 proto tcp from any to any keep state
pass out quick on xl0 proto udp from any to any keep state
pass out quick on xl0 proto icmp from any to any keep state
block in log level local6.info on xl0 from any to any
pass in on xl0 proto tcp from any to any port = 22 keep state
pass in on xl0 proto ipv6-icmp from any to any
```

Testing the firewall configuration should be done to ensure everything is working properly. The best way is from a remote machine. Make sure services you have open are working and try to utilize services you have blocked. The following is an example of blocked telnet attempts to my machine over both IPv4 and IPv6.

```
>tail  f /var/log/ipf4.log
Mar 27 05:52:22 news6 ipmon[50]: 05:52:22.331336 xl0 @0:1 b 192.168.25.5,32953 ->
192.168.25.6,23 PR tcp len 20 48 -S IN
Mar 27 05:52:26 news6 ipmon[50]: 05:52:25.692845 xl0 @0:1 b 192.168.25.5,32953 ->
192.168.25.6,23 PR tcp len 20 48 -S IN
Mar 27 05:52:32 news6 ipmon[50]: 05:52:32.442338 xl0 @0:1 b 192.168.25.5,32953 ->
192.168.25.6,23 PR tcp len 20 48 -S IN
>tail  f /var/log/ipf6.log
Mar 27 06:09:44 news6 ipmon[50]: 06:09:44.772488 xl0 @0:1 b 3ffe:80f0:1:1:201:2ff:
```

```
    fe00:2112,32955 -> 3ffe:80f0:1:1:201:2ff:fe00:2113,23 PR tcp len 40 28 -S IN
Mar 27 06:09:48 news6 ipmon[50]: 06:09:48.135094 xl0 @0:1 b 3ffe:80f0:1:1:201:2ff:
    fe00:2112,32955 -> 3ffe:80f0:1:1:201:2ff:fe00:2113,23 PR tcp len 40 28 -S IN
Mar 27 06:09:54 news6 ipmon[50]: 06:09:54.884650 xl0 @0:1 b 3ffe:80f0:1:1:201:2ff:
    fe00:2112,32955 -> 3ffe:80f0:1:1:201:2ff:fe00:2113,23 PR tcp len 40 28 -S IN
```

23.2.7 Configure FreeBSD to Boot IPF

Configuring ipmon and IPF for IPv4 at startup is already supported by the /etc/rc.network file and will be activated by inserting the following lines into /etc/rc.conf.

```
ipfilter_enable="YES"
ipfilter_program="/sbin/ipf -Fa -f"
ipfilter_flags=""
ipmon_enable="YES"
```

To get the IPv6 option of IPF to come up at boot time, you will need to tweak some startup scripts. Here is an example of how I got it to work using existing startup scripts. First, we need to back up the files we will be editing.

```
>cp /etc/rc.conf /etc/rc.conf.old
>cp /etc/rc.network /etc/rc.network.old
```

Insert these lines into the /etc/rc.conf file with your favorite text editor.

```
ipfilter6_program="/sbin/ipf -6f"
ipfilter6_enable="YES"
ipfilter6_rules="/etc/ipf6.rules"
```

Now all we need to do is insert the following into our /etc/rc.network file and we are finished. The earlier in the /etc/rc.network file you place this, the earlier it is executed in the network startup sequence. I have inserted this right after the ipfilter script block for IPv4 to ensure it comes up in the beginning of the network configuration.

```
case "${ipfilter6_enable}" in [Yy][Ee][Ss])
        if [ -r "${ipfilter6_rules}" ]; then
            ${ipfilter6_program} "${ipfilter6_rules}"
        fi
        ;; esac
```

23.2.8 TROUBLESHOOTING

If the installation does not work or breaks your current kernel configuration, change directories to where you have IPF's package source and follow these steps to revert all changes made (substitute GENERIC with your kernel name if needed).

```
>cd ip_fil3.4.16/FreeBSD-4.0/
>./kuninstall
>cd /sys/i386/conf
>cp GENERIC.bak GENERIC
```

Now rebuild the kernel with IPF.

23.3   Implementing IPsec on Sun Solaris (IPv4)[†]

IPsec provides IP-layer security for packets traversing a network—particularly useful when the network in question is insecure—like the Internet. The protection provided includes encryption (providing confidentiality), data-origin authentication (the receiving node can be sure the traffic originated at the node shown in the source address), data integrity (the data was not changed in transit), and antireplay (the traffic cannot be regenerated later and accepted as current by the receiver).

Native IPsec support is a key advantage of IPv6 over IPv4. Whereas in IPv4 IPsec support was an option, it is mandated in IPv6. There will be no IPv6-compliant (i.e., commercially marketable) network protocol implementations that do not support IPsec.

[†]This section is adapted from a document written by John E. Spence, © Zama Networks.

As we learned from the rapid adoption of the Internet—which followed the widespread adoption of IP networking—when technology is widely supported, the "network-effect" causes prolific growth in its use. I believe the growth of IPsec will be the same. Near-term future networks based on IPv6 will make widespread use of IPsec-based data security. The days where most traffic is carried unencrypted may, eventually, come to an end, and it will be a rare packet that will not be encrypted and authenticated. Just as you can't imaging sending important (read "most all") paper documents in "postcard" form through the mail, data on networks will be treated in the same way.

For now at least, most packets will still be transmitted in the clear. Although not all network data is confidential, *traffic analysis* attacks depend on having some volume of encrypted and/or unencrypted data to analyze. The absence of certain types of data in the unencrypted flows can be used to infer what the encrypted packets are carrying. Furthermore, encrypting only the confidential data simplifies the task of any attackers: They don't have to worry about trying to decrypt anything but the most valuable packets.

This section describes in detail how to obtain, install, and configure IPsec on Sun Solaris 8 (SPARC and Intel architecture) over IPv4.

23.3.1   KEY IPSEC CONCEPTS IN A NUTSHELL

IPsec provides two major components, ESP and AH. ESP stands for "Encapsulating Security Payload," which provides confidentiality, data integrity, and data source authentication of IP packets. AH stands for "Authentication Header," which provides data integrity and data source authentication of IP packets—but no confidentiality. We'll use ESP so we'll get all the protection we can.

Also required for IPsec are "Security Associations" (SAs). These specify the particular security association (called an SPI), packet destination, and protocol. SAs are unidirectional, so each host participating in an IPsec conversation must have at least two (and sometimes more) SAs.

Sun's current implementation only supports "manual SAs." That means we must create the SAs manually and manage them manually. Future releases will incorporate automatic systems for key management (notably Internet Key Exchange, or IKE).

23.3.2 ESTABLISH A BASELINE

We'll use "telnet" to test our IPsec connection, so, before we start make sure you can telnet in both directions between your machines. This will give us confidence if we have problems later that there are no non-IPsec-related problems with interface configurations, routes, cables, or anything else.

Set a performance baseline too. For my machines, I was able to achieve 3715 Kbytes/second while ftp'ing a 98MB file "in the clear." While using IPsec (DES encryption and MD5 authentication) my performance was reduced to 1601 KB/second.

23.3.3 COLLECT THE COMPONENTS YOU'LL NEED

You'll need the following.

- "Solaris 8 Supplemental Encryption Packages" from Sun, www.sun.com/software/solaris/get.html get the distribution you need for your platform.
- Regardless of which flavor of Solaris 8 you're using (SPARC or Intel), we need two machines to set up IPSec. Throughout this document we'll call them "sea-mach1" and "sea-mach2."

23.3.4 INSTALLING THE IPSEC COMPONENTS

After you have the packages on your machine, untar them. Change into the local directory "sparc/Packages." You'll be left with a directory that looks like this.

```
sea-mach1# ls

NSCPcomdo      SUNWamid      SUNWcrman SUNWcry64  SUNWcryrx   SUNWk5pkx    SUNWk5pux
NSCPfrcdo      SUNWamidx     SUNWcry   SUNWcryr   SUNWk5pk    SUNWk5pu
```

Run the "pkgadd" command as "pkgadd -d .," and you'll see this.

```
sea-mach1# pkgadd -d .

The following packages are available:
1    NSCPcomdo       Netscape Communicator
                     (sparc) 20.4.70,REV=1999.10.13.17.55
```

```
2    NSCPfrcdo           French Netscape Communicator (U.S. security)
                         (sparc) 20.4.70,REV=1999.11.05.13.36
3    SUNWamid            Authentication Management Infrastructure (domestic version)
                         (sparc) 11.8.0,REV=1999.12.07.04.22
4    SUNWamidx           Authentication Management Infrastructure
                            (64 bit domestic version)
                         (sparc) 11.8.0,REV=1999.12.07.04.22
5    SUNWcrman           Encryption Kit On-Line Manual Pages
                         (sparc) 6.0,REV=1
6    SUNWcry             Crypt Utilities
                         (sparc) 11.8.0,REV=1999.12.07.04.22
7    SUNWcry64           Prototype package for Crypt Library (64-bit)
                         (sparc) 11.8.0,REV=1999.12.07.04.22
8    SUNWcryr            Solaris Root Crypto
                         (sparc) 11.8.0,REV=1999.12.07.04.22
9    SUNWcryrx           Solaris Root Crypto (64-bit)
                         (sparc) 11.8.0,REV=1999.12.07.04.22
10   SUNWk5pk            kernel Kerberos V5 plug-in w/auth+privacy (32-bit)
                         (sparc) 11.8.0,REV=1999.12.07.04.22
... 3 more menu choices to follow;
<RETURN> for more choices, <CTRL-D> to stop display:
11   SUNWk5pkx           kernel Kerberos V5 plug-in w/auth+privacy (64-bit)
                         (sparc) 11.8.0,REV=1999.12.07.04.22
12   SUNWk5pu            user Kerberos V5 gss mechanism w/auth+privacy (32-bit)
                         (sparc) 11.8.0,REV=1999.12.07.04.22
13   SUNWk5pux           user Kerberos V5 gss mechanism w/auth+privacy (64-bit)
                         (sparc) 11.8.0,REV=1999.12.07.04.22
Select package(s) you wish to process (or 'all' to
process all packages). (default: all) [?,??,q]:
```

Choose 3, 4, 5, 6, 7, 8, and 9. We don't need the Kerberos products for IPsec. All the packages should install fine.

23.3.5 CONFIGURING IPSEC

Initial configurations for both machines are identical. We'll show details for sea-mach1, but sea-mach2 is similar. Later, we'll set up the

IPsec parameters and static SAs, and we'll show both machines for clarity.

Let's lay some groundwork. DNS can provide a security vulnerability. If a system relies on DNS to translate system names into IP addresses, and that DNS has been compromised, all kinds of problems can occur. For this reason, it is usually best to put entries in "/etc/hosts" for machines that are using IPsec. You'll also want to make sure that the machines "/etc/nsswitch.conf" file has this entry for "hosts."

```
hosts:        files dns
```

This means the machine will check the "/etc/hosts" records first when matching a name—before using DNS for address resolution. Here's our "/etc/hosts" file.

```
sea-mach1# cat /etc/hosts
# Internet host table
127.0.0.1           localhost
192.168.210.34      sea-mach1.zama6.com sea-mach1 ipv6s1.zama6.com ipv6s1 loghost
192.168.210.51      sea-mach2.zama6.com sea-mach2
```

You'll want a similar—but not identical—file on your IPsec partner system.

Next, we have to tell the machine to load the IPSec modules at boot-time. There should be a file in "/etc/inet" called "ipsecinit.sample." Copy this file to "ipsecinit.conf." To begin, the file can contain nothing (or nothing but comments). Just the fact that it exists will get IPsec loaded.

Create a place to put your IPsec config files. I'm using "/etc/ipsec-conf." You'll need two files—one to contain the SAs and one to contain the IPsec configuration.

23.3.6 CREATE THE SECURITY ASSOCIATIONS

Create the file "keys-all" (this file should have permissions 600—the keys must be kept private). This file will contain our SAs. Here's what mine looks like.

```
sea-mach1# cat keys-all
add esp spi 0x4444 src sea-mach2.zama6.com dst ipv6s1.zama6.com auth_alg md5 encr_alg
des \
```

```
authkey 1234567890abcdef1234567890abcdef encrkey 1234567890abcdef
add esp spi 0x5555 src ipv6s1.zama6.com dst sea-mach2.zama6.com auth_alg md5
     encr_alg
des \
authkey 1234567890abcdef1234567890abcdef encrkey 1234567890abcdef
```

Let's examine each line. The first line adds an SA for traffic headed for our IPsec partner. Let's look at each field in the first line—you can figure out the second line.

add   means we're adding an SA.

esp   specifies that this is an ESP SA, as opposed to an authentication-and-integrity (AH) SA.

0x4444   is the "SPI," which uniquely identifies this SA.

src sea-mach2.zama6.com   specifies the source for this SA is sea-mach2.

dst ipv6s1.zama6.com   specifies the destination for this SA.

auth_alg md5   specifies the authentication method we are using—md5 in this case.

encr_alg des   specifies the encryption method we are using—des (3des is also available).

authkey 1234567890abcdef1234567890abcdef   128-bit md5 key

encrkey 1234567890abcdef   64-bit des key

Put this file on both machines—exactly like this. Each encrypted packet will carry the "SPI" number used for the encryption/authentication, so the recipient machine must have the same keys associated with the same SPI. (By the way, these are lousy keys, used only for ease of demonstration. Choose a very random key.)

To enable these keys, use the command "ipseckey -f keys-all." To flush the keys, you can use "ipseckey flush" and then reload them.

23.3.7   CREATE THE SECURITY POLICIES

Now we'll create our IPsec configuration. Create the file "both-all." Here's what mine looks like.

```
sea-mach1# cat both-all
{
        saddr ipv6s1.zama6.com
```

```
            daddr sea-mach2.zama6.com
            ulp tcp
}apply {
            encr_algs des
            encr_auth_algs md5 sa shared
}
{
            saddr sea-mach2.zama6.com
            daddr ipv6s1.zama6.com
            ulp tcp
}permit {
            encr_algs des
            encr_auth_algs md5
}
```

Let's take this file apart. There are two policies in this file, each protecting traffic in one direction. The top policy is for ipv6 to sea-mach2. The "ulp tcp" says that we are only using IPsec for TCP traffic—UDP and ICMP traffic will not use IPsec. The "apply" statement simply says "Use IPsec for this traffic." The next line "encr_algs des" specifies the encryption algorithm to use; this has to match an SA (in our keys-all file). The last line in this policy specifies to use the "md5" authentication cipher. The "sa shared" tells IPsec to use any SA on the system that matches the parameters specified (source, destination, protocol, encryption cipher, and authentication cipher).

The second policy allows traffic returning from sea-mach2 to be decrypted and authenticated properly when it arrives back at ipv6s1.

To load the security policy, use the command "ipsecconf -a both-all." To unload them, use "ipsecconf -f," and then you can load them again. If the load goes well (no errors), you'll probably see this dialog.

```
sea-mach1# ipsecconf -a both-all
WARNING : New policy entries that are being added may
affect the existing connections. Existing connections
that are not subjected to policy constraints may be
```

subjected to policy constraints because of the new
policy. This can disrupt the communication of the
existing connections.

This looks pretty good so far. Let's just check our work by displaying the
configurations for these machines to the terminal. The commands for that
are "ipseckey dump" and "ipsecconf," as shown.

```
sea-mach1# ipseckey dump
Base message (version 2) type DUMP, SA type ESP.
Message length 152 bytes, seq=1, pid=1064.
SA: SADB_ASSOC spi=0x5555, replay=0, state=MATURE
SA: Authentication algorithm = HMAC-MD5
SA: Encryption algorithm = DES-CBC
SA: flags=0x80000000 < X_USED >
SRC: Source address (proto=0/<unspecified>)
SRC: AF_INET: port = 0, 192.168.210.34 (sea-mach1.zama6.com).
DST: Destination address (proto=0/<unspecified>)
DST: AF_INET: port = 0, 192.168.210.51 (sea-mach2.zama6.com).
AKY: Authentication key. AKY: 1234567890abcdef1234567890abcdef/128
EKY: Encryption key.
EKY: 1334577991abcdef/64
LT: Lifetime information
CLT: 52336 bytes protected, 0 allocations used.
CLT: SA added at time Fri Mar 02 10:05:55 2001
CLT: SA first used at time Fri Mar 02 10:06:16 2001
CLT: Time now is Fri Mar 02 16:04:47 2001
Base message (version 2) type DUMP, SA type ESP.
Message length 152 bytes, seq=1, pid=1064.
SA: SADB_ASSOC spi=0x4444, replay=0, state=MATURE
SA: Authentication algorithm = HMAC-MD5
SA: Encryption algorithm = DES-CBC
SA: flags=0x80000000 < X_USED >
SRC: Source address (proto=0/<unspecified>)
SRC: AF_INET: port = 0, 192.168.210.51 (sea-mach2.zama6.com).
```

```
DST: Destination address (proto=0/<unspecified>)
DST: AF_INET: port = 0, 192.168.210.34 (sea-mach1.zama6.com).
AKY: Authentication key.
AKY: 1234567890abcdef1234567890abcdef/128
EKY: Encryption key.
EKY: 1334577991abcdef/64
LT: Lifetime information
CLT: 15400 bytes protected, 0 allocations used.
CLT: SA added at time Fri Mar 02 10:05:55 2001
CLT: SA first used at time Fri Mar 02 10:06:16 2001
CLT: Time now is Fri Mar 02 16:04:47 2001
sea-mach1# ipsecconf
#INDEX 1
{
            saddr ipv6s1.zama6.com
            daddr sea-mach2.zama6.com
            ulp tcp
}apply {
            encr_algs des
            encr_auth_algs md5 sa shared
}
#INDEX 2
{
            saddr sea-mach2.zama6.com
            daddr ipv6s1.zama6.com
            ulp tcp
}permit {
            encr_algs des
            encr_auth_algs md5
}
```

You'll know if these don't look right.

Configuring IPsec on Machine 2 (Solaris 8 on Intel machine) is similar; everything works just the same—almost. I noticed that the "ipsecinit.conf" file was placed in the "/etc/inet" directory by the install program, so you can skip this step (well—check it to be sure) on Intel.

Configure this machine as you did ipv6s1. The "keys-all" file should be exactly identical. The "both-all" file is similar, but the src/dest fields are flipped. I'll show the contents of both files but omit the detailed instructions.

```
keys-all file
sea-mach2# more keys-all
add esp spi 0x4444 src sea-mach2.zama6.com dst ipv6s1.zama6.com auth_alg md5 encr_alg
des \
        authkey 1234567890abcdef1234567890abcdef \
        encrkey 1234567890abcdef
add esp spi 0x5555 src ipv6s1.zama6.com dst sea-mach2.zama6.com auth_alg md5 encr_alg
des \
        authkey 1234567890abcdef1234567890abcdef \
        encrkey 1234567890abcdef
both-all file
sea-mach2# more both-all
{
        saddr sea-mach2.zama6.com
        daddr ipv6s1.zama6.com
        ulp tcp
}apply {
        encr_algs des
        encr_auth_algs md5 sa shared
}
{
        saddr ipv6s1.zama6.com
        daddr sea-mach2.zama6.com
        ulp tcp
}permit {
        encr_algs des
        encr_auth_algs md5
}
ipseckey dump
```

```
sea-mach2# ipseckey dump
Base message (version 2) type DUMP, SA type ESP.
Message length 152 bytes, seq=1, pid=336.
SA: SADB_ASSOC spi=0x4444, replay=0, state=MATURE
SA: Authentication algorithm = HMAC-MD5
SA: Encryption algorithm = DES-CBC
SA: flags=0x80000000 < X_USED >
SRC: Source address (proto=0/<unspecified>)
SRC: AF_INET: port = 0, 192.168.210.51 (sea-mach2.zama6.com).
DST: Destination address (proto=0/<unspecified>)
DST: AF_INET: port = 0, 192.168.210.34 (ipv6s1.zama6.com).
AKY: Authentication key.
AKY: 1234567890abcdef1234567890abcdef/128
EKY: Encryption key.
EKY: 1334577991abcdef/64
LT: Lifetime information
CLT: 912 bytes protected, 0 allocations used.
CLT: SA added at time Fri Mar 02 10:50:18 2001
CLT: SA first used at time Fri Mar 02 10:50:43 2001
CLT: Time now is Fri Mar 02 16:12:58 2001
Base message (version 2) type DUMP, SA type ESP.
Message length 152 bytes, seq=1, pid=336.
SA: SADB_ASSOC spi=0x5555, replay=0, state=MATURE
SA: Authentication algorithm = HMAC-MD5
SA: Encryption algorithm = DES-CBC
SA: flags=0x80000000 < X_USED >
SRC: Source address (proto=0/<unspecified>)
SRC: AF_INET: port = 0, 192.168.210.34 (ipv6s1.zama6.com).
DST: Destination address (proto=0/<unspecified>)
DST: AF_INET: port = 0, 192.168.210.51 (sea-mach2.zama6.com).
AKY: Authentication key.
AKY: 1234567890abcdef1234567890abcdef/128
EKY: Encryption key.
EKY: 1334577991abcdef/64
LT: Lifetime information
CLT: 928 bytes protected, 0 allocations used.
```

```
CLT: SA added at time Fri Mar 02 10:50:18 2001

CLT: SA first used at time Fri Mar 02 10:50:43 2001

CLT: Time now is Fri Mar 02 16:12:58 2001

Dump succeeded for SA type 0.

ipsecconf

sea-mach2# ipsecconf

#INDEX 1

{

        saddr sea-mach2.zama6.com

        daddr ipv6s1.zama6.com

        ulp tcp

}apply {

        encr_algs des

        encr_auth_algs md5 sa shared

}

#INDEX 2

{

        saddr ipv6s1.zama6.com

        daddr sea-mach2.zama6.com

        ulp tcp

}permit {

        encr_algs des

        encr_auth_algs md5

}
```

23.3.8 GIVE IT A TRY

Let's use "snoop" on the box that is the target of your telnet—just to convince ourselves IPsec is really working. Run the command "snoop host sea-mach2" on the target machine.

Now, at the source machine, run the command "telnet ipv6s1." If you get the telnet login herald, then it works. Here's what you should see in your "snoop" window (this is just for the login herald, not the whole login process—I did a CNTRL-D).

```
sea-mach2.zama6.com -> sea-mach1.zama6.com ESP SPI=0x4444 Replay=53

sea-mach1.zama6.com -> sea-mach2.zama6.com ESP SPI=0x5555 Replay=389
```

```
sea-mach2.zama6.com -> sea-mach1.zama6.com ESP SPI=0x4444 Replay=54
sea-mach2.zama6.com -> sea-mach1.zama6.com ESP SPI=0x4444 Replay=55
sea-mach1.zama6.com -> sea-mach2.zama6.com ESP SPI=0x5555 Replay=390
sea-mach1.zama6.com -> sea-mach2.zama6.com ESP SPI=0x5555 Replay=391
sea-mach2.zama6.com -> sea-mach1.zama6.com ESP SPI=0x4444 Replay=56
sea-mach1.zama6.com -> sea-mach2.zama6.com ESP SPI=0x5555 Replay=392
sea-mach2.zama6.com -> sea-mach1.zama6.com ESP SPI=0x4444 Replay=57
sea-mach2.zama6.com -> sea-mach1.zama6.com ESP SPI=0x4444 Replay=58
sea-mach1.zama6.com -> sea-mach2.zama6.com ESP SPI=0x5555 Replay=393
```

You can see that the packets are tagged "ESP" and give the "SPI" number in our "keys-all" file. You also see the "Replay" field—these are sequential for each machine's source packets.

You learn even more if you use the command "snoop -v host sea-mach2." This is the "verbose" output, and it gives you much more insight. Here you see the details of the IP Header, ESP (Payload), and Ethernet Header. Note the line that says " ESP: . . . . ENCRYPTED DATA . . . ."—that's where your encrypted data lives.

```
      ----- IP Header -----
IP:
IP:      Version = 4
IP:      Header length = 20 bytes
IP:      Type of service = 0x00
IP:              xxx. .... = 0 (precedence)
IP:              ...0 .... = normal delay
IP:              .... 0... = normal throughput
IP:              .... .0.. = normal reliability
IP:      Total length = 72 bytes
IP:      Identification = 22733
IP:      Flags = 0x4
IP:              .1.. .... = do not fragment
IP:              ..0. .... = last fragment
IP:      Fragment offset = 0 bytes
IP:      Time to live = 64 seconds/hops
```

```
IP:      Protocol = 50 (ESP)
IP:      Header checksum = 2e44
IP:      Source address = 192.168.210.51, sea-mach2.zama6.com
IP:      Destination address = 192.168.210.34,
            sea-mach1.zama6.com
IP:      No options
IP:
ESP:     ----- Encapsulating Security Payload -----
ESP:
ESP:     SPI = 0x4444
ESP:     Replay = 71
ESP:          ....ENCRYPTED DATA....
ETHER:   ----- Ether Header -----
ETHER:
ETHER:   Packet 12 arrived at 16:26:8.41
ETHER:   Packet size = 102 bytes
ETHER:   Destination = 0:e0:18:d8:13:59,
ETHER:   Source = 8:0:20:fd:92:bb, Sun
ETHER:   Ethertype = 0800 (IP)
ETHER:
```

Try to telnet the other way—that should work too!

If the telnet session just hangs, use snoop to make sure that the ESP packets are making it to the target machine. If they are, you may have a problem with your SAs. If, for example, your ESP packet carries an SPI that doesn't exist on the target machine (i.e., if the source machine says "use SPI 0x2222" to the target machine), you'll see a message like this in "/var/adm/messages."

```
ESP: No association found for spi 0x4444, dst cb8e8e22
```

That pretty much does it. We've collected, installed, configured, and enabled encrypted, authenticated telnet services machine-to-machine. One thing we haven't done is to set this up so that the IPsec configuration is recovered if you reboot your machine. The "ipseckey" and "ipsecconf" configurations are not saved through a reboot cycle.

To configure the security policy to rebuild at boot-time, create a file called "/etc/rc2.d/S99IPSec-configure" that looks like this.

```
#/bin/ksh
ipseckey -f /etc/ipsec-config/keys-all
ipsecconf -a /etc/ipsec-config/both-all
```

Reboot your machine to check that it works.

23.4   Building TCP Wrapper for IPv6 on Solaris 8[‡]

This section describes in detail how to obtain, compile, and configure TCP Wrapper for use with IPv6.

23.4.1   Gathering the Pieces

Here's a brief list of what you'll need for this project.

- The ability to compile binaries from source code. This usually means a working gcc installation coupled with the necessary compilation utilities (e.g., make, ld, etc.).
- The ability to uncompress files with gzip.
- The ability to un-bundle file packages with tar.
- The IPv6-enabled TCP Wrapper source code. Version 7.6-ipv6.1 is the most recent version and can be found on Wietse Venema's Web site (http://www.porcupine.org).

23.4.2   BUILDING TCP WRAPPER

On the Internet today, whether you're communicating over IPv4 or IPv6, installing additional security measures on your system is never a bad thing. TCP Wrapper adds another layer of authentication to just about any service that's controlled by inetd. In addition, TCP Wrapper makes

---

[‡]This section is adapted from a document written by Robert C. Zilbauer Jr., © Zama Networks.

its authentication library available to any other application wishing to use Wrapper-style access control.

The first thing you need to do is to obtain the latest TCP Wrapper source code from the preceding Web site. For use with IPv6, you'll need the source package that contains the IPv6 modifications made by Casper Dik (version 7.6-ipv6.1).

Like most source packages, TCP Wrapper comes compressed and bundled into a tar file. If you're using the GNU version of tar, you can un-tar the package at the same time that you're uncompressing it. The following command will accomplish this.

```
% tar fxz tcp_wrappers_7.6-ipv6.1.tar.gz
```

Otherwise, you'll have to uncompress the package first and then proceed with the tar command.

```
% gzip  d tcp_wrappers_7.6-ipv6.1.tar.gz
% tar fx tcp_wrappers_7.6-ipv6.1.tar
```

Once you've uncompressed and extracted the source from the tar file, the process of compiling the code may be a little different from what you're used to. Unlike many source distributions, TCP Wrapper doesn't come with any automated configure script to set up your compilation environment for you. All this means is that you have to edit the Makefile by hand to suit your needs.

Drop down into the directory created by the preceding tar command and, using your favorite text editor (e.g., emacs or vi - not pico!), open the Makefile for editing. First, skip down to the "Advanced Installation" section and look for the "SysV.4 Solaris 2.x OSF AIX" definition. Uncomment (i.e., remove the # symbol from the beginning of the line) the definition for REAL_DAEMON_DIR so that it is set to /usr/sbin. Once you've made this change, your REAL_DAEMON_DIR line will look like this.

```
REAL_DAEMON_DIR=/usr/sbin
```

Now, move down quite a ways in the file until you come to the section entitled "System dependencies: selection of non-default object libraries."

Here, again, you'll want to uncomment the "SysV.4 Solaris 2.x" definition so that your LIBS looks like this.

```
LIBS = -lsocket  lnsl                    # SysV.4 Solaris 2.x
```

This next step is the reason you started reading this document in the first place. Skip down another few sections until you get to the one labeled "System dependencies: whether or not your system has IPV6." Since we're working with Solaris 8, uncomment the first definition of IPV6 so that it looks like this.

```
IPV6 = -DHAVE_IPV6
```

As far as enabling IPv6 in the code, that's all you have to do. As a matter of fact, you're done with all of the necessary changes to the Makefile as well. As a personal preference, I usually make one more change. In the "Optional: Changing the default disposition of logfile records" section, I'll change the FACILITY definition to LOG_LOCAL0. What this allows you to do is add a line like this

```
local0.info                              /var/adm/tcpd.log
```

to your /etc/syslog.conf file which will then record all messages coming from TCP Wrapper in their own log file (/var/adm/tcpd.log). This makes checking for security incidents a little easier. Of course, as the title of the section says, this is just an optional change. If you don't want to do it, I promise not to take it personally.

Once you've made all of the necessary, and any of the optional, changes to the Makefile, save the file and exit out of the text editor. Back at the command prompt, begin the compilation process with the appropriate make command. Since we're building the binaries for Solaris, you should use this command.

```
% make sunos5
```

23.4.3 INSTALLATION

Assuming that all goes well during compilation, you're ready to install the resulting binaries into their final resting places. The installation process, like the configuration you had to do, must be done by hand. Currently, there is no automated way to install the binaries after compiling. However, installation is as simple as a series of cp commands.

If you haven't already done so you'll have to become root to do the installation. First, install the actual executables in the standard directory, /usr/local/sbin. There are five executables that you'll want to copy in this step: tcpd, tcpdmatch, try-from, safe_finger, and tcpdchk. The command line to do this would look something like this.

```
# cp tcpd tcpdmatch try-from safe_finger tcpdchk /usr/local/sbin
```

tcpd is the actual wrapper program. tcpdmatch and try-from are both used in testing your installation once you have TCP Wrapper fully configured. safe_finger is a wrapper for the finger command and can be used if you want to do automatic fingering of questionable connections. The safe_finger wrapper makes the finger command more robust and secure for such use. Last, the tcpdchk program checks through your configuration files for errors.

Should another program wish to easily include TCP Wrapper–style authentication, it can use the libwrap.a library that was built during the compilation process. To make this library available to other packages, you need to put it in a standard directory for libraries. A good choice would be /usr/local/lib. To get the functionality out of this library the tcpd.h file must also be available. A standard place for header files like this one is /usr/local/include. Therefore, your next two commands will look something like this.

```
# cp libwrap.a /usr/local/lib
# cp tcpd.h /usr/local/include
```

All that's left to install are the documentation files. TCP Wrapper comes with several pages that need to be copied into the appropriate directories for the man command to use. The easiest way to install them is by man page section. There are files available for sections 3, 5, and 8, so your next three commands will look like this.

```
# cp *.3 /usr/local/man/man3
# cp *.5 /usr/local/man/man5
# cp *.8 /usr/local/man/man8
```

And that's that. You've just completed the installation of TCP Wrapper and all its man pages. All that remains is configuration. Luckily, that's the very next section.

23.4.4   CONFIGURATION

Before running recklessly into configuring your new software, you should make some decisions regarding what services you wish to wrap and what your end result should be. For our example, we'll assume we want the following.

- Telnet access allowed for people coming from 192.168.3.8
- Telnet access allowed for people coming from any IPv6 host under the 3ffe:80f0:1:1:: prefix
- FTP access allowed only for people coming from 3ffe:80f0:10:1: 201:2ff:dead:feed
- Everyone else denied for all services

The first thing you'll need to do is actually "wrap" the services in inetd.conf that you want wrapped. This is as simple as changing the value in the column that tells inetd which daemon it should run. To wrap a service, substitute the path to tcpd for the path to the daemon. For example, with the telnet service, the original line in /etc/inetd.conf looks like this.

```
telnet   stream   tcp6   nowait   root   /usr/sbin/in.telnetd in.telnetd
```

To wrap this service, you'd simply change the /usr/sbin/in.telnetd part to /usr/local/sbin/tcpd. Thus, the inetd.conf line for a wrapped telnet service would look like this.

```
telnet   stream   tcp6   nowait   root   /usr/local/sbin/tcpd in.telnetd
```

Piece of cake. Now, according to what we decided earlier, we also want to wrap the FTP service, so do the same for the ftp entry in your /etc/inetd.conf file. Once that's done, the inetd.conf lines for the telnet and FTP services will look like this.

```
ftp      stream   tcp6   nowait   root   /usr/local/sbin/tcpd   in.ftpd
telnet   stream   tcp6   nowait   root   /usr/local/sbin/tcpd   in.telnetd
```

Once you've made these changes, send the inetd process a HUP signal. This tells inetd to reread its configuration file. First, determine what process ID the inetd process is running under. Then send that process ID the HUP signal.

```
# ps -ef | grep inetd
root     164     1     0     Feb 05 ?              0:08 /usr/sbin/inetd-
s -t
# kill -HUP 164
```

You've just successfully wrapped ftp and telnet with TCP Wrapper. The last step is to set up the security rules that control connection authentication.

This part is accomplished using two different files: /etc/hosts.allow and /etc/hosts.deny. As the names suggest, the former indicates connections that are permitted, while the latter controls the denial of unwanted connections. When a connection attempt is made, the first rule that matches the connection information is the one that applies. Also, the first file to be checked is /etc/hosts.allow. Keep that in mind as you're creating your security rules.

Using the example requirements we just set for ourselves, we'll start with the easiest rules file first: /etc/hosts.deny. Chances are you don't have this file yet, so you'll have to create it. It's in this file that we'll specify our default "deny everyone from everything" rule. To make this happen, create /etc/hosts.deny and give it the following contents.

```
#
# /etc/hosts.deny
#
ALL: ALL
```

As the rule says, deny ALL hosts (the entry after the colon) from ALL services (the entry before the colon). While being very secure, it's not a terribly productive configuration, so let's continue. The next file you'll want to create is /etc/hosts.allow. It's in this file that you'll start to punch holes in your default deny rule to allow your friends and colleagues into your new IPv6 system.

First, we'll handle our telnet rules. Previously, we indicated that we wanted telnet open to people coming in from 192.168.3.8 as well as people coming in from any IPv6 host under the 3ffe:80f0:1:1:: prefix. To start things off, you need to indicate that this rule applies to the telnet service. Begin your line in /etc/hosts.allow with the name of the daemon for which this rule applies—in this case, the following.

```
in.telnetd:
```

Now follow that with the addresses of the hosts who should be allowed to use this service. In the case of IPv4 addresses, you can just enter them normally.

```
in.telnetd: 192.168.3.8
```

IPv6 addresses, on the other hand, must be surrounded by square brackets ([ ]). They can either be specified as a single IPv6 address, or you can specify a range of addresses by using a prefix/mask notation. In our case, we want everyone coming in from a host within the 3ffe:80f0:1:1:: network to be able to connect, so we'll be using the prefix/mask notation. Also, multiple hosts on the same line must be separated by spaces. Therefore, the final line in the rules file for telnet will look like this.

```
in.telnetd: 192.168.3.8 [3ffe:80f0:1:1::/64]
```

Our FTP rule will be much easier. As we defined earlier, we want anyone coming from 3ffe:80f0:10:1:201:2ff:dead:feed to be able to connect to our FTP service. Following the preceding format, the line in /etc/hosts.allow for the FTP service will look like this.

```
in.ftpd: [3ffe:80f0:10:1:201:2ff:dead:feed]
```

There are more options available for use in the hosts.deny and hosts.allow files, but these are the basics. For more information, I recommend taking a look at the hosts_access(5) man page. What you have just accomplished, however, fulfills all of the security requirements we set forth at the beginning of this section. For the sake of easy visualization, here's what the completed /etc/hosts.allow file looks like.

```
#
# /etc/hosts.allow
#
```

```
in.telnetd: 192.168.3.8 [3ffe:80f0:1:1::/64]
in.ftpd: [3ffe:80f0:10:1:201:2ff:dead:feed]
```

Also, since TCP Wrapper is run each time a wrapped service is requested, there's no need to start/stop a daemon or kill -HUP a process when you make a change to the rules files.

23.5   Summary

No prudent network administrator would skimp on security systems, and the use of packet filtering firewalls, IPsec, and TCP Wrappers as described here should be considered and adapted for any IPv6 network— even testbeds. Once the security systems are in place and routing is live, applications like DNS and email can be rolled out as described in the next chapter.

24

<hr>

Email and DNS Under IPv6

This chapter provides step-by-step instructions for setting up DNS services under IPv6, including setting up BIND, as well as a section detailing the process of setting up an email server under IPv6.

24.1 Building BIND 9 with OpenSSL Support*

This section explains in detail how to obtain and compile both OpenSSL and BIND 9 for use with an IPv6 DNS system.

<hr>

*This section is adapted from a document written by Robert C. Zilbauer Jr., © Zama Networks.

24.1.1 GATHERING THE PIECES

Here's a brief list of what you'll need for this project.

- The ability to compile binaries from source code. This usually means a working gcc installation coupled with the necessary compilation utilities (e.g., make, ld, etc.).
- The ability to uncompress files with gzip.
- The ability to un-bundle file packages with tar.
- The latest version of the Berkeley Internet Name Domain software (BIND). Currently, this is BIND 9.1.0 (http://www.isc.org/products/BIND/).
- OpenSSL release 0.9.5a or newer (http://www.openssl.org).

24.1.2 BUILDING OPENSSL

Although BIND 9 comes with its own version of SSL (for use with DNSSEC), that version contains no architecture-dependent optimizations. By compiling OpenSSL on your own, you'll be able to take advantage of assembly code optimizations that can dramatically speed up BIND's SSL operations (particularly on Intel and Sparc architectures).

The first thing you need to do is obtain the latest OpenSSL source code. You can find this code and a great deal of information about OpenSSL itself at the main OpenSSL Web site (http://www.openssl.org). For use with BIND 9, you'll need OpenSSL version 0.9.5a or higher. As just mentioned, the latest source release of OpenSSL is also available from http://www.zamanetworks.com.

Like most source packages, OpenSSL comes compressed and bundled into a tar file. If you're using the GNU version of tar, you can un-tar the package at the same time that you're uncompressing it. The following command will accomplish this.

```
% tar fxz openssl-0.9.6.tar.gz
```

Otherwise, you'll have to uncompress the package first and then proceed with the tar command.

```
% gzip  d openssl-0.9.6.tar.gz
% tar fx openssl-0.9.6.tar
```

Once you've uncompressed and extracted the source from the tar file, compiling the code is fairly straightforward. While in the directory created by un-tarring the source, configure the compilation process by running the supplied config script.

```
% cd openssl-0.9.6
% ./config
```

Once the configure script is finished, type "make" and the compilation of the source code into usable binaries will begin.

Once the make process is complete, test the resulting libraries and executables by doing a make test. Assuming everything goes well, do a make install and allow OpenSSL to install itself into the default location. This means that all of your OpenSSL libraries and executables will be found under /usr/local/ssl.

Building BIND   The BIND software is the meat of your new domain name server. This is the software that will be responding to DNS queries. Not only will it supply DNS information about your domain to external parties, but it will also resolve DNS information about external domains for you.

The first step is obtaining the source code. Currently, the package you want to use is BIND Version 9.1.0 or later. You can get this from the Internet Software Consortium's Web site (http://www.isc.org/products/BIND/). Just download the file and uncompress/un-tar it as you did with the OpenSSL software.

Once the source has been un-tarred, cd into the newly created directory and begin configuring the source for compilation. You want to make sure BIND uses the OpenSSL libraries you compiled earlier, so begin the configuration with the following command.

```
% cd bind-9.1.0
% ./configure  with-openssl=/usr/local/ssl
```

The configure script will now check your system for the elements required to build BIND and incorporate your previously compiled OpenSSL libraries.

Once the configure script is done, type make. This will start the compilation process. Assuming everything compiles correctly (i.e., you don't get any fatal errors), you should do a make check to run through the first part of the collection of test scripts that come with BIND. Check the output of these tests, and make sure there aren't any grievous errors. Toward the end of the testing, you'll get a number of errors regarding unconfigured interfaces, but you can ignore those. We'll deal with them next.

As a matter of fact, we'll deal with them now. If you've seen the unconfigured interface errors, your make check is probably finished. To run through the rest of the tests, you'll have to set up a bunch of virtual interfaces for the test scripts to use. Fortunately, the BIND installation comes with a script made to do just that. The script, ifconfig.sh, can be found in bin/tests/system/ from the top of the BIND 9 source tree. You may want to cd into that directory for the next few steps.

```
% cd bin/tests/system/
```

Unfortunately, as of BIND Version 9.1.1rc2, the ifconfig.sh script doesn't work at all for the Intel version of Solaris 8 and doesn't work completely for the Sun version of Solaris 8. The code maintainers have been notified, but just in case you're using unfixed code, you should be able to use the following script.

```
#!/bin/sh
#
# Copyright (C) 2000, 2001          Internet Software Consortium.
#
# Permission to use, copy, modify, and distribute this software for any
# purpose with or without fee is hereby granted, provided that the above
# copyright notice and this permission notice appear in all copies.
#
# THE SOFTWARE IS PROVIDED "AS IS" AND INTERNET SOFTWARE CONSORTIUM
# DISCLAIMS ALL WARRANTIES WITH REGARD TO THIS SOFTWARE INCLUDING ALL
# IMPLIED WARRANTIES OF MERCHANTABILITY AND FITNESS. IN NO EVENT SHALL
# INTERNET SOFTWARE CONSORTIUM BE LIABLE FOR ANY SPECIAL, DIRECT,
# INDIRECT, OR CONSEQUENTIAL DAMAGES OR ANY DAMAGES WHATSOEVER RESULTING
# FROM LOSS OF USE, DATA OR PROFITS, WHETHER IN AN ACTION OF CONTRACT,
# NEGLIGENCE OR OTHER TORTIOUS ACTION, ARISING OUT OF OR IN CONNECTION
# WITH THE USE OR PERFORMANCE OF THIS SOFTWARE.
```

```
# $Id: ifconfig.sh,v 1.25.4.1 2001/01/09 22:34:37 bwelling Exp $
#
# Set up interface aliases for bind9 system tests.
#
# If running on hp-ux, don't even try to run config.guess.
# It will try to create a temporary file in the current directory,
# which fails when running as root with the current directory
# on a NFS mounted disk.
case `uname -a` in
  *HP-UX*) sys=hpux ;;
  *) sys=`../../../config.guess` ;;
esac
case "$1" in
    start|up)
        for ns in 1 2 3 4 5
        do
                case "$sys" in
                    *-pc-solaris2.8)
                        ifconfig lo0:$ns plumb
                        ifconfig lo0:$ns 10.53.0.$ns up
                        ;;
                    *-sun-solaris2.8)
                        ifconfig lo0:$ns plumb
                        ifconfig lo0:$ns 10.53.0.$ns up
                        ;;
                    *)
                        echo "Don't know how to set up interface.
        Giving up."
                        exit 1
                esac
        done
        ;;
    stop|down)
```

```
for ns in 5 4 3 2 1
do
        case "$sys" in
            *-pc-solaris2.8)
                    ifconfig lo0:$ns 10.53.0.$ns down
                    ifconfig lo0:$ns 10.53.0.$ns unplumb
                    ;;
            *-sun-solaris2.8)
                    ifconfig lo0:$ns 10.53.0.$ns down
                    ifconfig lo0:$ns 10.53.0.$ns unplumb
                    ;;                              *)
                    echo "Don't know how to destroy interface.
    Giving up."
                    exit 1
        esac
done
;;
*)
        echo "Usage: $0 { up | down }"
        exit 1
esac
```

The preceding script is a stripped-down version of BIND's ifconfig.sh script. I've eliminated everything not pertaining to Solaris 8 and fixed the "down" section to properly unplumb the interfaces when you're done with them.

Armed with the proper ifconfig.sh script, you're ready to finish up with BIND's automated tests. First, run the script with the up argument. This will set up the required virtual interfaces BIND will use during the tests.

```
% ./ifconfig.sh up
```

Now, do a make test to run through the remaining tests. Once the tests have completed successfully, you'll want to clean up the virtual interfaces used in the tests. The same script will do this. Just give it the down argument instead of up.

```
% ./ifconfig.sh down
```

Finally, your newly built BIND package has been tested and is ready for installation. Move up to the top of the BIND source tree (assuming you dropped into the bin/tests/system directory) and issue the install command.

```
% cd ../../..
% make install
```

Several BIND executables will be installed in /usr/local/bin. The name server binary itself, named, will be installed in /usr/local/sbin, and several name server-related libraries will be put in /usr/local/lib. All that's left to do now is configure your new name server.

24.2   Configuring an IPv4/IPv6 DNS**

This section explains in detail how to configure BIND 9 for use as an IPv4/IPv6 domain name server. Configuration details will be given for both a master (primary) and a slave (secondary) server. In addition, example configuration files and a current root server list will be included at the end of this document.

24.2.1 GATHERING THE PIECES

Here's a brief list of what you'll need for this project.

- A working Solaris 8 (either Intel or Sun) machine for each server (master and slave).
- Both machines should have a correctly configured IPv4 interface.
- Both machines should have a properly configured IPv6 interface. It is recommended that both machines be configured with a static IPv6 address.

**This section is adapted from a document written by Robert C. Zilbauer Jr., © Zama Networks.

• The servers should also have the OpenSSL and BIND 9 packages compiled and installed on them.

24.2.2 CONFIGURING YOUR MASTER DNS

Once the preceding groundwork has been completed, you can move right into configuring your new DNS machines. By default BIND will look for its configuration file, named.conf, in /etc. A sample named.conf file has been included at the end of this document for your convenience. However, in the following section, we'll go over some of the highpoints of the configuration file and explain why they're in there.

All of the information that BIND will serve as your DNS (a.k.a., your zone records) can be kept anywhere you'd like. In this case, we'll create a directory, /var/named and instruct BIND to look there for its zone records. Also, we need to explicitly tell BIND to answer IPv6 queries. All of these things are done at the top of the named.conf file in an options section like this.

```
options
{
        listen-on-v6
{
any;
};
        directory "/var/named";
        notify yes;
        provide-ixfr yes;
};
```

The first line of the options section tells BIND to listen for IPv6 queries. The directory option tells it where to find its zone records. The notify and provide-ixfr options begin to define the relationship of your primary (or master) DNS with your secondary (or slave) DNS. The notify line says your master DNS should send notification to its slaves when a record has been updated, and the provide-ixfr option allows your slaves to request incremental updates (i.e., only the parts of the records that have been changed).

Make sure you have at least the default logging enabled. The following will allow BIND to send messages through syslog, which (usually) end up in your /var/adm/messages file.

```
logging
{
            category "default"
{
"default_syslog";
"default_debug";
                  };
};
```

Next, you must tell your name server where to look for root zone information. This is done with the root.hint file (the current version of which is included at the end of this document) and the following section in your named.conf file.

```
zone "."
{
          type hint;
          file "root.hint";
};
```

Now you'll need to start adding records for your DNS to serve. We'll start with the loopback addresses of your DNS.

```
zone "localhost"
{
          type master;
          file "db.localhost";
};
zone "0.0.127.in-addr.arpa"
{
          type master;
          file "db.127.0.0";
          notify no;
};
```

The config file definitions indicate that your forward localhost records can be found in a file named db.localhost and your reverse localhost records can be found in db.127.0.0. We'll describe the contents of these and the rest of your zone files later on in this paper. For now, just assume that the file names are correct and that they'll be there when we need them.

Since this is an IPv6 DNS, we'll need the IPv6 equivalent of the preceding files. So add the following lines to your config file for your IPv6 localhost lookups (only reverse is needed in this section; your forward IPv6 localhost lookups will be handled by the db.localhost file we defined earlier).

```
zone "0.0.0.0.0.0.0.0.0.0.0.0.0.0.0.0.ip6.int"
{
        type master;
        file "db.0000:0000:0000:0000.ip6.int";
        notify no;
};
zone "\[x0000000000000000/64].ip6.arpa"
{
        type master;
        file "db.0000:0000:0000:0000.ip6.arpa";
        notify no;
};
```

Officially, the ip6.int format (also known as "nibble format") is deprecated. However, it is still in use for compatibility with existing IPv6 applications.

Now identify the file name and other properties for your domain's zone records. For simplicity, we'll assume we're only setting up our DNS to answer queries for one (creatively named) domain, "mydomain.com."

```
zone "mydomain.com"
{
        type master;
        file "db.mydomain.com";
        notify yes;
        allow-transfer
        {
```

```
                                192.168.25.4;
                };
        };
```

Before going into further explanation, let's add in the reverse lookups for our IPv6 network. This document assumes that your IPv4 reverse DNS lookups are being handled by whoever gave you your addresses, so we won't be dealing with those. For our purposes, we'll use an IPv6 network beginning with 3ffe:80f0:1:1:... Notice that we're using both the "bitstring" format as well as the deprecated nibble format.

```
zone "\[x3ffe80f000010001/64].ip6.arpa"
{
        type master;
        file "db.3ffe:80f0:0001:0001.ip6.arpa";
        notify yes;
        allow-transfer
{
                        192.168.25.4;
                };
        };
zone "1.0.0.0.1.0.0.0.0.f.0.8.e.f.f.3.ip6.int"
{
        type master;
        file "db.3ffe:80f0:0001:0001.ip6.int";
        notify yes;
        allow-transfer
{
                        192.168.25.4;
                };
        };
```

If you take a look at the three zone definitions you've just created, you'll notice they all have several things in common. Since this is going to be your primary (or "master") DNS, each zone definition starts by indicating that this machine holds the master records for that zone (type master). Next, you've defined the name of the file in which the zone records will be kept. The notify yes line indicates that your master DNS should notify its slave DNS whenever records are updated within the given zone. And, last, the allow-transfer definition tells your server which machine is allowed to do zone transfers. This should be the IP address of your slave DNS.

24.2.3 CONFIGURING YOUR "localhost" ZONE

Now that your named.conf file is complete, it's time to start creating your zone files. Drop down into the directory you specified in your named.conf file as having your zone information. If you set up your named.conf file just like our examples, that would be /var/named.

The first two files you'll create are to facilitate lookups of your localhost. The info for your specific machine will (more than likely) be identical to what you see here. First, we handle the forward lookups (both IPv4 and IPv6) for your localhost. Create the db.localhost file and fill it with the following.

```
$ORIGIN localhost.
@          4h    IN     SOA     ns1.mydomain.com.        dns.mydomain.com.    (
                                2001012501      ; serial
                                28800           ; refresh
                                7200            ; retry
                                604800          ; expire
                                86400           ; minimum
                                        )
;
                 IN     NS      ns1.mydomain.com.
                 IN     NS      ns2.mydomain.com.
;
$TTL 1h
;
localhost        IN     A                       172.0.0.1
                 IN     AAAA                    0000:0000:0000:0000:0000:0000:0000:0001
                 IN     A6      0               0000:0000:0000:0000:0000:0000:0000:0001
```

At this point, we'll go over some of the key elements to be aware of in this file (as well as the other files you'll be creating). You'll notice the SOA indicator toward the top of the file. This stands for Start Of Authority. The machine name immediately following the SOA indicates the name of the machine, which should be considered "authoritative" for the information within the zone file. In all cases on your master DNS, this will be the name of your master DNS machine. The next element of the SOA line, "dns.mydomain.com," is actually the email address of the maintainer of the zone records. While it's written with periods as punctuation, it means dns@mydomain.com is the email address of the maintainer of the records within this zone file. This, too, will likely be the same throughout all of your zone files.

While we won't be going over all of the numbers within the parenthesized section of the SOA record, we will discuss one of them. Whenever you make updates to your zone records, you should adjust the serial number accordingly. As a general rule of thumb, use the current date as your serial number. Since you may be making more than one change to your files on a particular day, add a two-digit revision number to the end of the date. For example, the first change you make on March 23, 2001, would have a serial number of "2001032301" (YYYYMMDDRR, where RR is the double-digit revision number). Consequently, when you make the second change to the file on the same day, you'd change the serial number to "2001032302."

The reason for this has to do with the interaction between your master DNS and your slave DNS. In order for your slave DNS to know that there are new changes it needs to download from the master, the serial number must be incremented. If you've made changes to your master DNS and expect to see the changes propagate to your slave DNS but they don't, one of the first things you should check is your serial number on the master DNS. If you haven't incremented the serial number, the changes won't be reflected in your slave DNS's records.

For an explanation of the other numbers within the SOA block (e.g., refresh, retry, etc.), see the *BIND 9 Administrator Reference Manual*. This manual is available in PDF format from Nominum, Inc. (http://www.nominum.com).

The IN NS records define the name servers responsible for this zone. Chances are good that these lines will also be the same across all of your zone files.

Last, the entry beginning with "localhost" starts the actual localhost DNS information. In your forward lookup files, you will be defining the IPv4 address (the A record) as well as the IPv6 address. In the case of IPv6 forward lookups (just like with IPv6 reverse lookups), there are two address formats: the deprecated "quad-A" record (AAAA) and the A6 record. Both are used for compatibility reasons.

The IPv4 reverse lookup file for your localhost zone is much simpler. You'll notice that it contains a lot of the same information as the forward lookup zone. Create the file db.127.0.0 in your /var/named directory, and give it the following contents.

```
$ORIGIN 0.0.127.in-addr.arpa.
@        4h      IN      SOA     ns1.mydomain.com.        dns.mydomain.com.   (
                                 2001012501              ; serial
                                 28800                   ; refresh
                                 7200                    ; retry
                                 604800                  ; expire
                                 86400                   ; minimum
                                 )
;
         IN      NS      ns1.mydomain.com.
         IN      NS      ns2.mydomain.com.
;
$TTL 1h
;
1        IN      PTR     localhost.
```

The only thing different in this file is the actual zone data. The PTR record maps 127.0.0.1 to the name "localhost."

Now on to something a little more complicated: IPv6 reverse lookups for localhost. Remember that IPv6 reverse lookups (like forward lookups) have two formats that are both currently in use. We'll start with the older, nibble format. Create a new file in your /var/named directory named db.0000:0000:0000:0000.ip6.int with the following contents.

```
$ORIGIN 0.0.0.0.0.0.0.0.0.0.0.0.0.0.0.0.ip6.int.
@          4h      IN      SOA     ns1.mydomain.com. dns.mydomain.com. (
                                   2001012501      ; serial
                                   28800           ; refresh
                                   7200            ; retry
                                   604800          ; expire
                                   86400           ; minimum
                                   )
;
                   IN      NS      ns1.mydomain.com.
                   IN      NS      ns2.mydomain.com.
;
$TTL 1h
;
1.0.0.0.0.0.0.0.0.0.0.0.0.0.0.0.0 IN   PTR      localhost.
```

And then put the same information in the newer bitstring format. Create another file in /var/named with the name db.0000:0000:0000:0000.ip6.arpa containing this.

```
$ORIGIN \[x0000000000000000/64].ip6.arpa.
@  4h  IN      SOA     ns1.mydomain.com.    dns.mydomain.com. (
                                   2001012501      ; serial
                                   28800           ; refresh
                                   7200            ; retry
                                   604800          ; expire
                                   86400           ; minimum
                                   )
;
           IN      NS      ns1.mydomain.com.
           IN      NS      ns2.mydomain.com.
;
$TTL 1h
;
\[x0000000000000001/64] IN              PTR         localhost.
```

Both of these files are there for the same function: to map the IPv6 localhost address, 0000:0000:0000:0000:0000:0000:0000:0001, to the name "localhost."

24.2.4 Configuring Forward and Reverse DNS Lookups

Now that you've configured your localhost records, you're ready to set up the forward lookups for your domain, mydomain.com. Create a file in /var/named called db.mydomain.com with the following contents.

```
$ORIGIN mydomain.com.
@         4h    IN    SOA      ns1.mydomain.com.  dns.mydomain.com. (
                               2001021501      ; serial
                               28800           ; refresh
                               7200            ; retry
                               604800          ; expire
                               86400           ; minimum
                                        )
;
                IN    NS       ns1.mydomain.com.
                IN    NS       ns2.mydomain.com.
;
$TTL 1h
;
```

The rest of the file should be filled in with your domain information. First of all, you should add IPv4 and IPv6 entries for your master and slave DNS machines (ns1.mydomain.com and ns2.mydomain.com). Be sure to define your IPv6 addresses using both the older AAAA record type and the A6 record type. When you're done with that, your file will look something like this.

```
ns1       IN    A        192.168.25.5
          IN    AAAA     3ffe:80f0:1:1:201:2ff:fe00:2112
          IN    A6 0     3ffe:80f0:1:1:201:2ff:fe00:2112
```

```
ns2     IN      A          192.168.25.4
        IN      AAAA       3ffe:80f0:1:1:201:2ff:fe00:2111
        IN      A6 0       3ffe:80f0:1:1:201:2ff:fe00:2111
```

Now add entries for any other machines for which you'd like to have DNS entries. Let's say, for example, you want a Web server to answer at www.mydomain.com. Its DNS entry in this file would look something like this.

```
www     IN      A          192.168.25.7
        IN      AAAA       3ffe:80f0:1:1:201:2ff:fee8:efa1
        IN      A6 0       3ffe:80f0:1:1:201:2ff:fee8:efa1
```

The last thing to do is to configure the reverse lookups for your IPv6 network. Again, you should create two reverse lookup zone files: one for nibble format and one for bitstring format. First the nibble format. Create a file in /var/named called db.3ffe:80f0:0001:0001.ip6.int. Its contents will look something like this.

```
$ORIGIN 1.0.0.0.1.0.0.0.0.f.0.8.e.f.f.3.ip6.int.
@    4h   IN   SOA     ns1.mydomain.com. dns.mydomain.com. (
                       2001020201      ; serial
                       28800           ; refresh
                       7200            ; retry
                       604800          ; expire
                       86400           ; minimum
                       )
;
         IN   NS      ns1.mydomain.com.
         IN   NS      ns2.mydomain.com.
;
$TTL 1h
;
1.1.1.2.0.0.e.f.f.f.2.0.1.0.2.0
         IN   PTR     ns2.mydomain.com.
2.1.1.2.0.0.e.f.f.f.2.0.1.0.2.0
```

```
              IN    PTR    ns1.mydomain.com.
    1.a.f.e.8.e.e.f.f.f.2.0.1.0.2.0
              IN    PTR    www.mydomain.com.
```

And, finally, create a file in /var/named called db.3ffe:80f0:0001:0001.
ip6.arpa. This file will contain the reverse DNS information for your IPv6
network in bitstring format. Much like the preceding file, your bitstring
reverse DNS file will look something like this.

```
$ORIGIN \[x3ffe80f000010001/64].ip6.arpa.
@    4h    IN    SOA    ns1.mydomain.com. dns.mydomain.com. (
                        2001020201     ; serial
                        28800          ; refresh
                        7200           ; retry
                        604800         ; expire
                        86400          ; minimum
                        )
;
              IN    NS     ns1.mydomain.com.
              IN    NS     ns2.mydomain.com.
;
$TTL 1h
;
\[x020102fffe002111/64]
              IN    PTR    ns2.mydomain.com.
\[x020102fffe002112/64]
              IN    PTR    ns1.mydomain.com.
\[x020102fffee8efa1/64]
              IN    PTR    www.mydomain.com.
```

24.2.5 STARTING AND TESTING YOUR MASTER DNS

If you've gotten this far, you should have the following configuration files
ready to go.

- The BIND configuration file itself: /etc/named.conf
- localhost forward lookups: /var/named/db.localhost

- localhost IPv4 reverse lookups: /var/named/db.127.0.0
- localhost IPv6 reverse lookups (nibble format): /var/named/ db.0000:0000:0000:0000.ip6.int
- localhost IPv6 reverse lookups (bitstring format): /var/named/ db.0000:0000:0000:0000.ip6.arpa
- mydomain.com forward lookups: /var/named/db.mydomain.com
- IPv6 reverse lookups (nibble format): /var/named/db.3ffe:80f0:0001:0001.ip6.int
- IPv6 reverse lookups (bitstring format): /var/named/db.3ffe:80f0:0001:0001.ip6.arpa
- The root zone information file: /var/named/root.hint (see the end of this document)

Starting up the named process is as simple as typing in the name of the executable on the command line as root.

```
ns1# /usr/local/sbin/named
```

The named process will automatically look for its configuration file in /etc/named.conf and then load all of the zone files you've specified. Wait a few seconds for named to initialize itself and then check /var/adm/messages for any error messages. Assuming all looks good, you're ready to do some testing.

You can do some initial testing on the name server machine itself using the host command that comes with BIND 9. The host command takes the following arguments: options, item to lookup, and name server to use. Using the -a option with host will show you all of the information your new name server returns in response to a particular query. For example, to test your IPv6 lookups you would use the following command.

```
ns1# host -
a www.mydomain.com 3ffe:80f0:1:1:201:2ff:fe00:2112
```

That command will return something similar to the following.

```
Trying "www.mydomain.com."
Using domain server:
Name: 3ffe:80f0:1:1:201:2ff:fe00:2112
Address: 3ffe:80f0:1:1:201:2ff:fe00:2112#53
```

```
Aliases:

;;

->>HEADER<<- opcode: QUERY, status: NOERROR, id: 54299

;; flags: qr aa rd ra; QUERY: 1, ANSWER: 3, AUTHORITY: 2, ADDITIONAL: 6

;; QUESTION SECTION: ;www.mydomain.com.                    IN        ANY

;; ANSWER SECTION: www.mydomain.com.

    3600    IN    A      192.168.25.7 www.mydomain.com.

    3600    IN    AAAA   3ffe:80f0:10:1:201:2ff:fee8:efa1 www.mydomain.com.

    3600    IN    A6     0 3ffe:80f0:10:1:201:2ff:fee8:efa1

;; AUTHORITY SECTION:

    mydomain.com.        14400   IN    NS    ns2.mydomain.com.

    mydomain.com.        14400   IN    NS    ns1.mydomain.com.

;; ADDITIONAL SECTION:

    ns1.mydomain.com.    3600   IN    A     192.168.25.5

    ns1.mydomain.com.    3600   IN    A6    0 3ffe:80f0:1:1:201:2ff:fe00:2112

    ns1.mydomain.com.    3600   IN    AAAA  3ffe:80f0:1:1:201:2ff:fe00:2112

    ns2.mydomain.com.    3600   IN    A     192.168.25.4

    ns2.mydomain.com.    3600   IN    A6    0 3ffe:80f0:1:1:201:2ff:fe00:2111

    ns2.mydomain.com.    3600   IN    AAAA  3ffe:80f0:1:1:201:2ff:fe00:2111
Received 293 bytes from 3ffe:80f0:1:1:201:2ff:fe00:2112#53 in 3 ms
```

At the top of the output you'll see the IP address and port of the name server that host is using to look up the information. In this case the IP address is the IPv6 address you specified—3ffe:80f0:1:1:201:2ff:fe00:2112—and the port is the standard DNS port—53. The rest of the information shows you all of the records your new name server can return for that machine name.

Similar tests can be performed for the other machines you've defined. Also, you can (and should) test the reverse lookups for your machines as well. To test the IPv4 forward lookup for www.mydomain.com, you would use the IPv4 address of your new name server in the host command.

```
ns1# host a www.mydomain.com 192.168.25.5
```

To do a reverse lookup on the IPv6 address of www.mydomain.com, you would just specify its IP address in place of the machine name in the host command.

```
ns1# host -
a 3ffe:80f0:10:1:201:2ff:fee8:efa1 3ffe:80f0:1:1:201:2ff:fe00:2112
```

You can do similar tests from a separate machine. If that machine also has BIND9 installed, you can use the same exact host commands for your testing. Otherwise, you can use the standard nslookup command to do some rudimentary testing from a remote machine. I say *rudimentary* because nslookup won't generally understand IPv6 addresses. However, you can make sure your new DNS responds with IPv6 addresses from an IPv4 query. That's still a good sign you're set up correctly.

First, get into the nslookup command interpreter by typing nslookup at a prompt. Now, point nslookup at your new name server with the server <ip address> command. The next step is to tell nslookup to show you all the records it can by issuing a set type=any command. Now just type in the machine you want to test.

A test for www.mydomain.com with nslookup against your new name server will look something like this.

```
remotemachine.com> nslookup
Default Server: ns1.remotemachine.com Address: 216.65.257.1
> server 192.168.25.5
Default Server: [192.168.25.5]
Address: 192.168.25.5
> set type=any
> www.mydomain.com.
Server:       [192.168.25.5]
Address:       192.168.25.5
www.mydomain.com
        internet address = 192.168.25.7 www.mydomain.com
        IPv6 address = 3ffe:80f0:10:1:201:2ff:fee8:efa1
www.mydomain.com
        record type 38, interpreted as: www.mydomain.com.
     3600 IN 38 ?38? mydomain.com
          nameserver = ns2.mydomain.com mydomain.com
          nameserver = ns1.mydomain.com ns1.mydomain.com
```

```
        internet address = 192.168.25.5 ns1.mydomain.com
        record type 38, interpreted as: ns1.mydomain.com.
     3600 IN 38 ?38? ns1.mydomain.com
        IPv6 address = 3ffe:80f0:1:1:201:2ff:fe00:2112
ns2.mydomain.com
        internet address = 192.168.25.4 ns2.mydomain.com
        record type 38, interpreted as: ns2.mydomain.com.
     3600 IN 38 ?38? ns2.mydomain.com
        IPv6 address = 3ffe:80f0:1:1:201:2ff:fe00:2111
```

You'll notice in this output that the newer IPv6 record type, A6, is not understood. However, the IPv6 address comes through via the older AAAA record format.

You've now tested your master DNS both locally and remotely. Since I'm sure there's no chance of anything going wrong, you now have a working master domain name server capable of serving both IPv4 and IPv6 addresses. You're done!

24.2.6 CONFIGURING YOUR SLAVE DNS

Make that you're done unless you want to set up another machine as your slave DNS (a machine to answer DNS queries in case your master server is down or otherwise unavailable). The initial setup of the slave DNS machine will be identical to that of the master DNS machine. Check through the "Gathering the Pieces" section, and make sure the machine you want to use as your slave DNS meets all of the prerequisites. After that section is where things start to diverge.

You should still create a directory for your zone records as you did with the master DNS. Putting it in the same place, /var/named, is always a good idea. You should also copy over the root.hint file from your primary DNS into the /var/named directory of your new secondary DNS. Both the master and the slave need that file.

While you're copying files over, you may want to copy over the four files responsible for the localhost lookups. Although this machine is a slave DNS, it's still in charge of its own localhost lookups. The files you want are db.localhost, db.127.0.0.0, db.0000:0000:0000:0000.ip6.int, and db.0000:0000:0000:0000.ip6.arpa. The only change you should make to these files is in the SOA line at the top. In each of these four files, change the ns1.mydomain.com entry (immediately following the SOA element) to ns2.mydomain.com.

The rest of the files in /var/named on your slave DNS machine will be created automatically, however. So the only other file you need to change is the main BIND configuration file, /etc/named.conf.

The options section of the configuration file is different on a slave DNS machine. Basically, it doesn't need any of the options regarding zone transfers or slave notification. So the modified options section would look like this.

```
options
{
            listen-on-v6 {
any;
};
            directory "/var/named";
};
```

All of the following sections of the /etc/named.conf file on your slave DNS system will be identical to those on your master DNS machine.

- The "." zone section (which indicates the name of the root.hint file)
- The logging section
- The localhost zone (for forward localhost lookups)
- The zone responsible for reverse IPv4 localhost lookups
- The two zones responsible for reverse IPv6 localhost lookups (both the nibble and bitstring formats)

You can copy and paste those elements from your master DNS machine's /etc/named.conf file into your slave's. That sets up all of the basic BIND elements you need. Now, it's just a matter of setting up slave zones for the forward and reverse lookups of mydomain.com.

To do that, just add three zone definitions to your /etc/named.conf file. They will look similar to the following.

```
zone "mydomain.com"
{
            type slave;
```

```
           file "bk.mydomain.com";
           masters
{
192.168.25.5;
};
};
zone "\[x3ffe80f000010001/64].ip6.arpa"
{
           type slave;
           file "bk.3ffe:80f0:0001:0001.ip6.arpa";
           masters
{
192.168.25.5;
};
};
zone "1.0.0.0.1.0.0.0.0.f.0.8.e.f.f.3.ip6.int"
{
           type slave;
           file "bk.3ffe:80f0:0001:0001.ip6.int";
           masters
{
192.168.25.5;
};
};
```

The first one handles the forward lookups for mydomain.com, while the
last two take care of the different formats of IPv6 reverse lookups. In each
case, the type is set to slave, which indicates that this server should rely
on another for its information about these zones. The file is where it will
save that information once it is obtained, and the masters section tells it
from which machine it should get that information. The IP address in that
masters sections should be the IP address of your master DNS.

Now start the name server process (named) as root just like you did on
your master DNS.

```
ns1# /usr/local/sbin/named
```

After a few moments of initialization, you should see the three bk.* files show up in /var/named. Once they're in there, you can run some DNS query tests using the host command as you did with your master server. Just use the address of your slave server instead of the one for your master.

The final thing you should test is a zone transfer. Go over to your master server and make a change to one of your zone files. For example, add a test machine entry to db.mydomain.com. Important: Make sure you increment the serial number at the top of the file or the slave won't know the contents have changed.

Once you've made the appropriate changes, send the named process on your master server a HUP signal. This tells named to reread its configuration files. First, determine what process ID the named process is running under. Then send that process ID the HUP signal.

```
ns1:/var/named# ps -ef | grep named
  root  164  1  0  Feb 05 ?   0:08 /usr/local/sbin/named
ns1:/var/named# kill -HUP 164
```

Shortly after sending the HUP signal, you should see the changes propagate over to the appropriate bk.* file on your slave server. In this case, since we made the change to db.mydomain.com, you'll see the change reflected in bk.mydomain.com.

Now that you know your secondary server is correctly responding to queries and correctly handling zone transfers, you can pat yourself on the back. You've successfully set up an IPv6 capable master/slave DNS system!

24.2.7   EXAMPLE named.conf OPTIONS

Example named.conf (master) options

```
{
        listen-on-v6
{
any;
};
```

```
        directory "/var/named";
        notify yes;
        provide-ixfr yes;
};
logging
{
        category "default"
{
"default_syslog";
"default_debug";
        };
};
zone "."
{
        type hint;
        file "root.hint";
};
// IPv4 localhost and localhost reverse. zone "localhost"
{
        type master;
        file "db.localhost";
};
zone "0.0.127.in-addr.arpa"
{
        type master;
        file "db.127.0.0";
        notify no;
};
// IPv6 localhost and localhost reverse.
// .ip6.int is deprecated but kept for compatibility for now.
zone "0.0.0.0.0.0.0.0.0.0.0.0.0.0.0.0.ip6.int"
{
        type master;
```

```
            file "db.0000:0000:0000:0000.ip6.int";
            notify no;
};
zone "\[x0000000000000000/64].ip6.arpa"
{
            type master;
            file "db.0000:0000:0000:0000.ip6.arpa";
            notify no;
};
zone "mydomain.com"
{
            type master;
            file "db.mydomain.com";
            notify yes;
            allow-transfer
{
                    192.168.25.4;
            };
};
// Reverse lookups for 3ffe:80f0:0001:0001:
// ... zone "\[x3ffe80f000010001/64].ip6.arpa"
{
            type master;
            file "db.3ffe:80f0:0001:0001.ip6.arpa";
            notify yes;
            allow-transfer
{
                    192.168.25.4;
            };
};
zone "1.0.0.0.1.0.0.0.0.f.0.8.e.f.f.3.ip6.int"
{
            type master;
            file "db.3ffe:80f0:0001:0001.ip6.int";
```

```
                notify yes;
                allow-transfer
{
                        192.168.25.4;
                };
};
```

Example named.conf (slave) options

```
{
        listen-on-v6
{
any;
};
        directory "/var/named";
};
logging
{
        category "default"
{ "default_syslog"; "default_debug";
        };
};
zone "."
{
        type hint;
        file "root.hint";
};
// IPv4 localhost and localhost reverse.
zone "localhost"
{
        type master;
        file "db.localhost";
};
```

```
zone "0.0.127.in-addr.arpa"
{
        type master;
        file "db.127.0.0";
        notify no;
};
// IPv6 localhost and localhost reverse.
// .ip6.int is deprecated but kept for
// compatibility for now.
zone "0.0.0.0.0.0.0.0.0.0.0.0.0.0.0.0.ip6.int"
{
        type master;
        file "db.0000:0000:0000:0000.ip6.int";
        notify no;
};
zone "\[x0000000000000000/64].ip6.arpa"
{
        type master;
        file "db.0000:0000:0000:0000.ip6.arpa";
        notify no;
};
zone "mydomain.com"
{
        type slave;
file "bk.mydomain.com";
        masters
{
192.168.25.5;
};
};
// Reverse lookups for 3ffe:80f0:0001:0001:...
zone "\[x3ffe80f000010001/64].ip6.arpa"
{
        type slave;
        file "bk.3ffe:80f0:0001:0001.ip6.arpa";
        masters
```

```
{
192.168.25.5;
};
};
zone "1.0.0.0.1.0.0.0.0.f.0.8.e.f.f.3.ip6.int"
{
        type slave;
        file "bk.3ffe:80f0:0001:0001.ip6.int";
        masters
{
192.168.25.5;
};
};
```

Current root.hint file

```
;   This file holds the information on root name servers needed to
;   initialize cache of Internet domain name servers
;   (e.g. reference this file in the "cache . <file>"
;   configuration file of BIND domain name servers).
;
;   This file is made available by InterNIC registration services
;   under anonymous FTP as
;   file                    /domain/named.root
;   on server               FTP.RS.INTERNIC.NET
;   -OR- under Gopher at    RS.INTERNIC.NET
;   under menu              InterNIC Registration Services (NSI)
;   submenu                 InterNIC Registration Archives
;   file                    named.root
;
;   last update:   Aug 22, 1997
;   related version of root zone:      1997082200
;
;
```

```
; formerly NS.INTERNIC.NET
;
.                           3600000   IN   NS   A.ROOT-SERVERS.NET.
A.ROOT-SERVERS.NET.         3600000        A    198.41.0.4
;
; formerly NS1.ISI.EDU
;
.                           3600000        NS   B.ROOT-SERVERS.NET.
B.ROOT-SERVERS.NET.         3600000        A    128.9.0.107
;
; formerly C.PSI.NET
;
.                           3600000        NS   C.ROOT-SERVERS.NET.
C.ROOT-SERVERS.NET.         3600000        A    192.33.4.12
;
; formerly TERP.UMD.EDU
;
.                           3600000        NS   D.ROOT-SERVERS.NET.
D.ROOT-SERVERS.NET.         3600000        A    128.8.10.90
;
; formerly NS.NASA.GOV
;
.                           3600000        NS   E.ROOT-SERVERS.NET.
E.ROOT-SERVERS.NET.         3600000        A    192.203.230.10
;
; formerly NS.ISC.ORG
;
.                           3600000        NS   F.ROOT-SERVERS.NET.
F.ROOT-SERVERS.NET.         3600000        A    192.5.5.241
;
; formerly NS.NIC.DDN.MIL
;
.                           3600000        NS   G.ROOT-SERVERS.NET.
```

```
G.ROOT-SERVERS.NET.           3600000          A       192.112.36.4
;
; formerly AOS.ARL.ARMY.MIL
;
.                             3600000          NS      H.ROOT-SERVERS.NET.
H.ROOT-SERVERS.NET.           3600000          A       128.63.2.53
;
; formerly NIC.NORDU.NET
;
.                             3600000          NS      I.ROOT-SERVERS.NET.
I.ROOT-SERVERS.NET.           3600000          A       192.36.148.17
;
; temporarily housed at NSI (InterNIC)
;
.                             3600000          NS      J.ROOT-SERVERS.NET.
J.ROOT-SERVERS.NET.           3600000          A       198.41.0.10
;
; housed in LINX, operated by RIPE NCC
;
.                             3600000          NS      K.ROOT-SERVERS.NET.
K.ROOT-SERVERS.NET.           3600000          A       193.0.14.129
;
; temporarily housed at ISI (IANA)
;
.                             3600000          NS      L.ROOT-SERVERS.NET.
L.ROOT-SERVERS.NET.           3600000          A       198.32.64.12
;
; housed in Japan, operated by WIDE
;
.                             3600000          NS      M.ROOT-SERVERS.NET.
M.ROOT-SERVERS.NET.           3600000          A       202.12.27.33
; End of File
```

24.3   Designing and Implementing an IPv6 Email Server

This section explains in detail how to configure and install an IPv6-capable email server using Courier Mail Server.

24.3.1   GATHERING THE PIECES

Here's a brief list of what you'll need for this project.

- A working FreeBSD 4.2 machine (Intel) that is configured for IPv6
- db or gdbm (can be found on FreeBSD in /usr/ports/databases/)
- gcc 2.91 or higher (available from ftp://ftp.gnu.org/gnu/gcc/)
- gmake (can be found on FreeBSD in /usr/ports/devel/)
- Perl 5.6 (available from http://www.cpan.org/src/index.html)
- Gnupg (available from http://www.gnupg.org)
- OpenSSL 0.96 (available from www.openssl.org)
- Apache 1.3.19 source code that includes the IPv6 patch and the mod_ssl patch
- Courier Mail Server 0.32.0 or higher (available from http://sourceforge.net/projects/courier/)
- A static IPv6 ip address (obtain this from the Network Administrator or your IPv6 ISP)
- IPF Firewall configured for IPv4 and IPv6

24.3.2   "Pre-Courier" SOFTWARE INSTALLATION

Courier Mail Server is dependent on a number of other software packages that need to be configured and installed prior to unzipping and untarring Courier. Please refer to the iNSTALL files for the software for configuration and installation specifics.

This is the recommended order for installing the software prior to Courier Mail Server.

```
gcc
gmake
db or gdbm
```

```
gnupg

OpenSSL

Perl

Apache
```

Once OpenSSL is installed, there is a chance that you will have to manually seed the pseudo-random number generator (PRNG). If the PRNG is not seeded, you will see error messages when running scripts to create SSL certificates for Apache and Courier.

To seed the PRNG, do the following.

1. Create a file named .rand in /usr/local/ssl, and make sure that it is readable by root only.
2. Use a text editor, such as vi, and enter at least five lines of random gibberish.
3. Save the file, and then run the following command to finish seeding the PRNG.

```
$ openssl rand -out /usr/local/ssl/.rand -rand /usr/local/ssl/.rand -base64 1024
```

24.3.3 INSTALLING APACHE

For the Apache build, the installation instructions differ from those in the INSTALL file.

1. Make sure that root has /usr/local/ssl/lib and /usr/local/ssl/include contained in the LD_LIBRARY_PATH setting.
2. From within the build directory for Apache, run the script configure.v6 (this runs configure with the patch for IPv6 support and the mod_ssl patch).
3. Run make.
4. Run make certificate to generate a self-signed certificate. If you see an error message indicating that the PRNG is not seeded, see the section "Installing OpenSSL" for instructions to seed the PRNG.
5. Run make install to complete the install process.

Try starting Apache with the /usr/local/apache/bin/apachectl startssl command to see if it finds the SSL libraries that it needs to run

HTTPS connections. To avoid having to enter the passphrase each time you want to start Apache with SSL running (for instance, at boot up), you should remove the encryption from the RSA private key (while preserving the original file).

```
$ cp server.key server.key.org
$ openssl rsa -in server.key.org -out server.key
```

And also make sure the server.key file is now only readable by root.

```
$ chmod 400 server.key
```

Now server.key will contain an unencrypted copy of the key. If you point your server at this file it will not prompt you for a passphrase. However, if anyone gets this key, he or she will be able to impersonate you on the net. Please make sure that the permissions on that file are really such that only root or the Web server user can read it (preferably get your Web server to start as root but run as another server, and have the key readable only by root).

There will be modifications to the httpd.conf file, but that will be done once Courier Mail Server has been installed.

24.3.4 PREPARING TO INSTALL COURIER MAIL SERVER

Be sure to read the Courier Mail Server INSTALL document in its entirety before running configure and make (a "reader-friendly" version can be found on the Web at http://courier.sourceforge.net/install.html).

(Note: Keep in mind that configure and make are run as the user courier, whereas make install and make install-configure are run as root.)

Set up the PATH and LD_LIBRARY_PATH settings for both courier and root on your system in preparation for configuring and installing Courier Mail Server. The paths should look like the following examples.

```
PATH=/usr/local/src:/sbin:/usr/sbin:/bin:/usr/bin:/
usr/local/sbin:/usr/local/bin:/usr/X11R6/bin:/
usr/lib/courier/bin:/usr/lib/courier:/
usr/lib/courier-0.3x.x.xxxxxx:/usr/lib/courier/share
```

```
LD_LIBRARY_PATH=/usr/lib:/usr/local/ssl/lib:/usr/local/
ssl/include:/usr/local/lib:/usr/local/bin
```

24.3.5 PASSING OPTIONS: THE conf.script FILE

Once the Courier source code is unzipped and un-tarred, cd into the build directory and create a shell script called conf.script. This script will set flags for OpenSSL support, execute configure, and pass the desired options to configure. Here is an example conf.script.

```
#!/bin/sh
CPPFLAGS="-I/usr/local/ssl/include"
LDFLAGS="-L/usr/local/ssl/lib"
export CPPFLAGS
export LDFLAGS
./configure --with-mailuser=courier --with-mailgroup=courier
--with-mailuid=xxxx --with-mailgid=xxxx --without-authpam
--without-authldap --with-authpwd --without-authmysql
--without-authuserdb --without-authvchkpw --without-authcram
--with-waitfunc=wait --enable-webpass=yes --with-ipv6
```

Make the script executable by the courier user and then run it.

24.3.6 BUILDING COURIER MAIL SERVER

Refer to the steps in the Installation document for Courier Mail Server. If you run into problems while running configure or any of the makes, please read the FAQ page (http://courier.sourceforge.net/FAQ.html) or search the Courier users' mailing list (http://www.geocrawler.com/lists/3/SourceForge/3723/0/).

24.3.7 POSTINSTALLATION /etc FILE CONFIGURATION

Use a text editor, such as vi, to make configuration changes to the following files.

/usr/lib/courier/etc/authmodulelist

```
authpwd
```

/usr/lib/courier/etc/courierd

> DEFAULTDELIVERY="|/usr/lib/courier/bin/maildrop"

/usr/lib/courier/etc/esmtpd

> AUTHMODULES="authpwd"
>
> ...
>
> ESMTPDSTART=YES

/usr/lib/courier/etc/esmtpd.cnf

> RANDFILE = /usr/local/ssl.rnd
>
> ...
>
> CN=mail.zama6.com

/usr/lib/courier/etc/imap

> AUTHMODULES="authpwd"
>
> ...
>
> IMAPDSTART=YES

/usr/lib/courier/etc/imap.cnf

> RANDFILE = /usr/local/ssl.rnd
>
> ...
>
> CN=mail.zama6.com

/usr/lib/courier/etc/imap-ssl

> IMAPDSSLSTART=YES
>
> ...
>
> TLS_ALLOWSELFSIGNEDCERT=1 (uncomment this line)

/usr/lib/courier/etc/pop3d

> AUTHMODULES="authpwd"
>
> ...
>
> POP3DSTART=YES

/usr/lib/courier/etc/pop3.cnf

> RANDFILE = /usr/local/ssl.rnd
>
> ...
>
> CN=mail.zama6.com

/usr/lib/courier/etc/pop3d-ssl

> POP3DSSLSTART=YES
>
> ...
>
> TLS_ALLOWSELFSIGNEDCERT=1 (uncomment this line)

/usr/lib/courier/etc/aliases/system

```
postmaster:mailadmin
```

/usr/lib/courier/etc/smtpaccess/default:

```
172.16.12          allow,RELAYCLIENT
203.142.132        allow,RELAYCLIENT
203.142.142        allow,RELAYCLIENT
203.142.143        allow,RELAYCLIENT
```

Create the following files using a text editor.

/usr/lib/courier/etc/locals:

```
fully qualified hostname

hostname

fully qualified email domain (if different
   from hostname)

localhost
```

/usr/lib/courier/etc/esmtpdacceptmailfor.dir/default:

```
fully qualified email domain

email domain

localhost
```

24.3.8 POSTINSTALLATION SCRIPTS

Run the following scripts to read in the configuration changes made
in the etc/esmtpacceptmailfor.dir/default, etc/aliases/system, and
etc/smtpaccess/default files.

```
$ /usr/lib/courier/share/makeacceptmailfor
$ /usr/lib/courier/share/makealiases
$ /usr/lib/courier/share/makesmtpaccess
```

Run the following scripts to create the SSL certificate files for IMAP, POP3,
and SMTP.

```
$/usr/lib/courier/share/mkesmtpdcert
```

```
$/usr/lib/courier/share/mkeimapdcert

$/usr/lib/courier/share/mkepop3dcert
```

If these scripts fail, check them to verify that the path to the SSL executable is set to /usr/bin/openssl. If it is not, use vi to change the path in the scripts.

24.3.9 Final Configuration Checks

Set the directory permissions to 777 for each directory in the path to the SqWebMail executable /usr/lib/courier/libexec/courier/webmail/. Otherwise, users attempting to open an HTTP or HTTPS connection from their browsers will receive a message that they are forbidden from executing the webmail script.

Set the Courier Mail Server executable to executable by root.

```
$ (/usr/lib/courier-0.3x.x.xxxxxx/courier.sysvinit).
```

cd to /var and use mkdir to create a directory called lock. cd into lock and use mkdir to create a directory called subsys. cd into subsys and touch a file called courier. Set courier as the owner and group recursively for the /var/lock directory.

Use a text editor, such as vi, to make the following changes to /usr/local/apache/conf/httpd.conf.

```
ScriptAlias /cgi-bin/ "/usr/lib/courier/libexec/courier/webmail/"

...

<Directory "/usr/lib/courier/libexec/courier/webmail">

...

<Directory "/usr/local/apache/htdocs">

...

        Options FollowSymLinks MultiViews

...

User webuser

Group webuser
```

24.3.10 ADDING COURIER AND APACHE TO THE STARTUP SERVICES IN /etc/rc

Use a text editor, such as vi, to make the following entry in the /etc/rc file to start Courier at boot up.

```
if [ -x /usr/lib/courier-0.32.0.20010319/courier.sysvinit ]; then
    /usr/lib/courier-0.32.0.20010319/courier.sysvinit start
fi
```

Add the following entry in /etc/rc to start Apache at boot up.

```
if [ -x /usr/local/apache/bin/apachectl ]; then
   /usr/local/apache/bin/apachectl startssl
fi
```

You'll also need to modify sendmail on the machine so that it runs secondary to Courier's sendmail process and monitors the mail queue every 15 minutes. Make the following changes to the /etc/rc file's entry for running sendmail.

```
if [ -r /etc/mail/sendmail.cf ]; then
   echo -n ' sendmail';  /usr/sbin/sendmail -q15m
```

24.3.11 CONFIGURING THE FREEBSD KERNEL FOR FILESYSTEM QUOTA SUPPORT

Courier does not enforce any quota limits on user account size. It relies on the FreeBSD operating system to handle filesystem quotas. Therefore, quota support must be enabled at the OS level.

FreeBSD's default kernel configuration does not support filesystem quotas, so the option must be added to the configuration file and the kernel has to be recompiled to read in the new quota option.

cd to the /usr/src/sys/i386/conf/ directory. Copy the file GENERIC to GENERIC.bak so that the original configuration is preserved and may be used if the modified file becomes corrupted. Use a text editor to add the following line to the GENERIC file.

```
options QUOTA     # Filesystem quota support
```

Save the changes to the file and then run the following command.

```
$ config GENERIC
```

Then cd to the /usr/src/sys/compile/GENERIC directory and run the following commands.

```
$ make depend
$ make
$ make install
```

Enable quotas in the /etc/rc.conf file by using a text editor to add the following line.

```
enable_quotas="YES"
```

Edit the /etc/fstab file to enable quotas on a per-file system basis. To enable per-user quotas on a file system, add the userquota option to the options field in the /etc/fstab entry for the file system you want to enable quotas on. Here is an example.

```
/dev/ad0s1a / ufs rw,userquota 1 1
```

After the option has been added to the /etc/fstab file, type reboot to reboot the machine, and read in the new configuration changes for file system quotas.

Once the machine comes back up and you are logged in, type quota -v to verify that the quotas are enabled.

24.3.12   SETTING QUOTA LIMITS

The newuser script copies the quota attributes from a "model" Zama Mail user account called zmail. This account must exist before accounts can be created via the Web interface.

Create a user called zmail. Now create the Maildir for the zmail account. From the zmail home directory, run /usr/lib/courier/bin/maildirmake Maildir. Change the owner and group recursively on the Maildir to zmail.

Create a file called .courier in the zmail home directory that contains the following.

```
| /usr/bin/id > ID
| /usr/bin/env > ENV
| /usr/lib/courier/bin/maildrop
```

Change the owner and group of the .courier file to zmail. Now set the quota limits for the zmail user. Type edquota -u zmail. This will pull up the quota file for the user zmail. Use vi commands to set the soft limit to 4000 and the hard limit to 5000.

```
/: blocks in use: 67, limits (soft = 4000, hard = 5000)
```

Quit and save the changes for the zmail account.

Starting and Stopping Courier Mail Server Manually

To start Courier Mail Server manually, run this.

```
$ /usr/lib/courier-0.3x.x.xxxx/courier.sysvinit start
```

The services for esmtpd, imapd, imapd-ssl, pop3, and pop3d-ssl should start running on their appropriate ports.

To stop Courier, run this.

```
$ /usr/lib/courier-0.3x.x.xxxx/courier.sysvinit stop
```

This is a hard stop command.

To read in configuration changes, run this.

```
$ /usr/lib/courier-0.3x.x.xxxx/courier.sysvinit restart
```

This does stop and then start the services, but restart is a gentler way to stop the process than the stop option.

Set up a Maildir and a .courier file for each user that is owned by the user.

- If using the Web interface "create account" script, all of this will be done automatically.
- If not, from the user's home directory, run the following.

```
$ /usr/lib/courier/bin/maildirmake Maildir
```

Change the owner and group recursively on the Maildir to the user.

Copy the .courier file from /home/zmail/ to the user's home directory and change the owner and group to the user's.

24.3.13 TROUBLESHOOTING

If the installation for any of the software applications fails, please refer to their INSTALL or FAQ documents or user group mail lists.

For Apache (mod_ssl), the user group mail list URL is
`http://marc.theaimsgroup.com/`

For Courier Mail Server, the user group mail list URL is
`http://www.geocrawler.com/lists/3/SourceForge/3723/0/`

Also refer to the log files in /var/log and note the messages being logged for the different applications.

- Apache logs messages in /var/log/error_log and /var/log/access_log.
- Courier Mail Server logs messages in /var/log/maillog.

24.4   Summary

In this chapter, we looked at the Steps necessary to build an IPv6-capable DNS server as well as an IPv6-capable email server. Although applications and distributions change over time, and chances are good that the software described here may change as well, the broad outlines should give deployers guidance needed to roll out their own DNS and email services with whatever software they choose.

Having built, designed, installed and configured all the systems needed in an IPv6 network (nodes, servers, routers, security systems, and application servers), we move on in the next chapter to a discussion of the current state of the IPv6 world as well as a look at the future potential of IPv6.

25

The Present and the Future of IPv6

Over a decade after work began on IPng and the protocols that would ultimately comprise IPv6, there are still few production networks of any size or importance running IPv6. In this chapter, we look at what many considered the first big win for IPv6: the Third Generation Partnership Project (3GPP) for cellular communication, followed by a brief discussion of the few live IPv6 networks that are currently to be found. A section on the problems with IPv6 is followed by sections that list IPv6 implementations and IPv6 resources.

25.1 IPv6 and 3GPP

The Third Generation Partnership Project (3GPP) standards have long been anticipated by the IPv6 community. By 2001, it was said (back in 1998), support for IPv6 would be mandatory in all 3GPP cellular devices, from mobile telephones to roving wireless PDAs and laptops. By 2003, the degree to which IPv6 is deployed is considerably less than expected. RFC 3314, "Recommendations for IPv6 in Third Generation Partnership Project (3GPP) Standards," outlines the interoperation between wireless communication protocols and IPv6, with special attention to whether and how the protocols need to be modified. RFC 3316, "Internet Protocol Version 6 (IPv6) for Some Second and Third Generation Cellular Hosts," discusses how existing cellular hosts can be deployed with support for IPv6.

Both documents reflect optimism that the acceptance of IPv6 for these devices will be high and problems will all be surmountable. For example, RFC 3314 suggests that nodes will largely be able to use existing IPv6 implementations with little or no modification, making the process of migrating to IPv6 support painless.

However, by 2001, we were told, the 3GPP choice of IPv6 might not be as extensive as originally announced. Instead of deploying it on every 3GPP device, IPv6 would be used only for multimedia applications with most traditional wireless services still delivered by circuit-switched telecommunications networks. And there were indications that IPv6 would not even make the grade for the wireless vendors' backbones.

While in 2001, industry pundits anticipated 3GPP systems would be live by 2003, the drama is still playing out. Some IPv6 proponents foresaw IPv6 networks of as many as a billion or more wireless nodes by now; the dream of killer-applications for IPv6 has been deferred with many viewing Asia, especially China and India, as the force driving acceptance of IPv6.

25.2   Live IPv6 Networks

Ten years after the earliest IPv6 specifications and implementations, IPv6 remains on the extreme periphery of the mainstream portions of the global Internet. Large organizations willing to go on record as embracing IPv6 for their production networks remain as rare as hens' teeth. Although the number of ISPs and other connectivity providers announcing some form of IPv6 service or support continues to grow, the size of the actual market for IPv6 remains vanishingly small.

IPv6 implementers may be operating largely undetected by the rest of the Internet, but they are operating.

- Mobile telecommunications providers have begun using IPv6 to allocate addresses to mobile phones. IPv4 is simply incapable of supporting the millions (or hundreds of millions) of mobile devices that the wireless industry must support.
- Individuals and small businesses around the world have embraced IPv6, particularly among the open source movement. Linux and BSD operating systems have incorporated IPv6 support since the mid-1990s. These early implementers are adopting IPv6 for a number of reasons, from a desire to be on the bleeding edge of technology to the hope of developing new skills and products that will be in demand once IPv6 is accepted more generally. Many, if not most, believe in the inevitability of IPv6 as the successor to IPv4.
- Businesses, governments, and other groups that have been largely left out of the mainstream Internet view IPv6 as a viable alternative to attempting to support millions of IP nodes with a handful of IPv4 addresses.

A well-maintained and managed IP network, whether v4 or v6, should be transparent to the end user. Applications should work, and users should be able to accomplish their tasks without having to be aware of how their data is sent and received over the network. In many if not most cases, existing IPv4 networks may never have to support IPv6 except at their edges. New networks can be added, and are being added, that support IPv4 only.

It is possible, as of 2003, to implement IPv6-only or IPv6/IPv4 on production networks—but just barely. Significant research and preparation are necessary to locate IPv6-ready connectivity providers as well as IPv6-ready hardware and software. Much of that preparation may include creating solutions from scratch, but that is often the case when applying a new technology.

So where are the IPv6 network and connectivity providers? Attempting to list them in a chapter here would be as premature as someone trying to compile a comprehensive and authoritative list of manufacturers and types of automobiles 100 years ago. The data communication industry remains in flux, with established corporations merging, filing for bankruptcy, changing tactics, and spinning off or absorbing operations on a weekly basis.

One can only hope that by the time of this book's next edition some leading providers of IPv6 connectivity will have emerged, but for now the next generation IP network is still largely invisible.

25.3   The Problems with IPv6

Not everyone sees IPv6 as an inevitable upgrade. In fact, as the global IPv4 Internet continues to operate despite the gloomy predictions, more and more IPv6 is seen as a phantom menace much as the year 2000 "crisis" is now perceived.

However, there are problems with IPv6.

- IPv4 still works just fine. Sometimes backbones melt down, and sometimes attacks bring networks to their knees, but by and large IPv4 serves the needs of the Internet community.
- NAT seems to (mostly) work, and in conjunction with the un-allocated IPv4 address space, should provide enough elbow room for everyone who needs it.
- IPv6 is going to be an expensive hassle. At least, that's the perception, and given the costs associated with IT that were incurred to prepare for a Y2K crisis that never emerged (quite possibly because so many organizations prepared for it), managers are hard put to push for the budget necessary even to evaluate IPv6 for production networks.

And by 2001, IPv6 working group leaders were being quoted as saying that the one and only problem that IPv6 solves and IPv4 does not is that of address exhaustion. Clearly, no organization that already has enough address space for its needs could possibly justify the expense of solving a problem that it doesn't have.

25.4   IPv6 Promise and Potential

In the early summer of 2003, the Department of Defense announced that starting in October 2003 the DoD would only purchase IPv6-compliant network technologies, with the goal of full IPv6-compliance throughout the U.S. military by 2008.

With this announcement, IPv6 scored its first major public technology win—until mid-2003, IPv6 was only discussed as a technology that might be possible sometime in the future. There were no major corporations or other organizations committing to IPv6, and although vendors have been claiming IPv6 support for their products since the mid-1990s, never before has IPv6 support been on a list of required features for such a large consumer of networking technology.

The DoD, with its annual IT budget in excess of $30 billon, quite obviously will push the networking industry into a much higher commitment to IPv6 than ever before. What is not immediately obvious is the effect this decision will have on all the organizations that do business with the DoD. Every one of those businesses will now have to take a much more serious look at IPv6 and decide whether they want—or need—to migrate their own network infrastructures to support IPv6.

Even more than the selection of IPv6 by the 3GPP for deployment in large networks, the DoD's embrace of IPv6 for its internal and operational networks as well as for battlefield use ensures that IPv6 will (at the very least) be implemented and refined over the coming years.

25.5   IPv6 Resources

This section includes a list of Web links to sites of interest to the IPv6 networking community. These resources are offered as a selection; readers seeking the most up-to-date and complete Web resources are urged to use their favorite search engine. Invariably, many of the Web resources cited in printed books change or disappear by the time they arrive in bookstores; it is hoped that the sites referenced in Table 25–1 will still be useful to the reader.

25.6   Summary

It is becoming increasingly clear that, as explained in Chapter 1, IPv6 will succeed only if it can be applied to an entirely different field of endeavor. The global Internet is an IPv4 network; the costs involved in converting it are much too high. The only way IPv6 can stay off the trash heap of history

Site	URL
Microsoft Research Lab IPv6	www.research.microsoft.com/msripv6/
Microsoft IPv6 Support	www.microsoft.com/windowsserver2003/ technologies/ipv6/
Deep Space 6 (IPv6 Linux Portal)	www.deepspace6.net
IETF IPv6 Working Group	www.ietf.org/html.charters/ ipv6-charter.html
Additional IPv6 Working Group info	playground.sun.com/pub/ipv6/
IPv6 Forum (industry consortium)	www.ipv6forum.com
Peter Bieringer's Linux Section: IPv6	www.bieringer.de/linux/IPv6/
UK IPv6 Resource Centre (Lancaster University)	www.cs-ipv6.lancs.ac.uk
NetBSD IPv6 Networking	www.netbsd.org/Documentation/network/ ipv6/
KAME Project (BSD IPv6)	www.kame.net
Internet2 IPv6 Working Group	ipv6.internet2.edu
Links to Global IPv6 Taskforces	www.ipv6-taskforce.org
Searching the RFC Archive	www.rfc-editor.org/rfcsearch.html

Table 25–1: A selection of Web resources for IPv6.

is if someone figures out a way to use it for some entirely new application, where huge address spaces are mandatory. To date, promising starts have already been made in the mobile telecommunications market as well as the defense industry; whether those initiatives will be enough to propel IPv6 into every connected device on earth remains to be seen.

IV

Appendix

IPv6 RFCs

The following are all IPv6-related RFCs that had been published by the IETF as of mid-2003. The list was generated by searches on the RFC archive at www.rfc-editor.org. RFCs are listed in descending order, and each listing includes the RFC number, title, authors, date of publication, status (that is, whether it is updated or obsoleted by some other RFC or if it updates or obsoletes some other RFC), and type of document.

INFORMATIONAL RFCs provide information and are not to be interpreted as specifying an Internet standard.

PROPOSED STANDARD RFCs specify a protocol that has been implemented and that is being considered for use as an Internet standard.

DRAFT STANDARD RFCs specify a protocol that has been implemented in at least two different forms and that has a body of experience and research backing it up. It often represents a revision of a PROPOSED STANDARD.

STANDARD RFCs (also denoted as STDs) specify a protocol that has been accepted as a standard for the Internet community.

BEST CURRENT PRACTICES documents are published as RFCs as well as BCPs and contain information about recommended procedures, processes, or techniques for accomplishing networking goals.

EXPERIMENTAL RFCs specify a protocol that is being investigated by researchers. Experimental specifications should generally not be implemented or deployed in production networks and should be used with extreme caution in laboratory conditions.

RFCs published on April 1 are almost always "April Fool's" jokes and should be read for amusement only (however, there have been non-joke RFCs published on April 1 as well as joke RFCs with a publication date of April, without the date).

RFC 3572
Internet Protocol Version 6 over MAPOS (Multiple Access Protocol Over
   SONET/SDH)
T. Ogura, M. Maruyama, T. Yoshida
July 2003
INFORMATIONAL

RFC 3542
Advanced Sockets Application Program Interface (API) for IPv6
W. Stevens, M. Thomas, E. Nordmark, T. Jinmei
May 2003
Obsoletes RFC 2292
INFORMATIONAL

RFC 3531
A Flexible Method for Managing the Assignment of Bits of an IPv6
   Address Block
M. Blanchet
April 2003
INFORMATIONAL

RFC 3513
Internet Protocol Version 6 (IPv6) Addressing Architecture
R. Hinden, S. Deering
April 2003
Obsoletes RFC 2373
PROPOSED STANDARD

RFC 3493
Basic Socket Interface Extensions for IPv6
R. Gilligan, S. Thomson, J. Bound, J. McCann, W. Stevens
March 2003
Obsoletes RFC 2553
INFORMATIONAL

RFC 3484
Default Address Selection for Internet Protocol Version 6 (IPv6)
R. Draves
February 2003
PROPOSED STANDARD

RFC 3364
Tradeoffs in Domain Name System (DNS) Support for Internet Protocol
  version 6 (IPv6)
R. Austein
August 2002
Updates RFC 2673, RFC 2874
INFORMATIONAL

RFC 3363
Representing Internet Protocol version 6 (IPv6) Addresses in the Domain
  Name System (DNS)
R. Bush, A. Durand, B. Fink, O. Gudmundsson, T. Hain
August 2002
Updates RFC 2673, RFC 2874
INFORMATIONAL

RFC 3316
Internet Protocol Version 6 (IPv6) for Some Second and Third Generation
  Cellular Hosts
J. Arkko, G. Kuijpers, H. Soliman, J. Loughney, J. Wiljakka
April 2003
INFORMATIONAL

RFC 3314
Recommendations for IPv6 in Third Generation Partnership Project (3GPP)
  Standards
M. Wasserman, Ed.
September 2002
INFORMATIONAL

RFC 3307
Allocation Guidelines for IPv6 Multicast Addresses
B. Haberman
August 2002
PROPOSED STANDARD

RFC 3306
Unicast-Prefix-based IPv6 Multicast Addresses
B. Haberman, D. Thaler
August 2002
PROPOSED STANDARD

RFC 3266
Support for IPv6 in Session Description Protocol (SDP)
S. Olson, G. Camarillo, A. B. Roach
June 2002
Updates RFC 2327
PROPOSED STANDARD

RFC 3226
DNSSEC and IPv6 A6 aware server/resolver message size requirements
O. Gudmundsson
December 2001
Updates RFC 2535, RFC 2874
PROPOSED STANDARD

RFC 3194
The H-Density Ratio for Address Assignment Efficiency: An Update on the
  H ratio
A. Durand, C. Huitema
November 2001
Updates RFC 1715
INFORMATIONAL

RFC 3178
IPv6 Multihoming Support at Site Exit Routers
J. Hagino, H. Snyder
October 2001
INFORMATIONAL

RFC 3177
IAB/IESG Recommendations on IPv6 Address
IAB, IESG
September 2001
INFORMATIONAL

RFC 3175
Aggregation of RSVP for IPv4 and IPv6 Reservations
F. Baker, C. Iturralde, F. Le Faucheur, B. Davie
September 2001
PROPOSED STANDARD

RFC 3162
RADIUS and IPv6
B. Aboba, G. Zorn, D. Mitton
August 2001
PROPOSED STANDARD

RFC 3146
Transmission of IPv6 Packets over IEEE 1394 Networks
K. Fujisawa, A. Onoe
October 2001
PROPOSED STANDARD

RFC 3142
An IPv6-to-IPv4 Transport Relay Translator
J. Hagino, K. Yamamoto
June 2001
INFORMATIONAL

RFC 3122
Extensions to IPv6 Neighbor Discovery for Inverse Discovery
  Specification
A. Conta
June 2001
PROPOSED STANDARD

RFC 3111
Service Location Protocol Modifications for IPv6
E. Guttman
May 2001
PROPOSED STANDARD

RFC 3089
A SOCKS-based IPv6/IPv4 Gateway Mechanism
H. Kitamura
April 2001
INFORMATIONAL

RFC 3056
Connection of IPv6 Domains via IPv4 Clouds
B. Carpenter, K. Moore
February 2001
PROPOSED STANDARD

RFC 3053
IPv6 Tunnel Broker
A. Durand, P. Fasano, I. Guardini, D. Lento
January 2001
INFORMATIONAL

RFC 3041
Privacy Extensions for Stateless Address Autoconfiguration
  in IPv6
T. Narten, R. Draves
January 2001
PROPOSED STANDARD

RFC 3019
IP Version 6 Management Information Base for The Multicast Listener
  Discovery Protocol
B. Haberman, R. Worzella
January 2001
PROPOSED STANDARD

RFC 2928
Initial IPv6 Sub-TLA ID Assignments
R. Hinden, S. Deering, R. Fink, T. Hain
September 2000
INFORMATIONAL

RFC 2921
6BONE pTLA and pNLA Formats (pTLA)
B. Fink
September 2000
INFORMATIONAL

RFC 2894
Router Renumbering for IPv6
M. Crawford
August 2000
PROPOSED STANDARD

RFC 2893
Transition Mechanisms for IPv6 Hosts and Routers
R. Gilligan, E. Nordmark
August 2000
Obsoletes RFC 1933
PROPOSED STANDARD

RFC 2874
DNS Extensions to Support IPv6 Address Aggregation and Renumbering
M. Crawford, C. Huitema
July 2000
Updates RFC 1886, Updated by RFC 3152, RFC 3226, RFC 3363, RFC 3364
    EXPERIMENTAL
[pub as:PROPOSED STANDARD]

RFC 2767
Dual Stack Hosts using the Bump-In-the-Stack Technique (BIS)
K. Tsuchiya, H. Higuchi, Y. Atarashi
February 2000
INFORMATIONAL

RFC 2766
Network Address Translation—Protocol Translation (NAT-PT)
G. Tsirtsis, P. Srisuresh
February 2000
Updated by RFC 3152
PROPOSED STANDARD

RFC 2765
Stateless IP/ICMP Translation Algorithm (SIIT)
E. Nordmark
February 2000
PROPOSED STANDARD

RFC 2740
OSPF for IPv6
R. Coltun, D. Ferguson, J. Moy
December 1999
PROPOSED STANDARD

RFC 2732
Format for Literal IPv6 Addresses in URL's
R. Hinden, B. Carpenter, L. Masinter
December 1999
PROPOSED STANDARD

RFC 2711
IPv6 Router Alert Option
C. Partridge, A. Jackson
October 1999
PROPOSED STANDARD

RFC 2710
Multicast Listener Discovery (MLD) for IPv6
S. Deering, W. Fenner, B. Haberman
October 1999
PROPOSED STANDARD

RFC 2675
IPv6 Jumbograms
D. Borman, S. Deering, R. Hinden
August 1999
Obsoletes RFC 2147
PROPOSED STANDARD

RFC 2590
Transmission of IPv6 Packets over Frame Relay Networks Specification
A. Conta, A. Malis, M. Mueller
May 1999
PROPOSED STANDARD

RFC 2553
Basic Socket Interface Extensions for IPv6
R. Gilligan, S. Thomson, J. Bound, W. Stevens
March 1999
Obsoletes RFC 2133, Obsoleted by RFC 3493, Updated by RFC 3152
INFORMATIONAL

RFC 2546
6Bone Routing Practice
A. Durand, B. Buclin
March 1999
Obsoleted by RFC 2772
INFORMATIONAL

RFC 2545
Use of BGP-4 Multiprotocol Extensions for IPv6 Inter-Domain Routing
P. Marques, F. Dupont
March 1999
PROPOSED STANDARD

RFC 2529
Transmission of IPv6 over IPv4 Domains without Explicit Tunnels
B. Carpenter, C. Jung
March 1999
PROPOSED STANDARD

RFC 2526
Reserved IPv6 Subnet Anycast Addresses
D. Johnson, S. Deering
March 1999
PROPOSED STANDARD

RFC 2497
Transmission of IPv6 Packets over ARCnet Networks
I. Souvatzis
January 1999
PROPOSED STANDARD

RFC 2492
IPv6 over ATM Networks
G. Armitage, P. Schulter, M. Jork
January 1999
PROPOSED STANDARD

RFC 2491
IPv6 over Non-Broadcast Multiple Access (NBMA) networks
G. Armitage, P. Schulter, M. Jork, G. Harter
January 1999
PROPOSED STANDARD

RFC 2474
Definition of the Differentiated Services Field (DS Field) in the IPv4
  and IPv6 Headers
K. Nichols, S. Blake, F. Baker, D. Black
December 1998
Obsoletes RFC 1455, RFC 1349, Updated by RFC 3168, RFC 3260
PROPOSED STANDARD

RFC 2473
Generic Packet Tunneling in IPv6 Specification
A. Conta, S. Deering
December 1998
PROPOSED STANDARD

RFC 2472
IP Version 6 over PPP
D. Haskin, E. Allen
December 1998
Obsoletes RFC 2023
PROPOSED STANDARD

RFC 2471
IPv6 Testing Address Allocation
R. Hinden, R. Fink, J. Postel (deceased)
December 1998
Obsoletes RFC 1897
EXPERIMENTAL

RFC 2470
Transmission of IPv6 Packets over Token Ring Networks
M. Crawford, T. Narten, S. Thomas
December 1998
PROPOSED STANDARD

RFC 2467
Transmission of IPv6 Packets over FDDI Networks
M. Crawford
December 1998
Obsoletes RFC 2019
PROPOSED STANDARD

RFC 2466
Management Information Base for IP Version 6: ICMPv6 Group
D. Haskin, S. Onishi
December 1998
PROPOSED STANDARD

RFC 2465
Management Information Base for IP Version 6: Textual Conventions and
   General Group
D. Haskin, S. Onishi
December 1998
PROPOSED STANDARD

RFC 2464
Transmission of IPv6 Packets over Ethernet Networks
M. Crawford
December 1998
Obsoletes RFC 1972
PROPOSED STANDARD

RFC 2463
Internet Control Message Protocol (ICMPv6) for the Internet Protocol
   Version 6 (IPv6) Specification
A. Conta, S. Deering
December 1998
Obsoletes RFC 1885
DRAFT STANDARD

RFC 2462
IPv6 Stateless Address Autoconfiguration
S. Thomson, T. Narten
December 1998
Obsoletes RFC 1971
DRAFT STANDARD

RFC 2461
Neighbor Discovery for IP Version 6 (IPv6)
T. Narten, E. Nordmark, W. Simpson
December 1998
Obsoletes RFC 1970
DRAFT STANDARD

RFC 2460
Internet Protocol, Version 6 (IPv6) Specification
S. Deering, R. Hinden
December 1998
Obsoletes RFC 1883
DRAFT STANDARD

RFC 2454
IP Version 6 Management Information Base for the User Datagram
  Protocol
M. Daniele
December 1998
PROPOSED STANDARD

RFC 2452
IP Version 6 Management Information Base for the Transmission
  Control Protocol
M. Daniele
December 1998
PROPOSED STANDARD

RFC 2450
Proposed TLA and NLA Assignment Rule
R. Hinden
December 1998
INFORMATIONAL

RFC 2428
FTP Extensions for IPv6 and NATs
M. Allman, S. Ostermann, C. Metz
September 1998
PROPOSED STANDARD

RFC 2406
IP Encapsulating Security Payload (ESP)
S. Kent, R. Atkinson
November 1998
Obsoletes RFC 1827
PROPOSED STANDARD

RFC 2402
IP Authentication Header
S. Kent, R. Atkinson
November 1998
Obsoletes RFC 1826
PROPOSED STANDARD

RFC 2401
Security Architecture for the Internet Protocol
S. Kent, R. Atkinson
November 1998
Obsoletes RFC 1825, Updated by RFC 3168
PROPOSED STANDARD

RFC 2375
IPv6 Multicast Address Assignments
R. Hinden, S. Deering
July 1998
INFORMATIONAL

RFC 2374
An IPv6 Aggregatable Global Unicast Address Format
R. Hinden, M. O'Dell, S. Deering
July 1998
Obsoletes RFC 2073
PROPOSED STANDARD

RFC 2365
BCP0023
Administratively Scoped IP Multicast
D. Meyer
July 1998
BEST CURRENT PRACTICE

RFC 2292
Advanced Sockets API for IPv6
W. Stevens, M. Thomas
February 1998
Obsoleted by RFC 3542
INFORMATIONAL

RFC 2185
Routing Aspects of IPv6 Transition
R. Callon, D. Haskin
September 1997
INFORMATIONAL

RFC 2147
TCP and UDP over IPv6 Jumbograms
D. Borman
May 1997
Obsoleted by RFC 2675
PROPOSED STANDARD

RFC 2133
Basic Socket Interface Extensions for IPv6
R. Gilligan, S. Thomson, J. Bound, W. Stevens
April 1997
Obsoleted by RFC 2553
INFORMATIONAL

RFC 2080
RIPng for IPv6
G. Malkin, R. Minnear
January 1997
PROPOSED STANDARD

RFC 2073
An IPv6 Provider-Based Unicast Address Format
Y. Rekhter, P. Lothberg, R. Hinden, S. Deering, J. Postel
January 1997
Obsoleted by RFC 2374
PROPOSED STANDARD

RFC 2030
Simple Network Time Protocol (SNTP) Version 4 for IPv4, IPv6 and OSI
D. Mills
October 1996
Obsoletes RFC 1769
INFORMATIONAL

RFC 2023
IP Version 6 Over PPP
D. Haskin, E. Allen
October 1996
Obsoleted by RFC 2472
PROPOSED STANDARD

RFC 2019
Transmission of IPv6 Packets over FDDI
M. Crawford
October 1996
Obsoleted by RFC 2467
PROPOSED STANDARD

RFC 1981
Path MTU Discovery for IP version 6
J. McCann, S. Deering, J. Mogul
August 1996
PROPOSED STANDARD

RFC 1972
A Method for the Transmission of IPv6 Packets over Ethernet Networks
M. Crawford
August 1996
Obsoleted by RFC 2464
PROPOSED STANDARD

RFC 1971
IPv6 Stateless Address Autoconfiguration
S. Thomson, T. Narten
August 1996
Obsoleted by RFC 2462
PROPOSED STANDARD

RFC 1970
Neighbor Discovery for IP Version 6 (IPv6)
T. Narten, E. Nordmark, W. Simpson
August 1996
Obsoleted by RFC 2461
PROPOSED STANDARD

RFC 1955
New Scheme for Internet Routing and Addressing (ENCAPS) for IPNG
R. Hinden
June 1996
INFORMATIONAL

RFC 1933
Transition Mechanisms for IPv6 Hosts and Routers
R. Gilligan, E. Nordmark
April 1996
Obsoleted by RFC 2893
PROPOSED STANDARD

RFC 1924
A Compact Representation of IPv6 Addresses
R. Elz
Apr-01-1996
INFORMATIONAL

RFC 1897
IPv6 Testing Address Allocation
R. Hinden, J. Postel
January 1996
Obsoleted by RFC 2471
EXPERIMENTAL

RFC 1888
OSI NSAPs and IPv6
J. Bound, B. Carpenter, D. Harrington, J. Houldsworth, A. Lloyd
August 1996
EXPERIMENTAL

RFC 1887
An Architecture for IPv6 Unicast Address Allocation
Y. Rekhter, T. Li, Eds.
December 1995
INFORMATIONAL

RFC 1886
DNS Extensions to support IP version 6
S. Thomson, C. Huitema
December 1995
Updated by RFC 2874, RFC 3152
PROPOSED STANDARD

RFC 1885
Internet Control Message Protocol (ICMPv6) for the Internet Protocol
  Version 6 (IPv6)
A. Conta, S. Deering
December 1995
Obsoleted by RFC 2463
PROPOSED STANDARD

RFC 1884
IP Version 6 Addressing Architecture
R. Hinden, S. Deering, Eds.
December 1995
Obsoleted by RFC 2373
HISTORIC
[pub as:PROPOSED STANDARD]

RFC 1883
Internet Protocol, Version 6 (IPv6) Specification
S. Deering, R. Hinden
December 1995
Obsoleted by RFC 2460
PROPOSED STANDARD

RFC 1881
IPv6 Address Allocation Management
IAB, IESG
December 1995
INFORMATIONAL

RFC 1827
IP Encapsulating Security Payload (ESP)
R. Atkinson
August 1995
Obsoleted by RFC 2406
PROPOSED STANDARD

RFC 1826
IP Authentication Header
R. Atkinson
August 1995
Obsoleted by RFC 2402
PROPOSED STANDARD

RFC 1825
Security Architecture for the Internet Protocol
R. Atkinson
August 1995
Obsoleted by RFC 2401
PROPOSED STANDARD

RFC 1810
Report on MD5 Performance
J. Touch
June 1995
INFORMATIONAL

RFC 1809
Using the Flow Label Field in IPv6
C. Partridge
June 1995
INFORMATIONAL

RFC 1776
The Address is the Message
S. Crocker
Apr-01-1995
INFORMATIONAL

RFC 1753
IPng Technical Requirements Of the Nimrod Routing and Addressing
  Architecture
N. Chiappa
December 1994
INFORMATIONAL

RFC 1752
The Recommendation for the IP Next Generation Protocol
S. Bradner, A. Mankin
January 1995
PROPOSED STANDARD

RFC 1726
Technical Criteria for Choosing IP The Next Generation (IPng)
C. Partridge, F. Kastenholz
December 1994
INFORMATIONAL

RFC 1719
A Direction for IPng
P. Gross
December 1994
INFORMATIONAL

RFC 1715
The H Ratio for Address Assignment Efficiency
C. Huitema
November 1994
Updated by RFC 3194
INFORMATIONAL

RFC 1710
Simple Internet Protocol Plus White Paper
R. Hinden
October 1994
INFORMATIONAL

RFC 1707
CATNIP: Common Architecture for the Internet
M. McGovern, R. Ullmann
October 1994
INFORMATIONAL

RFC 1705
Six Virtual Inches to the Left: The Problem with IPng
R. Carlson, D. Ficarella
October 1994
INFORMATIONAL

RFC 1688
IPng Mobility Considerations
W. Simpson
August 1994
INFORMATIONAL

RFC 1687
A Large Corporate User's View of IPng
E. Fleischman
August 1994
INFORMATIONAL

RFC 1686
IPng Requirements: A Cable Television Industry Viewpoint
M. Vecchi
August 1994
INFORMATIONAL

RFC 1683
Multiprotocol Interoperability In IPng
R. Clark, M. Ammar, K. Calvert
August 1994
INFORMATIONAL

RFC 1682
IPng BSD Host Implementation Analysis
J. Bound
August 1994
INFORMATIONAL

RFC 1680
IPng Support for ATM Services
C. Brazdziunas
August 1994
INFORMATIONAL

RFC 1679
HPN Working Group Input to the IPng Requirements Solicitation
D. Green, P. Irey, D. Marlow, K. O'Donoghue
August 1994
INFORMATIONAL

RFC 1678
IPng Requirements of Large Corporate Networks
E. Britton, J. Tavs
August 1994
INFORMATIONAL

RFC 1677
Tactical Radio Frequency Communication Requirements for IPng
B. Adamson
August 1994
INFORMATIONAL

RFC 1676
INFN Requirements for an IPng
A. Ghiselli, D. Salomoni, C. Vistoli
August 1994
INFORMATIONAL

RFC 1675
Security Concerns for IPng
S. Bellovin
August 1994
INFORMATIONAL

RFC 1674
A Cellular Industry View of IPng
M. Taylor
August 1994
INFORMATIONAL

RFC 1673
Electric Power Research Institute Comments on IPng
R. Skelton
August 1994
INFORMATIONAL

RFC 1672
Accounting Requirements for IPng
N. Brownlee
August 1994
INFORMATIONAL

RFC 1671
IPng White Paper on Transition and Other Considerations
B. Carpenter
August 1994
INFORMATIONAL

RFC 1670
Input to IPng Engineering Considerations
D. Heagerty
August 1994
INFORMATIONAL

RFC 1669
Market Viability as a IPng Criteria
J. Curran
August 1994
INFORMATIONAL

RFC 1668
Unified Routing Requirements for IPng
D. Estrin, T. Li, Y. Rekhter
August 1994
INFORMATIONAL

RFC 1667
Modeling and Simulation Requirements for IPng
S. Symington, D. Wood, M. Pullen
August 1994
INFORMATIONAL

RFC 1622
Pip Header Processing
P. Francis
May 1994
INFORMATIONAL

RFC 1621
Pip Near-term Architecture
P. Francis
May 1994
INFORMATIONAL

RFC 1550
IP: Next Generation (IPng) White Paper Solicitation
S. Bradner, A. Mankin
December 1993
INFORMATIONAL

RFC 1475
TP/IX: The Next Internet
R. Ullmann
June 1993
EXPERIMENTAL

RFC 1454
Comparison of Proposals for Next Version of IP
T. Dixon
May 1993
INFORMATIONAL

Index